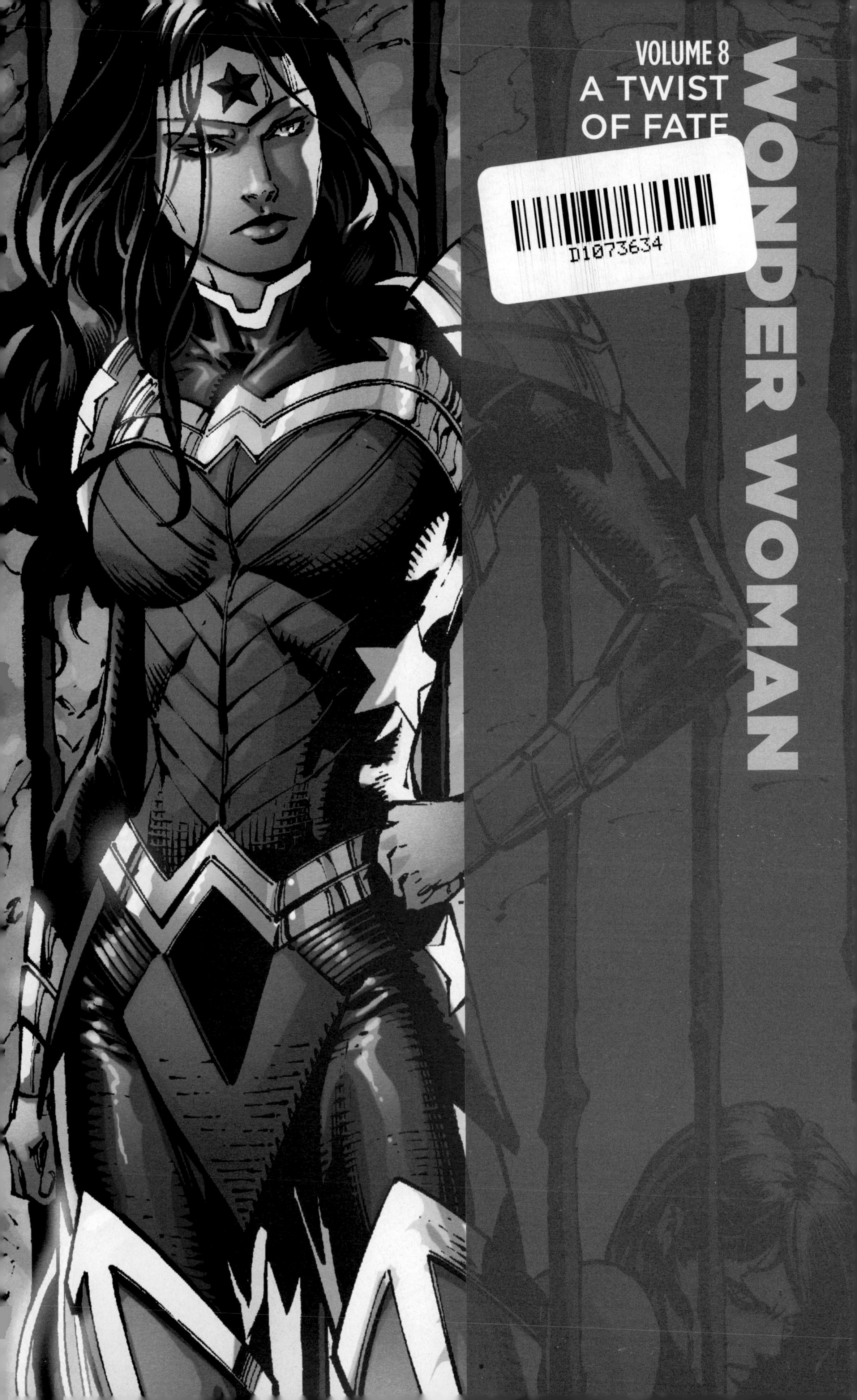

VOLUME 8
A TWIST OF FATE
WONDER WOMAN

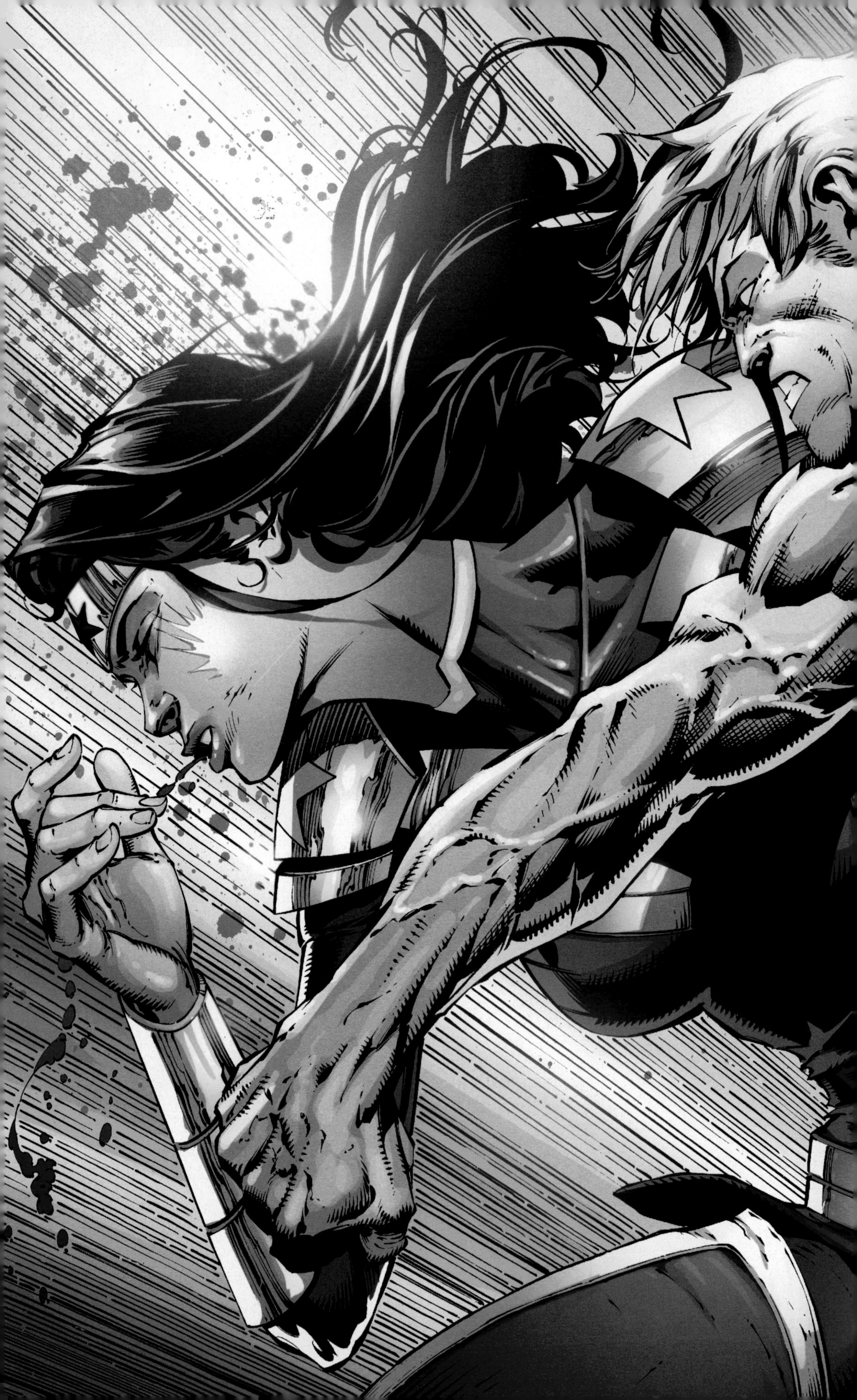

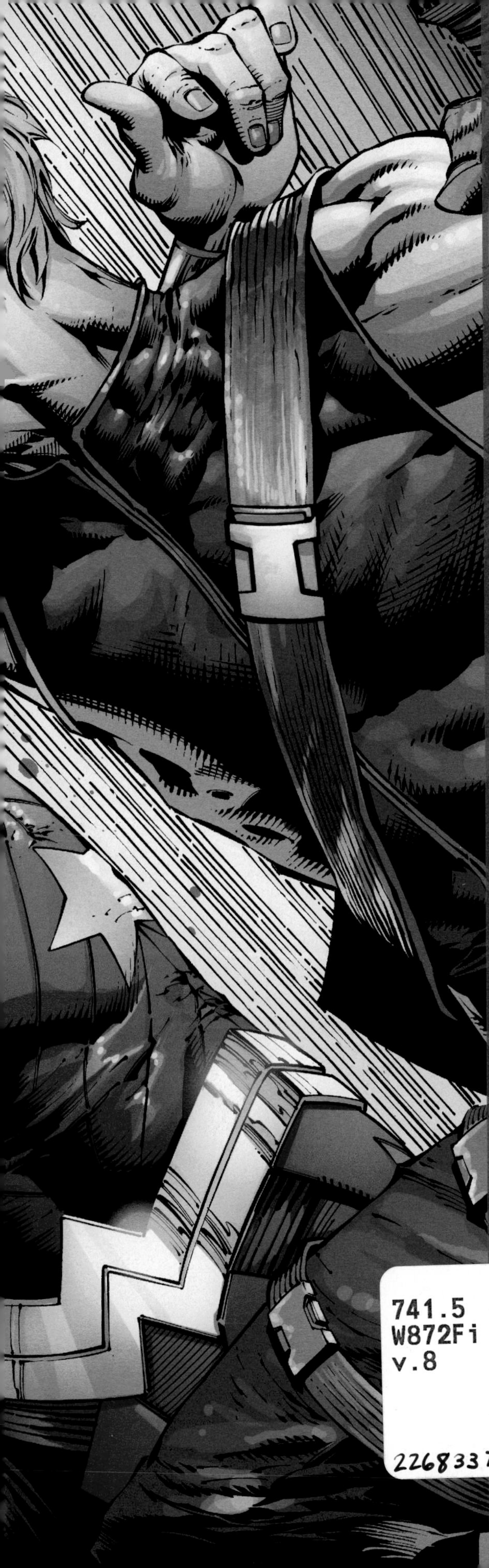

WONDER WOMAN

VOLUME 8
A TWIST OF FATE

WRITTEN BY
MEREDITH FINCH

PENCILS BY
DAVID FINCH
IAN CHURCHILL
MIGUEL MENDONÇA

INKS BY
JONATHAN GLAPION
JOHNNY DESJARDINS
RICK BRYANT
ANDREW HENNESSY
MARK IRWIN
TREVOR SCOTT
SCOTT HANNA
DEXTER VINES

COLOR BY
BRAD ANDERSON
BETH SOTELO

LETTERS BY
ROB LEIGH

COLLECTION COVER ART BY
FINCH, GLAPION & ANDERSON

WONDER WOMAN CREATED BY
WILLIAM MOULTON MARSTON

MIKE COTTON Editor – Original Series
PAUL KAMINSKI Associate Editor – Original Series
JEB WOODARD Group Editor – Collected Editions
LIZ ERICKSON Editor – Collected Edition
STEVE COOK Design Director – Books
DAMIAN RYLAND Publication Design

BOB HARRAS Senior VP – Editor-in-Chief, DC Comics

DIANE NELSON President
DAN DIDIO and JIM LEE Co-Publishers
GEOFF JOHNS Chief Creative Officer
AMIT DESAI Senior VP – Marketing & Global Franchise Management
NAIRI GARDINER Senior VP – Finance
SAM ADES VP – Digital Marketing
BOBBIE CHASE VP – Talent Development
MARK CHIARELLO Senior VP – Art, Design & Collected Editions
JOHN CUNNINGHAM VP – Content Strategy
ANNE DEPIES VP – Strategy Planning & Reporting
DON FALLETTI VP – Manufacturing Operations
LAWRENCE GANEM VP – Editorial Administration & Talent Relations
ALISON GILL Senior VP – Manufacturing & Operations
HANK KANALZ Senior VP – Editorial Strategy & Administration
JAY KOGAN VP – Legal Affairs
DEREK MADDALENA Senior VP – Sales & Business Development
JACK MAHAN VP – Business Affairs
DAN MIRON VP – Sales Planning & Trade Development
NICK NAPOLITANO VP – Manufacturing Administration
CAROL ROEDER VP – Marketing
EDDIE SCANNELL VP – Mass Account & Digital Sales
COURTNEY SIMMONS Senior VP – Publicity & Communications
JIM (SKI) SOKOLOWSKI VP – Comic Book Specialty & Newsstand Sales
SANDY YI Senior VP – Global Franchise Management

WONDER WOMAN VOLUME 8: A TWIST OF FATE

Published by DC Comics. Compilation and all new material Copyright © 2016 DC Comics. All Rights Reserved.

Originally published in single magazine form in WONDER WOMAN 41-47 © 2015 DC Comics. All Rights Reserved. All characters, their
distinctive likenesses and related elements featured in this publication are trademarks of DC Comics. The stories, characters and incidents
featured in this publication are entirely fictional. DC Comics does not read or accept unsolicited ideas, stories or artwork.

DC Comics, 2900 West Alameda Ave., Burbank, CA 91505
Printed by RR Donnelley, Salem, VA, USA. 8/12/16. First Printing.
ISBN: 978-1-4012-6583-0

Library of Congress Cataloging-in-Publication Data is available

PEFC Certified

Printed on paper from
sustainably managed
forests and controlled
sources

PEFC/29-31-75   www.pefc.org

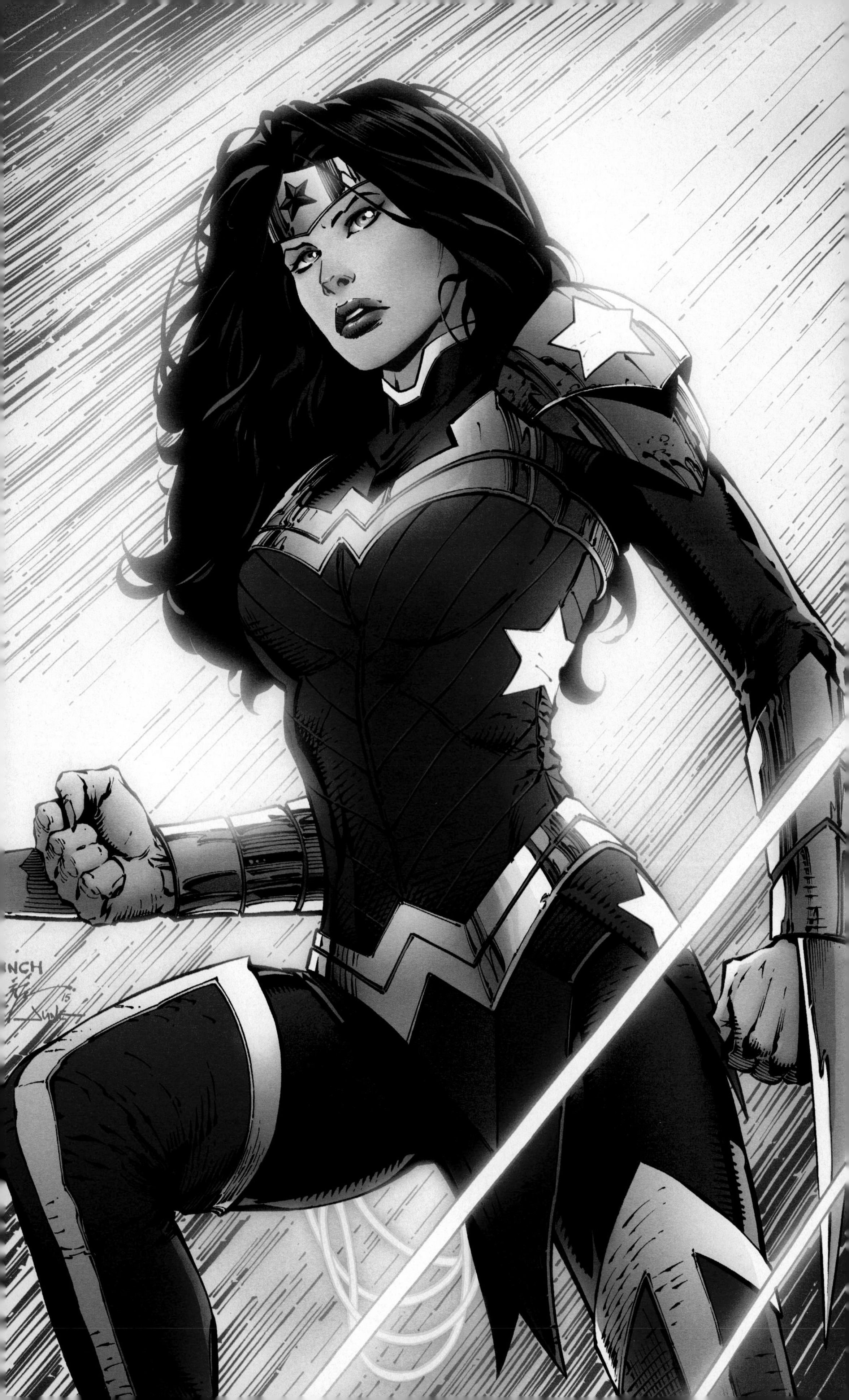

BALANCE

MEREDITH FINCH writer DAVID FINCH penciller JONATHAN GLAPION JOHNNY DESJARDINS inkers BRAD ANDERSON colorist ROB LEIGH letterer
cover by FINCH, GLAPION & ANDERSON

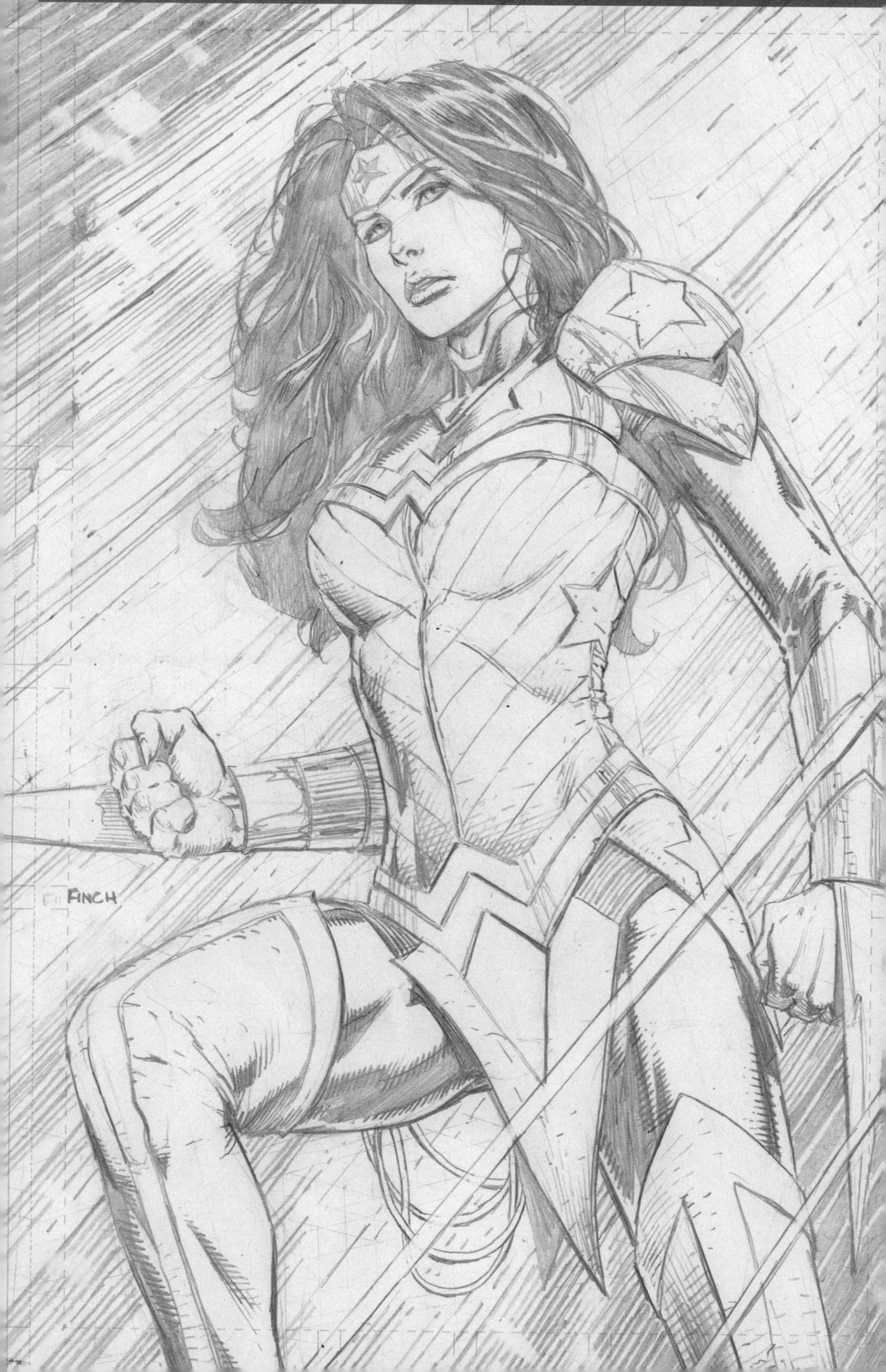
FINCH

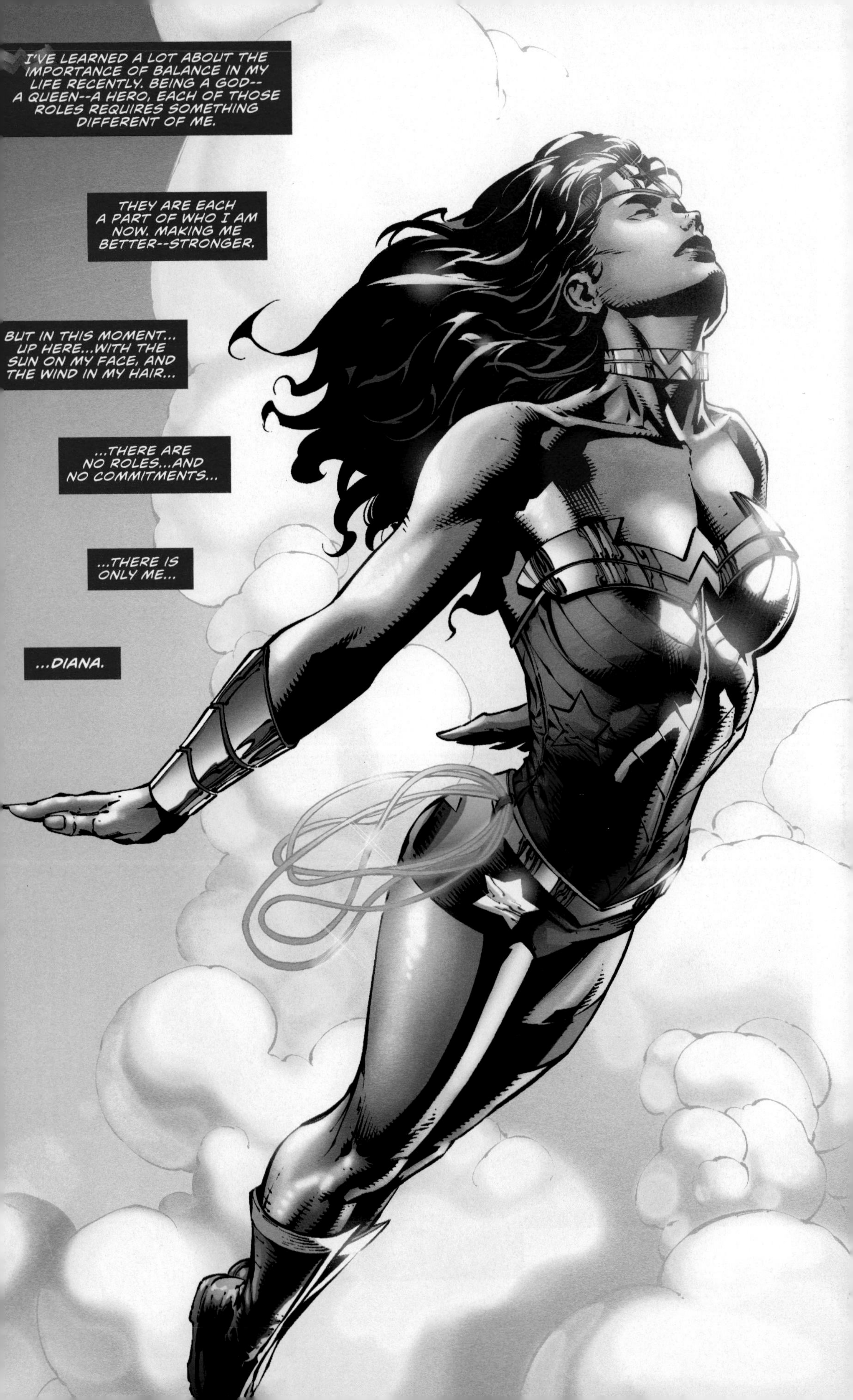
I'VE LEARNED A LOT ABOUT THE IMPORTANCE OF BALANCE IN MY LIFE RECENTLY. BEING A GOD-- A QUEEN--A HERO, EACH OF THOSE ROLES REQUIRES SOMETHING DIFFERENT OF ME.
THEY ARE EACH A PART OF WHO I AM NOW. MAKING ME BETTER--STRONGER.
BUT IN THIS MOMENT... UP HERE...WITH THE SUN ON MY FACE, AND THE WIND IN MY HAIR...
...THERE ARE NO ROLES...AND NO COMMITMENTS...
...THERE IS ONLY ME...
...DIANA.

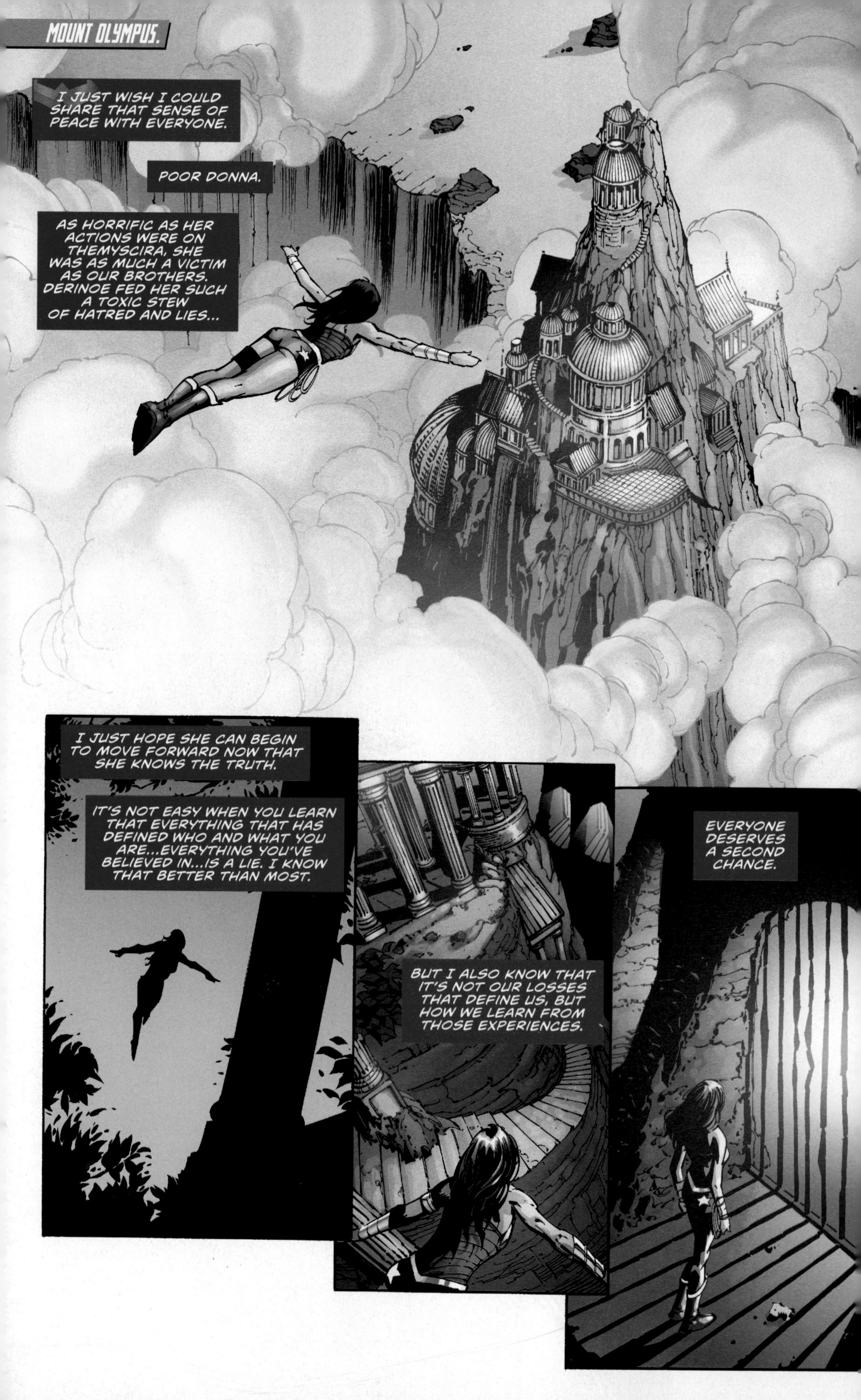
MOUNT OLYMPUS.
I JUST WISH I COULD SHARE THAT SENSE OF PEACE WITH EVERYONE.
POOR DONNA.
AS HORRIFIC AS HER ACTIONS WERE ON THEMYSCIRA, SHE WAS AS MUCH A VICTIM AS OUR BROTHERS. DERINOE FED HER SUCH A TOXIC STEW OF HATRED AND LIES...
I JUST HOPE SHE CAN BEGIN TO MOVE FORWARD NOW THAT SHE KNOWS THE TRUTH.
IT'S NOT EASY WHEN YOU LEARN THAT EVERYTHING THAT HAS DEFINED WHO AND WHAT YOU ARE...EVERYTHING YOU'VE BELIEVED IN...IS A LIE. I KNOW THAT BETTER THAN MOST.
BUT I ALSO KNOW THAT IT'S NOT OUR LOSSES THAT DEFINE US, BUT HOW WE LEARN FROM THOSE EXPERIENCES.
EVERYONE DESERVES A SECOND CHANCE.

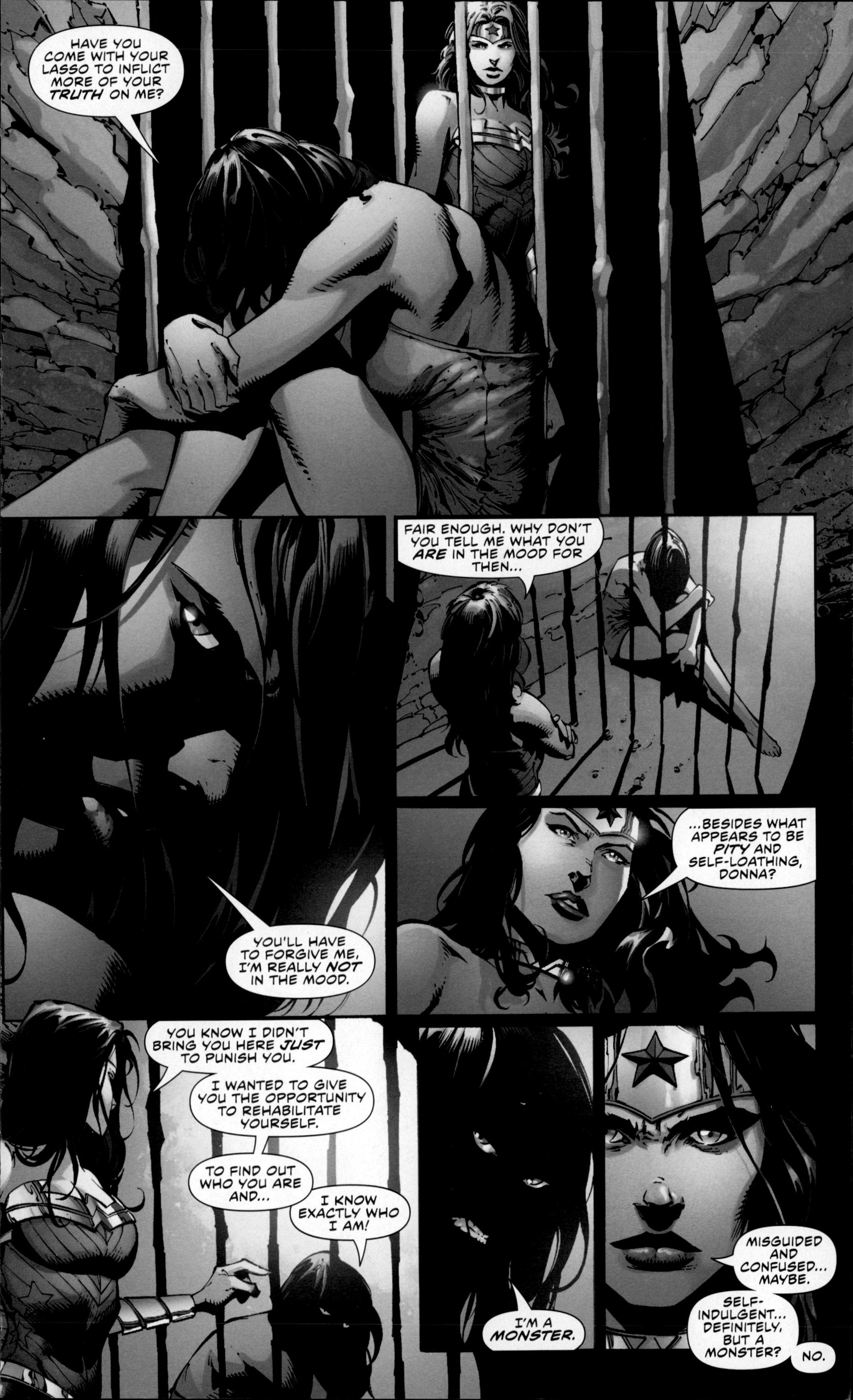
HAVE YOU COME WITH YOUR LASSO TO INFLICT MORE OF YOUR *TRUTH* ON ME?
YOU'LL HAVE TO FORGIVE ME, I'M REALLY *NOT* IN THE MOOD.
FAIR ENOUGH. WHY DON'T YOU TELL ME WHAT YOU *ARE* IN THE MOOD FOR THEN...
...BESIDES WHAT APPEARS TO BE *PITY* AND SELF-LOATHING, DONNA?
YOU KNOW I DIDN'T BRING YOU HERE *JUST* TO PUNISH YOU.
I WANTED TO GIVE YOU THE OPPORTUNITY TO REHABILITATE YOURSELF.
TO FIND OUT WHO YOU ARE AND...
I KNOW EXACTLY WHO I AM!
I'M A *MONSTER.*
MISGUIDED AND CONFUSED... MAYBE.
SELF-INDULGENT... DEFINITELY, BUT A MONSTER?
NO.

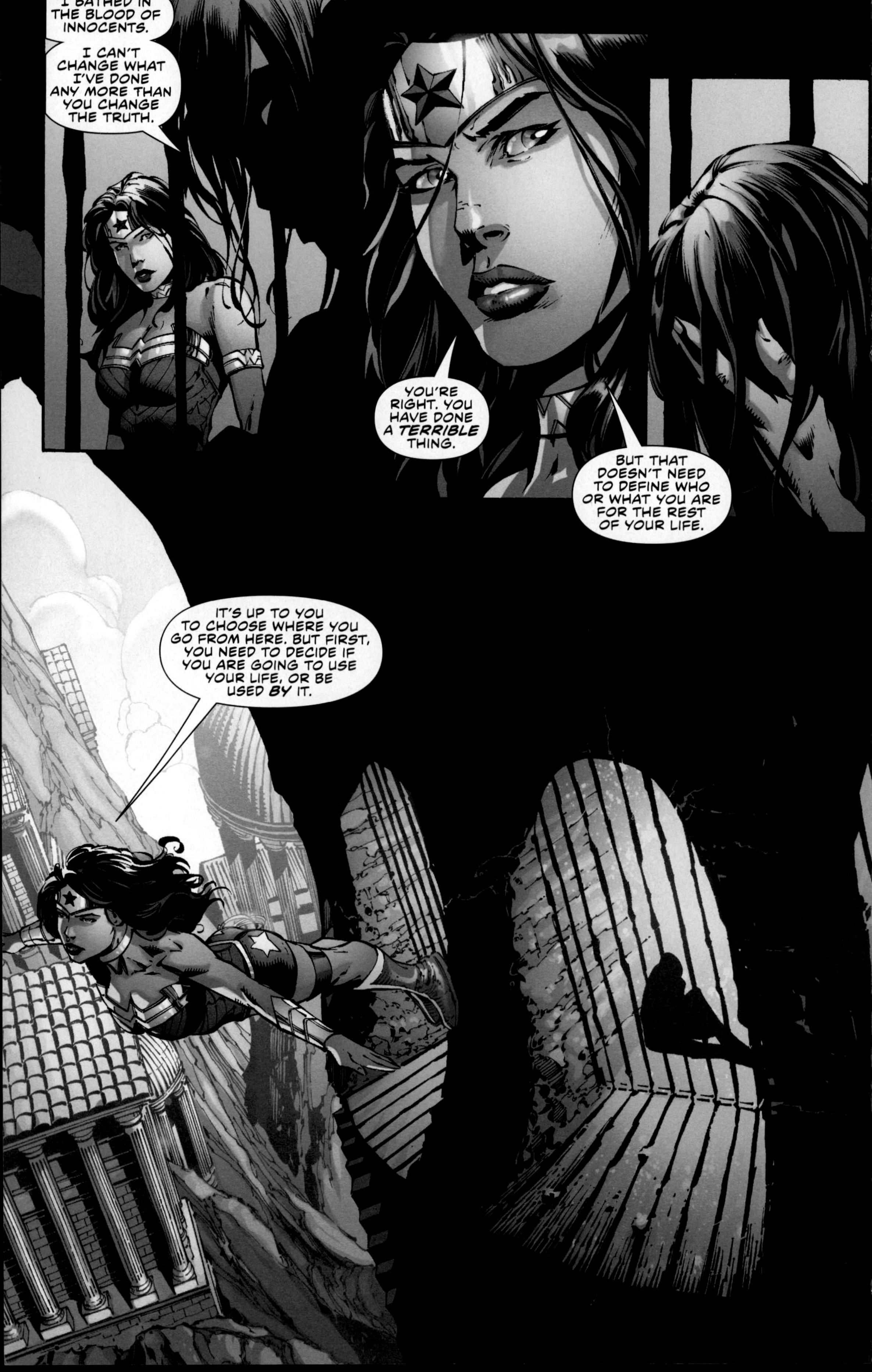
I BATHED IN THE BLOOD OF INNOCENTS.
I CAN'T CHANGE WHAT I'VE DONE ANY MORE THAN YOU CHANGE THE TRUTH.
YOU'RE RIGHT. YOU HAVE DONE A TERRIBLE THING.
BUT THAT DOESN'T NEED TO DEFINE WHO OR WHAT YOU ARE FOR THE REST OF YOUR LIFE.
IT'S UP TO YOU TO CHOOSE WHERE YOU GO FROM HERE. BUT FIRST, YOU NEED TO DECIDE IF YOU ARE GOING TO USE YOUR LIFE, OR BE USED BY IT.

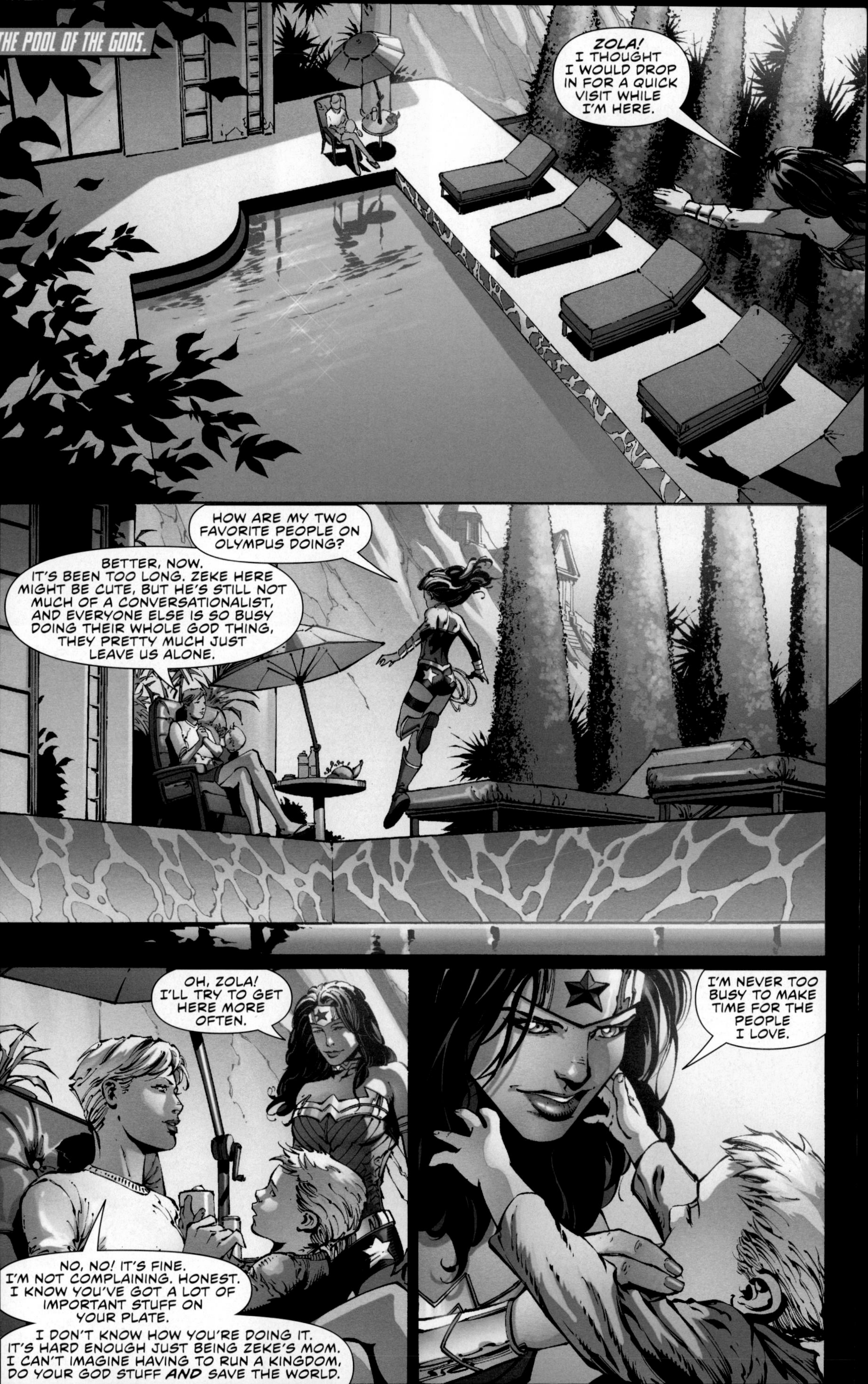
THE POOL OF THE GODS.
ZOLA! I THOUGHT I WOULD DROP IN FOR A QUICK VISIT WHILE I'M HERE.
HOW ARE MY TWO FAVORITE PEOPLE ON OLYMPUS DOING?
BETTER, NOW. IT'S BEEN TOO LONG. ZEKE HERE MIGHT BE CUTE, BUT HE'S STILL NOT MUCH OF A CONVERSATIONALIST, AND EVERYONE ELSE IS SO BUSY DOING THEIR WHOLE GOD THING, THEY PRETTY MUCH JUST LEAVE US ALONE.
OH, ZOLA! I'LL TRY TO GET HERE MORE OFTEN.
NO, NO! IT'S FINE. I'M NOT COMPLAINING. HONEST. I KNOW YOU'VE GOT A LOT OF IMPORTANT STUFF ON YOUR PLATE.
I DON'T KNOW HOW YOU'RE DOING IT. IT'S HARD ENOUGH JUST BEING ZEKE'S MOM. I CAN'T IMAGINE HAVING TO RUN A KINGDOM, DO YOUR GOD STUFF AND SAVE THE WORLD.
I'M NEVER TOO BUSY TO MAKE TIME FOR THE PEOPLE I LOVE.

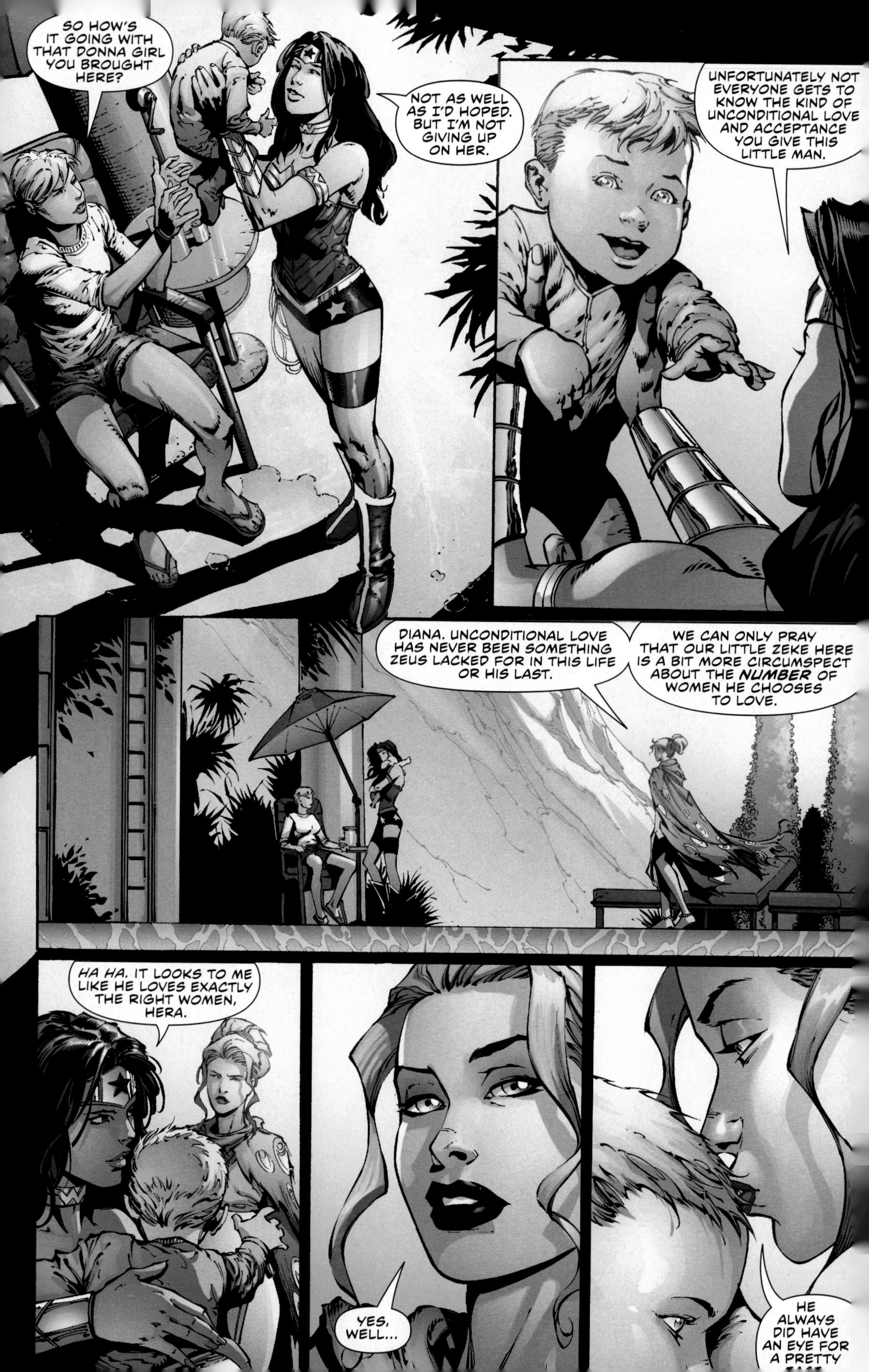
SO HOW'S IT GOING WITH THAT DONNA GIRL YOU BROUGHT HERE?
NOT AS WELL AS I'D HOPED. BUT I'M NOT GIVING UP ON HER.
UNFORTUNATELY NOT EVERYONE GETS TO KNOW THE KIND OF UNCONDITIONAL LOVE AND ACCEPTANCE YOU GIVE THIS LITTLE MAN.
DIANA. UNCONDITIONAL LOVE HAS NEVER BEEN SOMETHING ZEUS LACKED FOR IN THIS LIFE OR HIS LAST.
WE CAN ONLY PRAY THAT OUR LITTLE ZEKE HERE IS A BIT MORE CIRCUMSPECT ABOUT THE NUMBER OF WOMEN HE CHOOSES TO LOVE.
HA HA. IT LOOKS TO ME LIKE HE LOVES EXACTLY THE RIGHT WOMEN, HERA.
YES, WELL...
HE ALWAYS DID HAVE AN EYE FOR A PRETTY

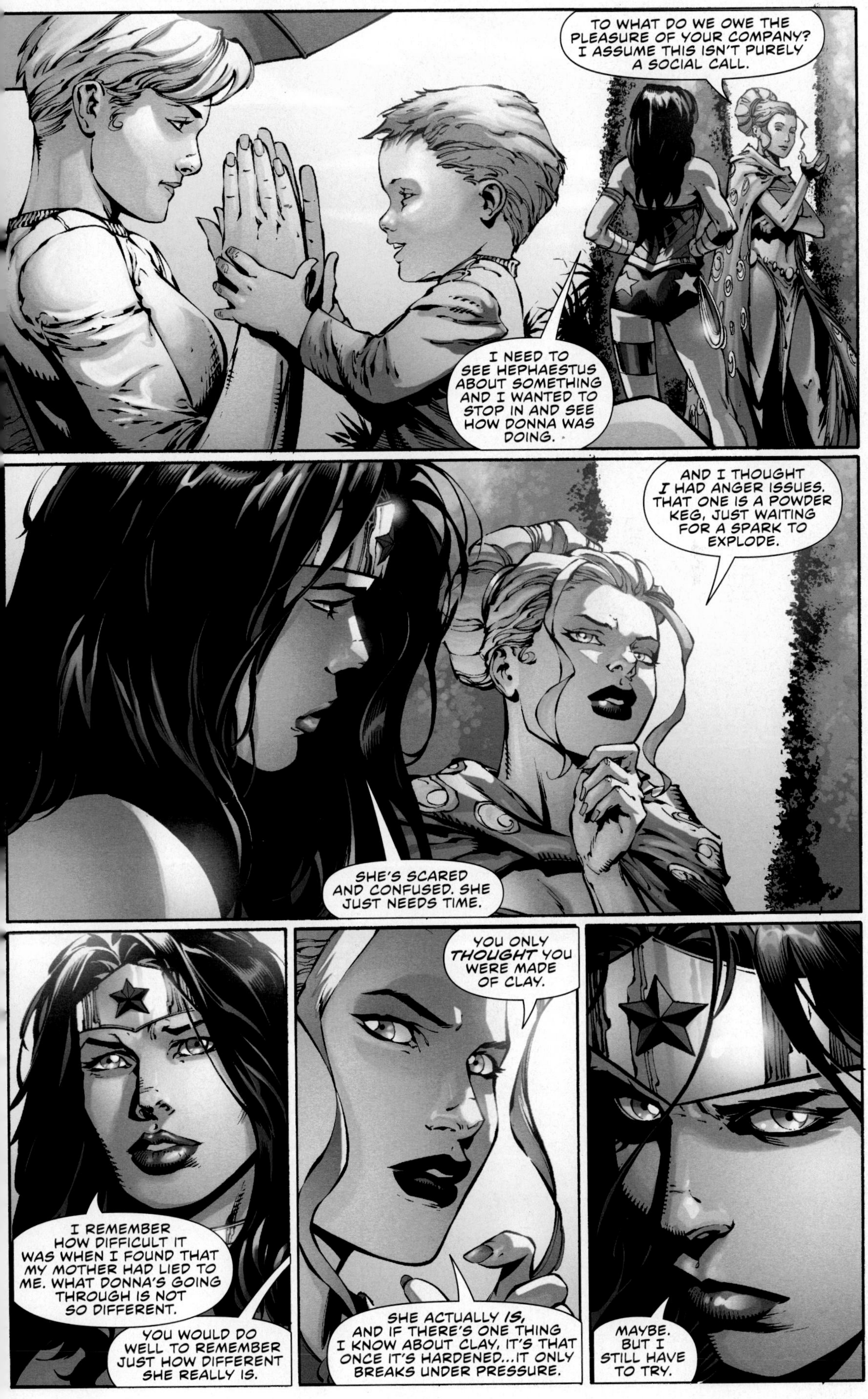
TO WHAT DO WE OWE THE PLEASURE OF YOUR COMPANY? I ASSUME THIS ISN'T PURELY A SOCIAL CALL.
I NEED TO SEE HEPHAESTUS ABOUT SOMETHING AND I WANTED TO STOP IN AND SEE HOW DONNA WAS DOING.
AND I THOUGHT *I* HAD ANGER ISSUES. THAT ONE IS A POWDER KEG, JUST WAITING FOR A SPARK TO EXPLODE.
SHE'S SCARED AND CONFUSED. SHE JUST NEEDS TIME.
I REMEMBER HOW DIFFICULT IT WAS WHEN I FOUND THAT MY MOTHER HAD LIED TO ME. WHAT DONNA'S GOING THROUGH IS NOT SO DIFFERENT.
YOU WOULD DO WELL TO REMEMBER JUST HOW DIFFERENT SHE REALLY IS.
YOU ONLY *THOUGHT* YOU WERE MADE OF CLAY.
SHE ACTUALLY *IS*, AND IF THERE'S ONE THING I KNOW ABOUT CLAY, IT'S THAT ONCE IT'S HARDENED...IT ONLY BREAKS UNDER PRESSURE.
MAYBE. BUT I STILL HAVE TO TRY.

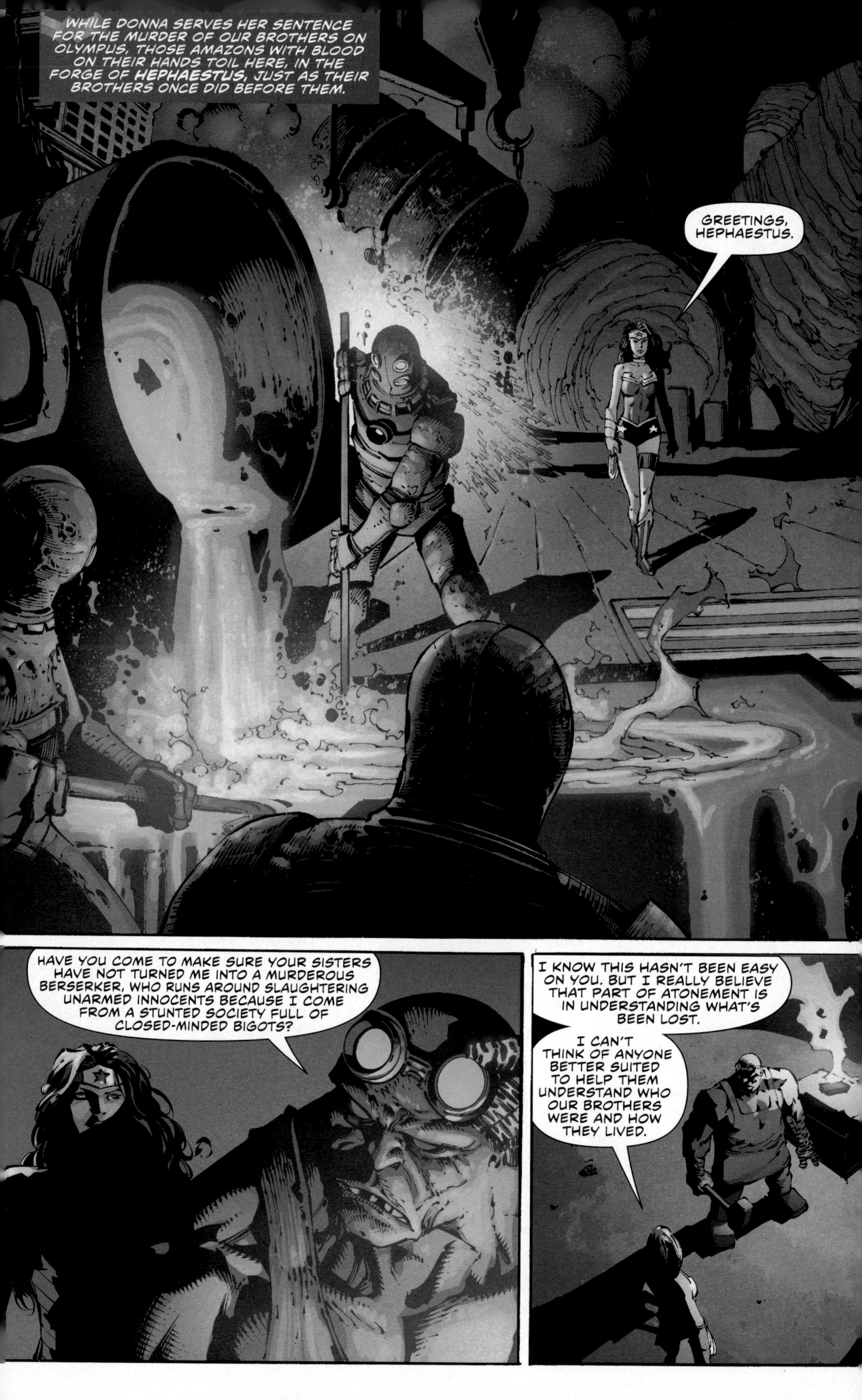
WHILE DONNA SERVES HER SENTENCE FOR THE MURDER OF OUR BROTHERS ON OLYMPUS, THOSE AMAZONS WITH BLOOD ON THEIR HANDS TOIL HERE, IN THE FORGE OF HEPHAESTUS, JUST AS THEIR BROTHERS ONCE DID BEFORE THEM.
GREETINGS, HEPHAESTUS.
HAVE YOU COME TO MAKE SURE YOUR SISTERS HAVE NOT TURNED ME INTO A MURDEROUS BERSERKER, WHO RUNS AROUND SLAUGHTERING UNARMED INNOCENTS BECAUSE I COME FROM A STUNTED SOCIETY FULL OF CLOSED-MINDED BIGOTS?
I KNOW THIS HASN'T BEEN EASY ON YOU. BUT I REALLY BELIEVE THAT PART OF ATONEMENT IS IN UNDERSTANDING WHAT'S BEEN LOST.
I CAN'T THINK OF ANYONE BETTER SUITED TO HELP THEM UNDERSTAND WHO OUR BROTHERS WERE AND HOW THEY LIVED.

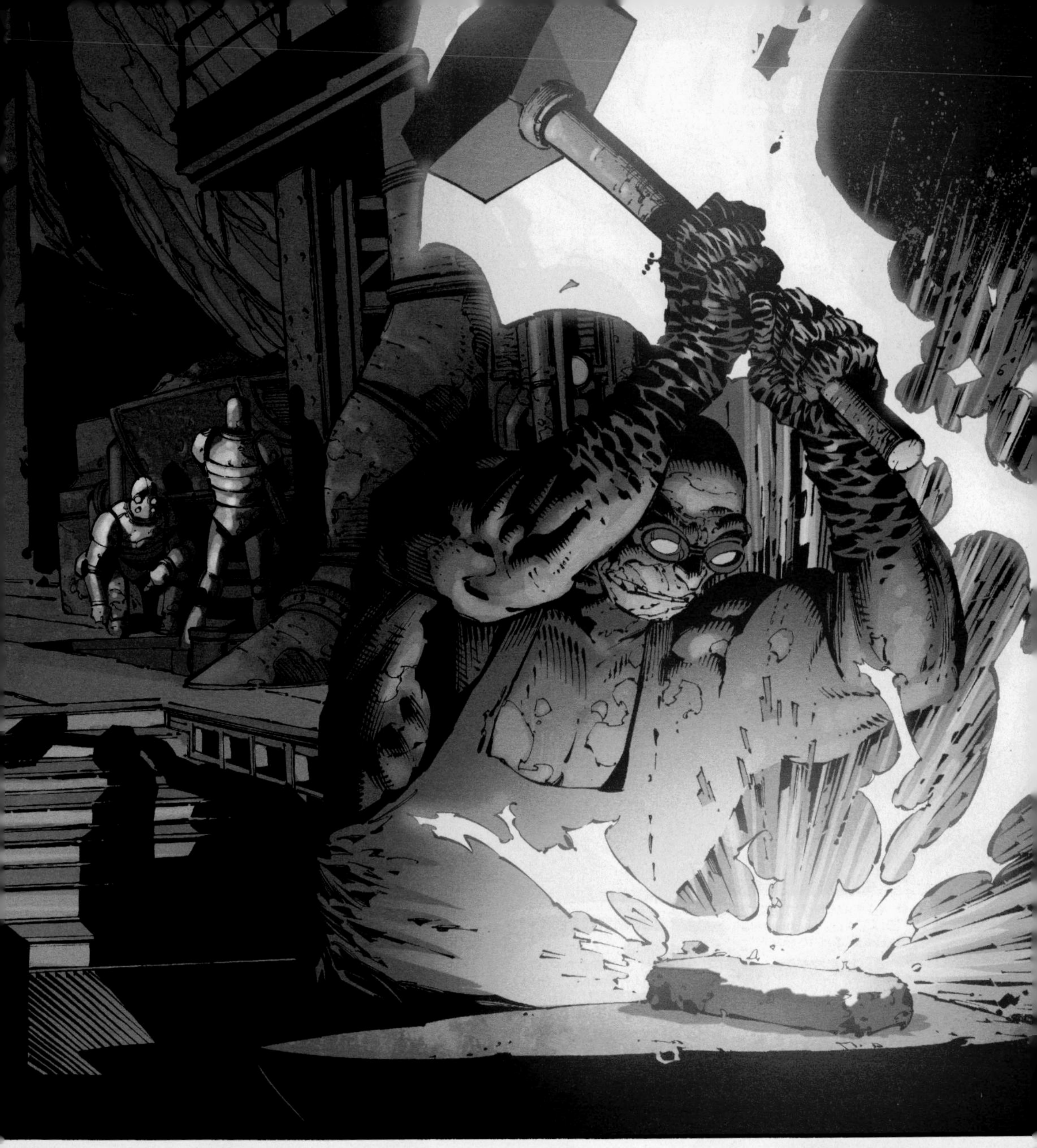

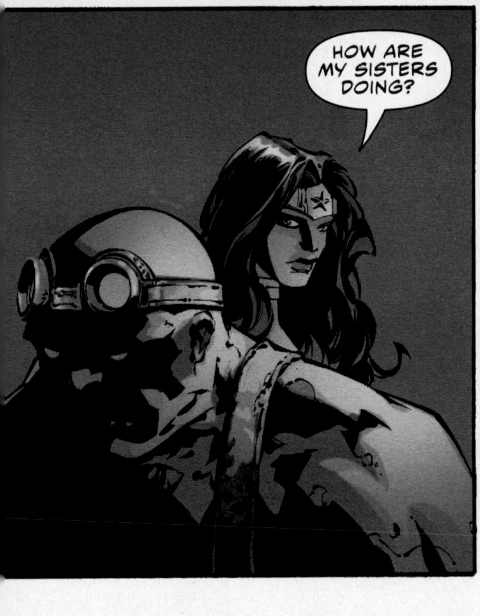
HOW ARE MY SISTERS DOING?

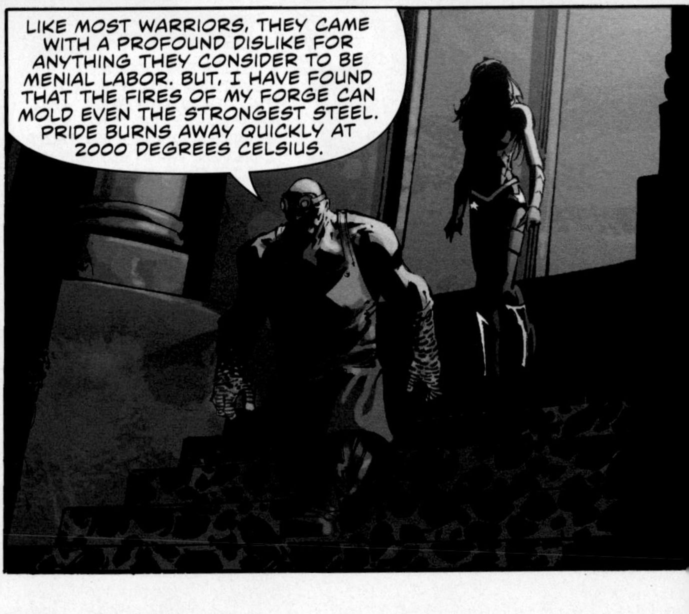
LIKE MOST WARRIORS, THEY CAME WITH A PROFOUND DISLIKE FOR ANYTHING THEY CONSIDER TO BE MENIAL LABOR. BUT, I HAVE FOUND THAT THE FIRES OF MY FORGE CAN MOLD EVEN THE STRONGEST STEEL. PRIDE BURNS AWAY QUICKLY AT 2000 DEGREES CELSIUS.

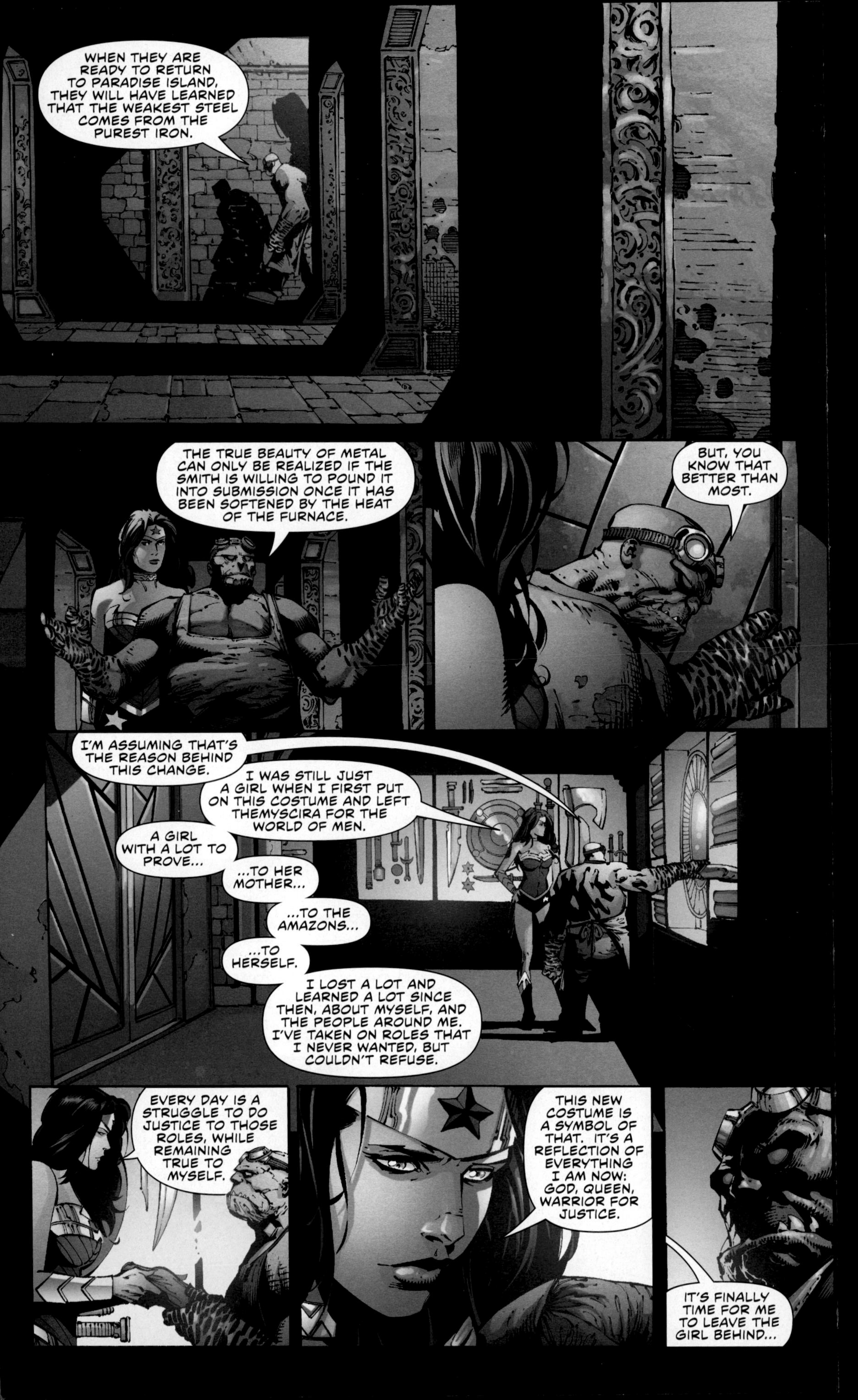
WHEN THEY ARE READY TO RETURN TO PARADISE ISLAND, THEY WILL HAVE LEARNED THAT THE WEAKEST STEEL COMES FROM THE PUREST IRON.
THE TRUE BEAUTY OF METAL CAN ONLY BE REALIZED IF THE SMITH IS WILLING TO POUND IT INTO SUBMISSION ONCE IT HAS BEEN SOFTENED BY THE HEAT OF THE FURNACE.
BUT, YOU KNOW THAT BETTER THAN MOST.
I'M ASSUMING THAT'S THE REASON BEHIND THIS CHANGE.
I WAS STILL JUST A GIRL WHEN I FIRST PUT ON THIS COSTUME AND LEFT THEMYSCIRA FOR THE WORLD OF MEN.
A GIRL WITH A LOT TO PROVE...
...TO HER MOTHER...
...TO THE AMAZONS...
...TO HERSELF.
I LOST A LOT AND LEARNED A LOT SINCE THEN, ABOUT MYSELF, AND THE PEOPLE AROUND ME. I'VE TAKEN ON ROLES THAT I NEVER WANTED, BUT COULDN'T REFUSE.
EVERY DAY IS A STRUGGLE TO DO JUSTICE TO THOSE ROLES, WHILE REMAINING TRUE TO MYSELF.
THIS NEW COSTUME IS A SYMBOL OF THAT. IT'S A REFLECTION OF EVERYTHING I AM NOW: GOD, QUEEN, WARRIOR FOR JUSTICE.
IT'S FINALLY TIME FOR ME TO LEAVE THE GIRL BEHIND...

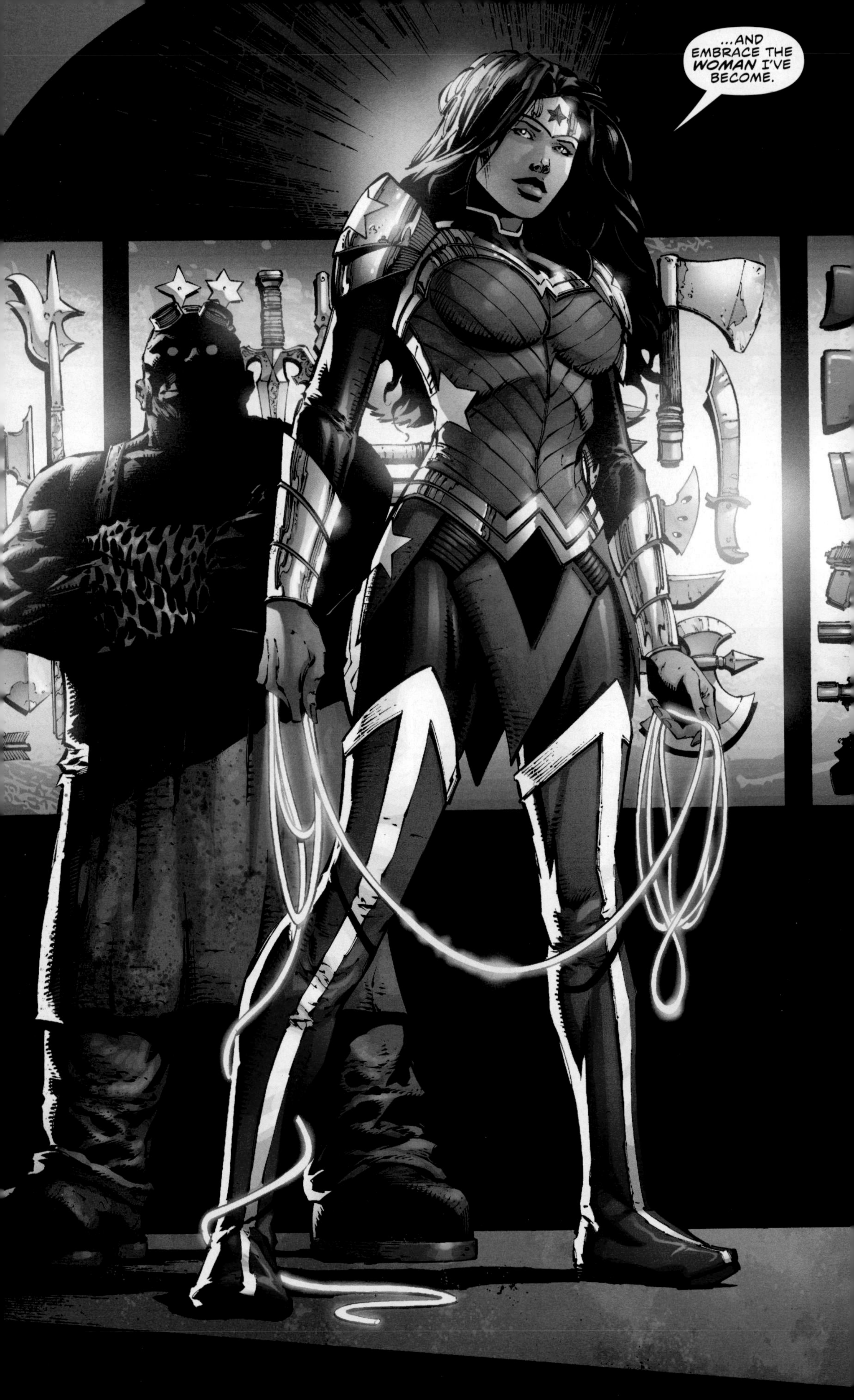
...AND EMBRACE THE WOMAN I'VE BECOME.

ON MY WAY HOME FROM OLYMPUS, I GOT A CALL FROM *CYBORG.* HE HEARD ON THE POLICE SCANNERS THAT SOME KID HAS THREATENED TO BLOW HIMSELF UP UNLESS HE GETS TO MEET WONDER WOMAN.

I DON'T USUALLY INTERFERE IN POLICE BUSINESS, BUT IN THIS CASE...I COULDN'T LIVE WITH THE POSSIBILITY OF FAILURE.

WE REALLY DON'T WANT TO BOTHER YOU, WONDER WOMAN. I'M SURE MY GUYS CAN HANDLE THIS.

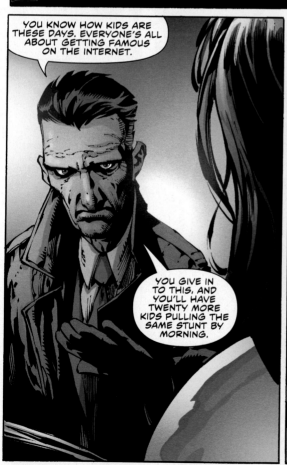

YOU KNOW HOW KIDS ARE THESE DAYS. EVERYONE'S ALL ABOUT GETTING FAMOUS ON THE INTERNET.

YOU GIVE IN TO THIS, AND YOU'LL HAVE TWENTY MORE KIDS PULLING THE SAME STUNT BY MORNING.

MAYBE. BUT I'M NOT WILLING TO TAKE THAT CHANCE. NOT WHEN I CAN HELP.

JUST KEEP YOUR MEN CLEAR.

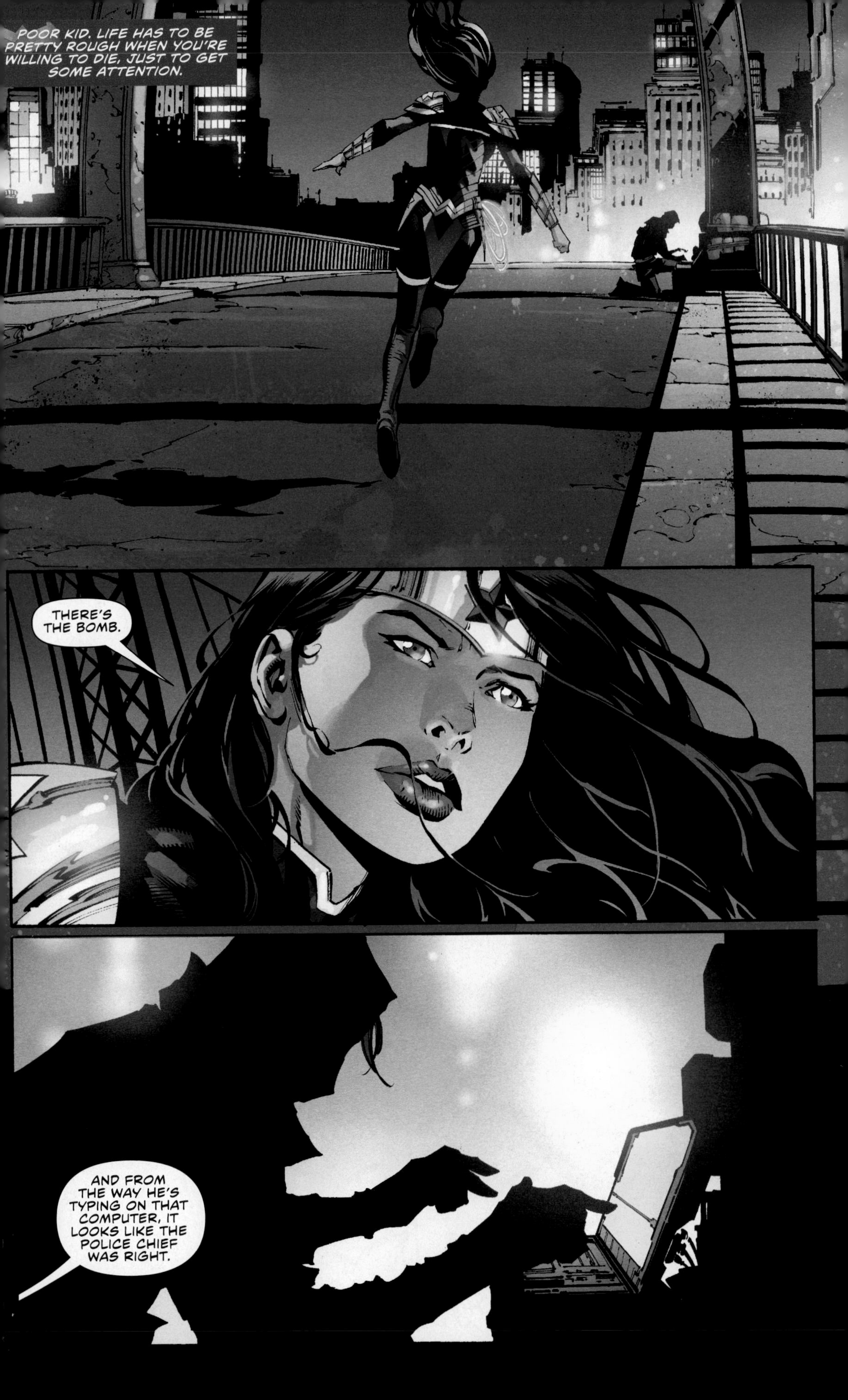
POOR KID. LIFE HAS TO BE PRETTY ROUGH WHEN YOU'RE WILLING TO DIE, JUST TO GET SOME ATTENTION.
THERE'S THE BOMB.
AND FROM THE WAY HE'S TYPING ON THAT COMPUTER, IT LOOKS LIKE THE POLICE CHIEF WAS RIGHT.

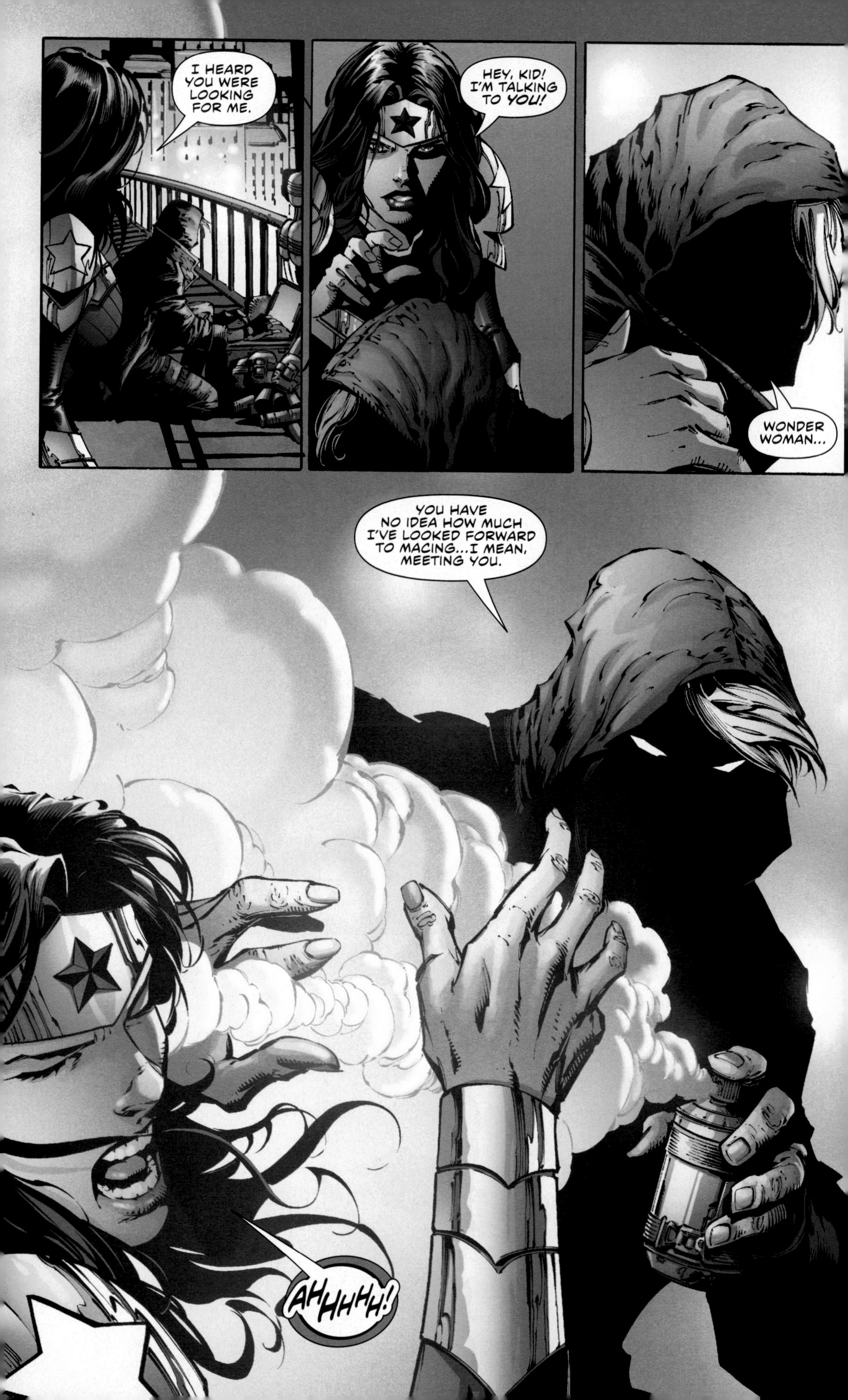
I HEARD YOU WERE LOOKING FOR ME.
HEY, KID! I'M TALKING TO *YOU!*
WONDER WOMAN...
YOU HAVE NO IDEA HOW MUCH I'VE LOOKED FORWARD TO MACING...I MEAN, MEETING YOU.
AHHHHH!

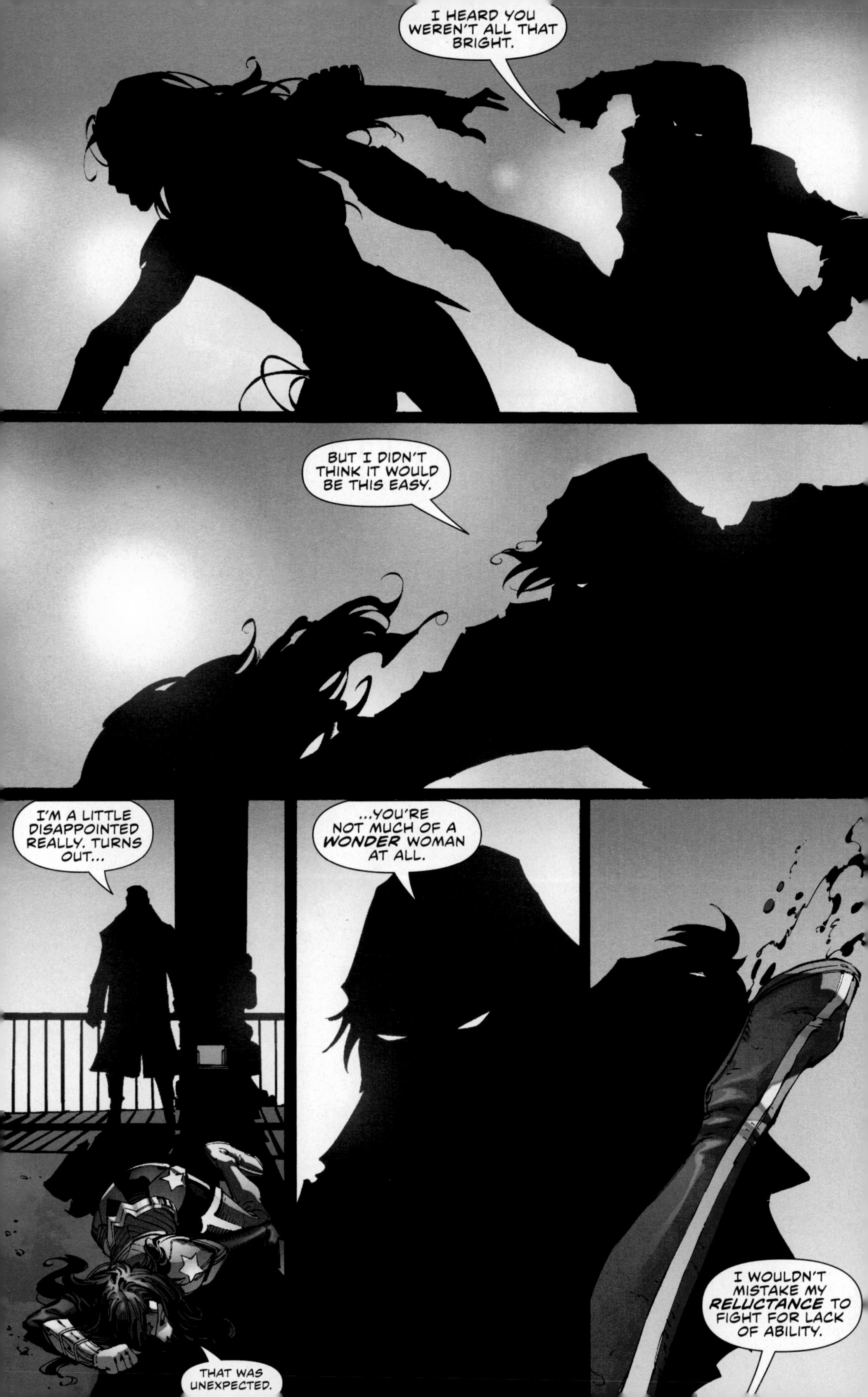
I HEARD YOU WEREN'T ALL THAT BRIGHT.
BUT I DIDN'T THINK IT WOULD BE THIS EASY.
I'M A LITTLE DISAPPOINTED REALLY. TURNS OUT...
THAT WAS UNEXPECTED.
...YOU'RE NOT MUCH OF A WONDER WOMAN AT ALL.
I WOULDN'T MISTAKE MY RELUCTANCE TO FIGHT FOR LACK OF ABILITY.

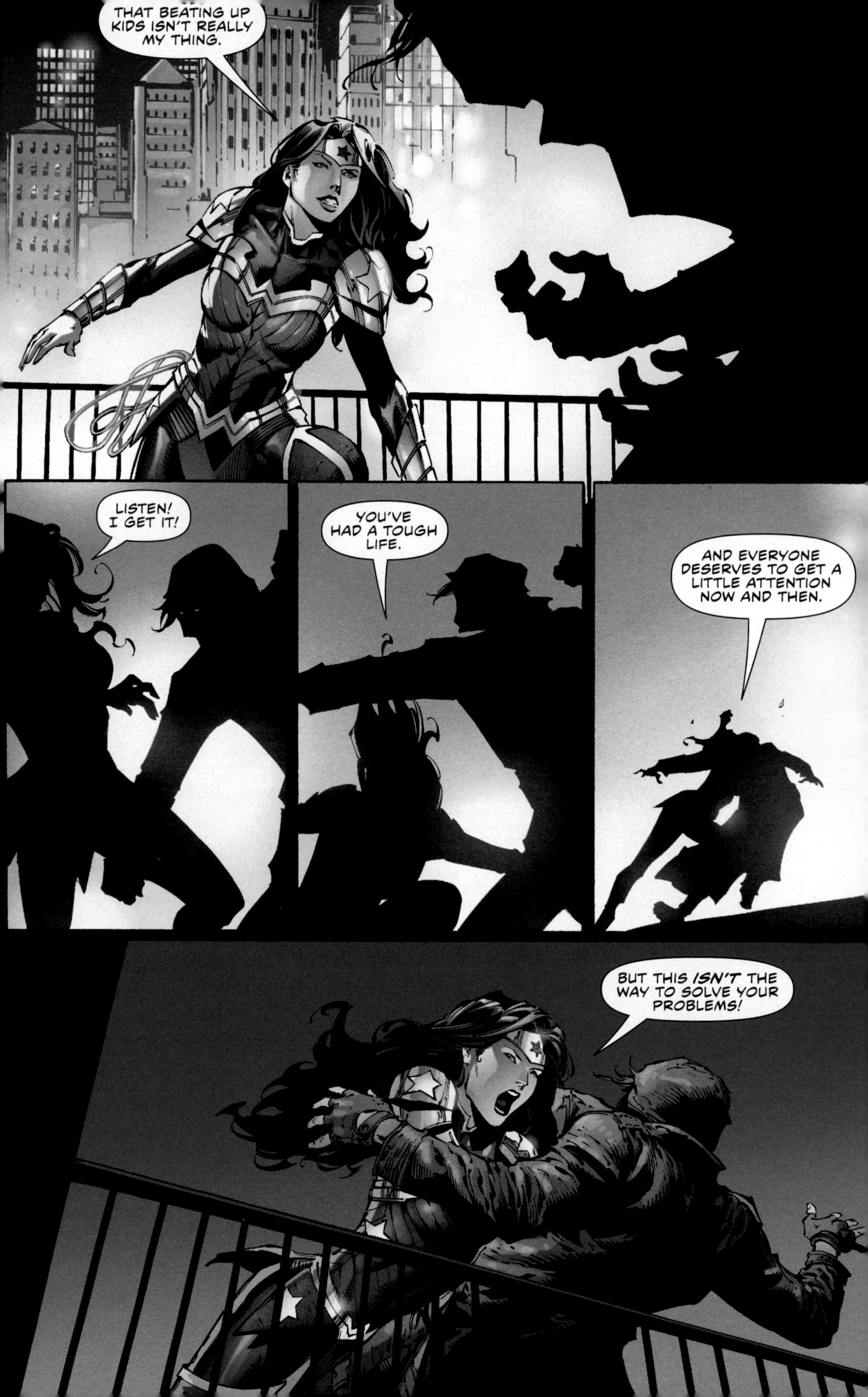
THAT BEATING UP KIDS ISN'T REALLY MY THING.
LISTEN! I GET IT!
YOU'VE HAD A TOUGH LIFE.
AND EVERYONE DESERVES TO GET A LITTLE ATTENTION NOW AND THEN.
BUT THIS *ISN'T* THE WAY TO SOLVE YOUR PROBLEMS!

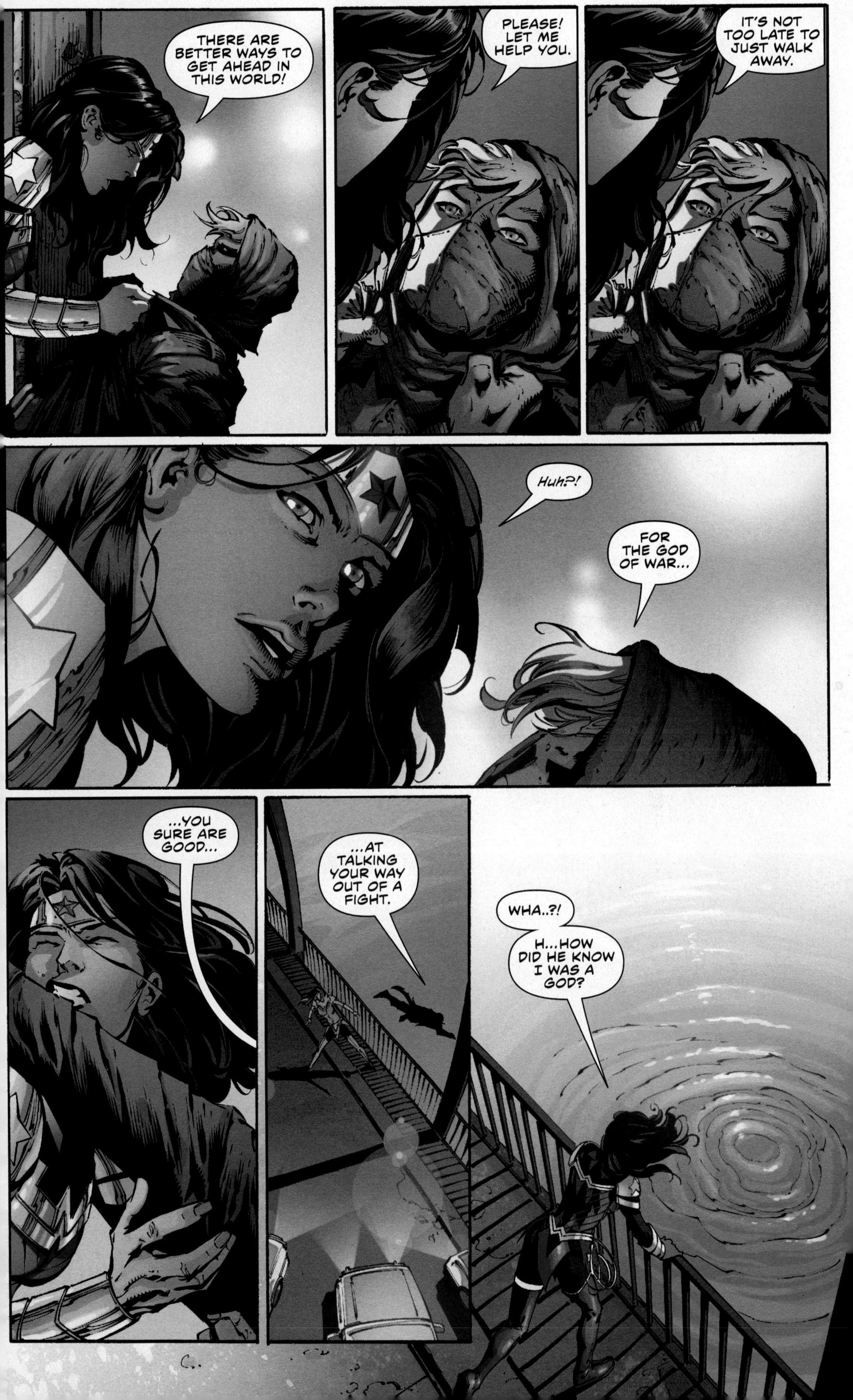
THERE ARE BETTER WAYS TO GET AHEAD IN THIS WORLD!
PLEASE! LET ME HELP YOU.
IT'S NOT TOO LATE TO JUST WALK AWAY.
Huh?!
FOR THE GOD OF WAR...
...YOU SURE ARE GOOD...
...AT TALKING YOUR WAY OUT OF A FIGHT.
WHA..?!
H...HOW DID HE KNOW I WAS A GOD?

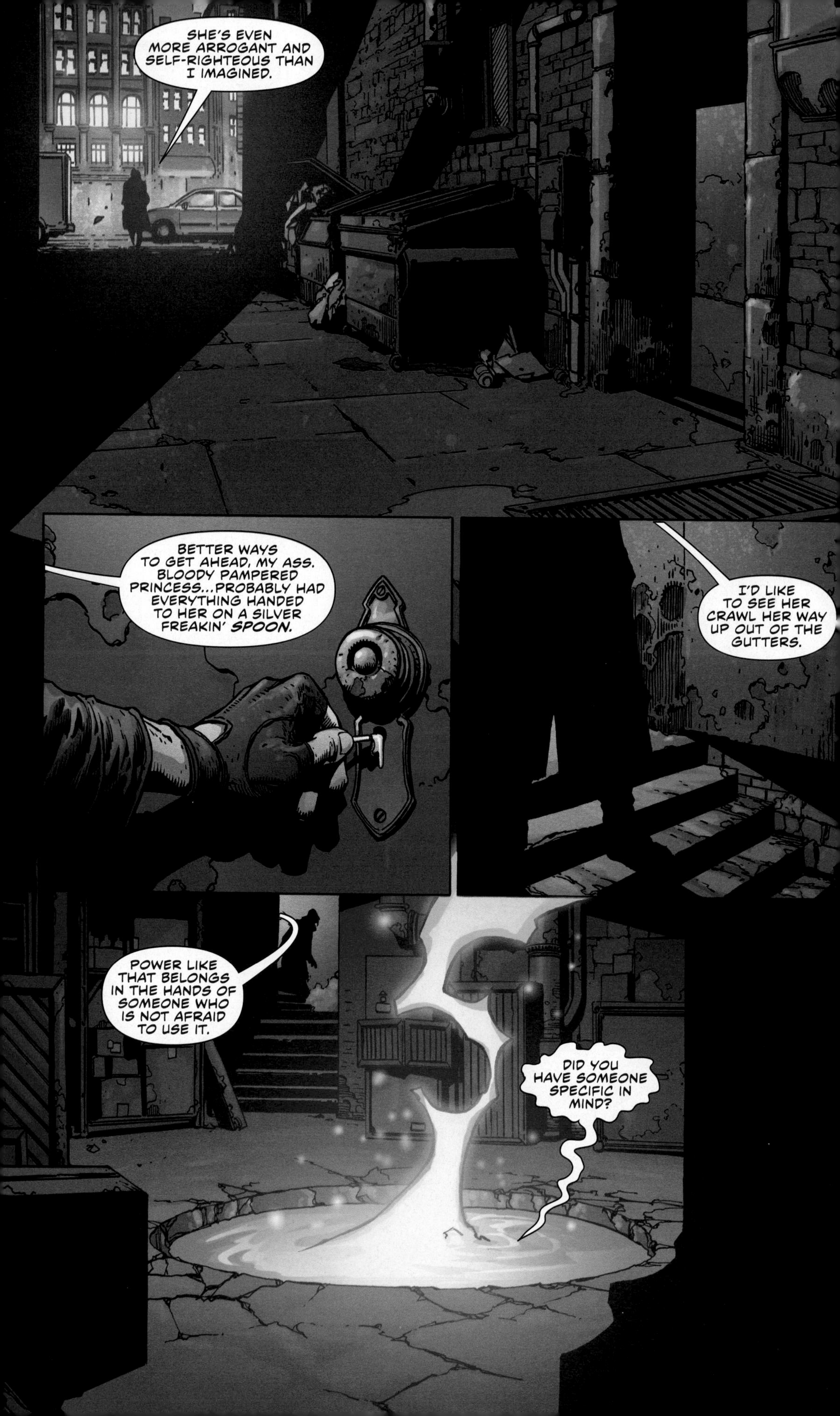

SHE'S EVEN MORE ARROGANT AND SELF-RIGHTEOUS THAN I IMAGINED.
BETTER WAYS TO GET AHEAD, MY ASS. BLOODY PAMPERED PRINCESS...PROBABLY HAD EVERYTHING HANDED TO HER ON A SILVER FREAKIN' *SPOON.*
I'D LIKE TO SEE HER CRAWL HER WAY UP OUT OF THE GUTTERS.
POWER LIKE THAT BELONGS IN THE HANDS OF SOMEONE WHO IS NOT AFRAID TO USE IT.
DID YOU HAVE SOMEONE SPECIFIC IN MIND?

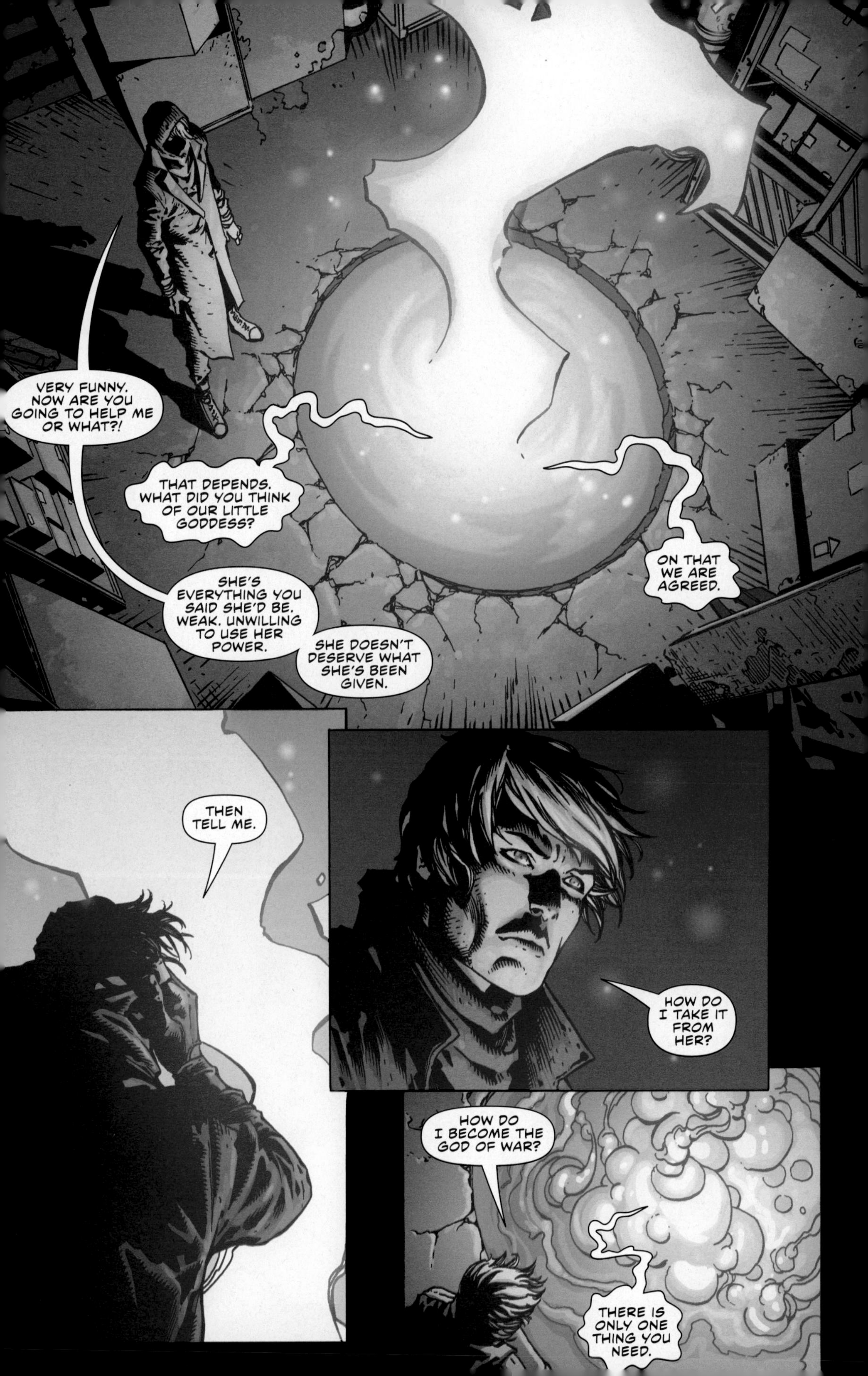
VERY FUNNY. NOW ARE YOU GOING TO HELP ME OR WHAT?!
THAT DEPENDS. WHAT DID YOU THINK OF OUR LITTLE GODDESS?
SHE'S EVERYTHING YOU SAID SHE'D BE. WEAK. UNWILLING TO USE HER POWER.
SHE DOESN'T DESERVE WHAT SHE'S BEEN GIVEN.
ON THAT WE ARE AGREED.
THEN TELL ME.
HOW DO I TAKE IT FROM HER?
HOW DO I BECOME THE GOD OF WAR?
THERE IS ONLY ONE THING YOU NEED.

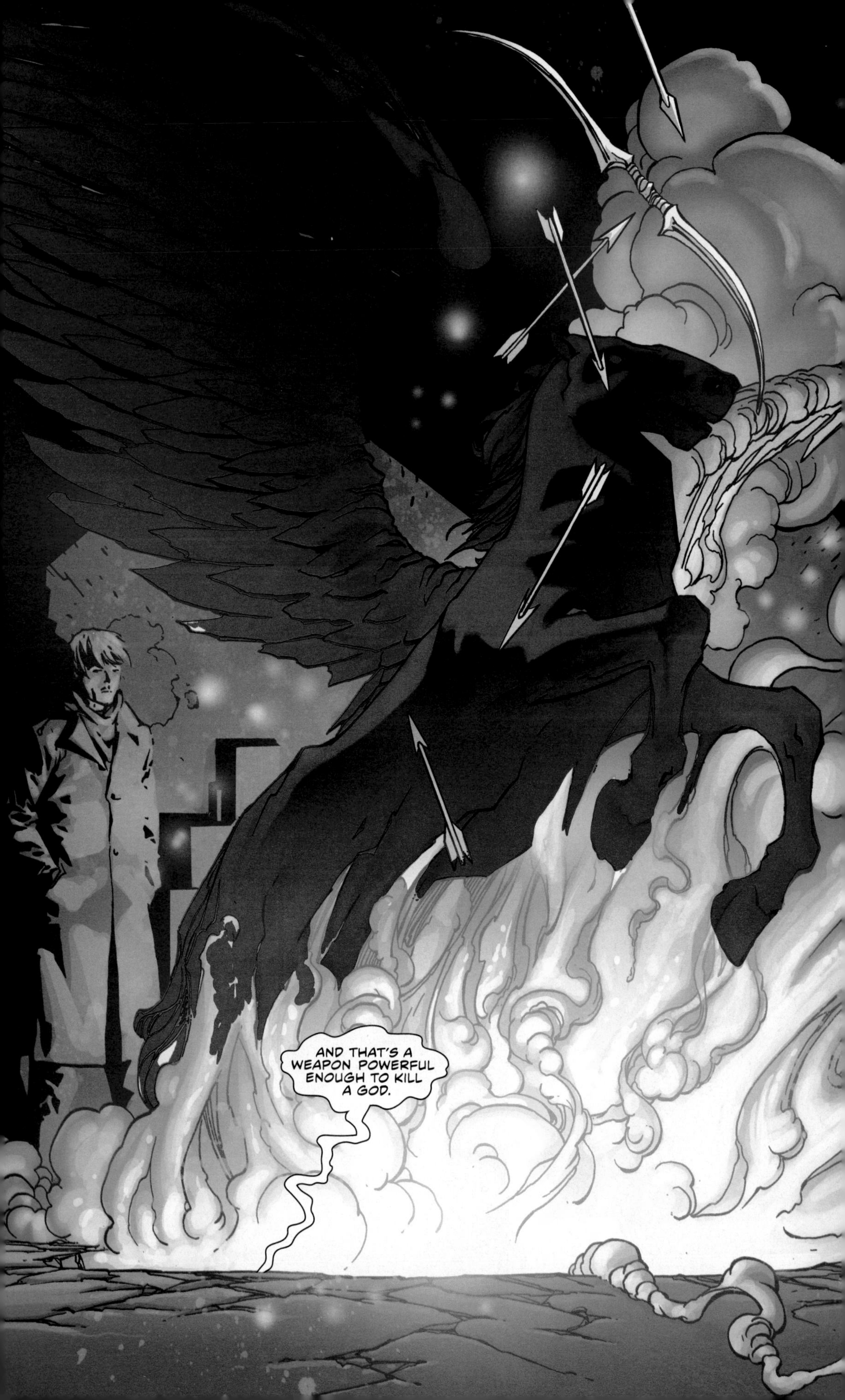
AND THAT'S A WEAPON POWERFUL ENOUGH TO KILL A GOD.

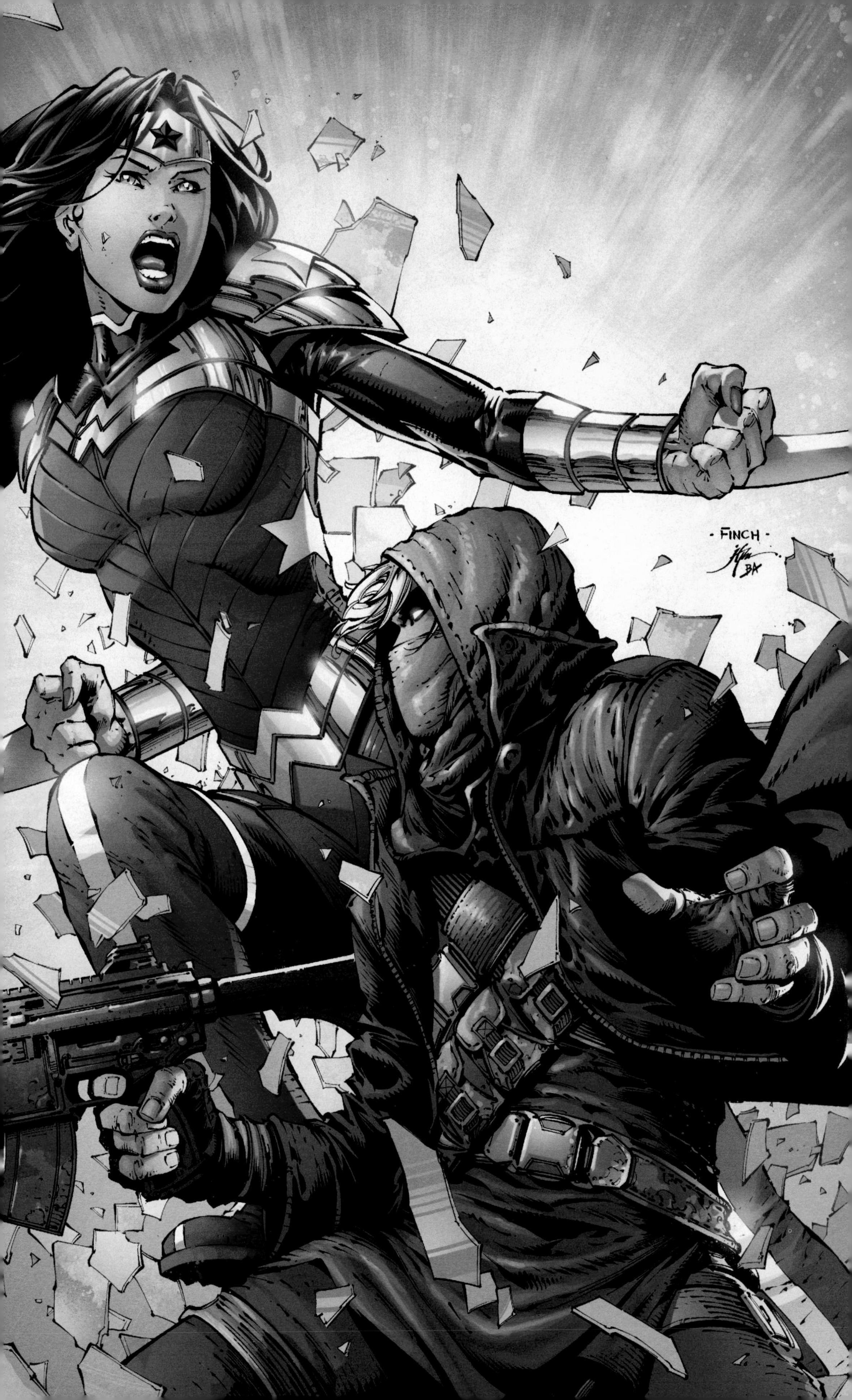
-FINCH-

STRUGGLE & STRIFE

MEREDITH FINCH writer DAVID FINCH penciller JONATHAN GLAPION JOHNNY DESJARDINS inkers BRAD ANDERSON colorist ROB LEIGH letterer
cover by FINCH, GLAPION & ANDERSON

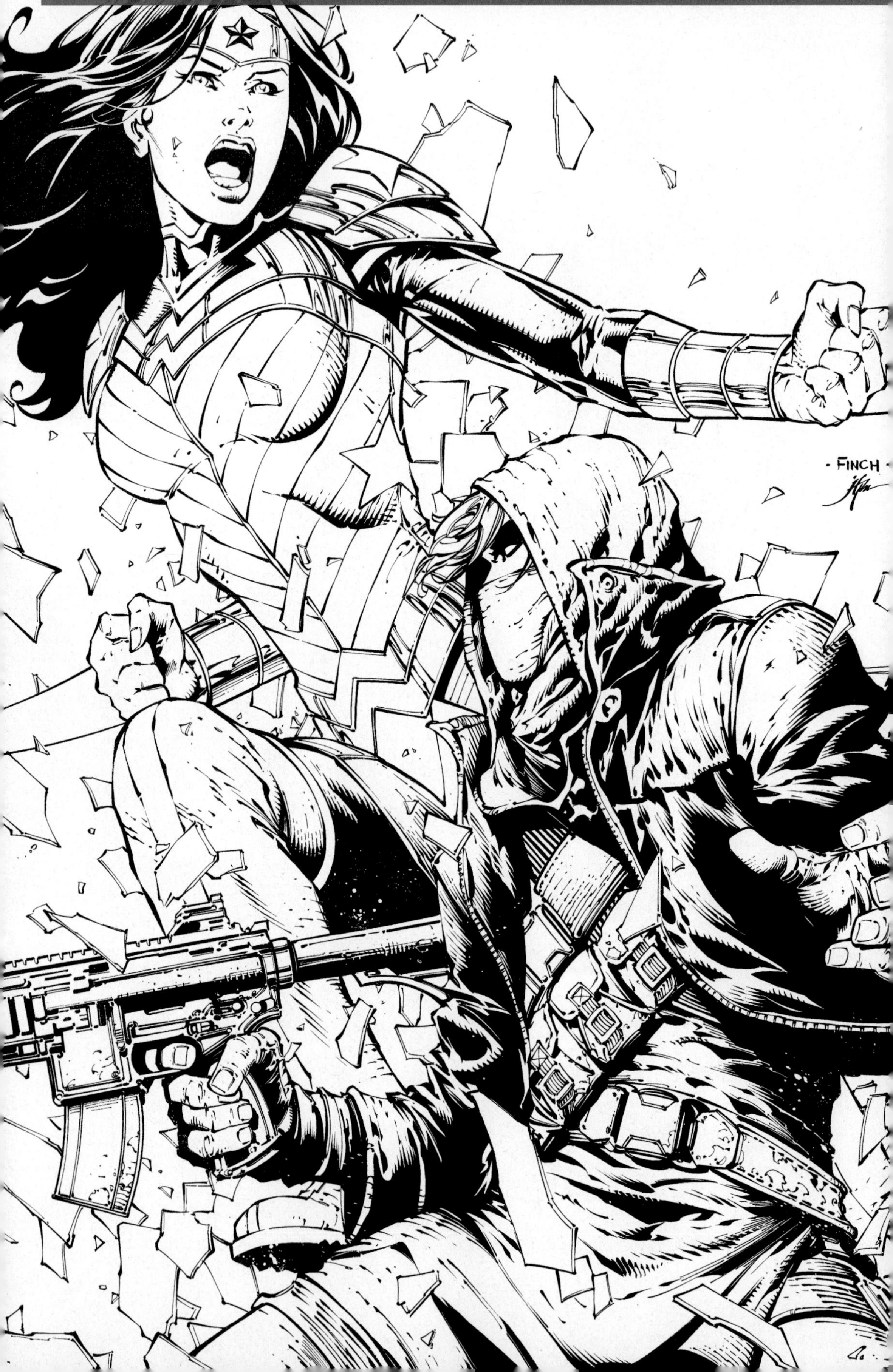

- FINCH -

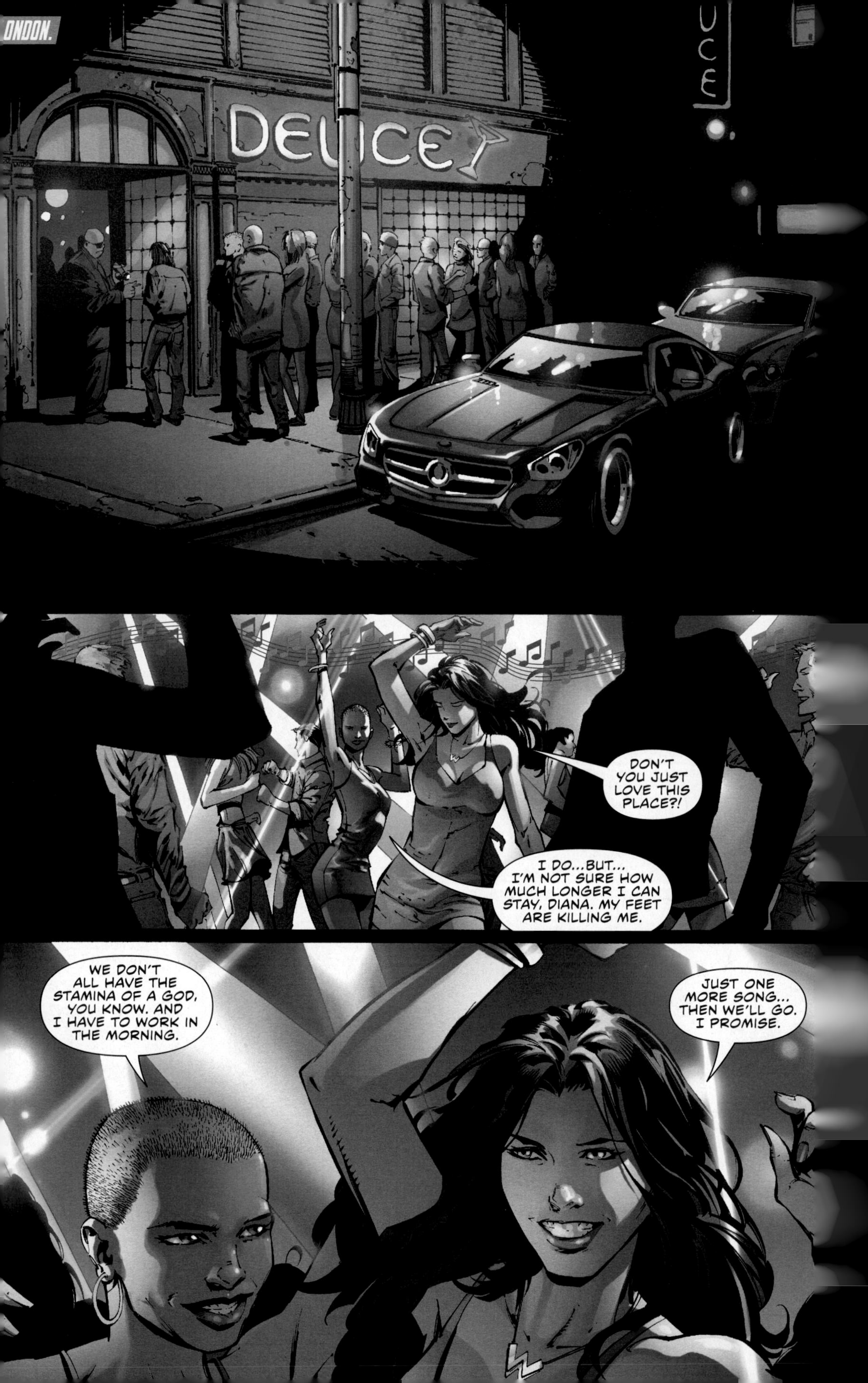
ONDON.
DEUCE
UCE
DON'T YOU JUST LOVE THIS PLACE?!
I DO...BUT... I'M NOT SURE HOW MUCH LONGER I CAN STAY, DIANA. MY FEET ARE KILLING ME.
WE DON'T ALL HAVE THE STAMINA OF A GOD, YOU KNOW. AND I HAVE TO WORK IN THE MORNING.
JUST ONE MORE SONG... THEN WE'LL GO. I PROMISE.

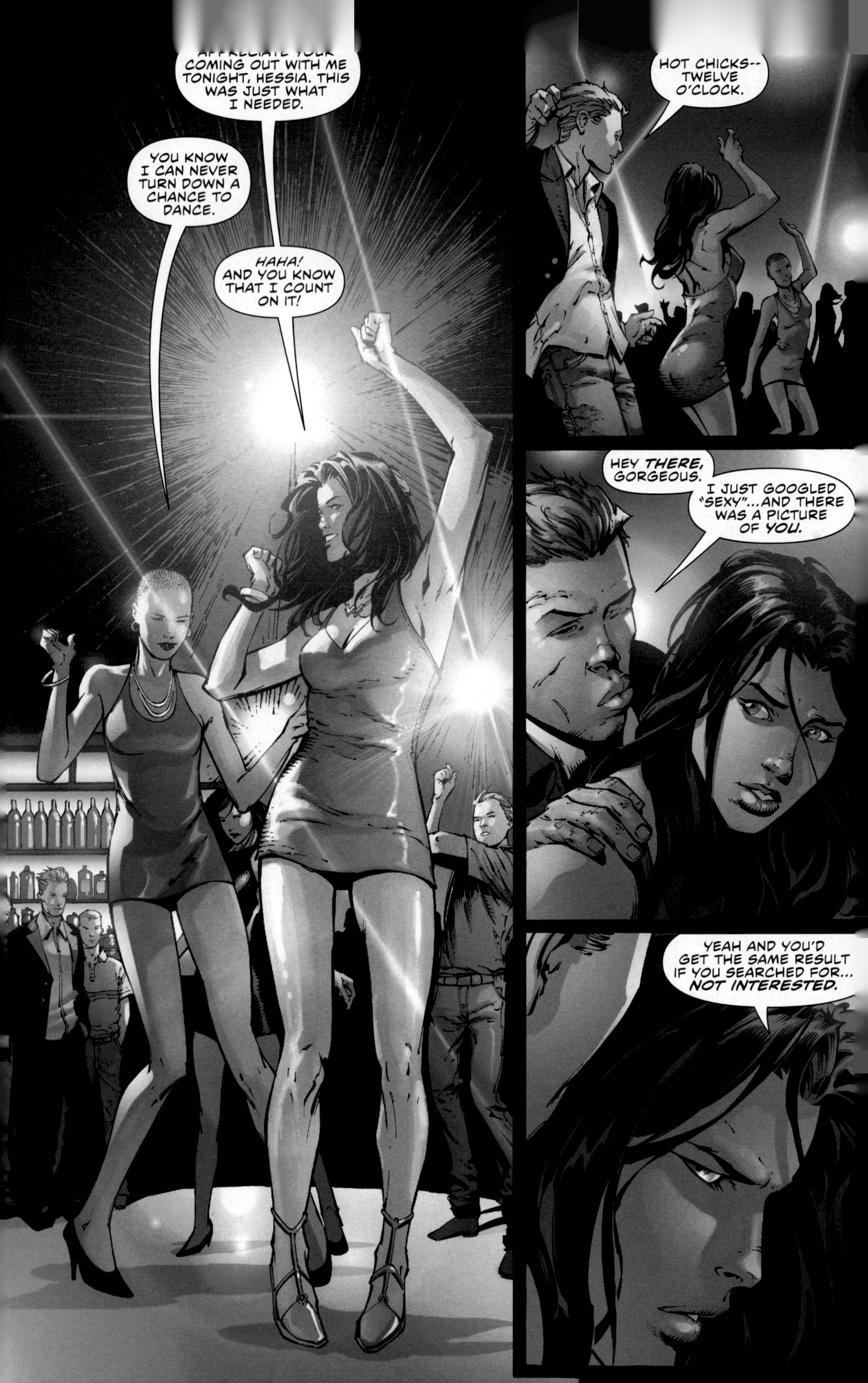
COMING OUT WITH ME TONIGHT, HESSIA. THIS WAS JUST WHAT I NEEDED.
YOU KNOW I CAN NEVER TURN DOWN A CHANCE TO DANCE.
HAHA! AND YOU KNOW THAT I COUNT ON IT!
HOT CHICKS-- TWELVE O'CLOCK.
HEY ***THERE,*** GORGEOUS.
I JUST GOOGLED "SEXY"...AND THERE WAS A PICTURE OF ***YOU.***
YEAH AND YOU'D GET THE SAME RESULT IF YOU SEARCHED FOR... ***NOT INTERESTED.***

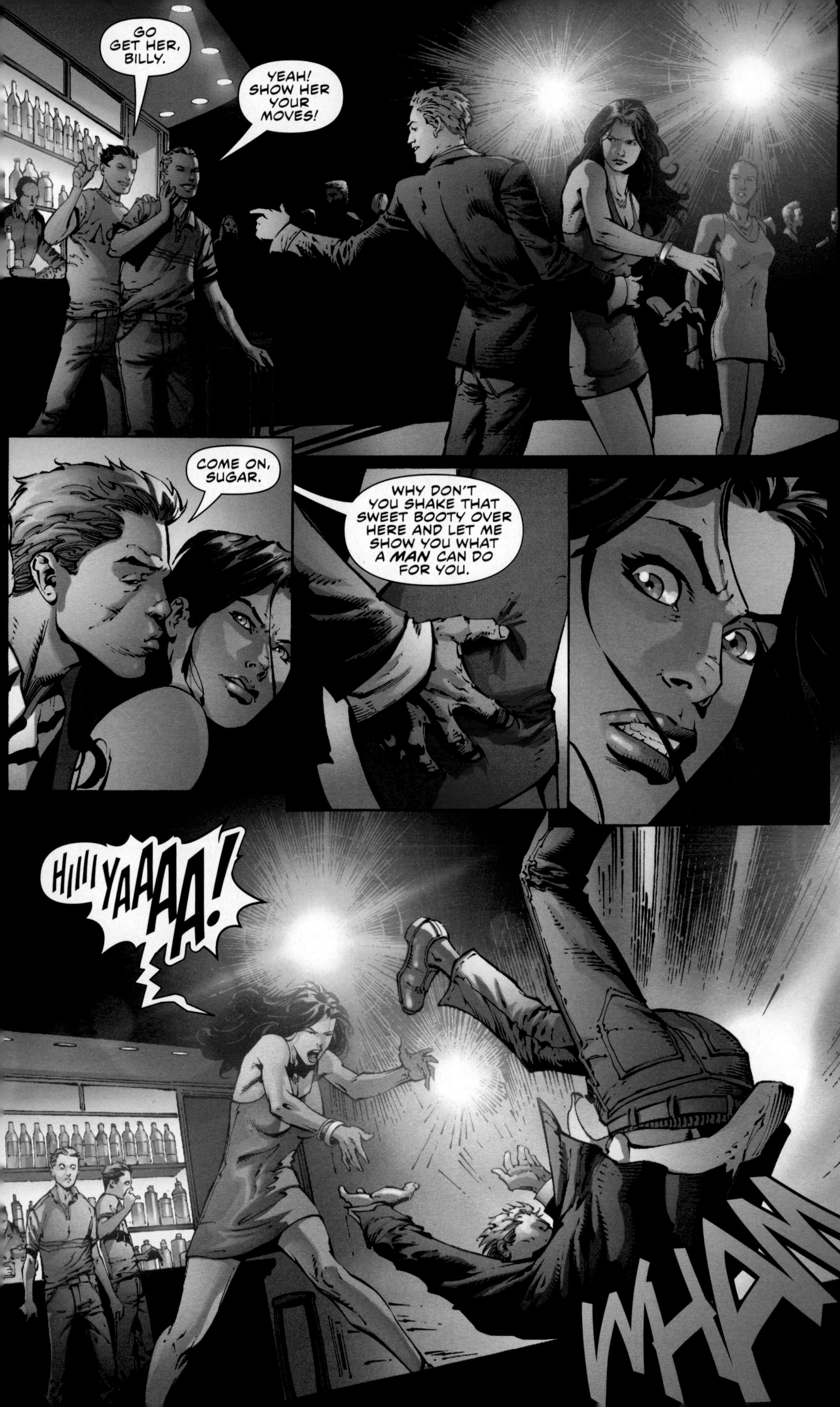
GO GET HER, BILLY.
YEAH! SHOW HER YOUR MOVES!
COME ON, SUGAR.
WHY DON'T YOU SHAKE THAT SWEET BOOTY OVER HERE AND LET ME SHOW YOU WHAT A *MAN* CAN DO FOR YOU.
HIIIIYAAAAA!
WHAM

THE ONLY *THING* YOU CAN *DO* FOR ME...

...IS TO GIVE YOUR HEAD A SHAKE THE NEXT TIME YOU EVEN *THINK* ABOUT PUTTING YOUR HANDS ON A WOMAN WITHOUT HER *PERMISSION*.

NICE WORK, LADY D.

NEXT TIME WE'RE LOOKING FOR A BOUNCER... I KNOW JUST THE GIRL FOR THE JOB.

YOU KNOW IT, J.T.!

I'LL SEE YOU NEXT WEEK.

WELL, *THAT* WAS AN EVENTFUL WAY TO END THE EVENING.

I'D LIKE TO SAY HE WAS HARMLESS...BUT THAT KIND OF THING ALWAYS HURTS SOMEONE.

HE'S JUST LUCKY THE ONLY THING I HURT TONIGHT WAS HIS PRIDE.

HOMELESS VET HUNGRY PLEASE HELP

CAN EITHER OF YOU LOVELY LADIES SPARE A BIT O' CHANGE FOR A POOR BUGGER, DOWN ON HIS LUCK?

HOMELESS VET HUNGRY PLEASE HELP

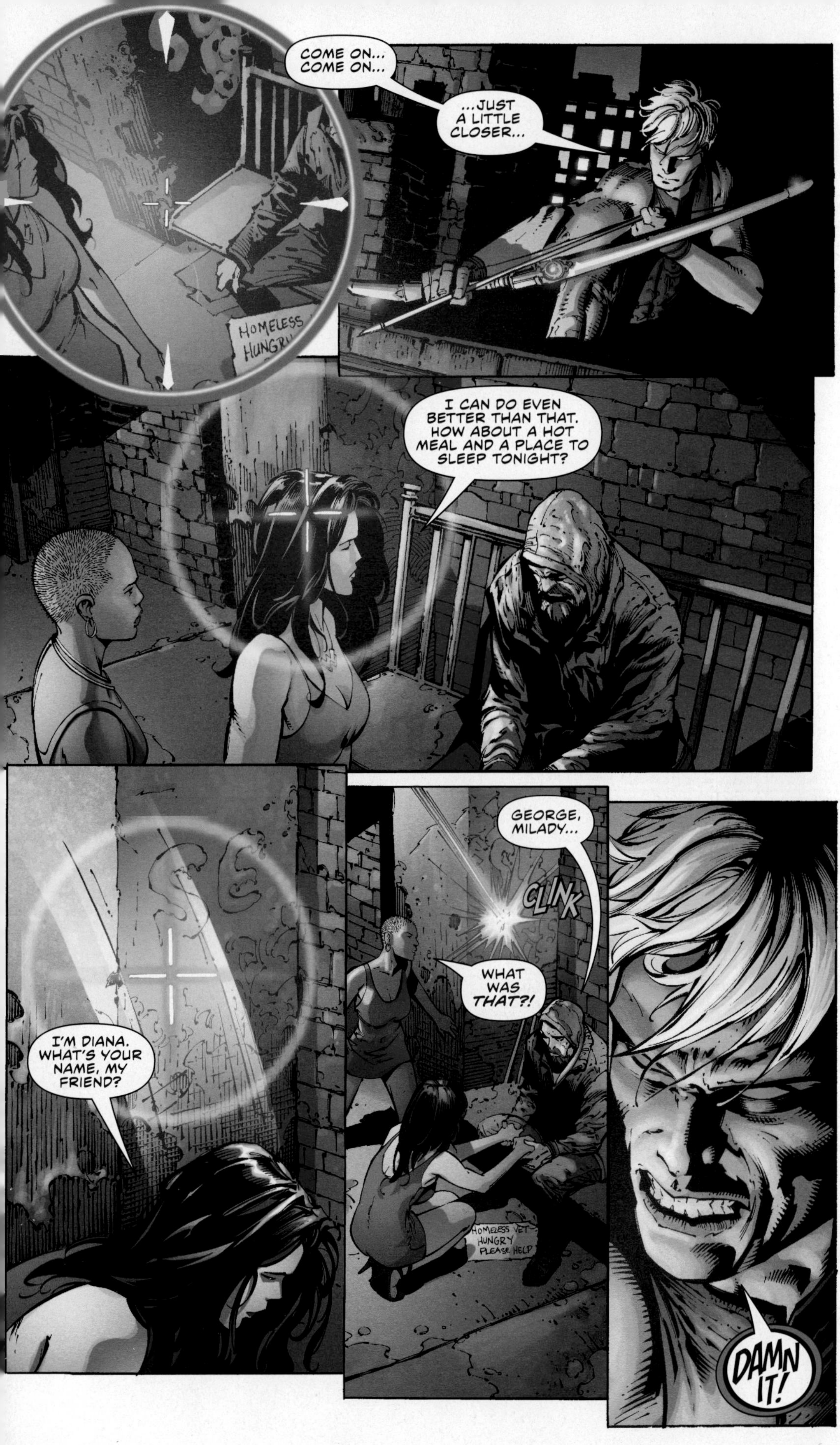
COME ON...
COME ON...
...JUST
A LITTLE
CLOSER...
HOMELESS
HUNGRY
I CAN DO EVEN
BETTER THAN THAT.
HOW ABOUT A HOT
MEAL AND A PLACE TO
SLEEP TONIGHT?
I'M DIANA.
WHAT'S YOUR
NAME, MY
FRIEND?
GEORGE,
MILADY...
CLINK
WHAT
WAS
THAT?!
HOMELESS VET
HUNGRY
PLEASE HELP
DAMN
IT!

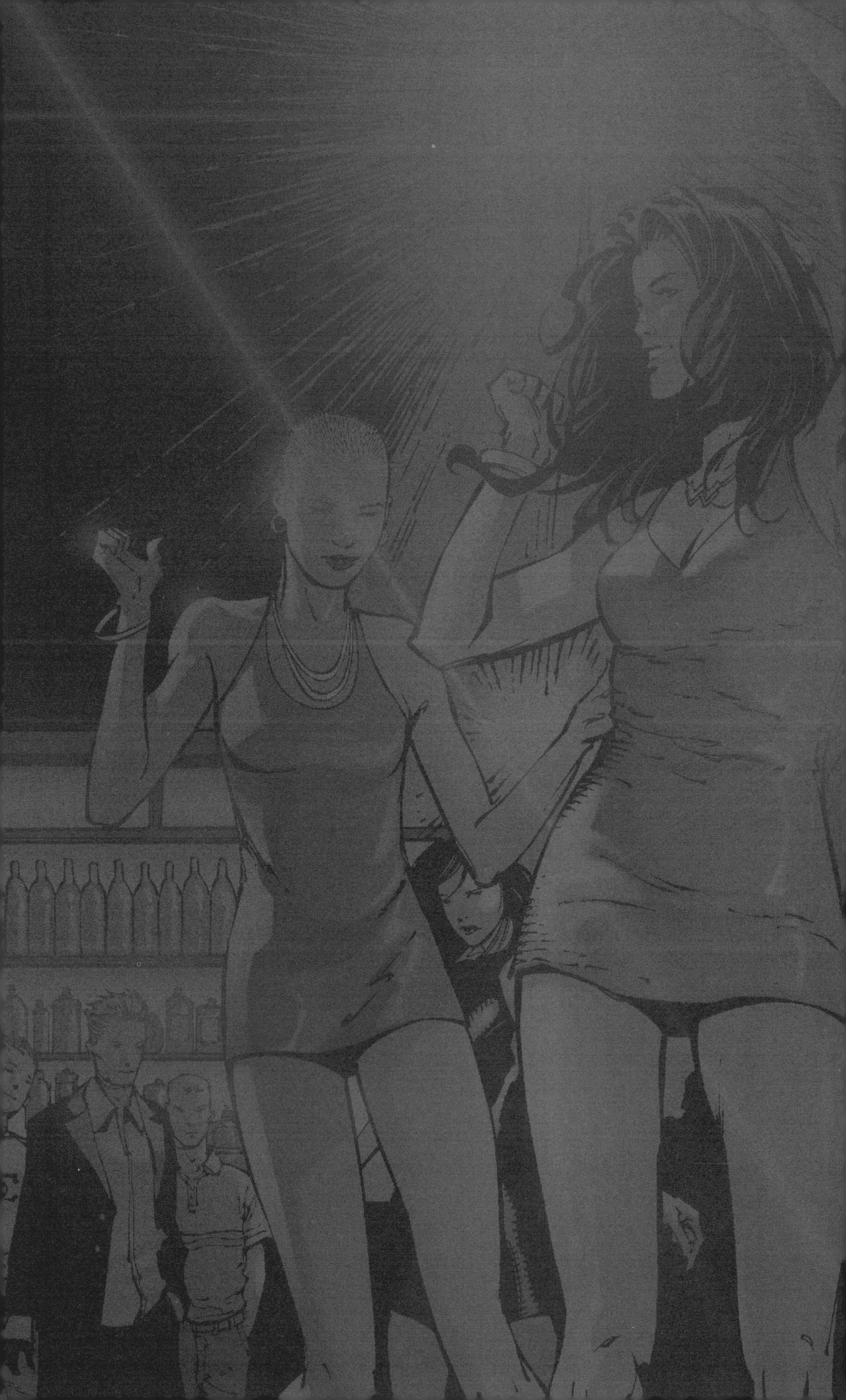

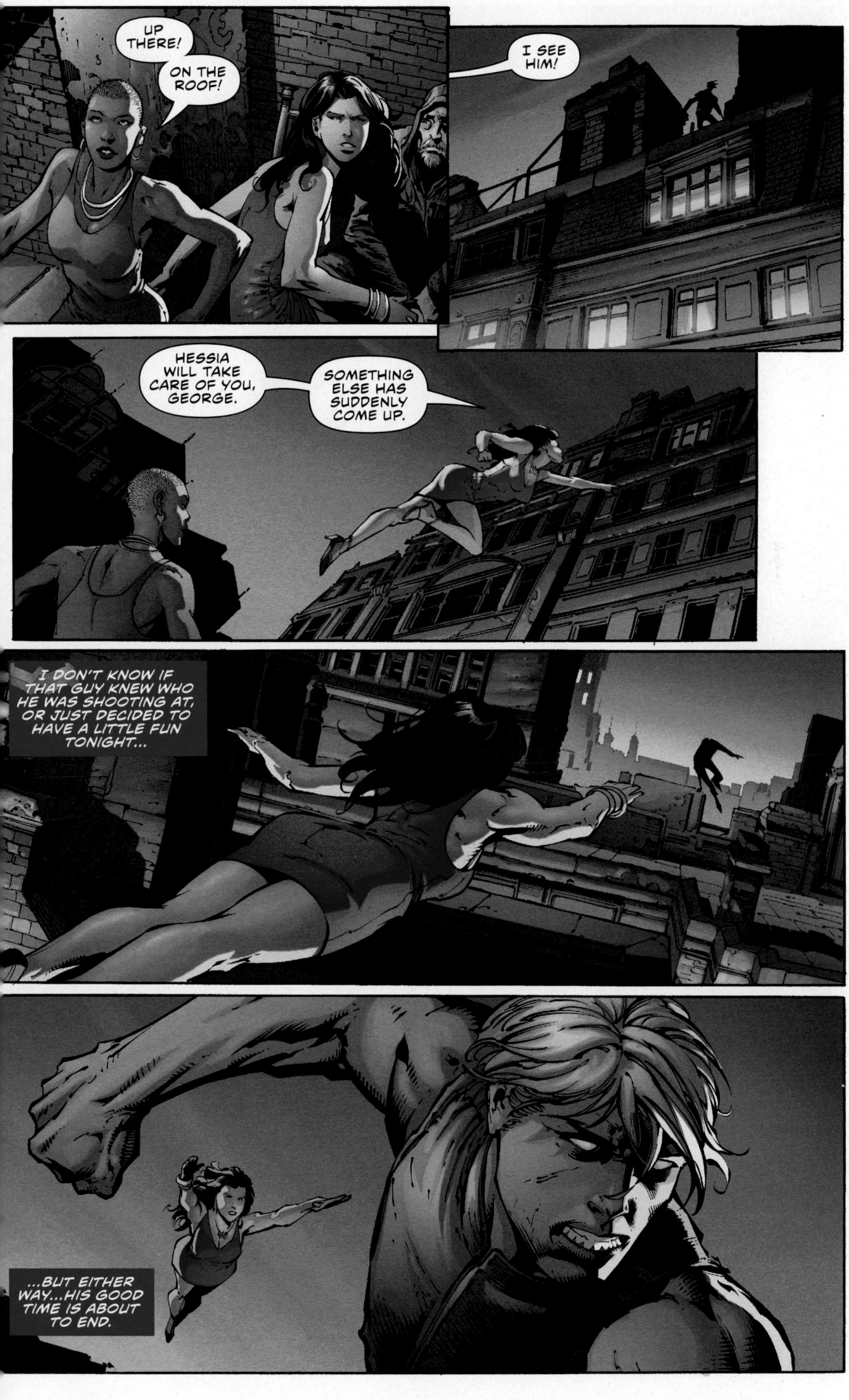
UP THERE!
ON THE ROOF!
I SEE HIM!
HESSIA WILL TAKE CARE OF YOU, GEORGE.
SOMETHING ELSE HAS SUDDENLY COME UP.
I DON'T KNOW IF THAT GUY KNEW WHO HE WAS SHOOTING AT, OR JUST DECIDED TO HAVE A LITTLE FUN TONIGHT...
...BUT EITHER WAY...HIS GOOD TIME IS ABOUT TO END.

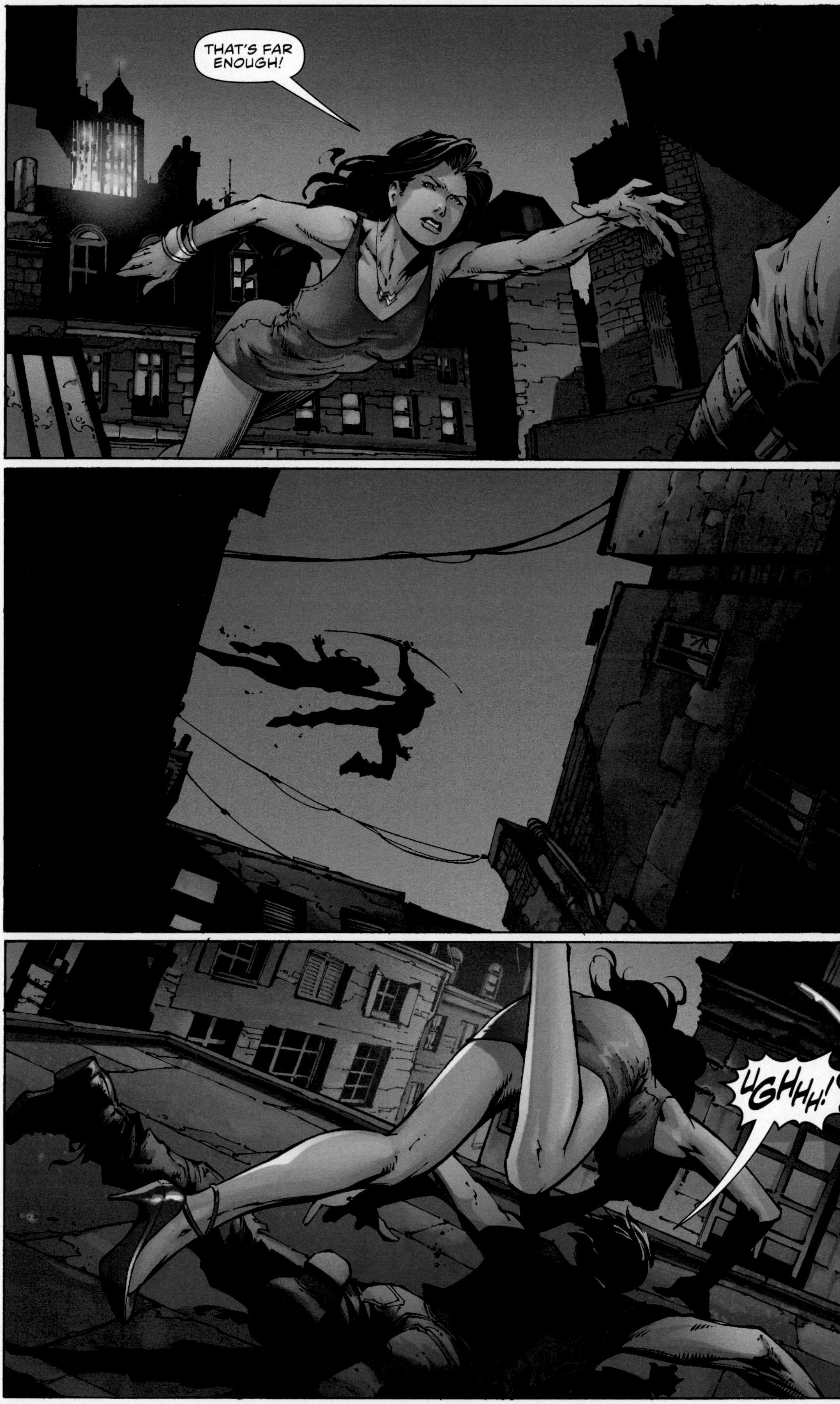
THAT'S FAR ENOUGH!
UGHHH!

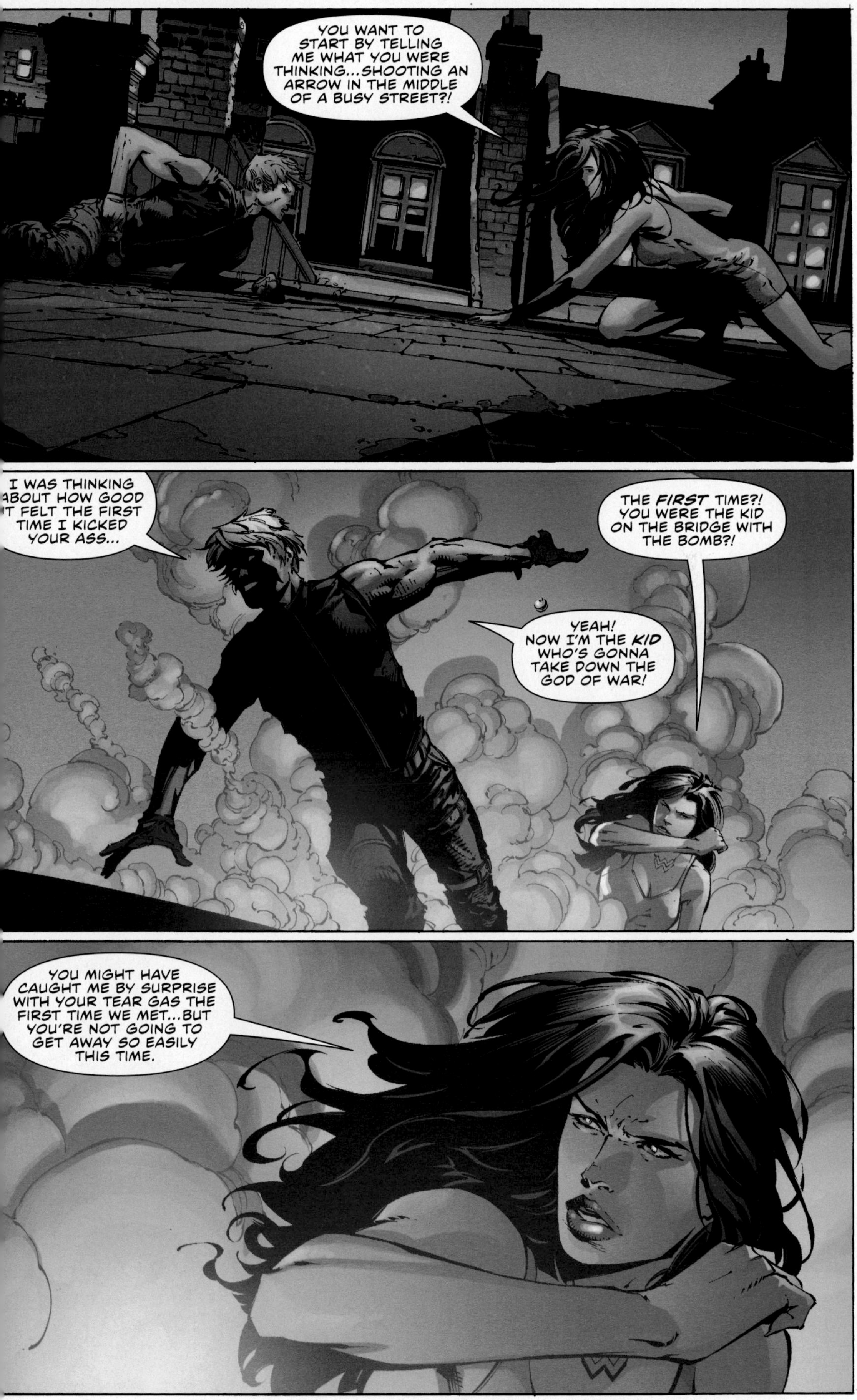
YOU WANT TO START BY TELLING ME WHAT YOU WERE THINKING...SHOOTING AN ARROW IN THE MIDDLE OF A BUSY STREET?!
I WAS THINKING ABOUT HOW GOOD IT FELT THE FIRST TIME I KICKED YOUR ASS...
THE FIRST TIME?! YOU WERE THE KID ON THE BRIDGE WITH THE BOMB?!
YEAH! NOW I'M THE KID WHO'S GONNA TAKE DOWN THE GOD OF WAR!
YOU MIGHT HAVE CAUGHT ME BY SURPRISE WITH YOUR TEAR GAS THE FIRST TIME WE MET...BUT YOU'RE NOT GOING TO GET AWAY SO EASILY THIS TIME.

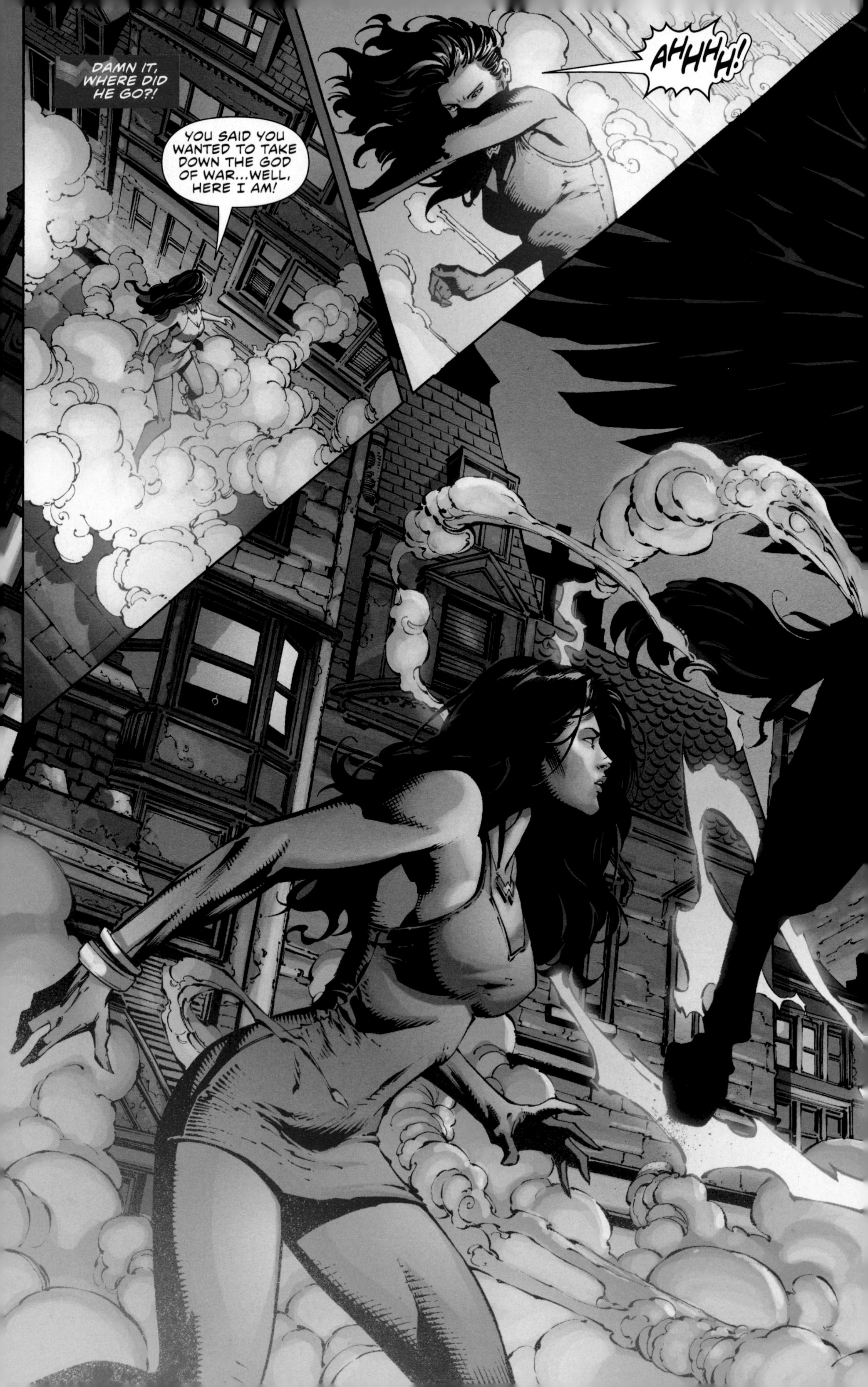
DAMN IT, WHERE DID HE GO?!
AHHHH!
YOU SAID YOU WANTED TO TAKE DOWN THE GOD OF WAR...WELL, HERE I AM!

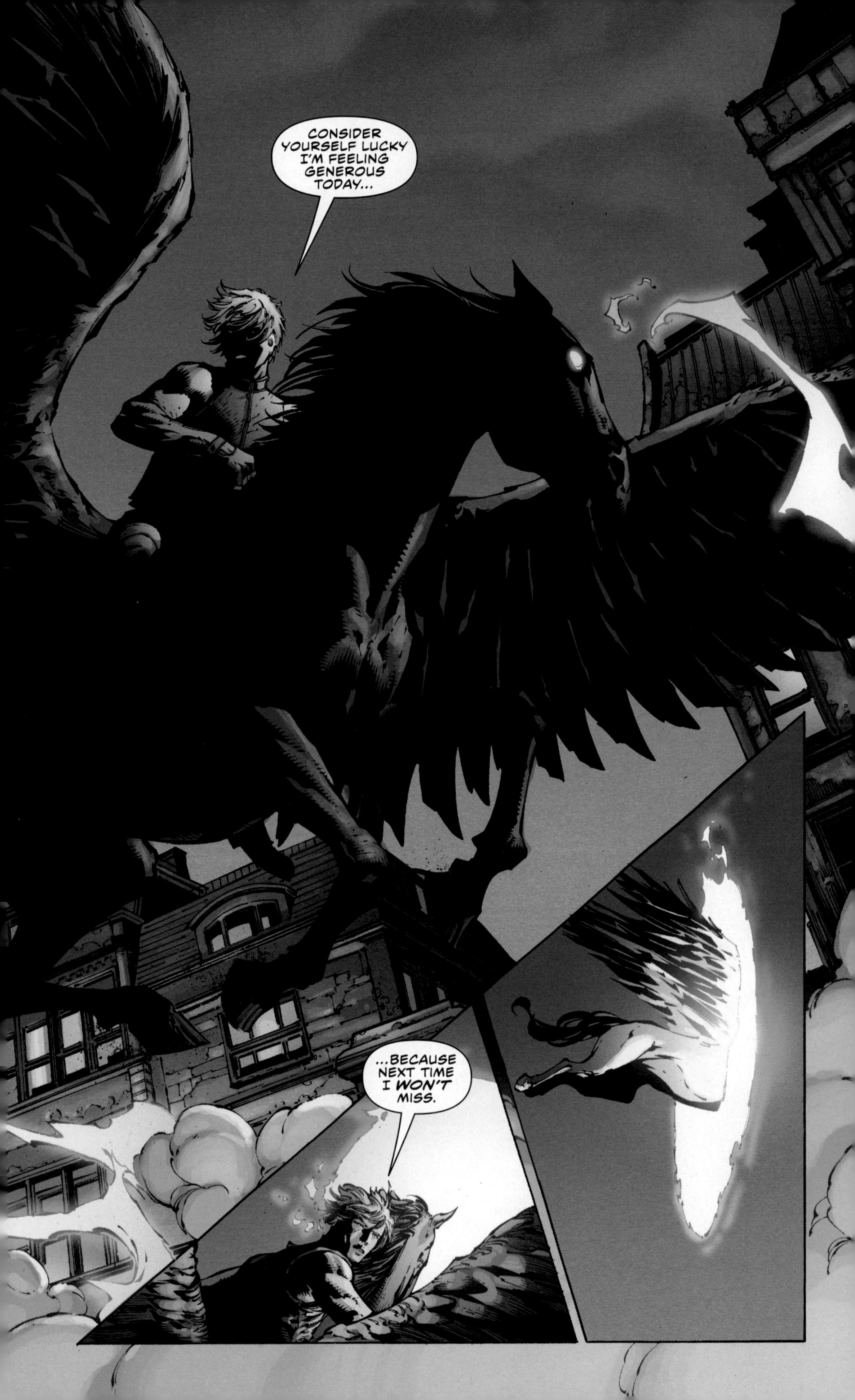
CONSIDER YOURSELF LUCKY I'M FEELING GENEROUS TODAY...
...BECAUSE NEXT TIME I *WON'T* MISS.

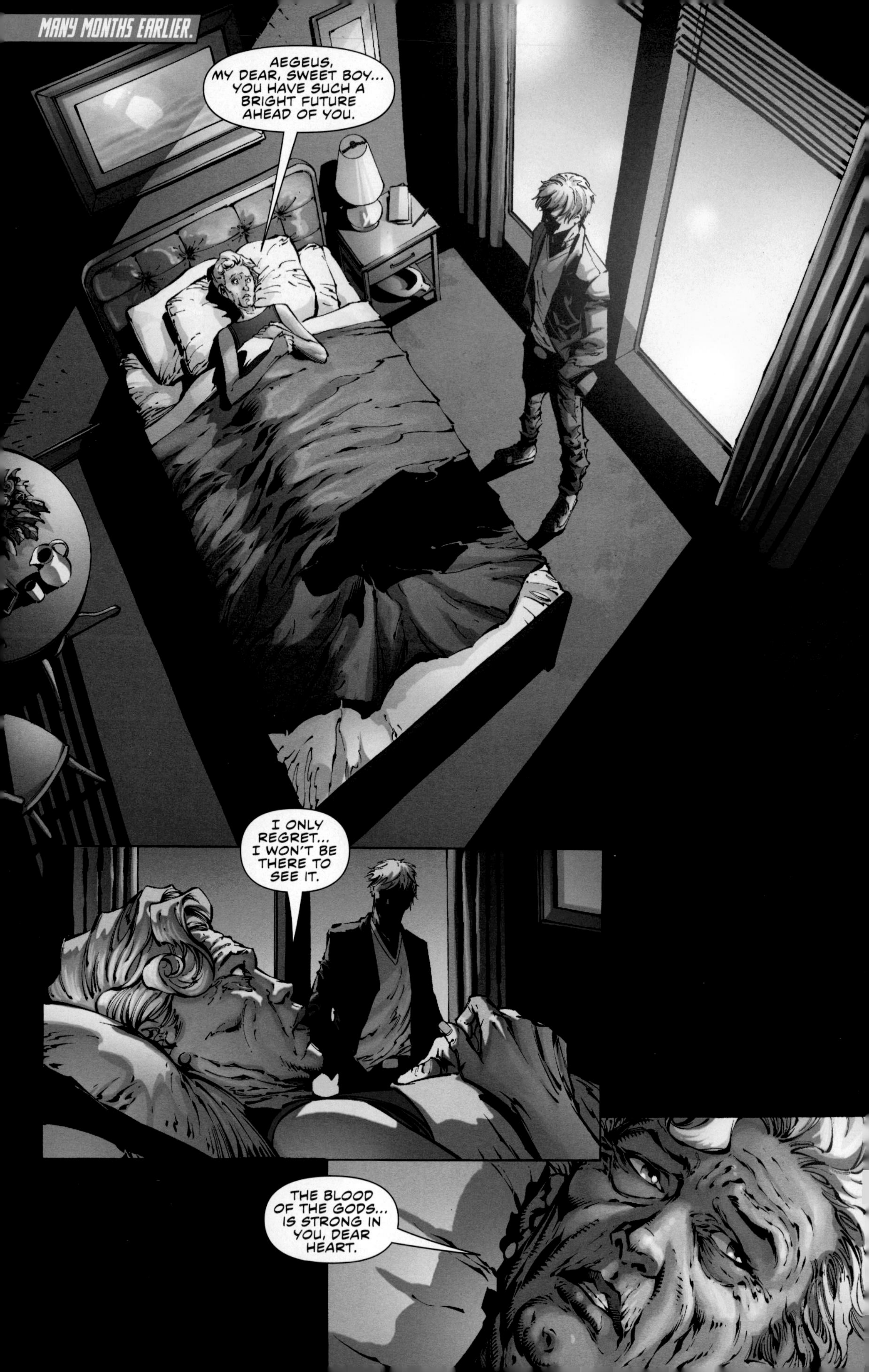
MANY MONTHS EARLIER.
AEGEUS, MY DEAR, SWEET BOY... YOU HAVE SUCH A BRIGHT FUTURE AHEAD OF YOU.
I ONLY REGRET... I WON'T BE THERE TO SEE IT.
THE BLOOD OF THE GODS... IS STRONG IN YOU, DEAR HEART.

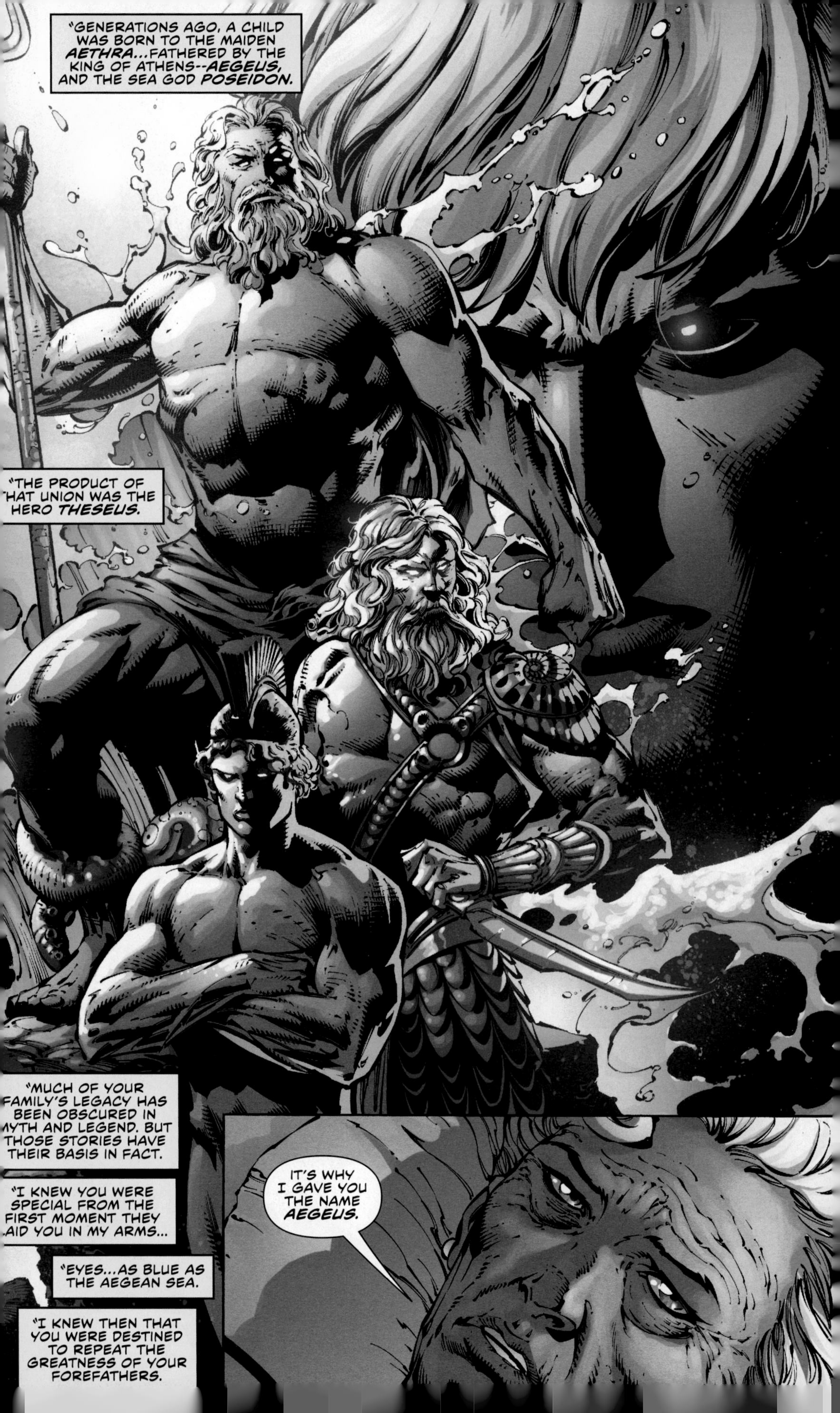
"GENERATIONS AGO, A CHILD WAS BORN TO THE MAIDEN AETHRA...FATHERED BY THE KING OF ATHENS--AEGEUS, AND THE SEA GOD POSEIDON.
"THE PRODUCT OF THAT UNION WAS THE HERO THESEUS.
"MUCH OF YOUR FAMILY'S LEGACY HAS BEEN OBSCURED IN MYTH AND LEGEND. BUT THOSE STORIES HAVE THEIR BASIS IN FACT.
"I KNEW YOU WERE SPECIAL FROM THE FIRST MOMENT THEY LAID YOU IN MY ARMS...
"EYES...AS BLUE AS THE AEGEAN SEA.
"I KNEW THEN THAT YOU WERE DESTINED TO REPEAT THE GREATNESS OF YOUR FOREFATHERS.
IT'S WHY I GAVE YOU THE NAME AEGEUS.

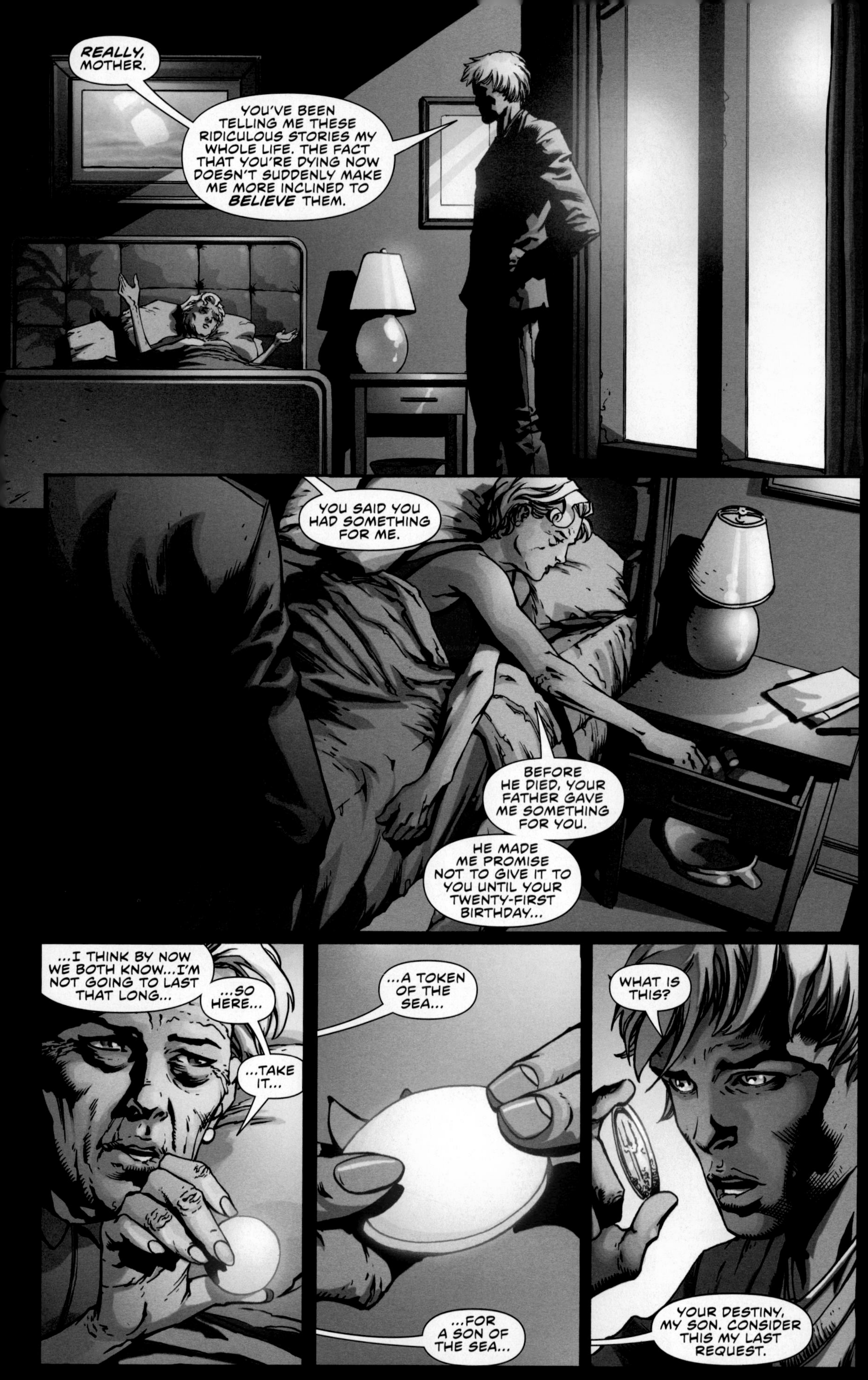
REALLY, MOTHER.
YOU'VE BEEN TELLING ME THESE RIDICULOUS STORIES MY WHOLE LIFE. THE FACT THAT YOU'RE DYING NOW DOESN'T SUDDENLY MAKE ME MORE INCLINED TO BELIEVE THEM.
YOU SAID YOU HAD SOMETHING FOR ME.
BEFORE HE DIED, YOUR FATHER GAVE ME SOMETHING FOR YOU.
HE MADE ME PROMISE NOT TO GIVE IT TO YOU UNTIL YOUR TWENTY-FIRST BIRTHDAY...
...I THINK BY NOW WE BOTH KNOW...I'M NOT GOING TO LAST THAT LONG...
...SO HERE...
...TAKE IT...
...A TOKEN OF THE SEA...
...FOR A SON OF THE SEA...
WHAT IS THIS?
YOUR DESTINY, MY SON. CONSIDER THIS MY LAST REQUEST.

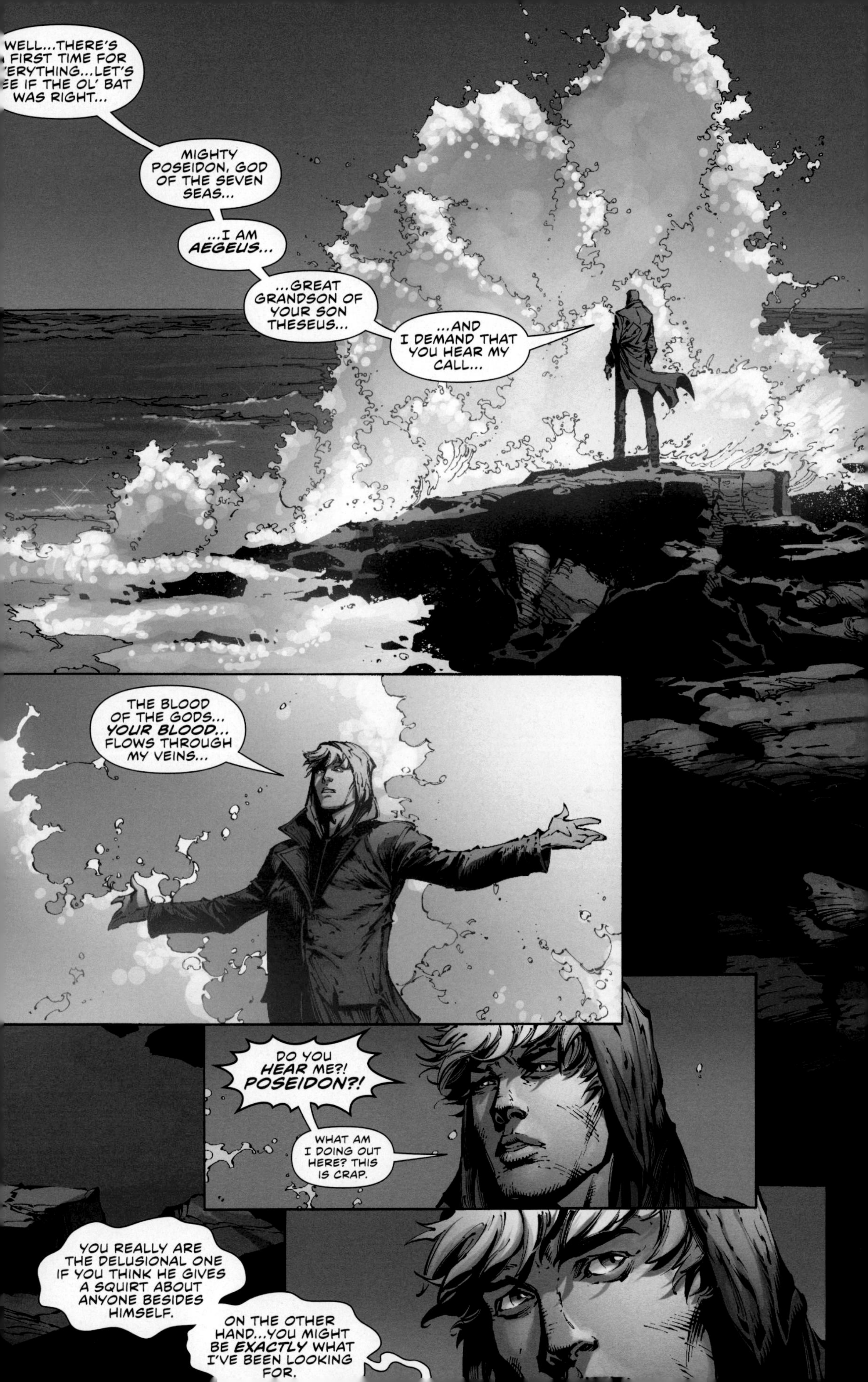
WELL...THERE'S A FIRST TIME FOR EVERYTHING...LET'S SEE IF THE OL' BAT WAS RIGHT...
MIGHTY POSEIDON, GOD OF THE SEVEN SEAS...
...I AM *AEGEUS*...
...GREAT GRANDSON OF YOUR SON THESEUS...
...AND I DEMAND THAT YOU HEAR MY CALL...
THE BLOOD OF THE GODS... *YOUR BLOOD*... FLOWS THROUGH MY VEINS...
DO YOU *HEAR* ME?! *POSEIDON?!*
WHAT AM I DOING OUT HERE? THIS IS CRAP.
YOU REALLY ARE THE DELUSIONAL ONE IF YOU THINK HE GIVES A SQUIRT ABOUT ANYONE BESIDES HIMSELF.
ON THE OTHER HAND...YOU MIGHT BE *EXACTLY* WHAT I'VE BEEN LOOKING FOR.

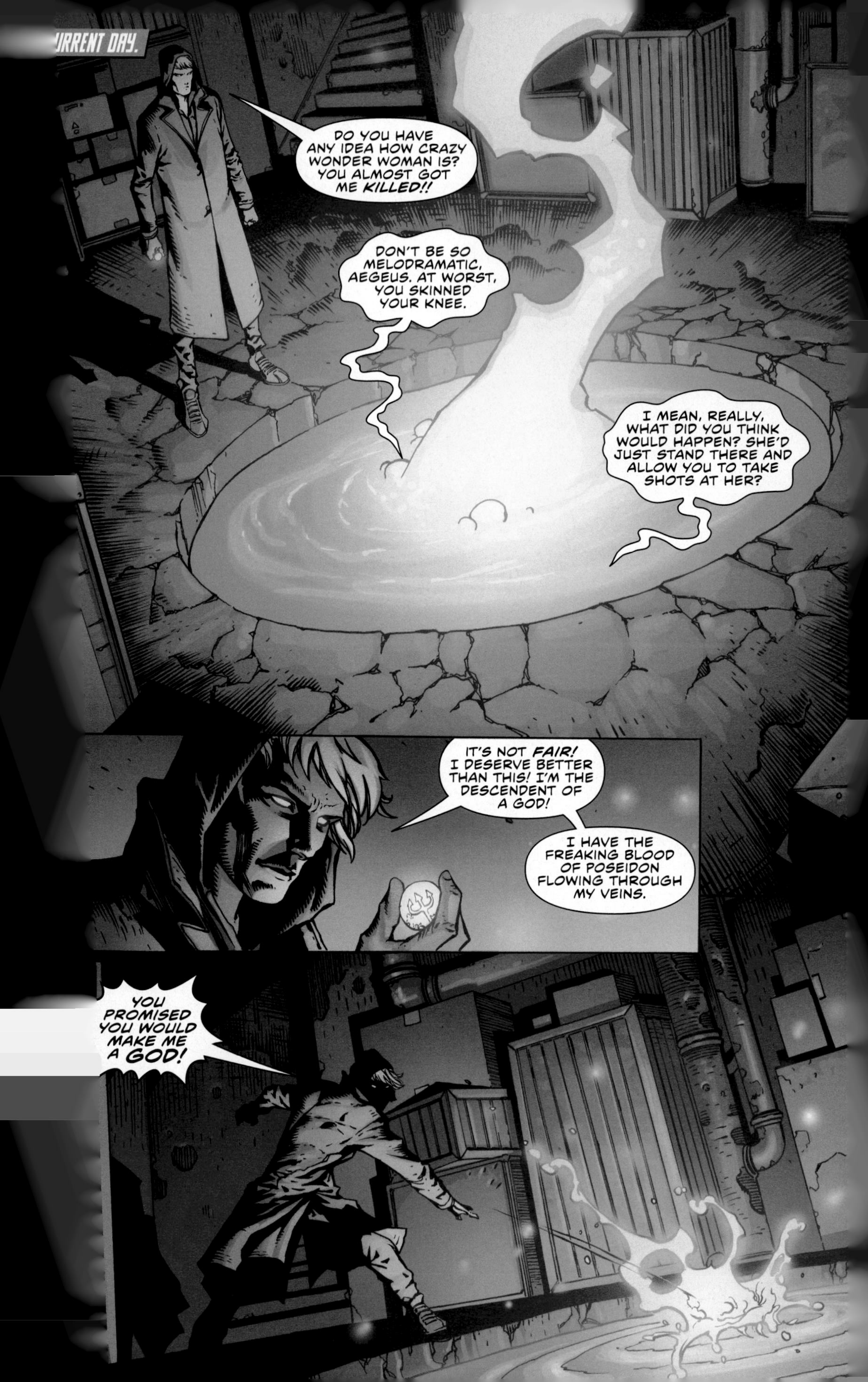

URRENT DAY.
DO YOU HAVE ANY IDEA HOW CRAZY WONDER WOMAN IS? YOU ALMOST GOT ME KILLED!!
DON'T BE SO MELODRAMATIC, AEGEUS. AT WORST, YOU SKINNED YOUR KNEE.
I MEAN, REALLY, WHAT DID YOU THINK WOULD HAPPEN? SHE'D JUST STAND THERE AND ALLOW YOU TO TAKE SHOTS AT HER?
IT'S NOT FAIR! I DESERVE BETTER THAN THIS! I'M THE DESCENDENT OF A GOD!
I HAVE THE FREAKING BLOOD OF POSEIDON FLOWING THROUGH MY VEINS.
YOU PROMISED YOU WOULD MAKE ME A GOD!

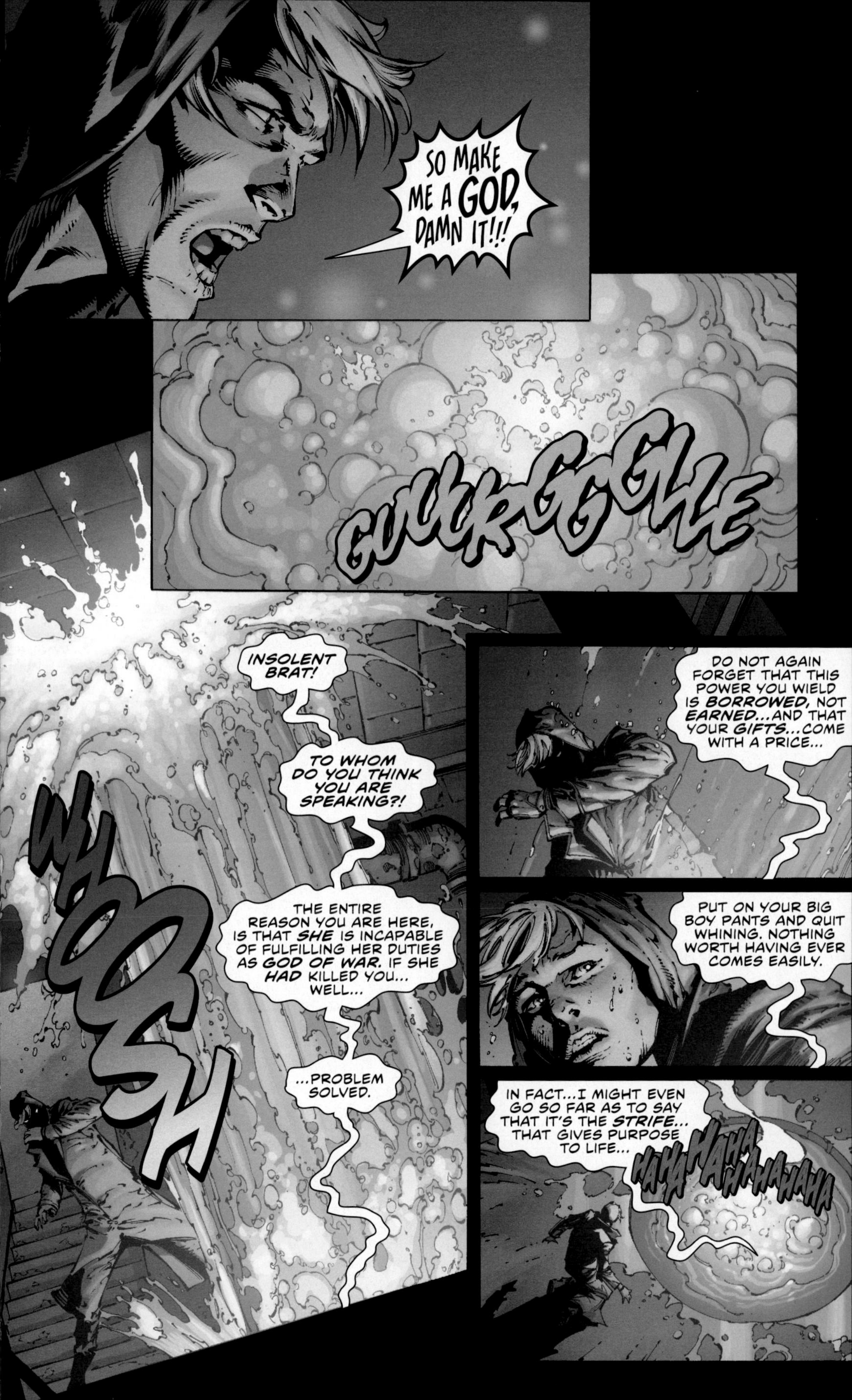
SO MAKE ME A GOD, DAMN IT!!!
GULLRGGGLLE
INSOLENT BRAT!
TO WHOM DO YOU THINK YOU ARE SPEAKING?!
THE ENTIRE REASON YOU ARE HERE, IS THAT SHE IS INCAPABLE OF FULFILLING HER DUTIES AS GOD OF WAR. IF SHE HAD KILLED YOU... WELL...
...PROBLEM SOLVED.
WHOOOSH
DO NOT AGAIN FORGET THAT THIS POWER YOU WIELD IS BORROWED, NOT EARNED...AND THAT YOUR GIFTS...COME WITH A PRICE...
PUT ON YOUR BIG BOY PANTS AND QUIT WHINING. NOTHING WORTH HAVING EVER COMES EASILY.
IN FACT...I MIGHT EVEN GO SO FAR AS TO SAY THAT IT'S THE STRIFE... THAT GIVES PURPOSE TO LIFE...
HAHAHAHAHAHAHAHAHA

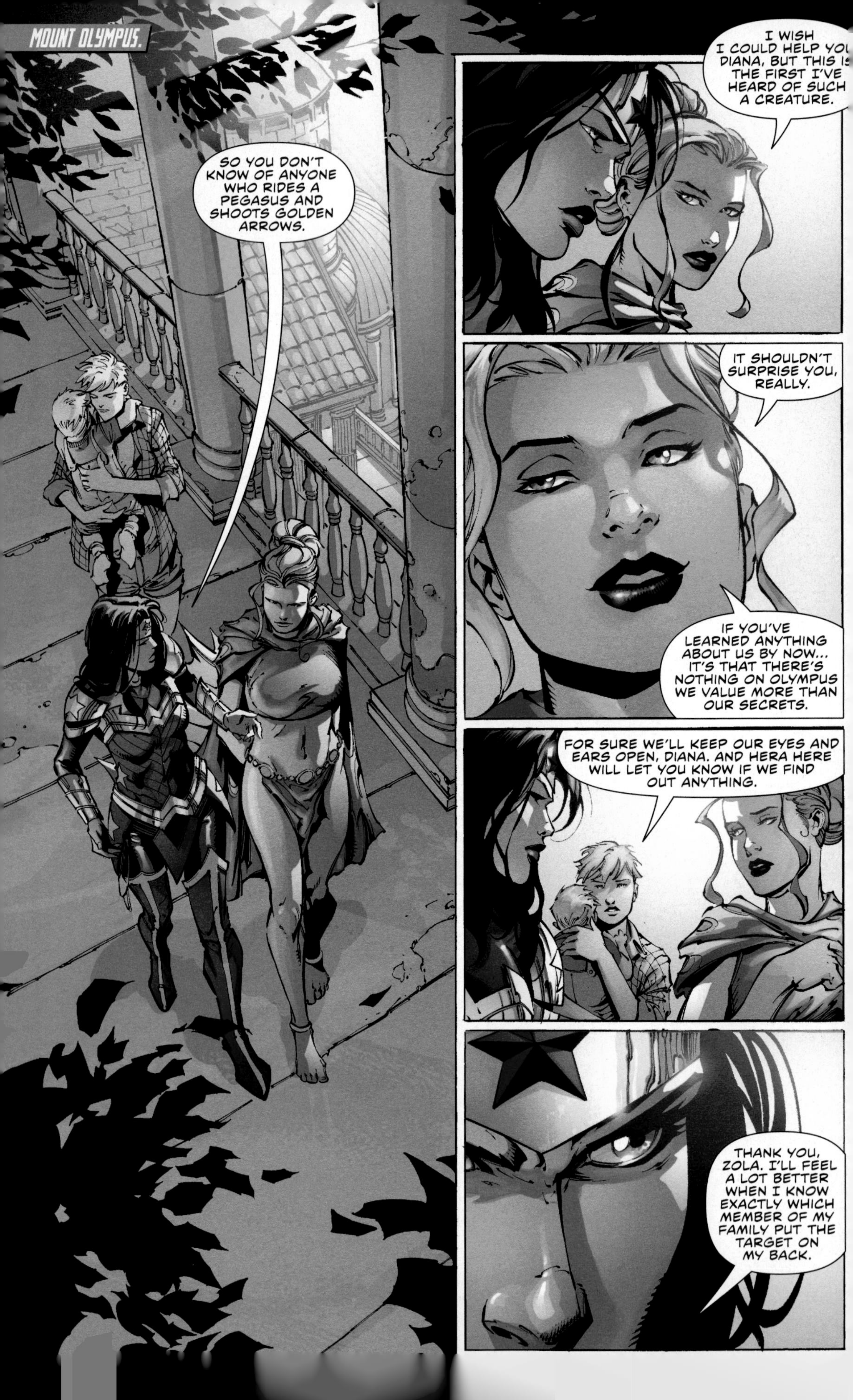
MOUNT OLYMPUS.
SO YOU DON'T KNOW OF ANYONE WHO RIDES A PEGASUS AND SHOOTS GOLDEN ARROWS.
I WISH I COULD HELP YOU DIANA, BUT THIS IS THE FIRST I'VE HEARD OF SUCH A CREATURE.
IT SHOULDN'T SURPRISE YOU, REALLY.
IF YOU'VE LEARNED ANYTHING ABOUT US BY NOW... IT'S THAT THERE'S NOTHING ON OLYMPUS WE VALUE MORE THAN OUR SECRETS.
FOR SURE WE'LL KEEP OUR EYES AND EARS OPEN, DIANA. AND HERA HERE WILL LET YOU KNOW IF WE FIND OUT ANYTHING.
THANK YOU, ZOLA. I'LL FEEL A LOT BETTER WHEN I KNOW EXACTLY WHICH MEMBER OF MY FAMILY PUT THE TARGET ON MY BACK.

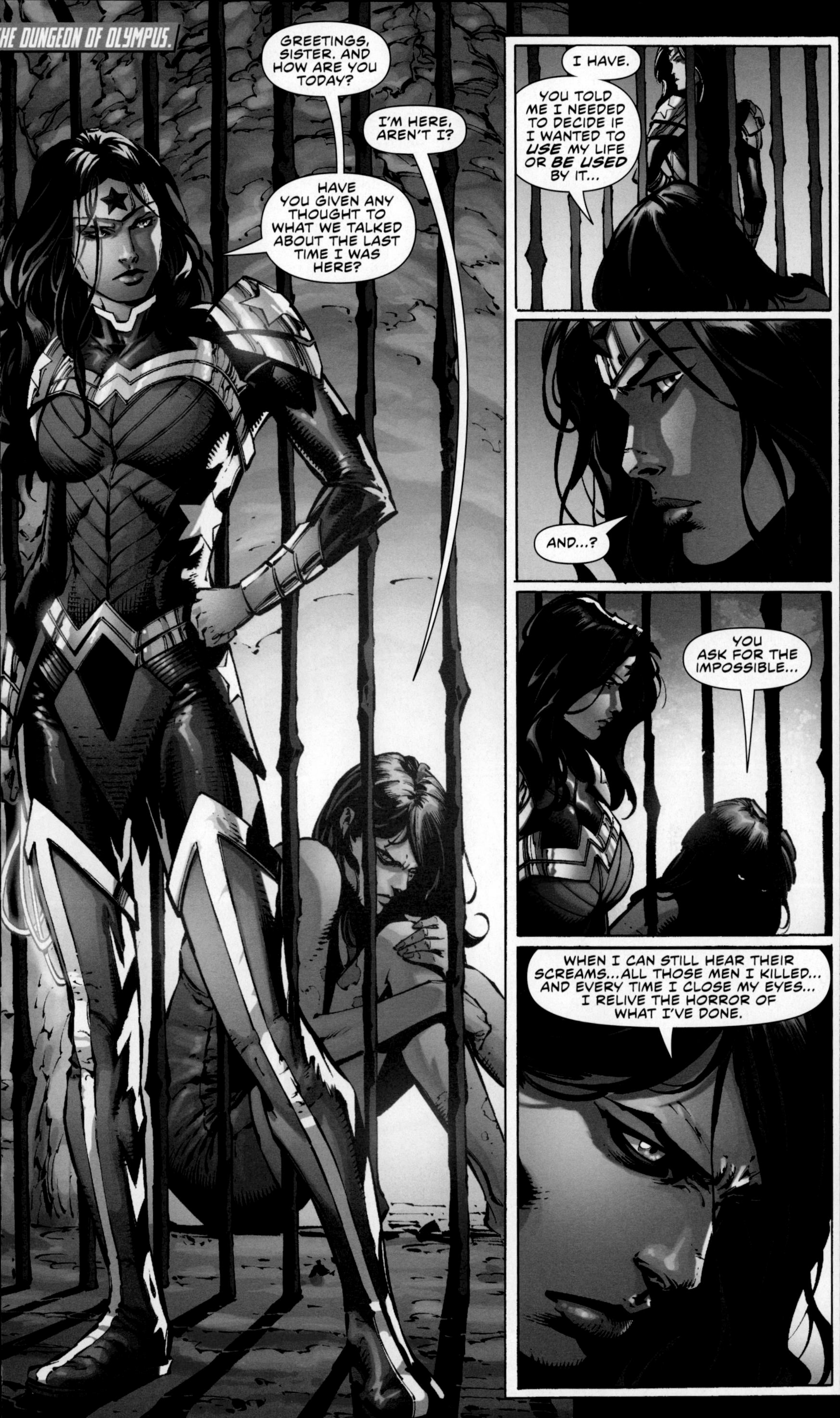
THE DUNGEON OF OLYMPUS.
GREETINGS, SISTER. AND HOW ARE YOU TODAY?
I'M HERE, AREN'T I?
HAVE YOU GIVEN ANY THOUGHT TO WHAT WE TALKED ABOUT THE LAST TIME I WAS HERE?
I HAVE.
YOU TOLD ME I NEEDED TO DECIDE IF I WANTED TO USE MY LIFE OR BE USED BY IT...
AND...?
YOU ASK FOR THE IMPOSSIBLE...
WHEN I CAN STILL HEAR THEIR SCREAMS...ALL THOSE MEN I KILLED... AND EVERY TIME I CLOSE MY EYES... I RELIVE THE HORROR OF WHAT I'VE DONE.

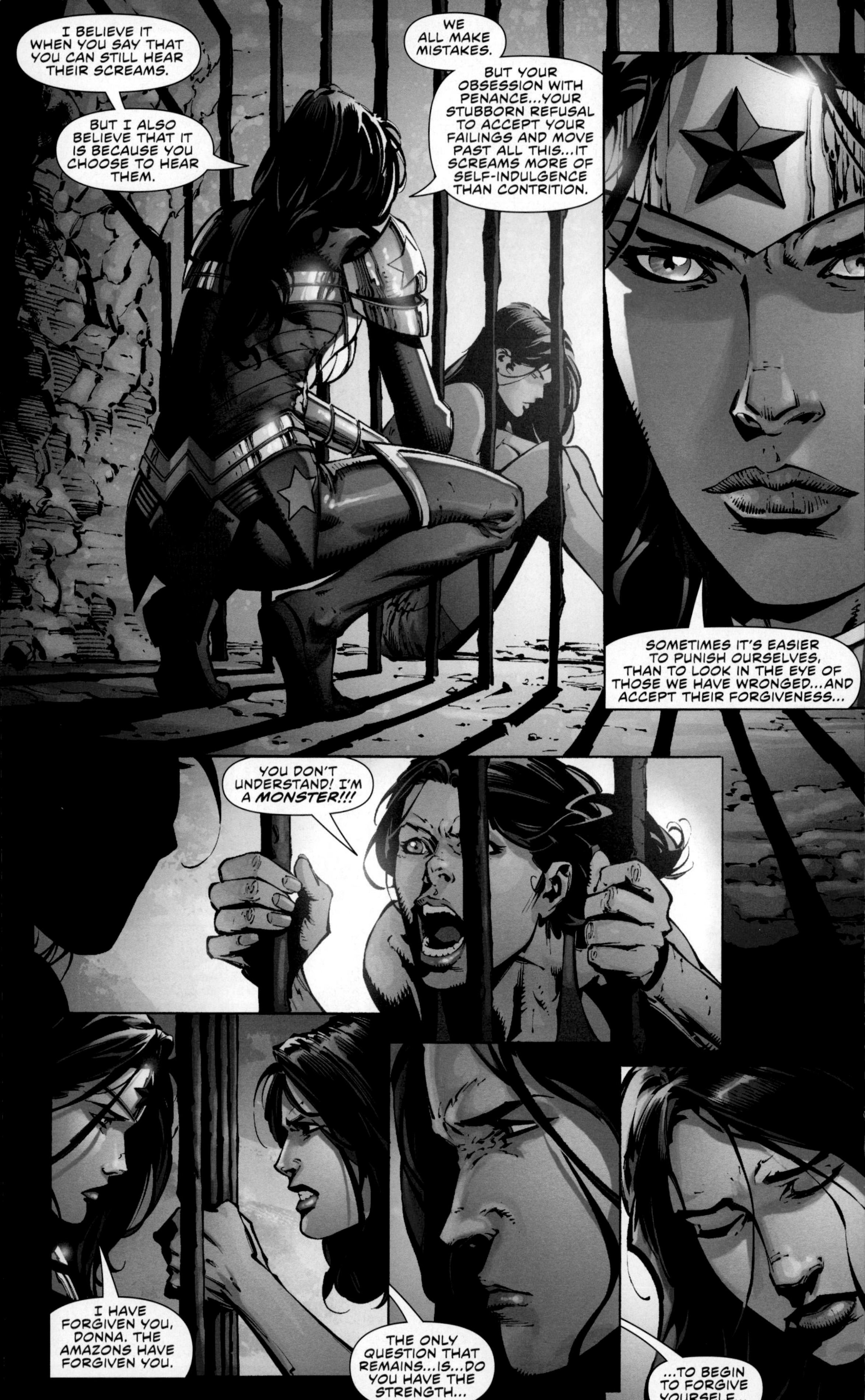
I BELIEVE IT WHEN YOU SAY THAT YOU CAN STILL HEAR THEIR SCREAMS.
BUT I ALSO BELIEVE THAT IT IS BECAUSE YOU CHOOSE TO HEAR THEM.
WE ALL MAKE MISTAKES.
BUT YOUR OBSESSION WITH PENANCE...YOUR STUBBORN REFUSAL TO ACCEPT YOUR FAILINGS AND MOVE PAST ALL THIS...IT SCREAMS MORE OF SELF-INDULGENCE THAN CONTRITION.
SOMETIMES IT'S EASIER TO PUNISH OURSELVES, THAN TO LOOK IN THE EYE OF THOSE WE HAVE WRONGED...AND ACCEPT THEIR FORGIVENESS...
YOU DON'T UNDERSTAND! I'M A MONSTER!!!
I HAVE FORGIVEN YOU, DONNA. THE AMAZONS HAVE FORGIVEN YOU.
THE ONLY QUESTION THAT REMAINS...IS...DO YOU HAVE THE STRENGTH...
...TO BEGIN TO FORGIVE

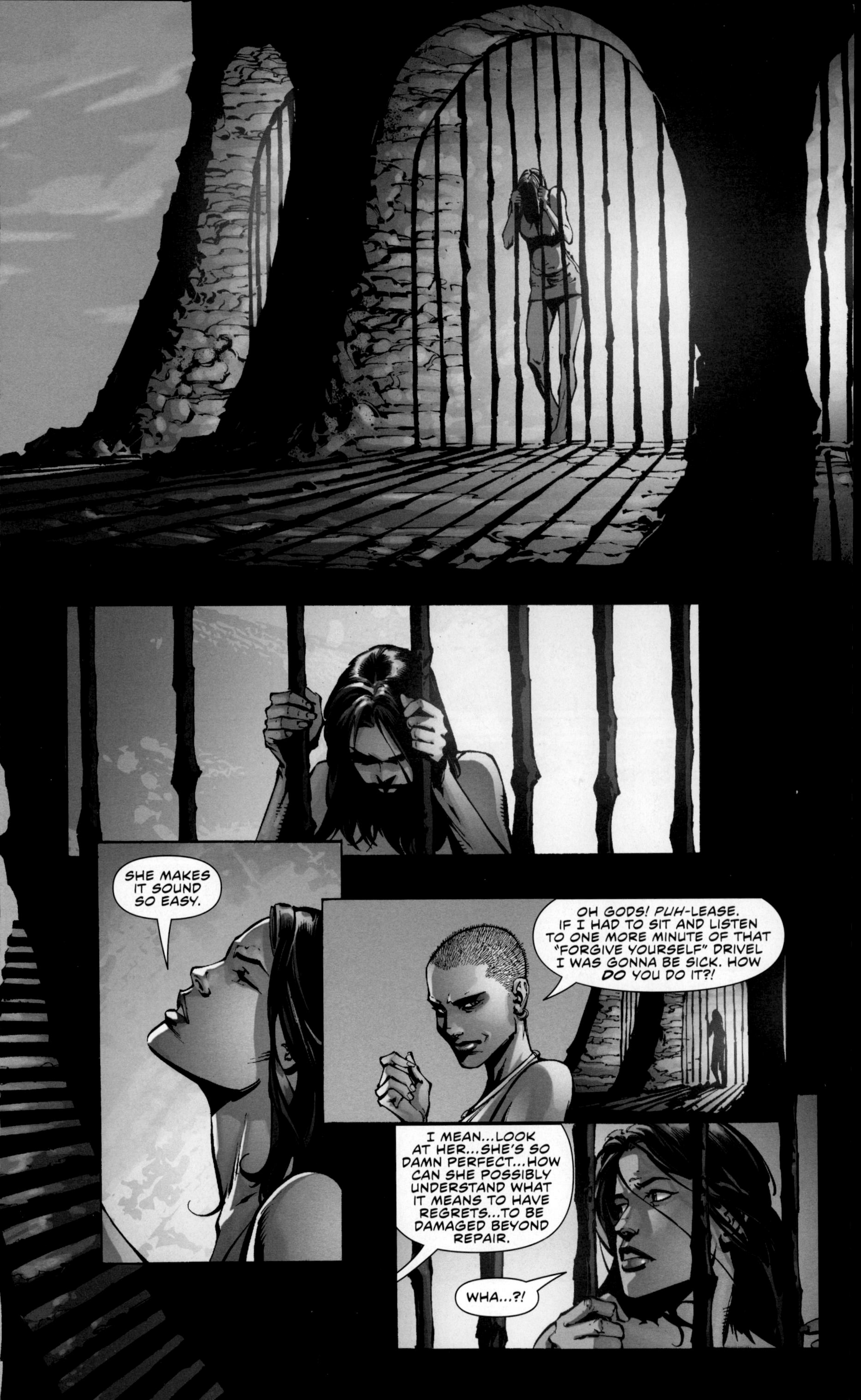
SHE MAKES IT SOUND SO EASY.
OH GODS! PUH-LEASE. IF I HAD TO SIT AND LISTEN TO ONE MORE MINUTE OF THAT "FORGIVE YOURSELF" DRIVEL I WAS GONNA BE SICK. HOW DO YOU DO IT?!
I MEAN...LOOK AT HER...SHE'S SO DAMN PERFECT...HOW CAN SHE POSSIBLY UNDERSTAND WHAT IT MEANS TO HAVE REGRETS...TO BE DAMAGED BEYOND REPAIR.
WHA...?!

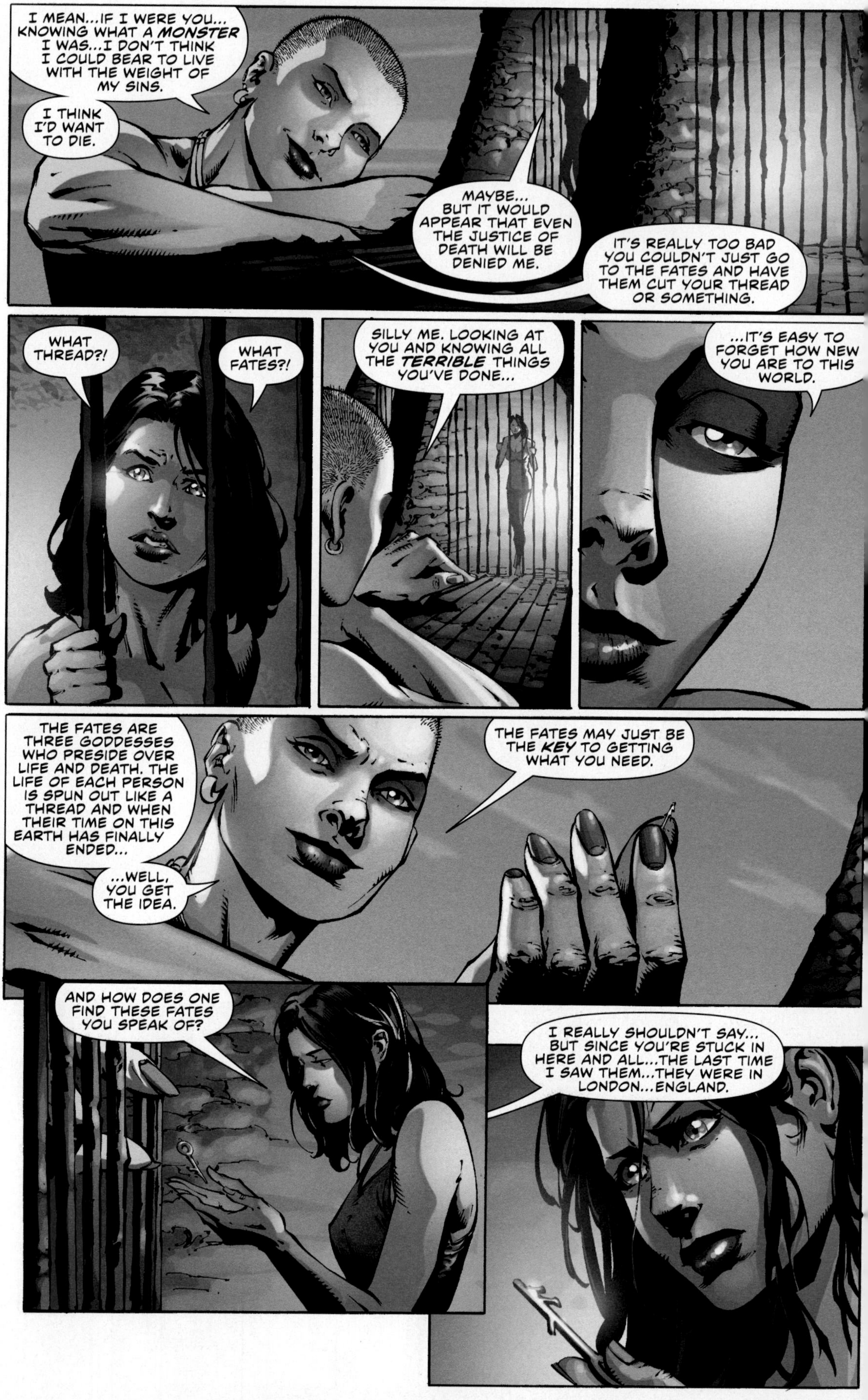
I MEAN...IF I WERE YOU... KNOWING WHAT A MONSTER I WAS...I DON'T THINK I COULD BEAR TO LIVE WITH THE WEIGHT OF MY SINS.
I THINK I'D WANT TO DIE.
MAYBE... BUT IT WOULD APPEAR THAT EVEN THE JUSTICE OF DEATH WILL BE DENIED ME.
IT'S REALLY TOO BAD YOU COULDN'T JUST GO TO THE FATES AND HAVE THEM CUT YOUR THREAD OR SOMETHING.
WHAT THREAD?!
WHAT FATES?!
SILLY ME. LOOKING AT YOU AND KNOWING ALL THE TERRIBLE THINGS YOU'VE DONE...
...IT'S EASY TO FORGET HOW NEW YOU ARE TO THIS WORLD.
THE FATES ARE THREE GODDESSES WHO PRESIDE OVER LIFE AND DEATH. THE LIFE OF EACH PERSON IS SPUN OUT LIKE A THREAD AND WHEN THEIR TIME ON THIS EARTH HAS FINALLY ENDED...
...WELL, YOU GET THE IDEA.
THE FATES MAY JUST BE THE KEY TO GETTING WHAT YOU NEED.
AND HOW DOES ONE FIND THESE FATES YOU SPEAK OF?
I REALLY SHOULDN'T SAY... BUT SINCE YOU'RE STUCK IN HERE AND ALL...THE LAST TIME I SAW THEM...THEY WERE IN LONDON...ENGLAND.

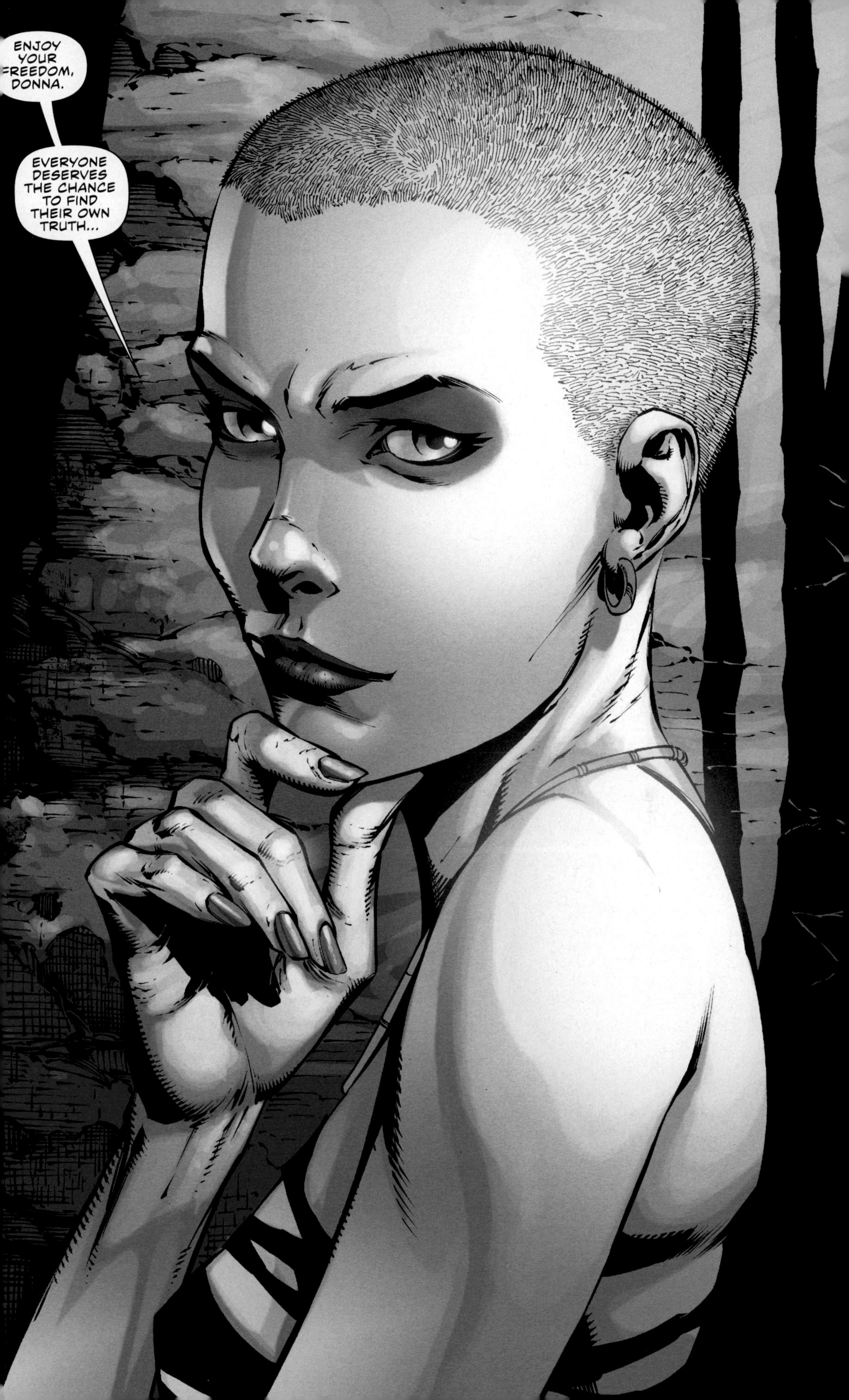
ENJOY YOUR FREEDOM, DONNA.
EVERYONE DESERVES THE CHANCE TO FIND THEIR OWN TRUTH...

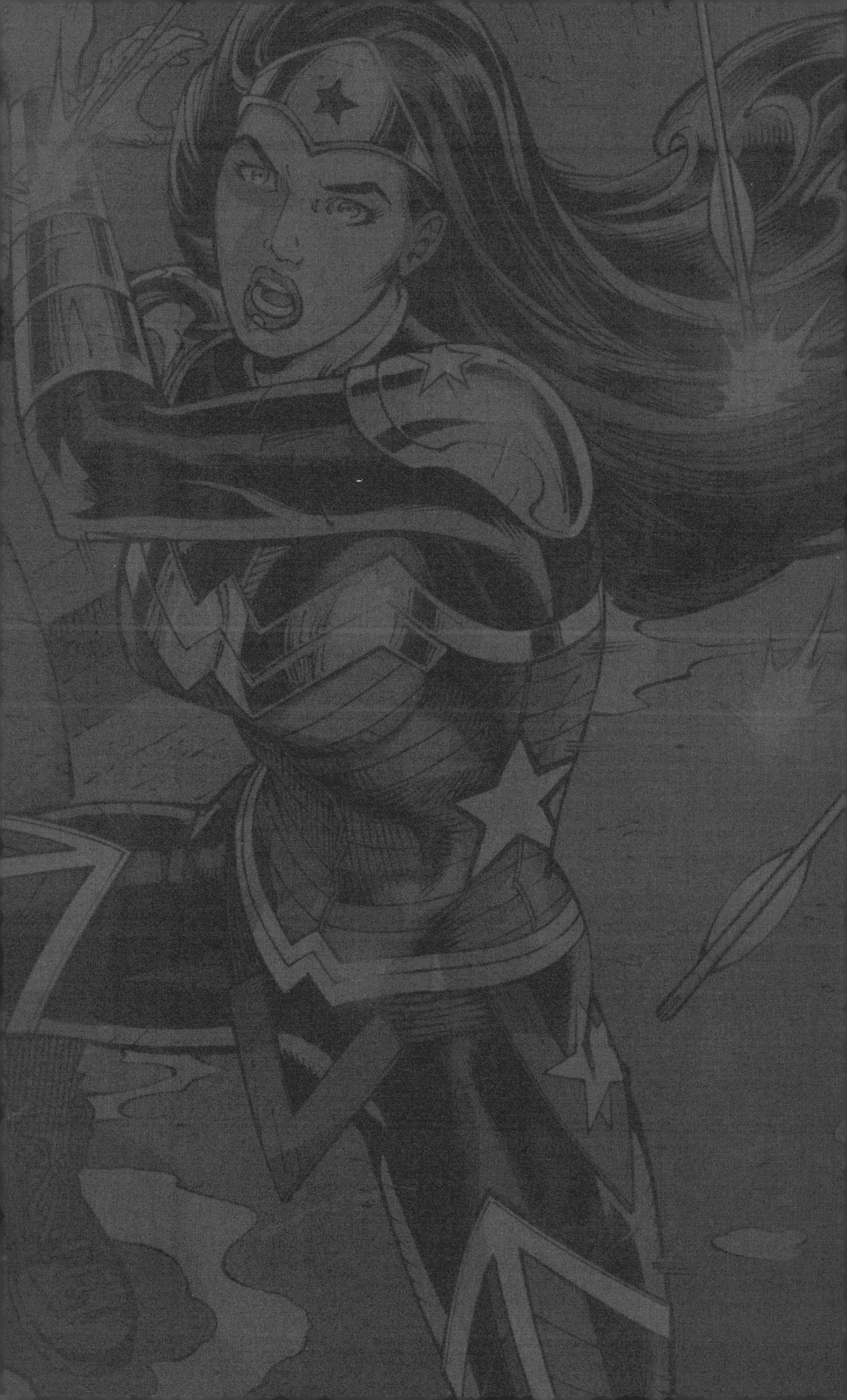

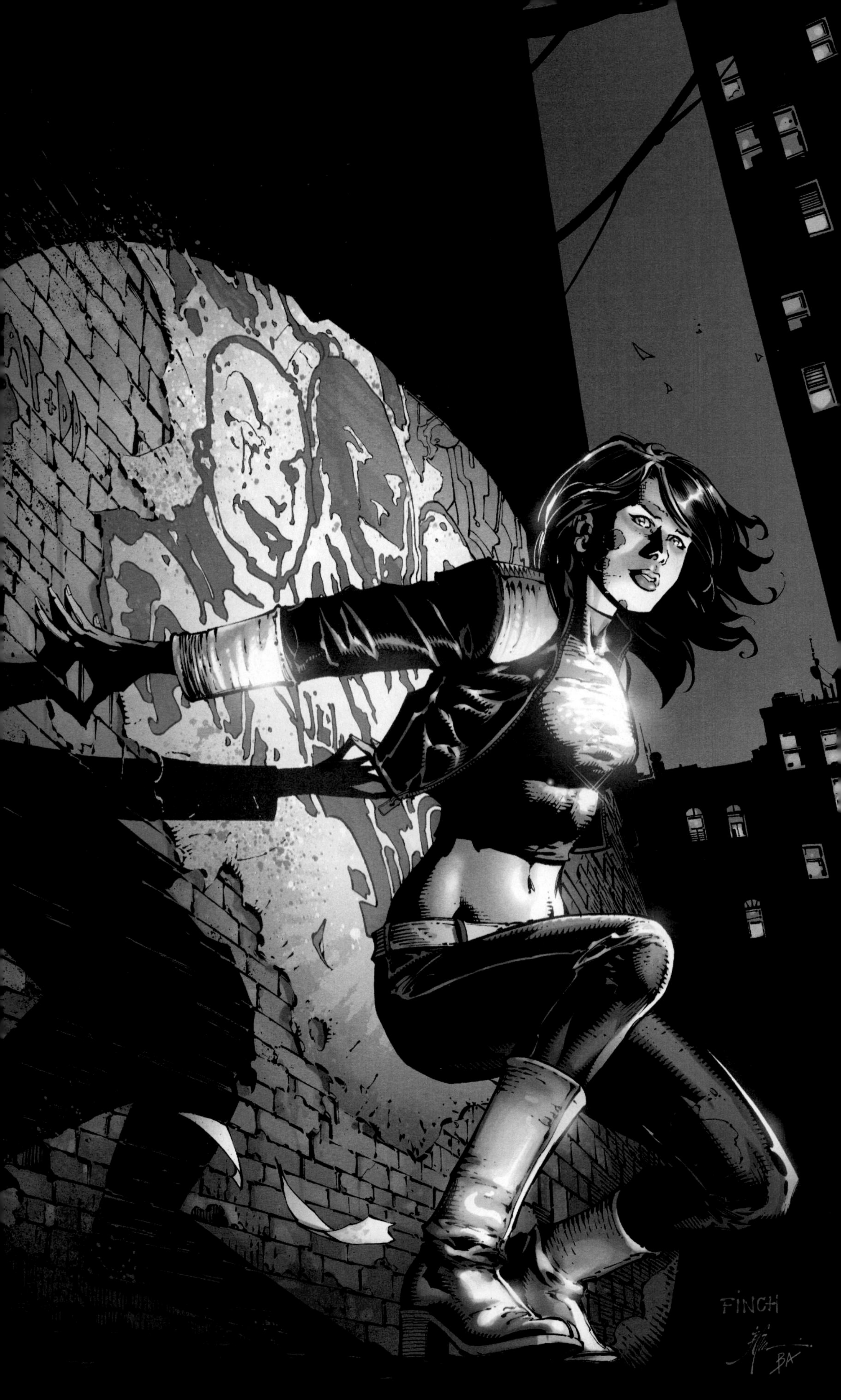
FINCH

A TWIST OF FATE

MEREDITH FINCH writer **IAN CHURCHILL** penciller **RICK BRYANT ANDREW HENNESSY MARK IRWIN** inkers **BRAD ANDERSON** colorist **ROB LEIGH** letterer
cover by **FINCH, GLAPION & ANDERSON**

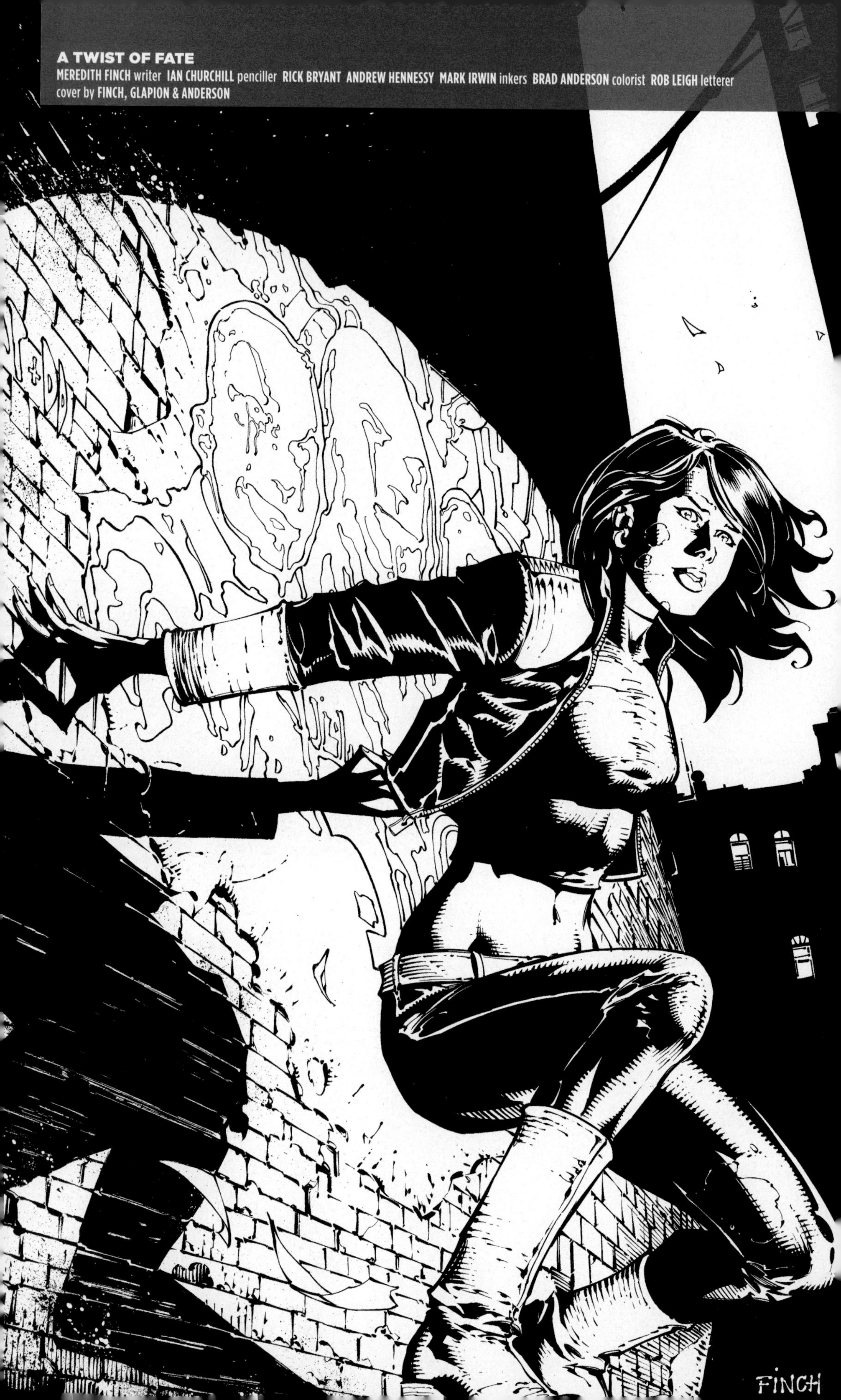
FINCH

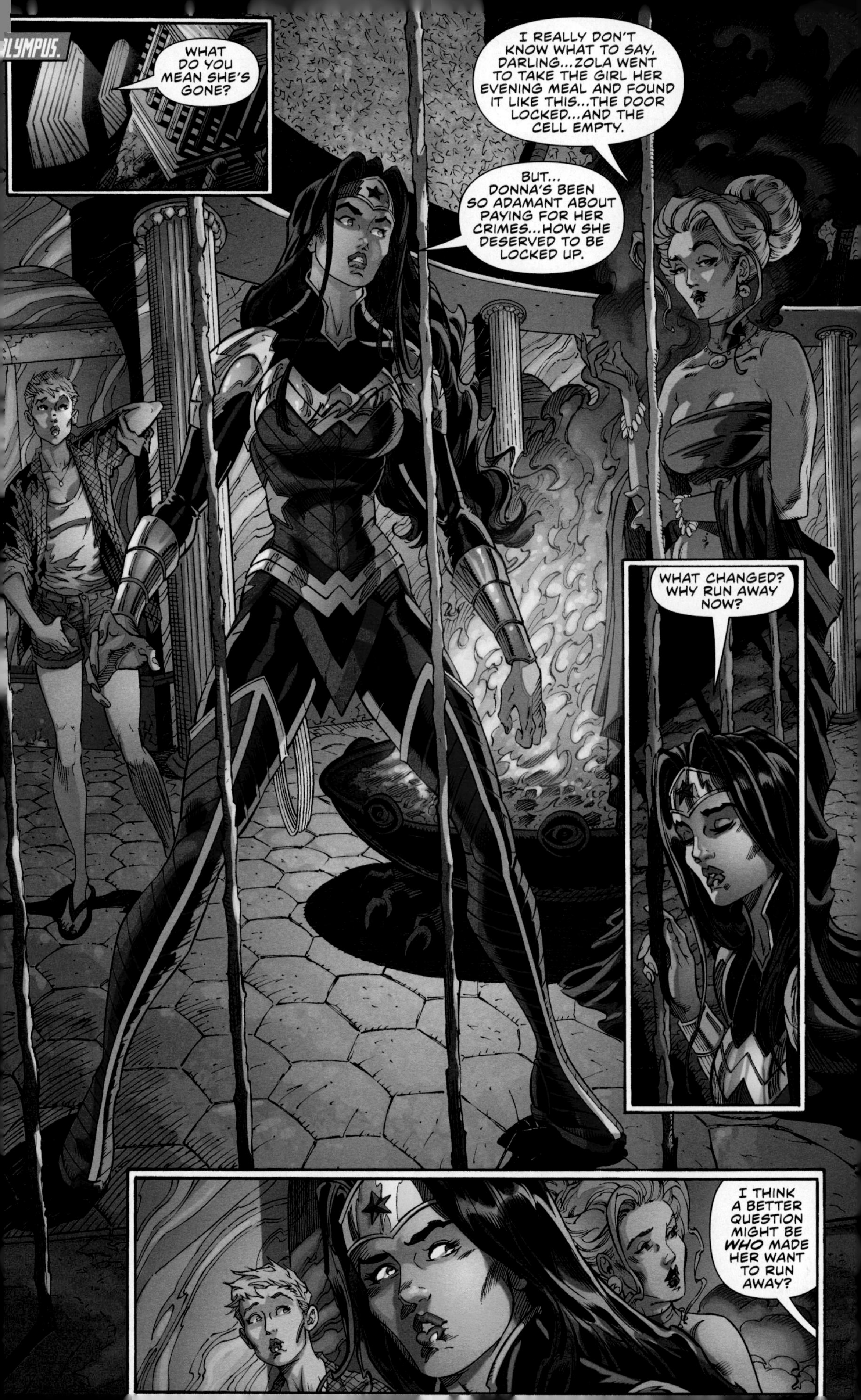
OLYMPUS.
WHAT DO YOU MEAN SHE'S GONE?
I REALLY DON'T KNOW WHAT TO SAY, DARLING...ZOLA WENT TO TAKE THE GIRL HER EVENING MEAL AND FOUND IT LIKE THIS...THE DOOR LOCKED...AND THE CELL EMPTY.
BUT... DONNA'S BEEN SO ADAMANT ABOUT PAYING FOR HER CRIMES...HOW SHE DESERVED TO BE LOCKED UP.
WHAT CHANGED? WHY RUN AWAY NOW?
I THINK A BETTER QUESTION MIGHT BE WHO MADE HER WANT TO RUN AWAY?

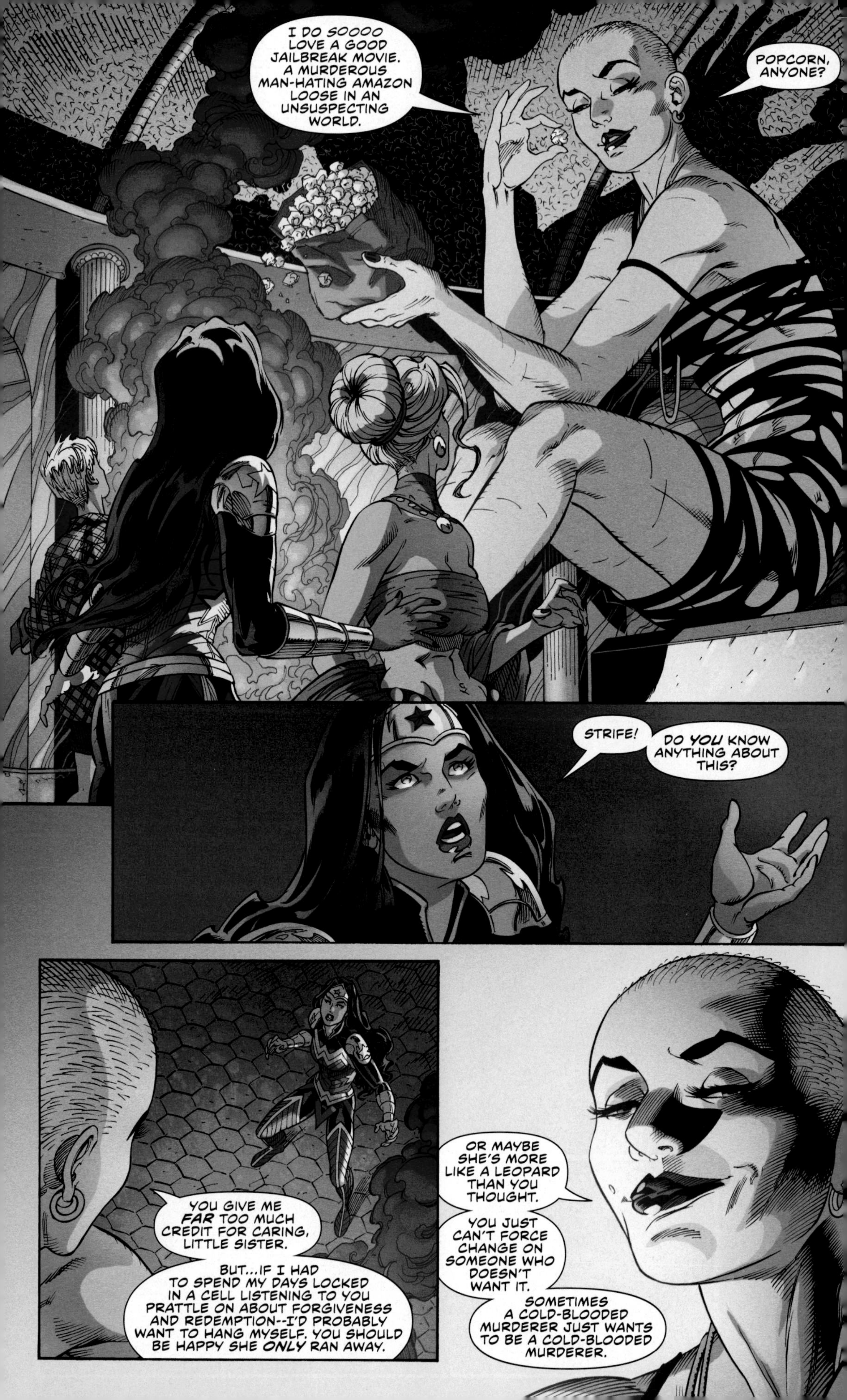
I DO SOOOO LOVE A GOOD JAILBREAK MOVIE. A MURDEROUS MAN-HATING AMAZON LOOSE IN AN UNSUSPECTING WORLD.
POPCORN, ANYONE?
STRIFE!
DO YOU KNOW ANYTHING ABOUT THIS?
YOU GIVE ME FAR TOO MUCH CREDIT FOR CARING, LITTLE SISTER.
BUT...IF I HAD TO SPEND MY DAYS LOCKED IN A CELL LISTENING TO YOU PRATTLE ON ABOUT FORGIVENESS AND REDEMPTION--I'D PROBABLY WANT TO HANG MYSELF. YOU SHOULD BE HAPPY SHE ONLY RAN AWAY.
OR MAYBE SHE'S MORE LIKE A LEOPARD THAN YOU THOUGHT.
YOU JUST CAN'T FORCE CHANGE ON SOMEONE WHO DOESN'T WANT IT.
SOMETIMES A COLD-BLOODED MURDERER JUST WANTS TO BE A COLD-BLOODED MURDERER.

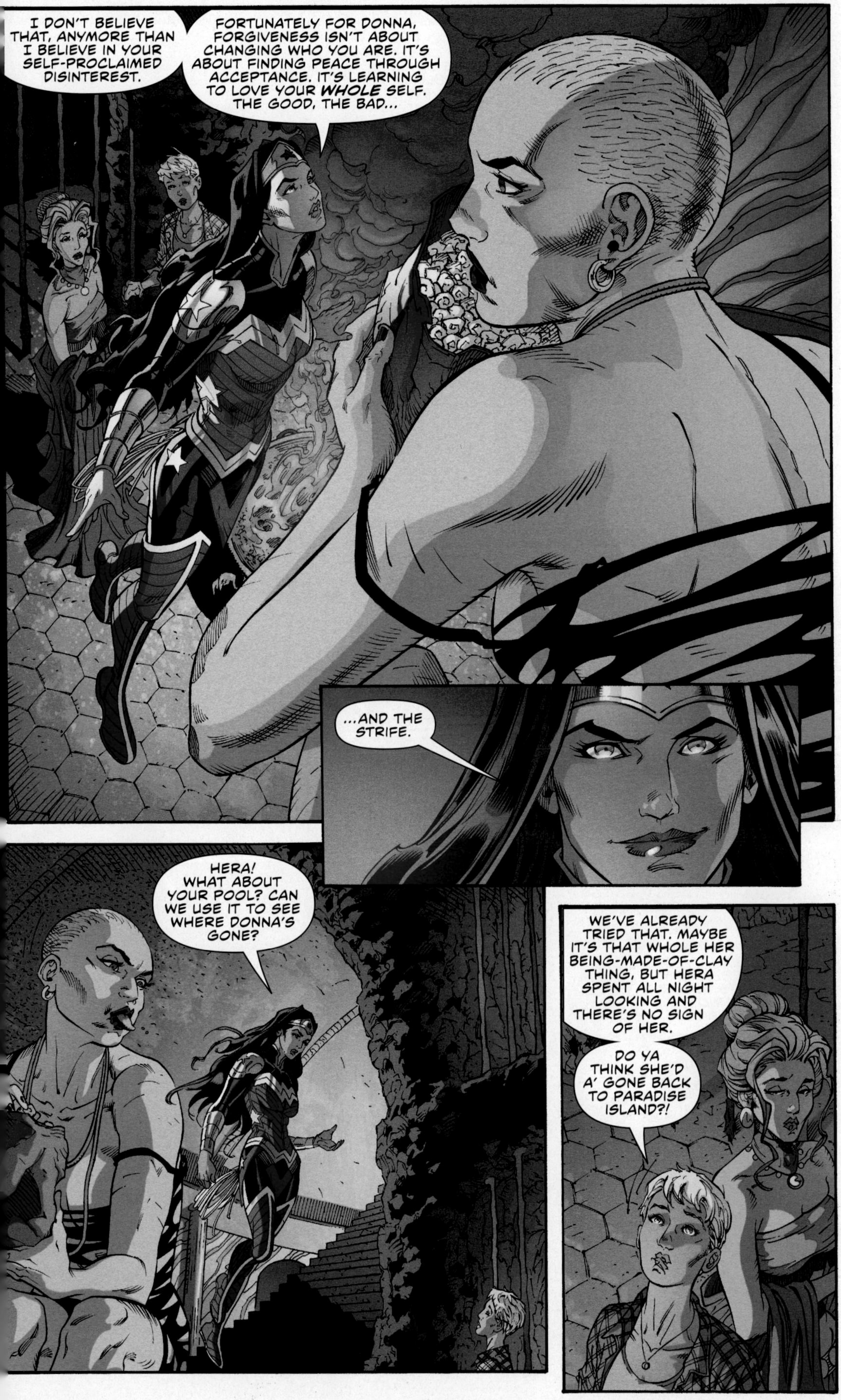
I DON'T BELIEVE THAT, ANYMORE THAN I BELIEVE IN YOUR SELF-PROCLAIMED DISINTEREST.
FORTUNATELY FOR DONNA, FORGIVENESS ISN'T ABOUT CHANGING WHO YOU ARE. IT'S ABOUT FINDING PEACE THROUGH ACCEPTANCE. IT'S LEARNING TO LOVE YOUR *WHOLE* SELF. THE GOOD, THE BAD...
...AND THE STRIFE.
HERA! WHAT ABOUT YOUR POOL? CAN WE USE IT TO SEE WHERE DONNA'S GONE?
WE'VE ALREADY TRIED THAT. MAYBE IT'S THAT WHOLE HER BEING-MADE-OF-CLAY THING, BUT HERA SPENT ALL NIGHT LOOKING AND THERE'S NO SIGN OF HER.
DO YA THINK SHE'D A' GONE BACK TO PARADISE ISLAND?!

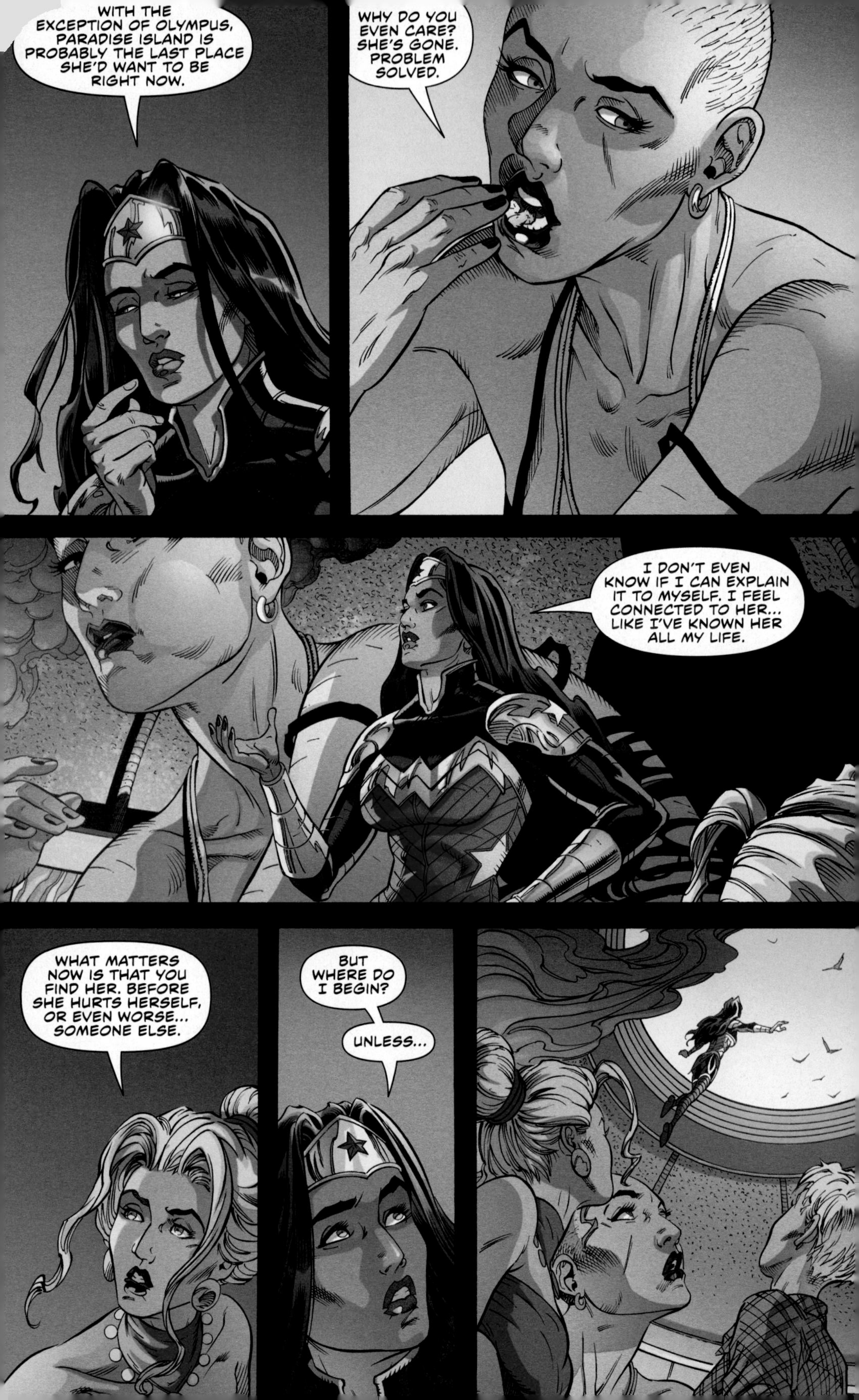
WITH THE EXCEPTION OF OLYMPUS, PARADISE ISLAND IS PROBABLY THE LAST PLACE SHE'D WANT TO BE RIGHT NOW.
WHY DO YOU EVEN CARE? SHE'S GONE. PROBLEM SOLVED.
I DON'T EVEN KNOW IF I CAN EXPLAIN IT TO MYSELF. I FEEL CONNECTED TO HER... LIKE I'VE KNOWN HER ALL MY LIFE.
WHAT MATTERS NOW IS THAT YOU FIND HER. BEFORE SHE HURTS HERSELF, OR EVEN WORSE... SOMEONE ELSE.
BUT WHERE DO I BEGIN?
UNLESS...

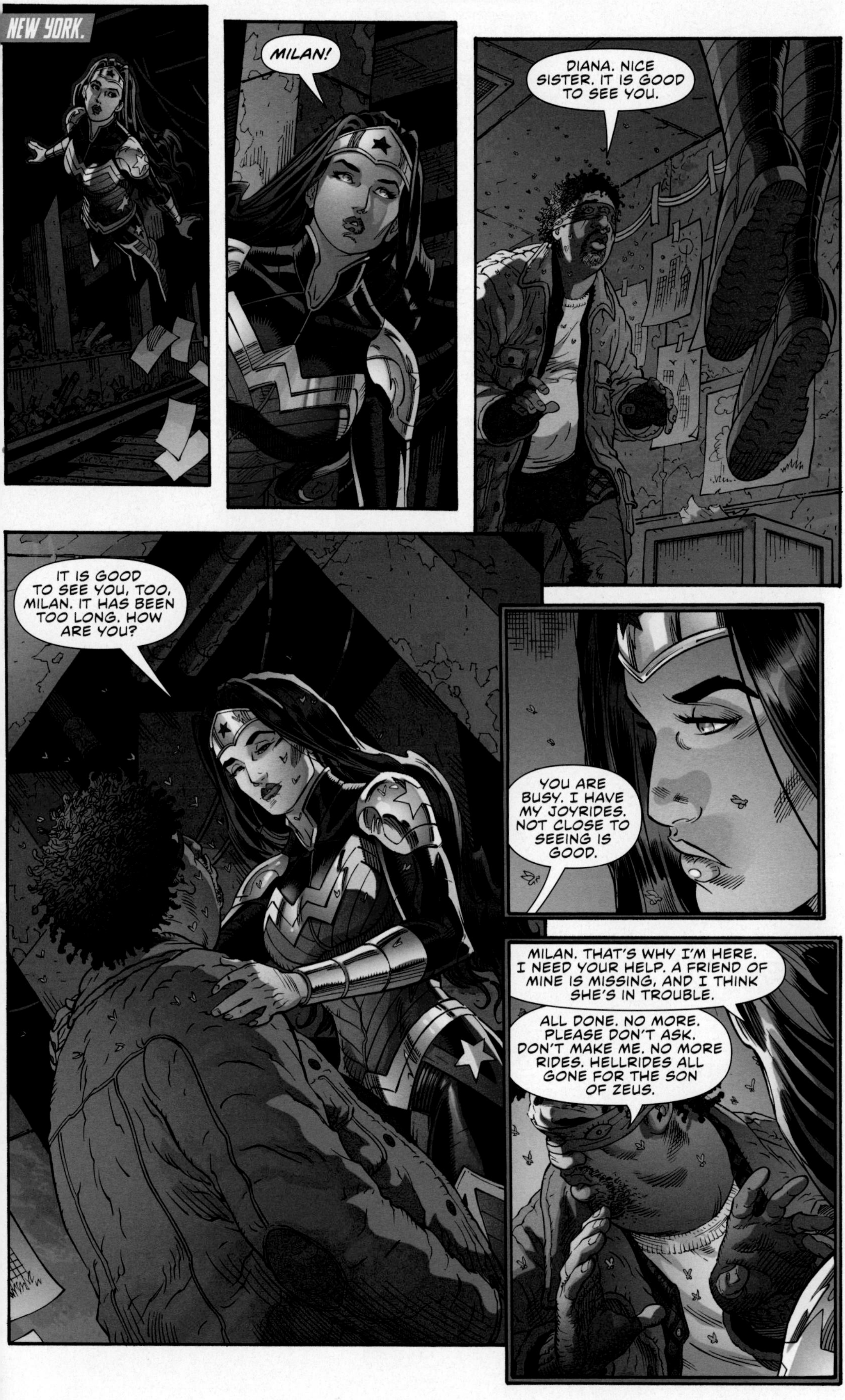
NEW YORK.
MILAN!
DIANA. NICE SISTER. IT IS GOOD TO SEE YOU.
IT IS GOOD TO SEE YOU, TOO, MILAN. IT HAS BEEN TOO LONG. HOW ARE YOU?
YOU ARE BUSY. I HAVE MY JOYRIDES. NOT CLOSE TO SEEING IS GOOD.
MILAN. THAT'S WHY I'M HERE. I NEED YOUR HELP. A FRIEND OF MINE IS MISSING, AND I THINK SHE'S IN TROUBLE.
ALL DONE. NO MORE. PLEASE DON'T ASK. DON'T MAKE ME. NO MORE RIDES. HELLRIDES ALL GONE FOR THE SON OF ZEUS.

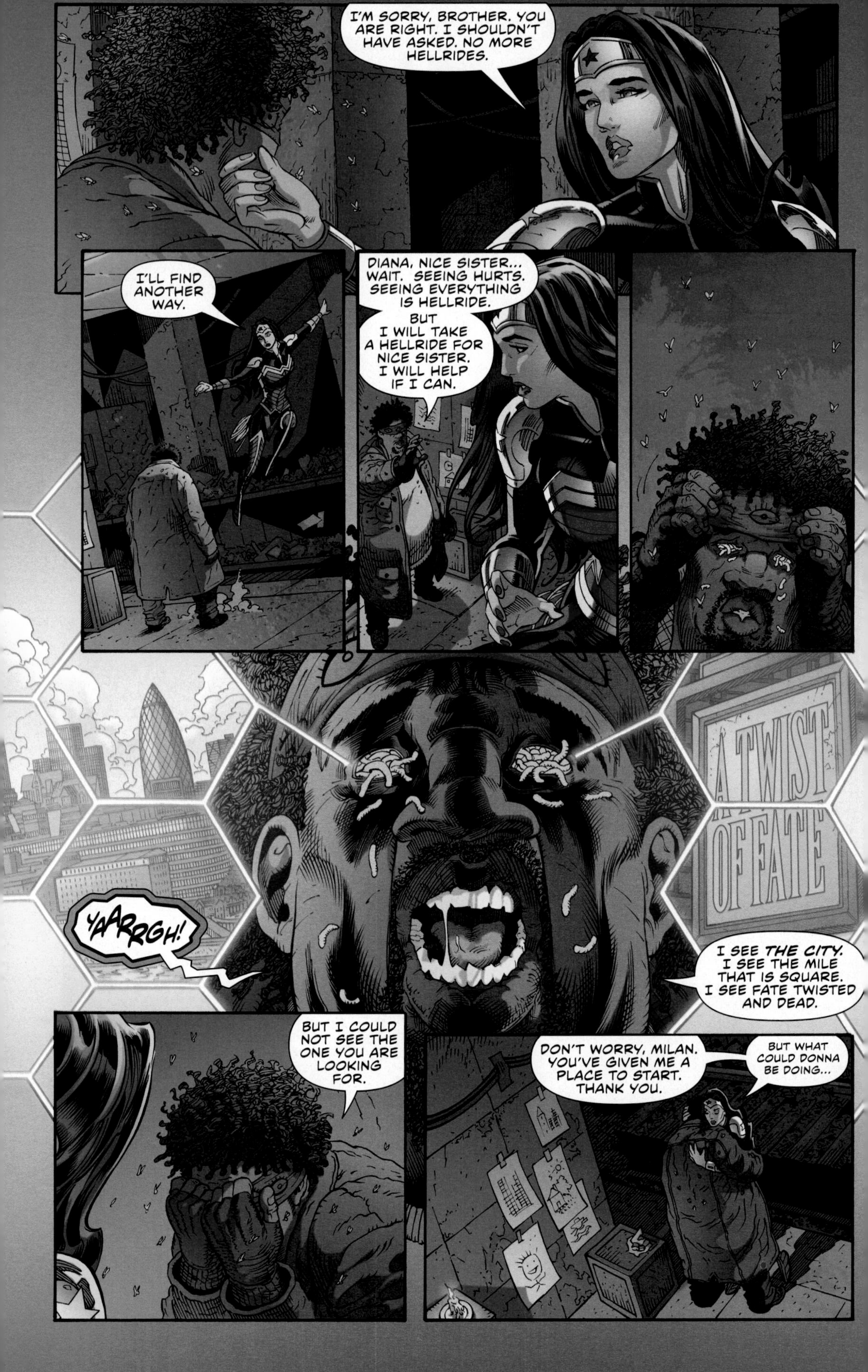
I'M SORRY, BROTHER. YOU ARE RIGHT. I SHOULDN'T HAVE ASKED. NO MORE HELLRIDES.
I'LL FIND ANOTHER WAY.
DIANA, NICE SISTER... WAIT. SEEING HURTS. SEEING EVERYTHING IS HELLRIDE.
BUT I WILL TAKE A HELLRIDE FOR NICE SISTER. I WILL HELP IF I CAN.
A TWIST OF FATE
YAARRGH!
I SEE THE CITY. I SEE THE MILE THAT IS SQUARE. I SEE FATE TWISTED AND DEAD.
BUT I COULD NOT SEE THE ONE YOU ARE LOOKING FOR.
DON'T WORRY, MILAN. YOU'VE GIVEN ME A PLACE TO START. THANK YOU.
BUT WHAT COULD DONNA BE DOING...

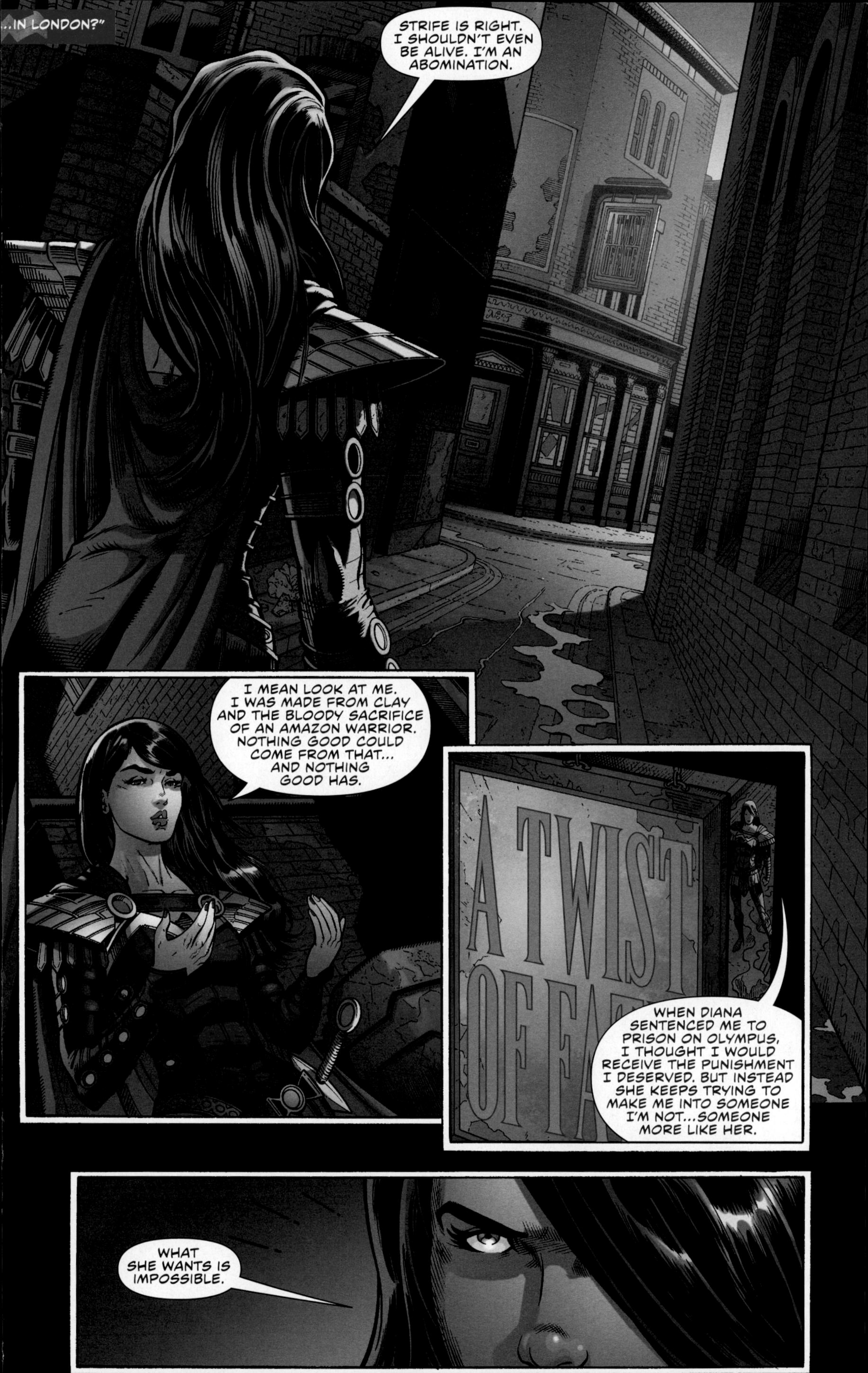
...IN LONDON?"
STRIFE IS RIGHT. I SHOULDN'T EVEN BE ALIVE. I'M AN ABOMINATION.
A TWIST OF FATE
I MEAN LOOK AT ME. I WAS MADE FROM CLAY AND THE BLOODY SACRIFICE OF AN AMAZON WARRIOR. NOTHING GOOD COULD COME FROM THAT... AND NOTHING GOOD HAS.
WHEN DIANA SENTENCED ME TO PRISON ON OLYMPUS, I THOUGHT I WOULD RECEIVE THE PUNISHMENT I DESERVED. BUT INSTEAD SHE KEEPS TRYING TO MAKE ME INTO SOMEONE I'M NOT...SOMEONE MORE LIKE HER.
WHAT SHE WANTS IS IMPOSSIBLE.

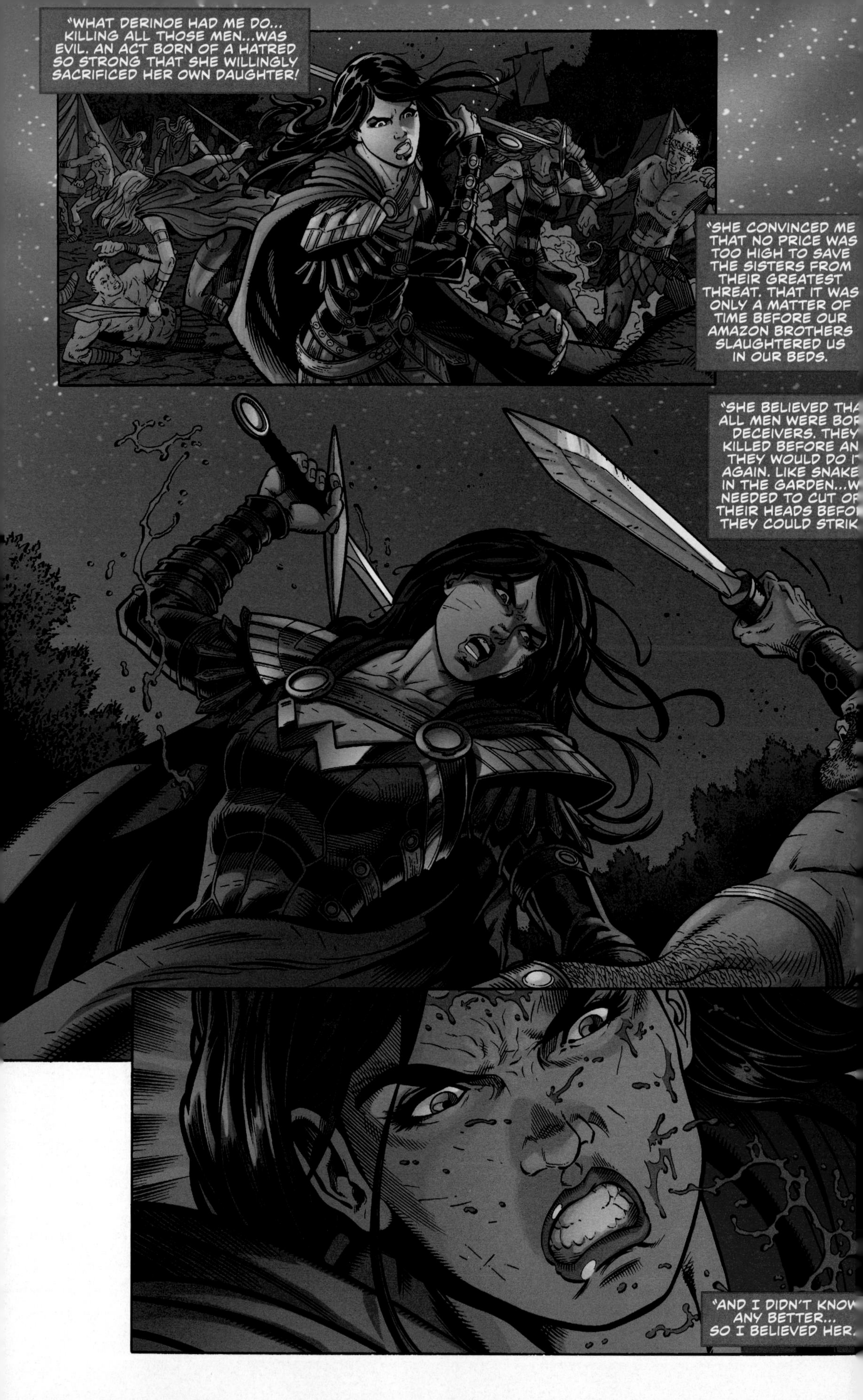
"WHAT DERINOE HAD ME DO... KILLING ALL THOSE MEN...WAS EVIL. AN ACT BORN OF A HATRED SO STRONG THAT SHE WILLINGLY SACRIFICED HER OWN DAUGHTER!
"SHE CONVINCED ME THAT NO PRICE WAS TOO HIGH TO SAVE THE SISTERS FROM THEIR GREATEST THREAT. THAT IT WAS ONLY A MATTER OF TIME BEFORE OUR AMAZON BROTHERS SLAUGHTERED US IN OUR BEDS.
"SHE BELIEVED THA ALL MEN WERE BOR DECEIVERS. THEY KILLED BEFORE AN THEY WOULD DO I AGAIN. LIKE SNAKE IN THE GARDEN...W NEEDED TO CUT OF THEIR HEADS BEFO THEY COULD STRIK
"AND I DIDN'T KNOW ANY BETTER... SO I BELIEVED HER.

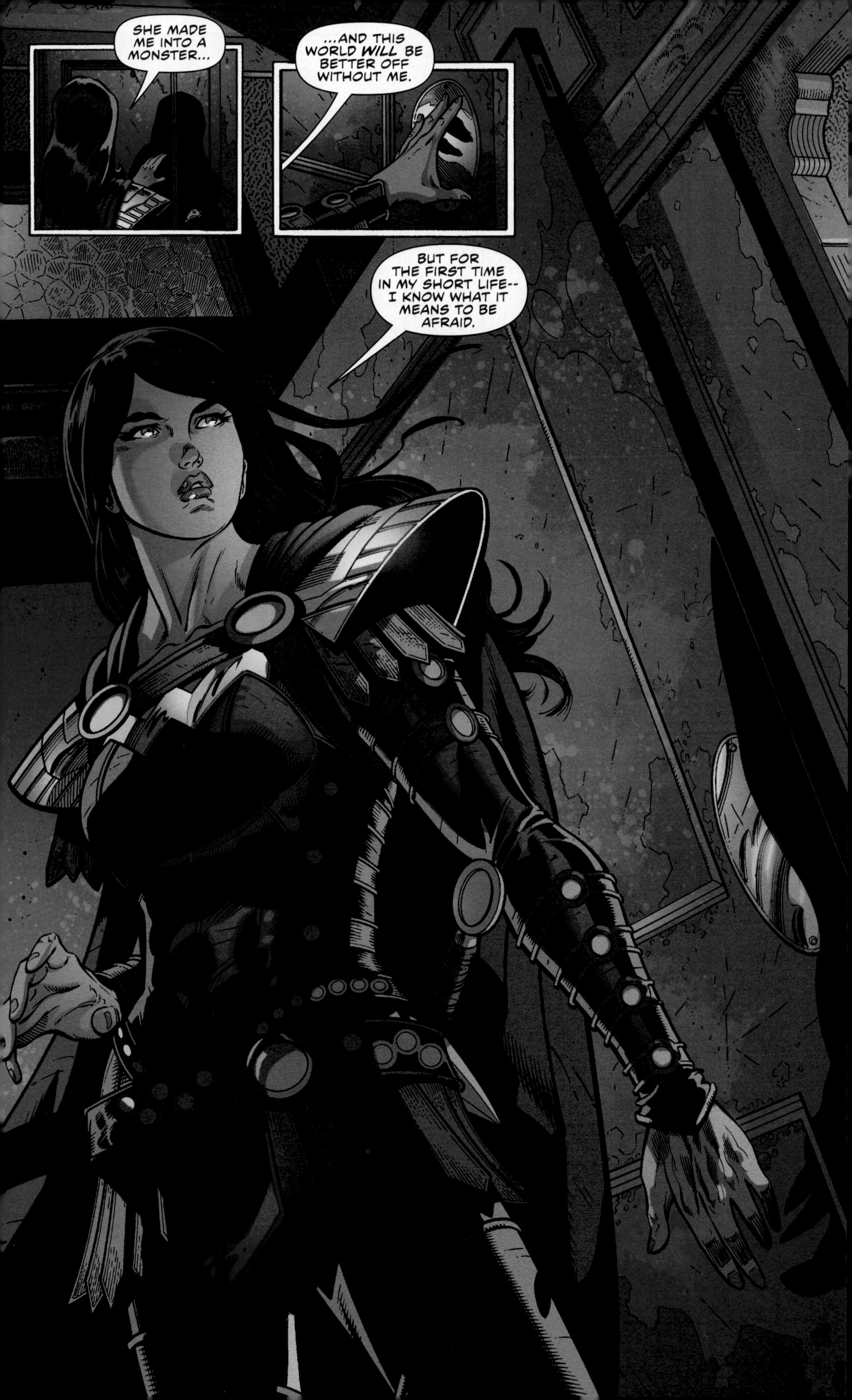
SHE MADE ME INTO A MONSTER...
...AND THIS WORLD WILL BE BETTER OFF WITHOUT ME.
BUT FOR THE FIRST TIME IN MY SHORT LIFE-- I KNOW WHAT IT MEANS TO BE AFRAID.

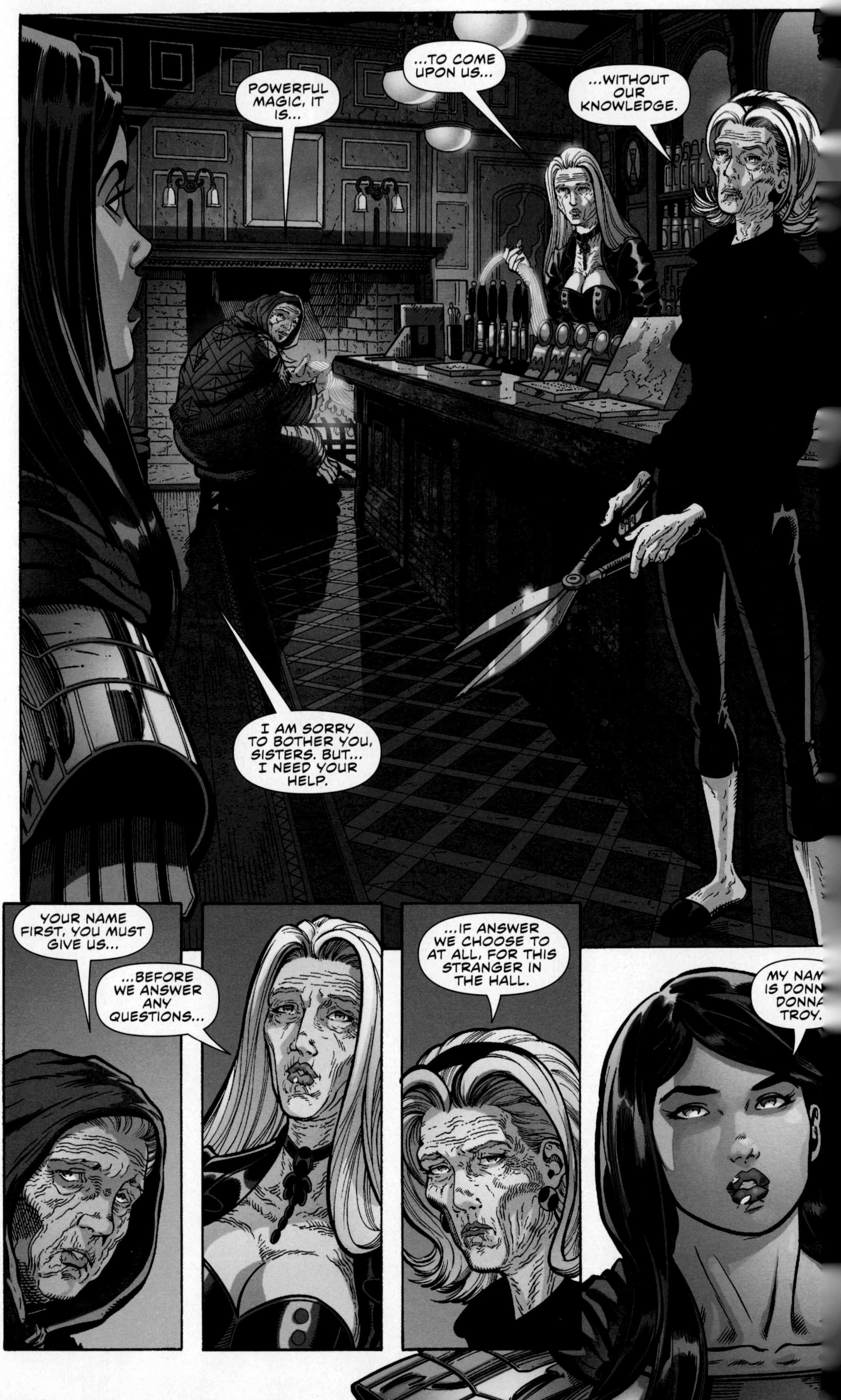
POWERFUL MAGIC, IT IS...
...TO COME UPON US...
...WITHOUT OUR KNOWLEDGE.
I AM SORRY TO BOTHER YOU, SISTERS. BUT... I NEED YOUR HELP.
YOUR NAME FIRST, YOU MUST GIVE US...
...BEFORE WE ANSWER ANY QUESTIONS...
...IF ANSWER WE CHOOSE TO AT ALL, FOR THIS STRANGER IN THE HALL.
MY NAM IS DONN DONNA TROY.

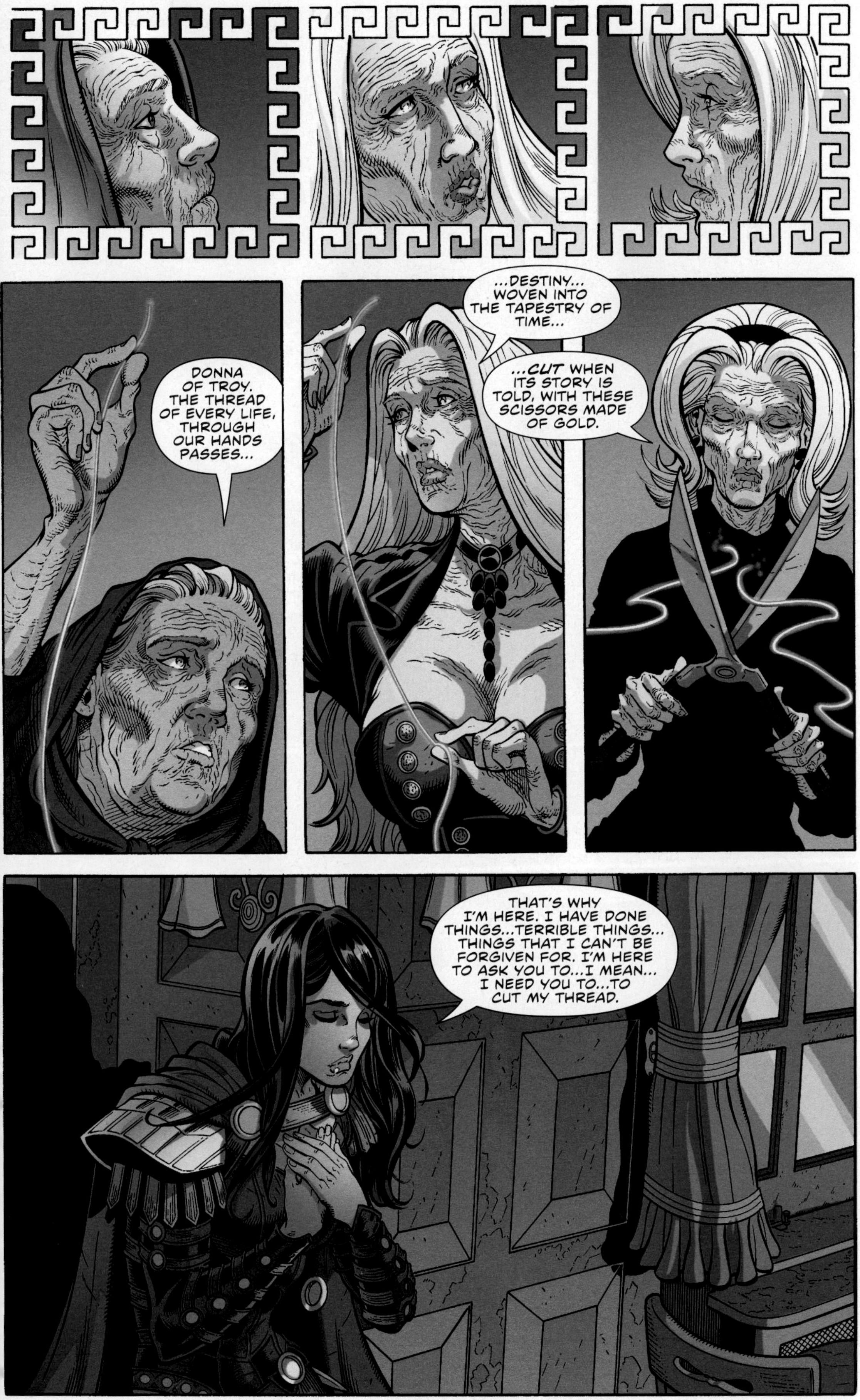
DONNA OF TROY. THE THREAD OF EVERY LIFE, THROUGH OUR HANDS PASSES...
...DESTINY... WOVEN INTO THE TAPESTRY OF TIME...
...CUT WHEN ITS STORY IS TOLD, WITH THESE SCISSORS MADE OF GOLD.
THAT'S WHY I'M HERE. I HAVE DONE THINGS...TERRIBLE THINGS... THINGS THAT I CAN'T BE FORGIVEN FOR. I'M HERE TO ASK YOU TO...I MEAN... I NEED YOU TO...TO CUT MY THREAD.

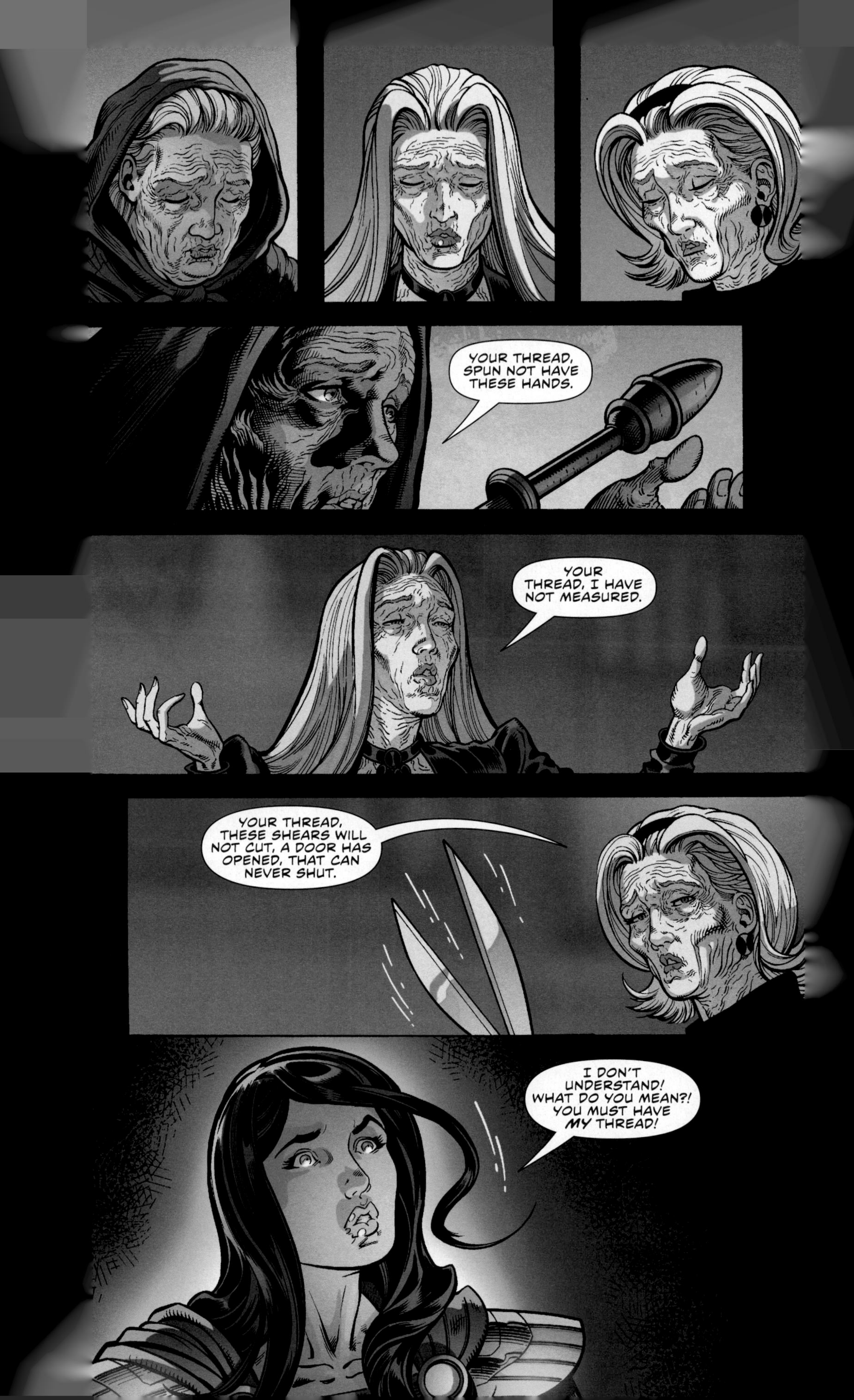
YOUR THREAD, SPUN NOT HAVE THESE HANDS.
YOUR THREAD, I HAVE NOT MEASURED.
YOUR THREAD, THESE SHEARS WILL NOT CUT, A DOOR HAS OPENED, THAT CAN NEVER SHUT.
I DON'T UNDERSTAND! WHAT DO YOU MEAN?! YOU MUST HAVE MY THREAD!

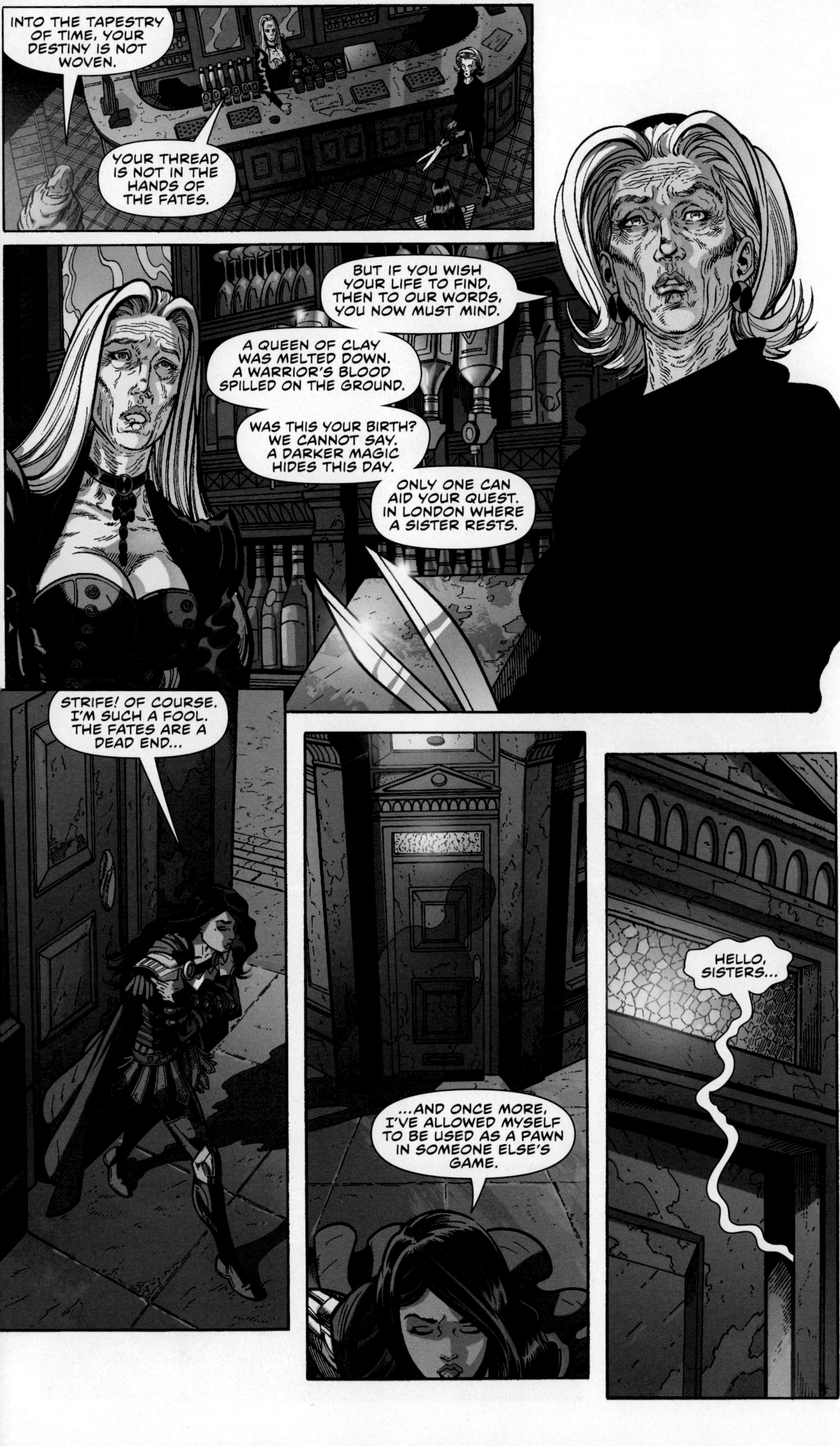

INTO THE TAPESTRY OF TIME, YOUR DESTINY IS NOT WOVEN.
YOUR THREAD IS NOT IN THE HANDS OF THE FATES.
BUT IF YOU WISH YOUR LIFE TO FIND, THEN TO OUR WORDS, YOU NOW MUST MIND.
A QUEEN OF CLAY WAS MELTED DOWN. A WARRIOR'S BLOOD SPILLED ON THE GROUND.
WAS THIS YOUR BIRTH? WE CANNOT SAY. A DARKER MAGIC HIDES THIS DAY.
ONLY ONE CAN AID YOUR QUEST. IN LONDON WHERE A SISTER RESTS.
STRIFE! OF COURSE. I'M SUCH A FOOL. THE FATES ARE A DEAD END...
...AND ONCE MORE, I'VE ALLOWED MYSELF TO BE USED AS A PAWN IN SOMEONE ELSE'S GAME.
HELLO, SISTERS...

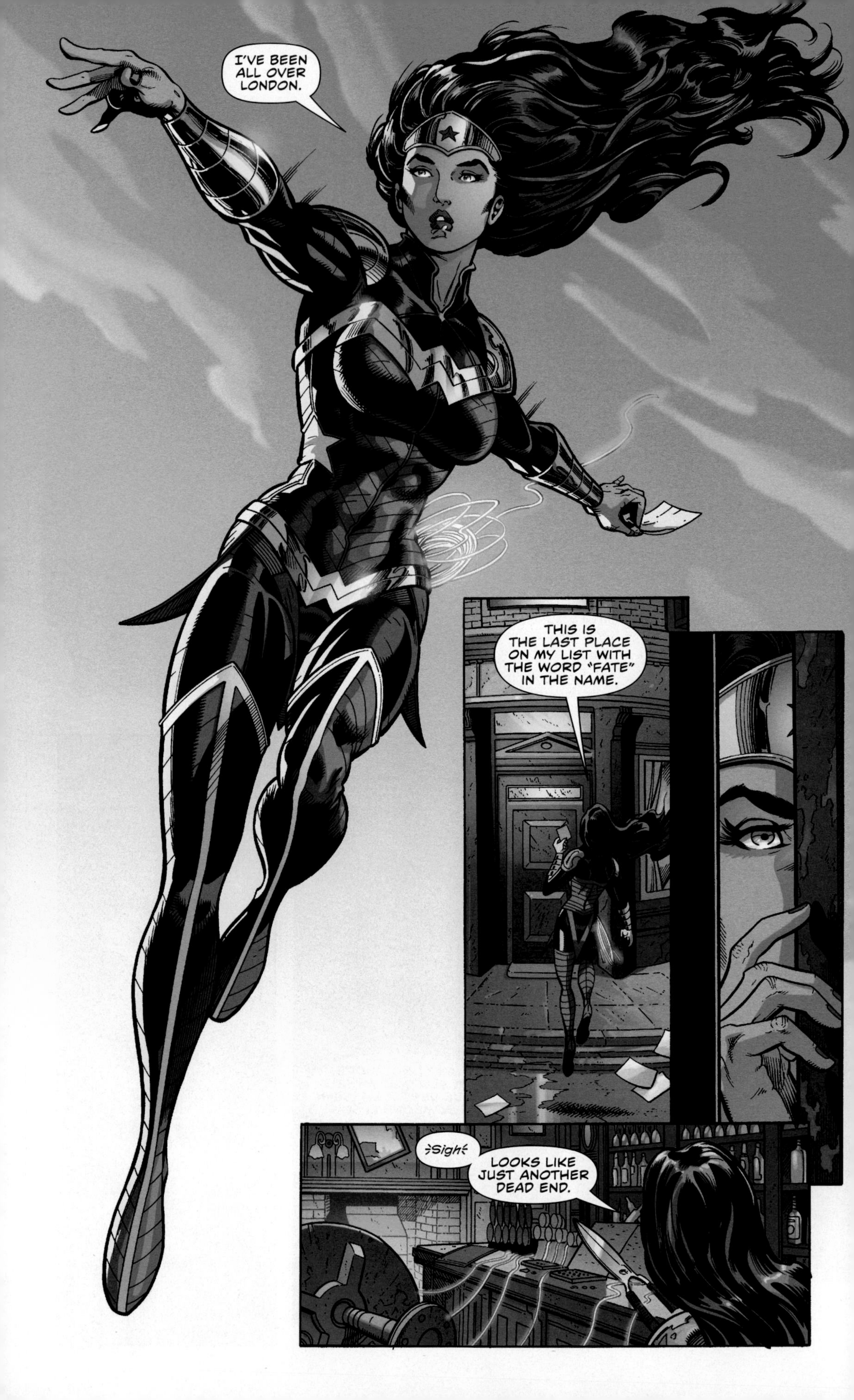
I'VE BEEN ALL OVER LONDON.
THIS IS THE LAST PLACE ON MY LIST WITH THE WORD "FATE" IN THE NAME.
Sigh
LOOKS LIKE JUST ANOTHER DEAD END.

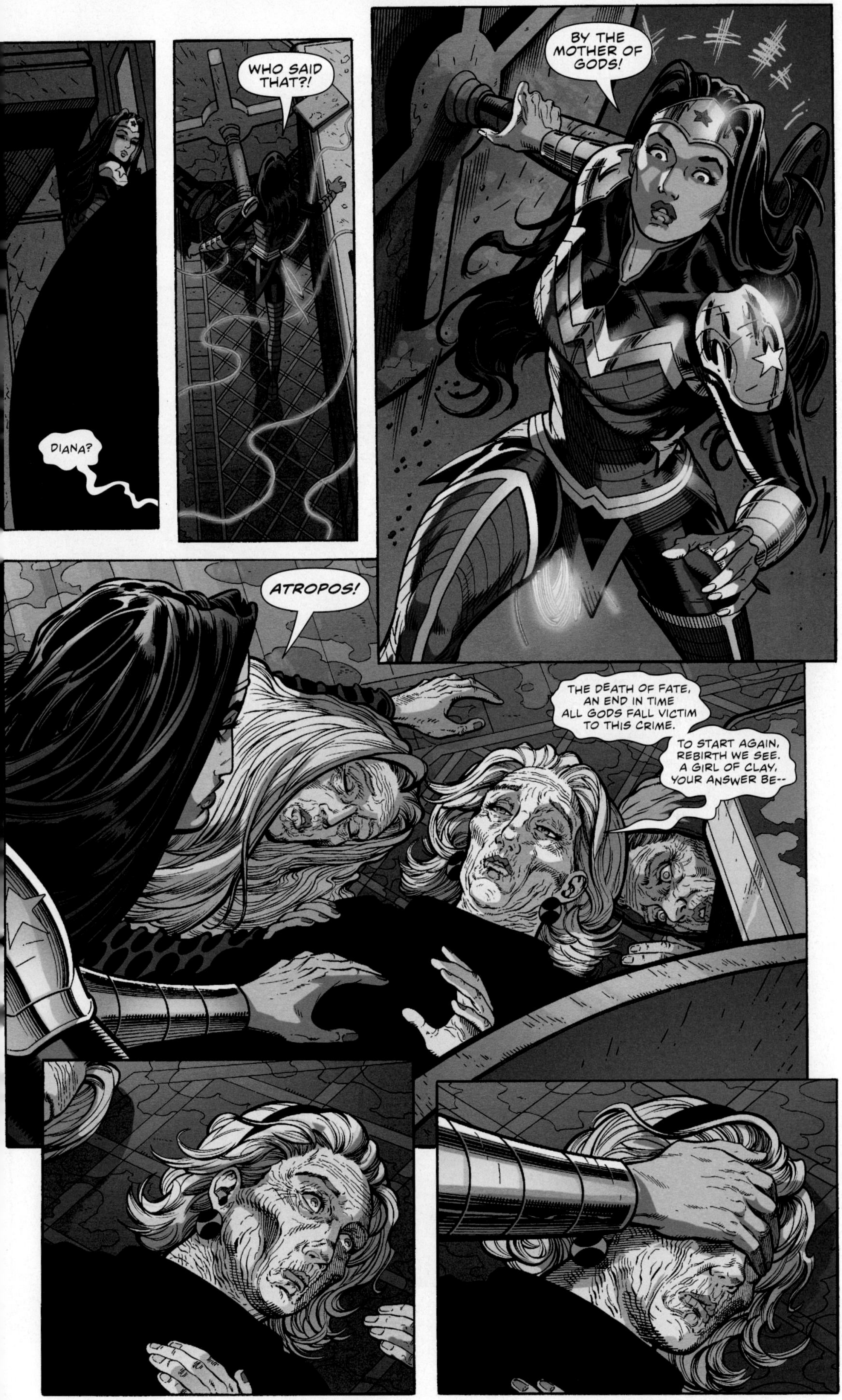
DIANA?
WHO SAID THAT?!
BY THE MOTHER OF GODS!
ATROPOS!
THE DEATH OF FATE, AN END IN TIME ALL GODS FALL VICTIM TO THIS CRIME.
TO START AGAIN, REBIRTH WE SEE. A GIRL OF CLAY, YOUR ANSWER BE--

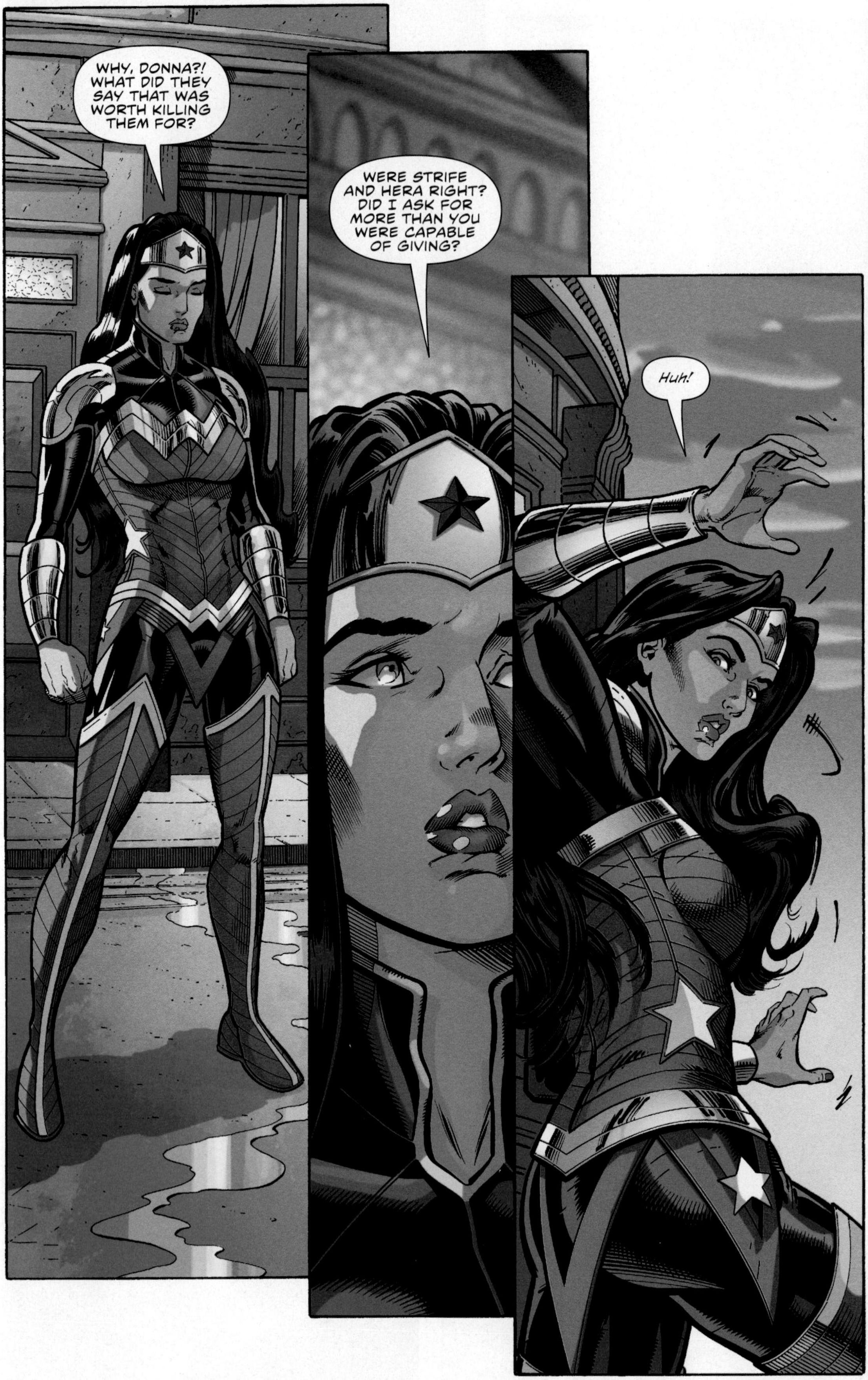
WHY, DONNA?! WHAT DID THEY SAY THAT WAS WORTH KILLING THEM FOR?
WERE STRIFE AND HERA RIGHT? DID I ASK FOR MORE THAN YOU WERE CAPABLE OF GIVING?
Huh!

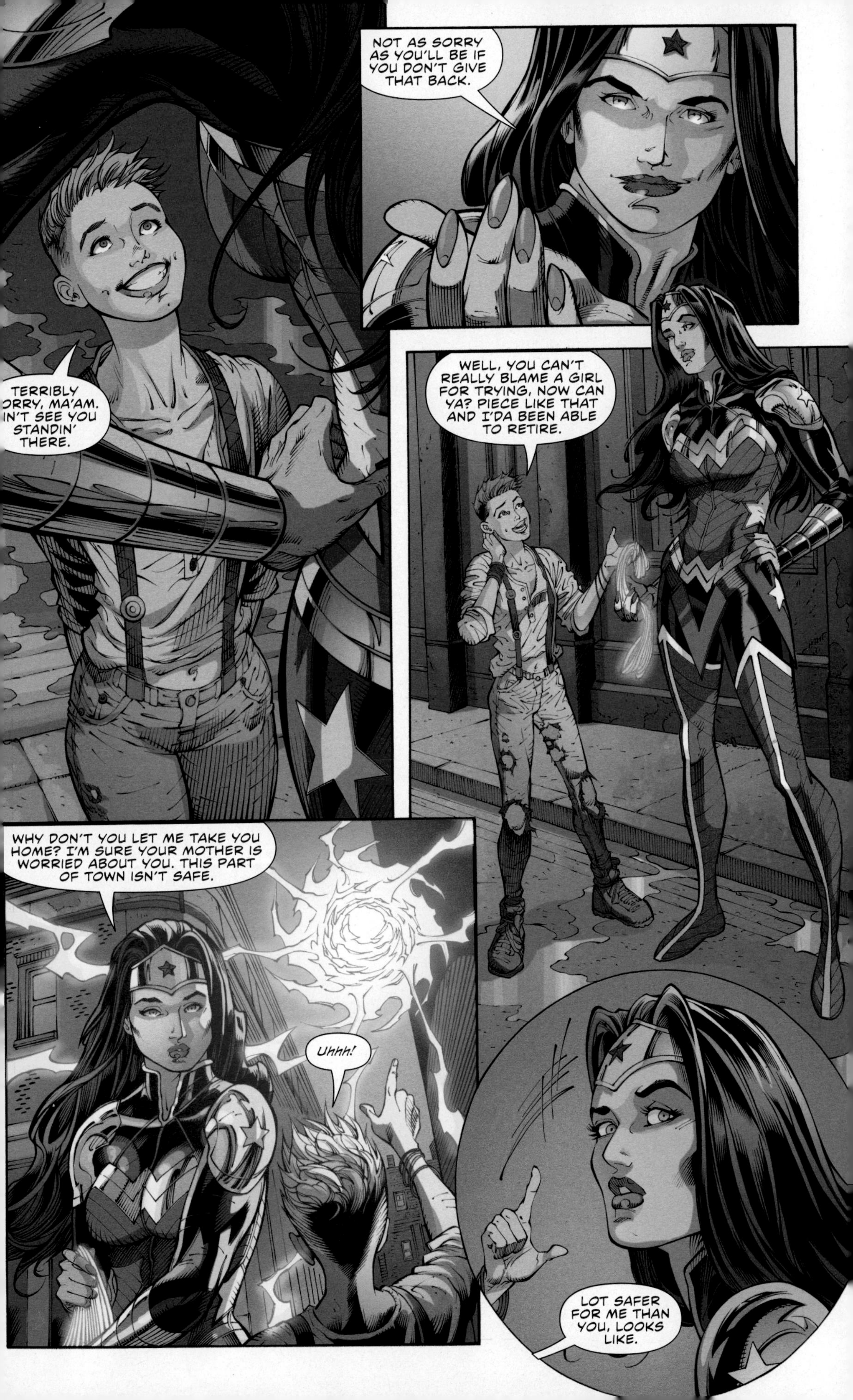
TERRIBLY
SORRY, MA'AM.
DIDN'T SEE YOU
STANDIN'
THERE.
NOT AS SORRY
AS YOU'LL BE IF
YOU DON'T GIVE
THAT BACK.
WELL, YOU CAN'T
REALLY BLAME A GIRL
FOR TRYING, NOW CAN
YA? PIECE LIKE THAT
AND I'DA BEEN ABLE
TO RETIRE.
WHY DON'T YOU LET ME TAKE YOU
HOME? I'M SURE YOUR MOTHER IS
WORRIED ABOUT YOU. THIS PART
OF TOWN ISN'T SAFE.
Uhhh!
LOT SAFER
FOR ME THAN
YOU, LOOKS
LIKE.

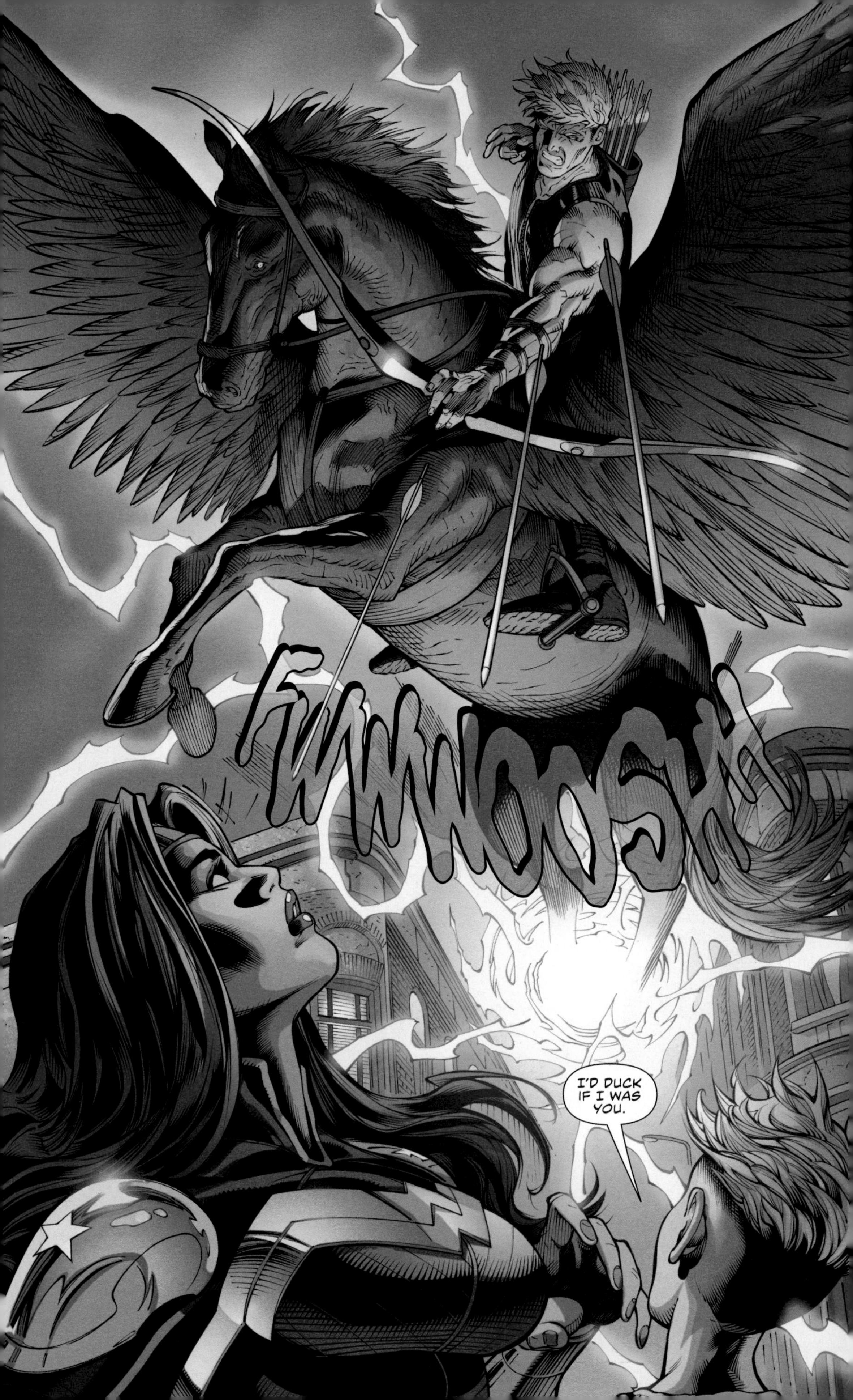
FWWOOSH!
I'D DUCK IF I WAS YOU.

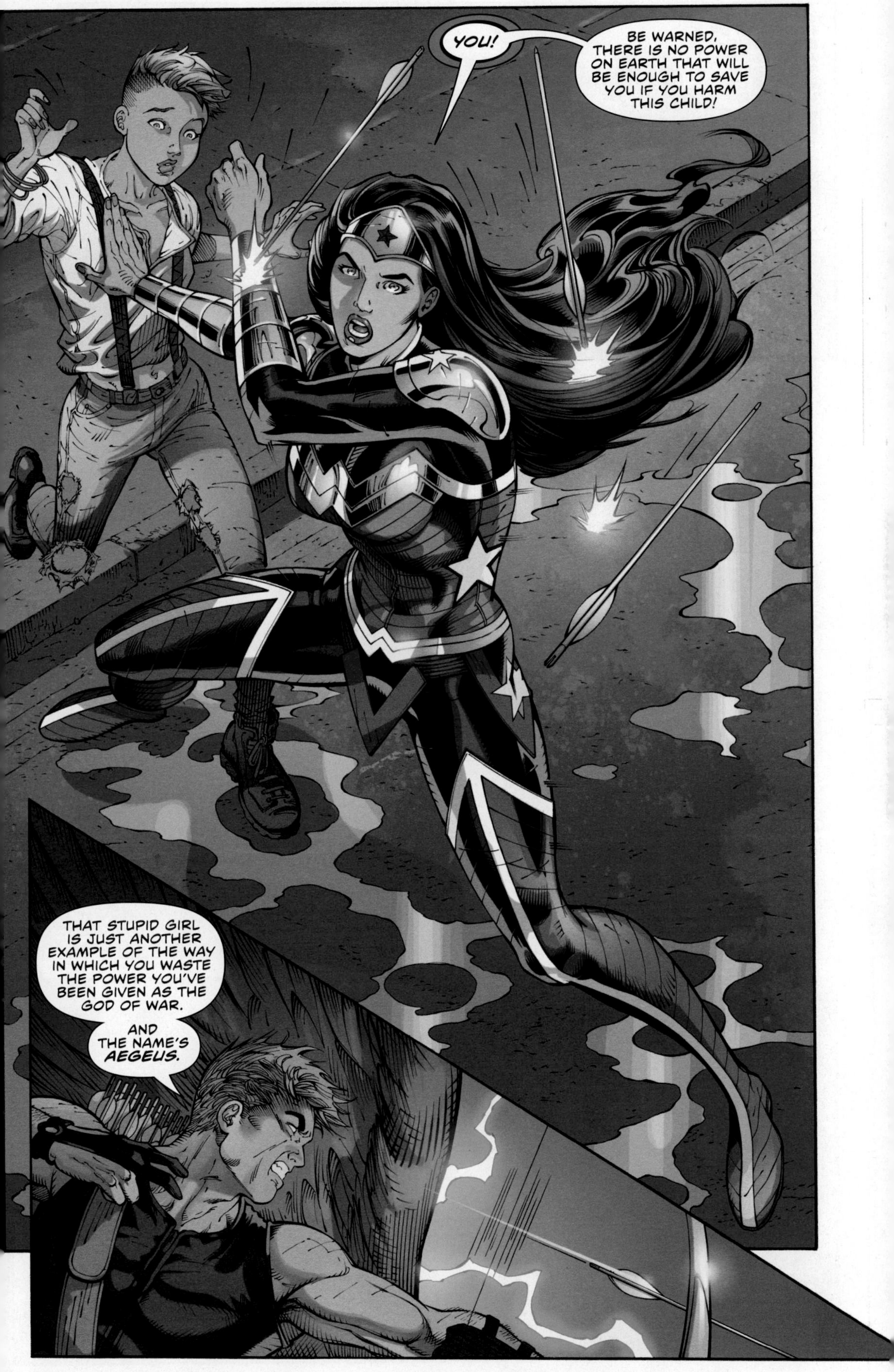
YOU!
BE WARNED, THERE IS NO POWER ON EARTH THAT WILL BE ENOUGH TO SAVE YOU IF YOU HARM THIS CHILD!
THAT STUPID GIRL IS JUST ANOTHER EXAMPLE OF THE WAY IN WHICH YOU WASTE THE POWER YOU'VE BEEN GIVEN AS THE GOD OF WAR.
AND THE NAME'S AEGEUS.

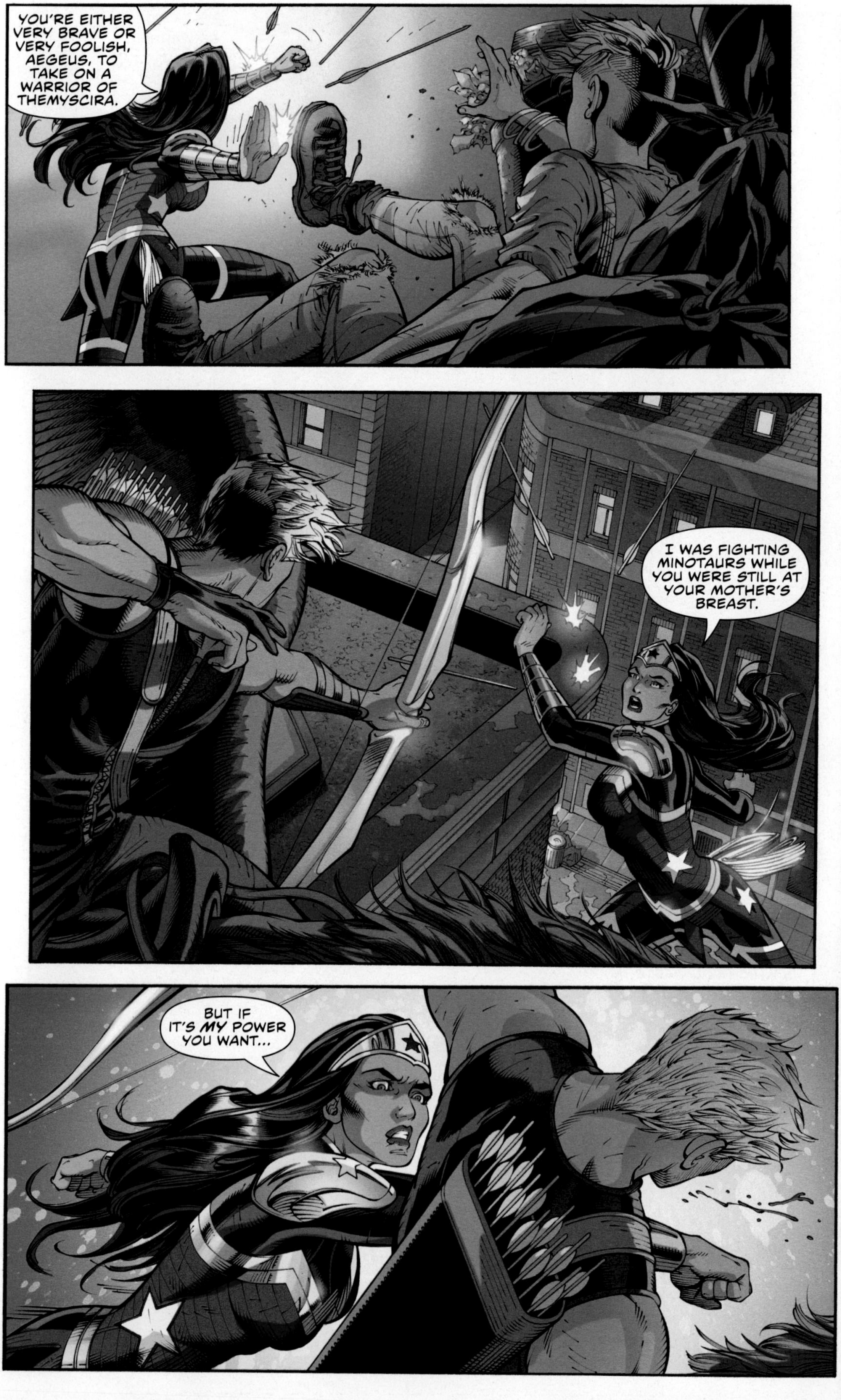
YOU'RE EITHER VERY BRAVE OR VERY FOOLISH, AEGEUS, TO TAKE ON A WARRIOR OF THEMYSCIRA.
I WAS FIGHTING MINOTAURS WHILE YOU WERE STILL AT YOUR MOTHER'S BREAST.
BUT IF IT'S *MY* POWER YOU WANT...

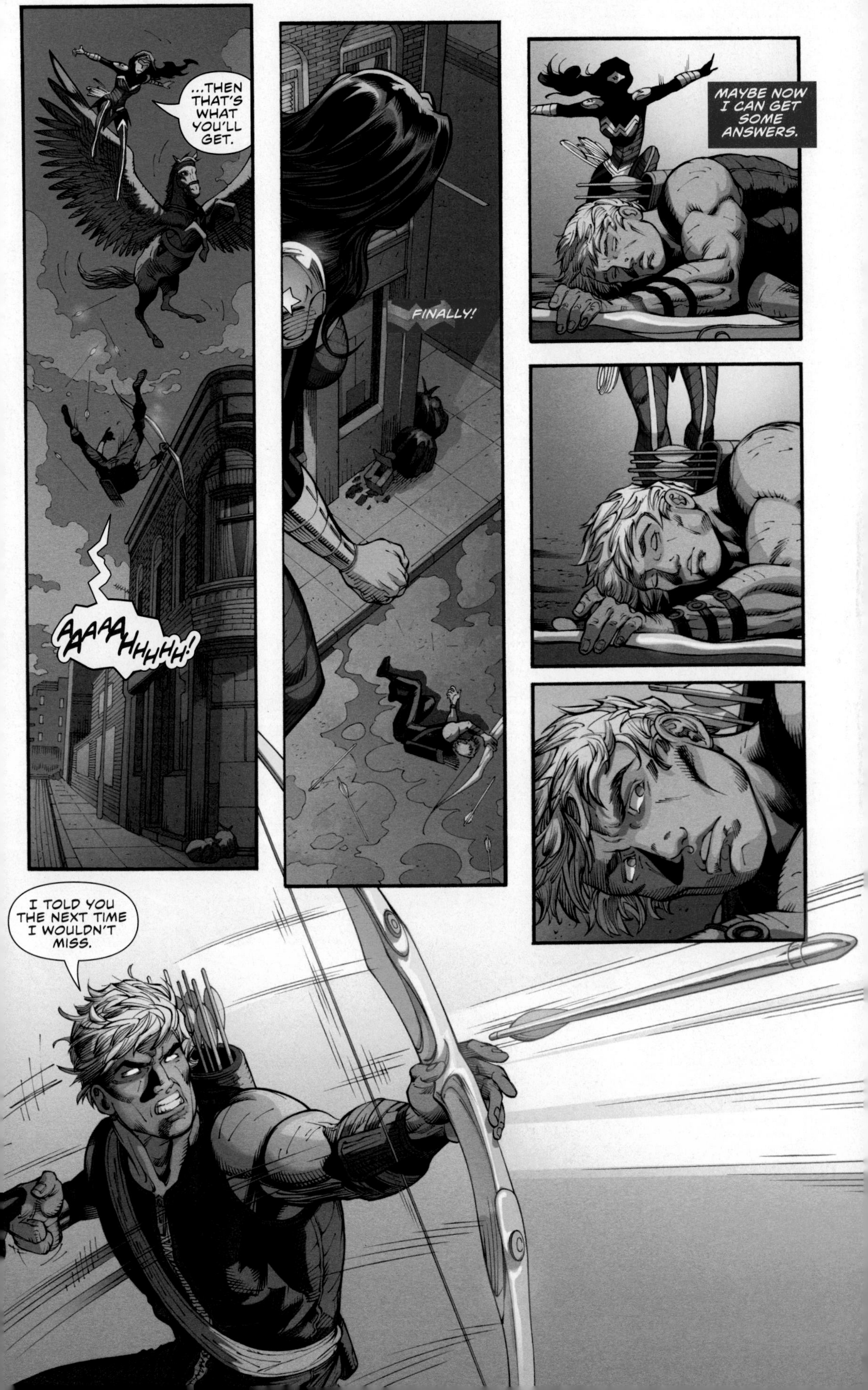
...THEN THAT'S WHAT YOU'LL GET.
AAAAAHHHHH!
FINALLY!
MAYBE NOW I CAN GET SOME ANSWERS.
I TOLD YOU THE NEXT TIME I WOULDN'T MISS.

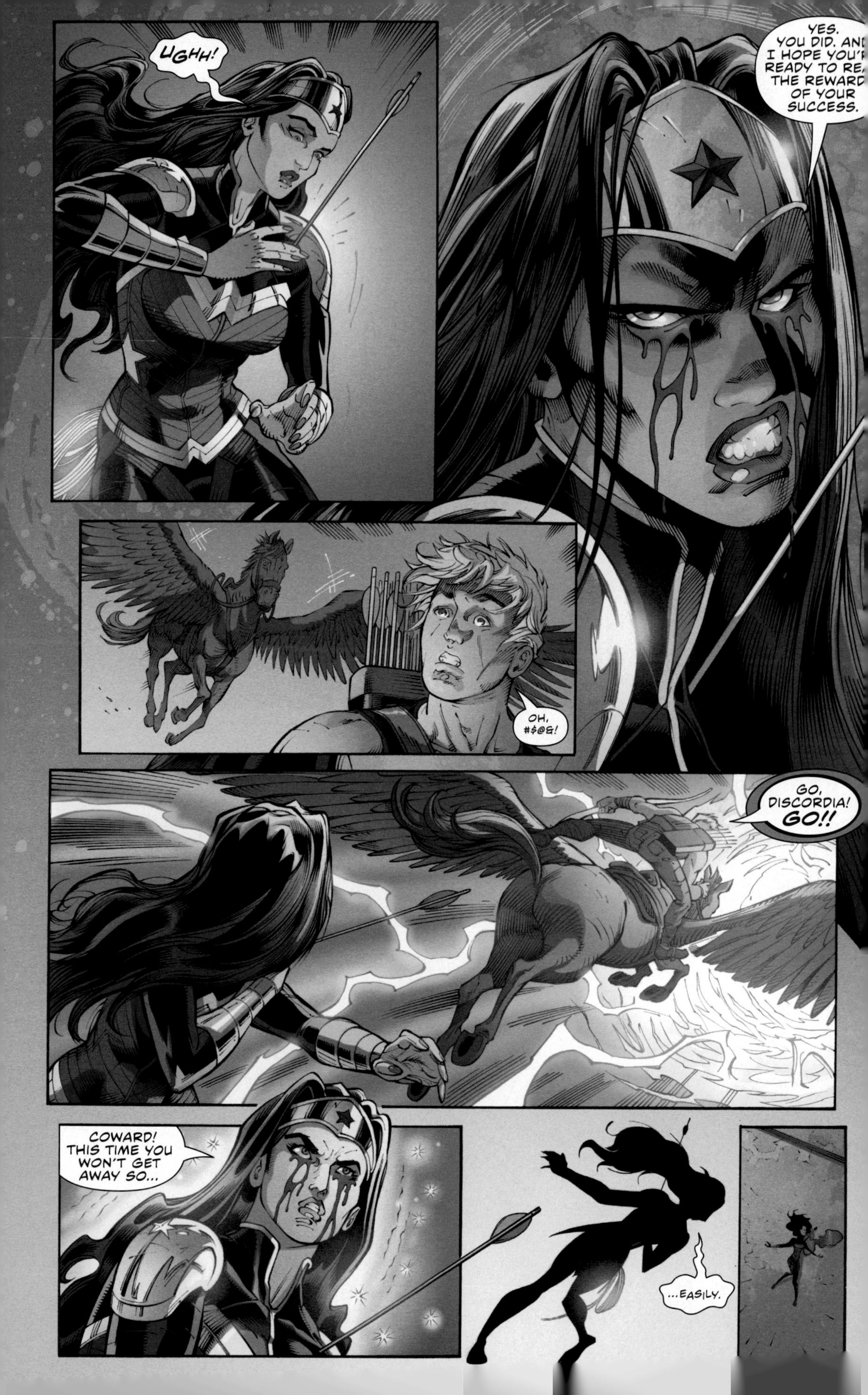
UGHH!
YES. YOU DID. AND I HOPE YOU'RE READY TO REAP THE REWARDS OF YOUR SUCCESS.
OH, #$@&!
GO, DISCORDIA! GO!!
COWARD! THIS TIME YOU WON'T GET AWAY SO...
...EASILY.

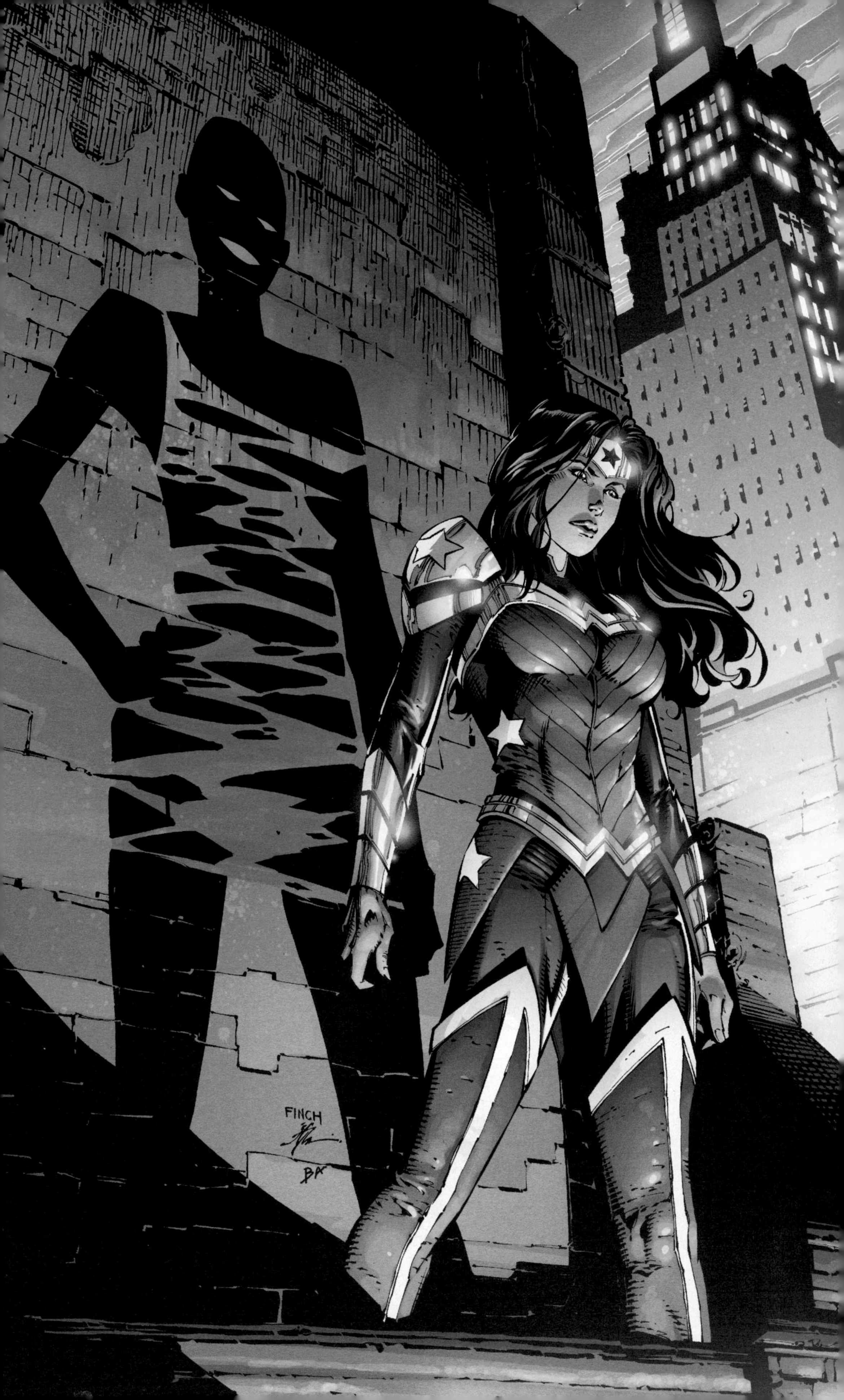
FINCH
BA

PATH TO DESTINY

MEREDITH FINCH writer DAVID FINCH penciller JONATHAN GLAPION inker BRAD ANDERSON colorist ROB LEIGH letterer
cover by FINCH, GLAPION & ANDERSON

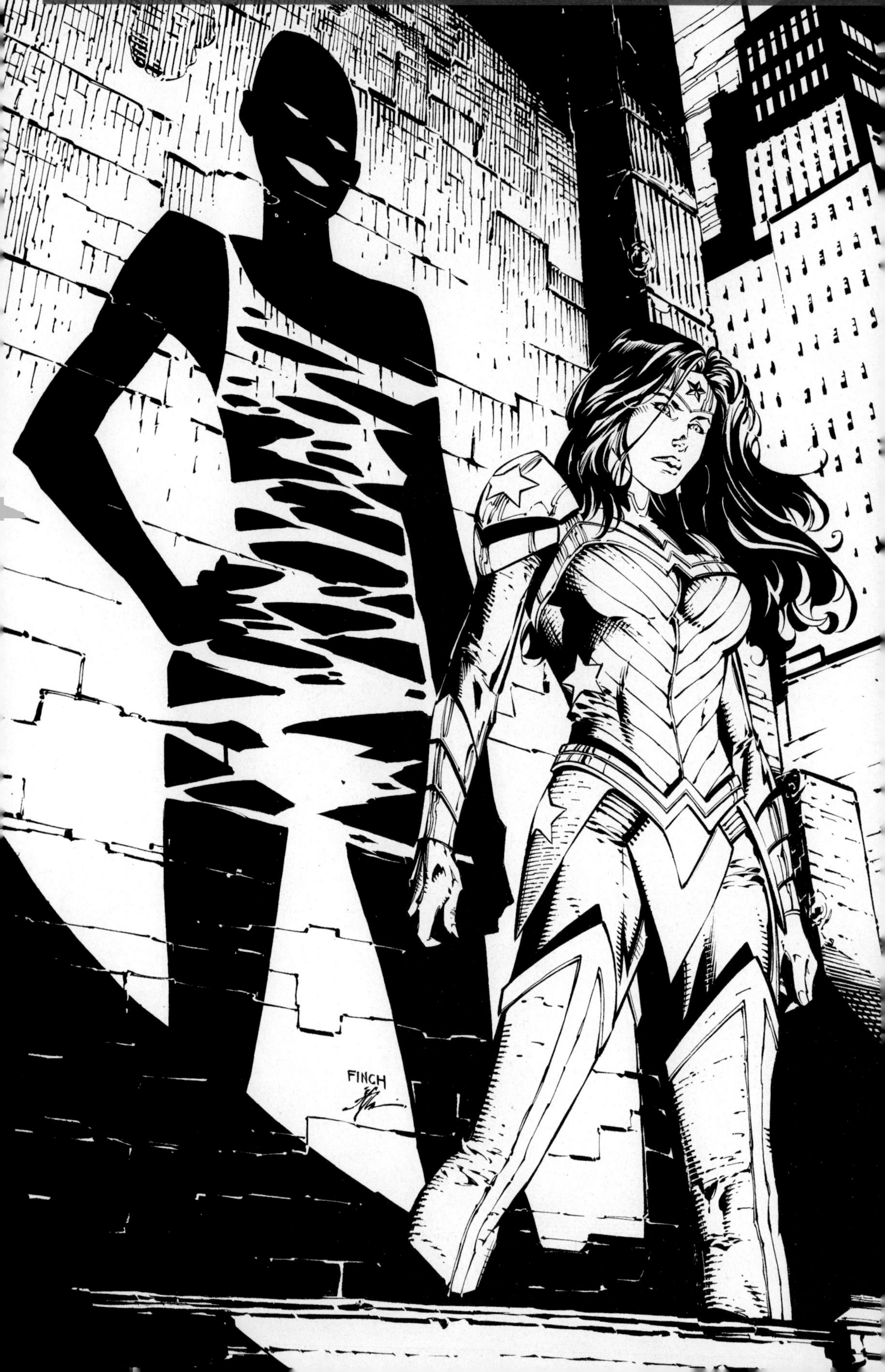
FINCH

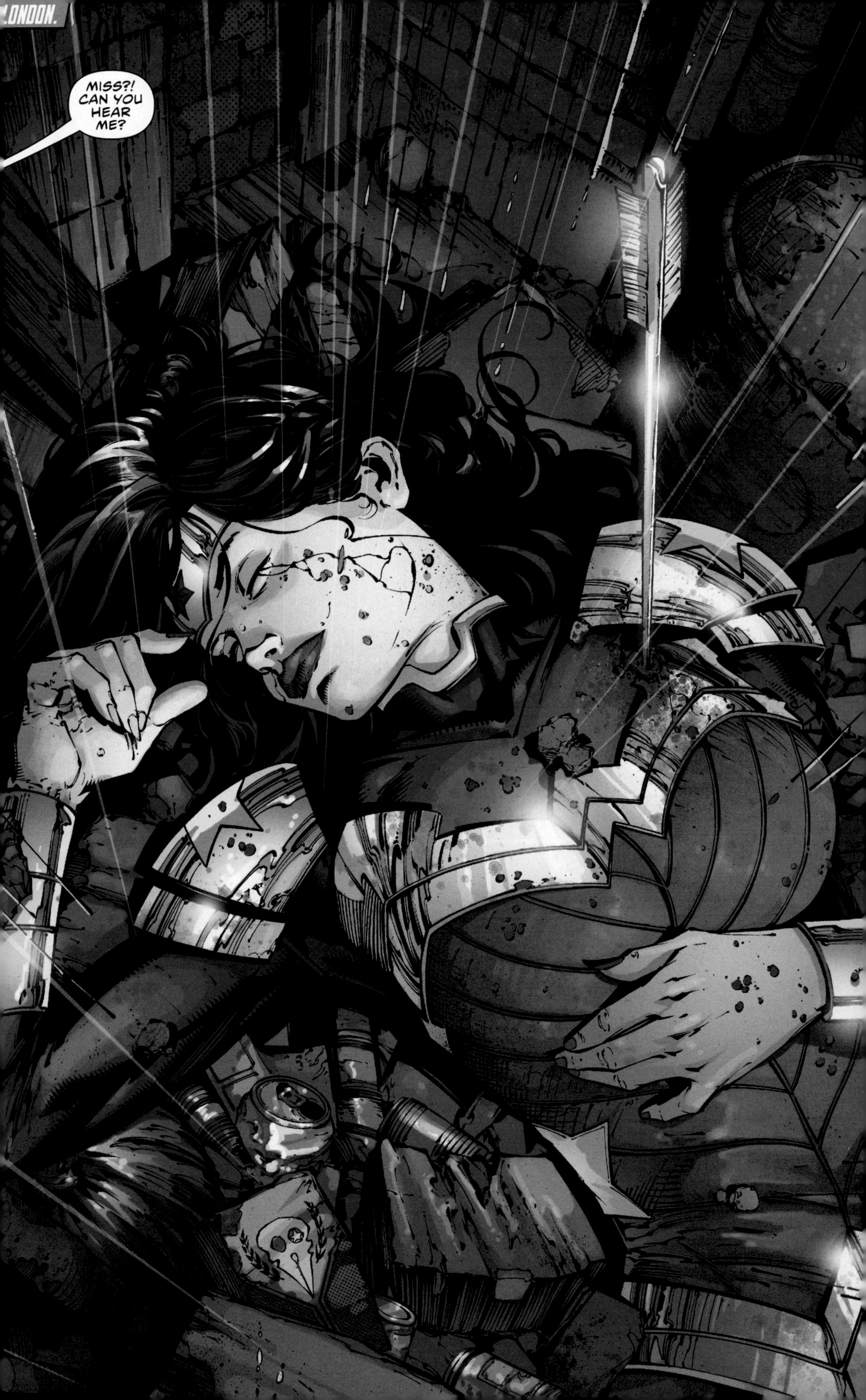
LONDON.
MISS?! CAN YOU HEAR ME?

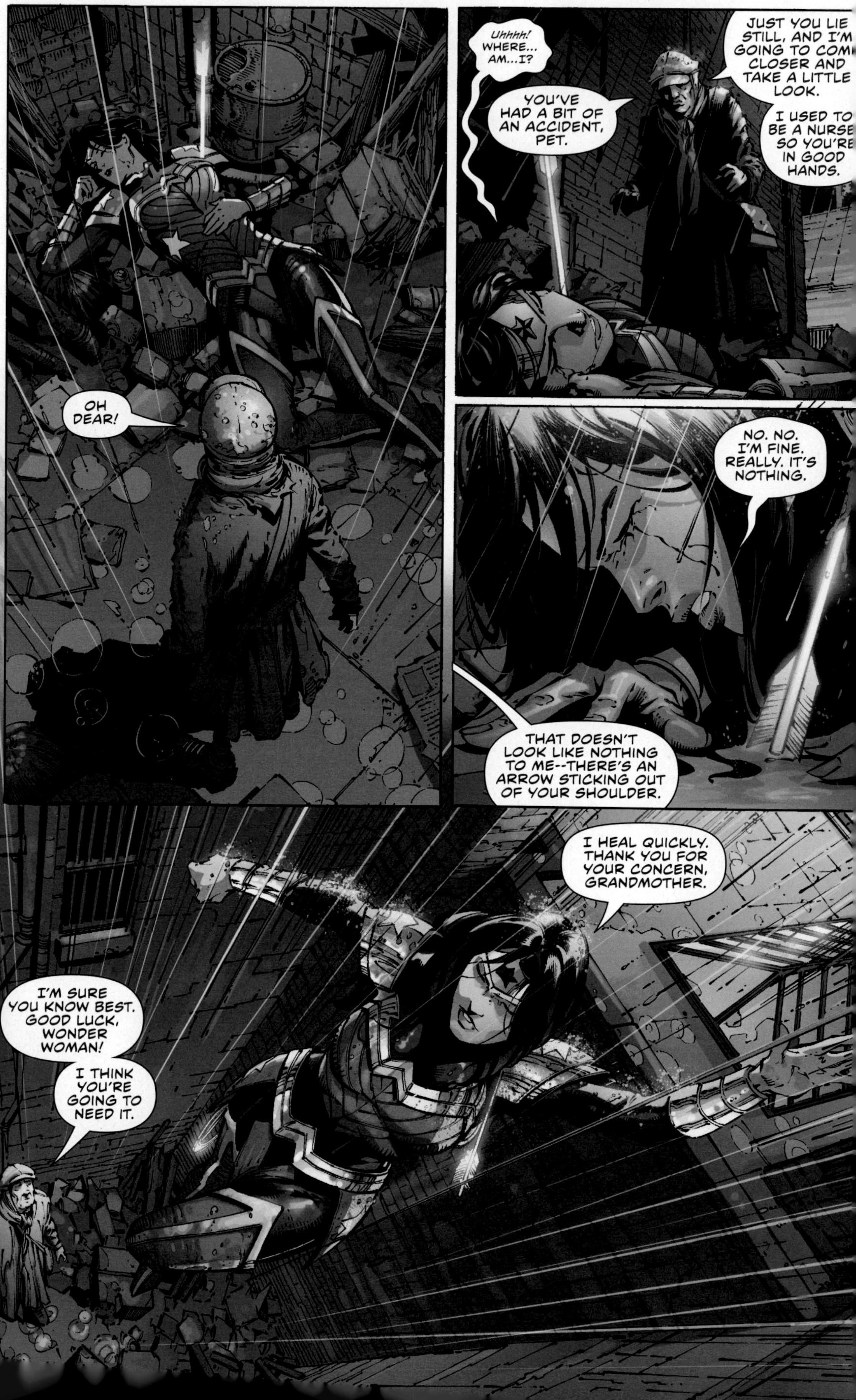
OH DEAR!
Uhhhh! WHERE... AM...I?
YOU'VE HAD A BIT OF AN ACCIDENT, PET.
JUST YOU LIE STILL, AND I'M GOING TO COM CLOSER AND TAKE A LITTLE LOOK.
I USED TO BE A NURSE SO YOU'RE IN GOOD HANDS.
NO. NO. I'M FINE. REALLY. IT'S NOTHING.
THAT DOESN'T LOOK LIKE NOTHING TO ME--THERE'S AN ARROW STICKING OUT OF YOUR SHOULDER.
I HEAL QUICKLY. THANK YOU FOR YOUR CONCERN, GRANDMOTHER.
I'M SURE YOU KNOW BEST. GOOD LUCK, WONDER WOMAN!
I THINK YOU'RE GOING TO NEED IT.

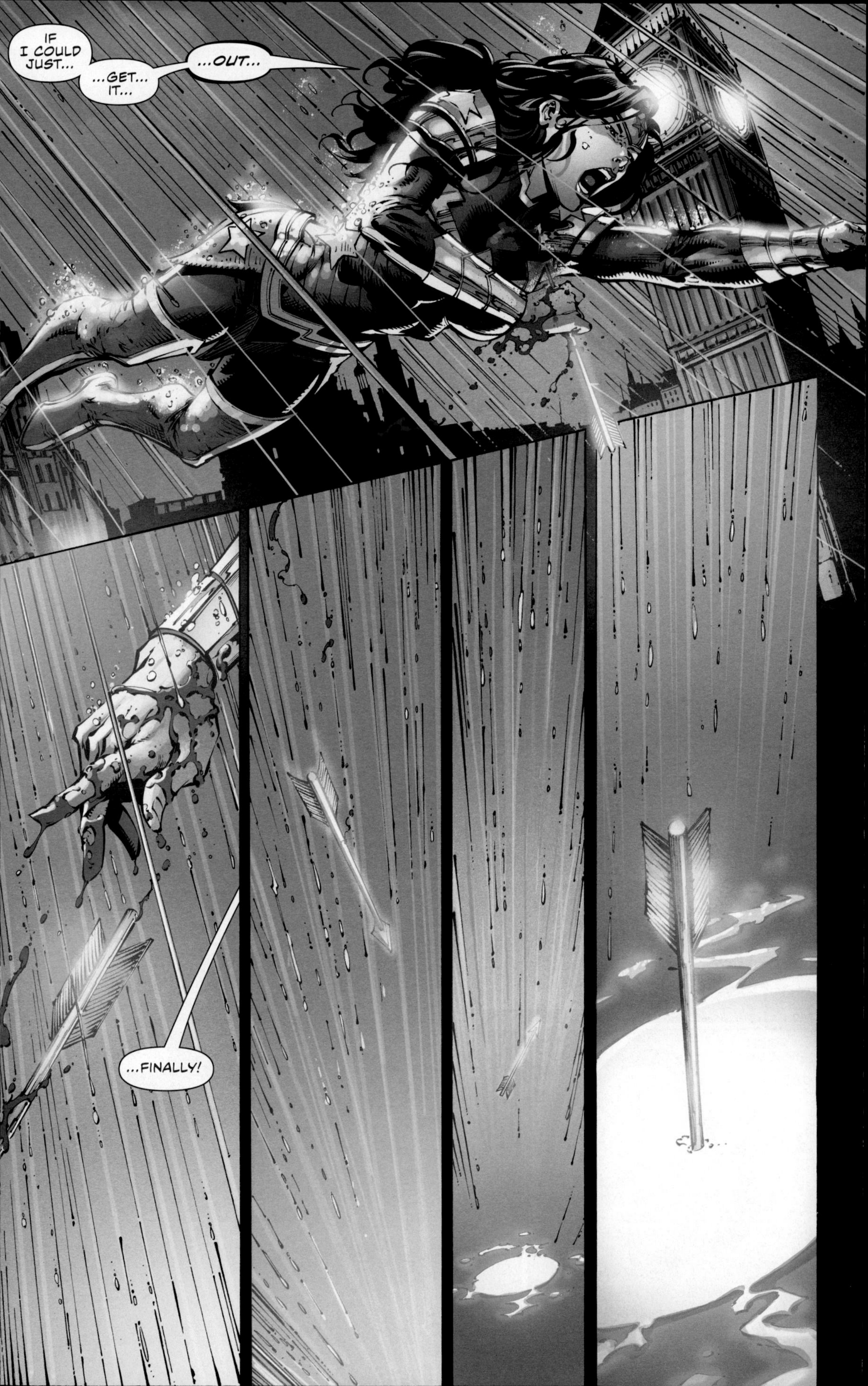
IF I COULD JUST...
...GET... IT...
...OUT...
...FINALLY!

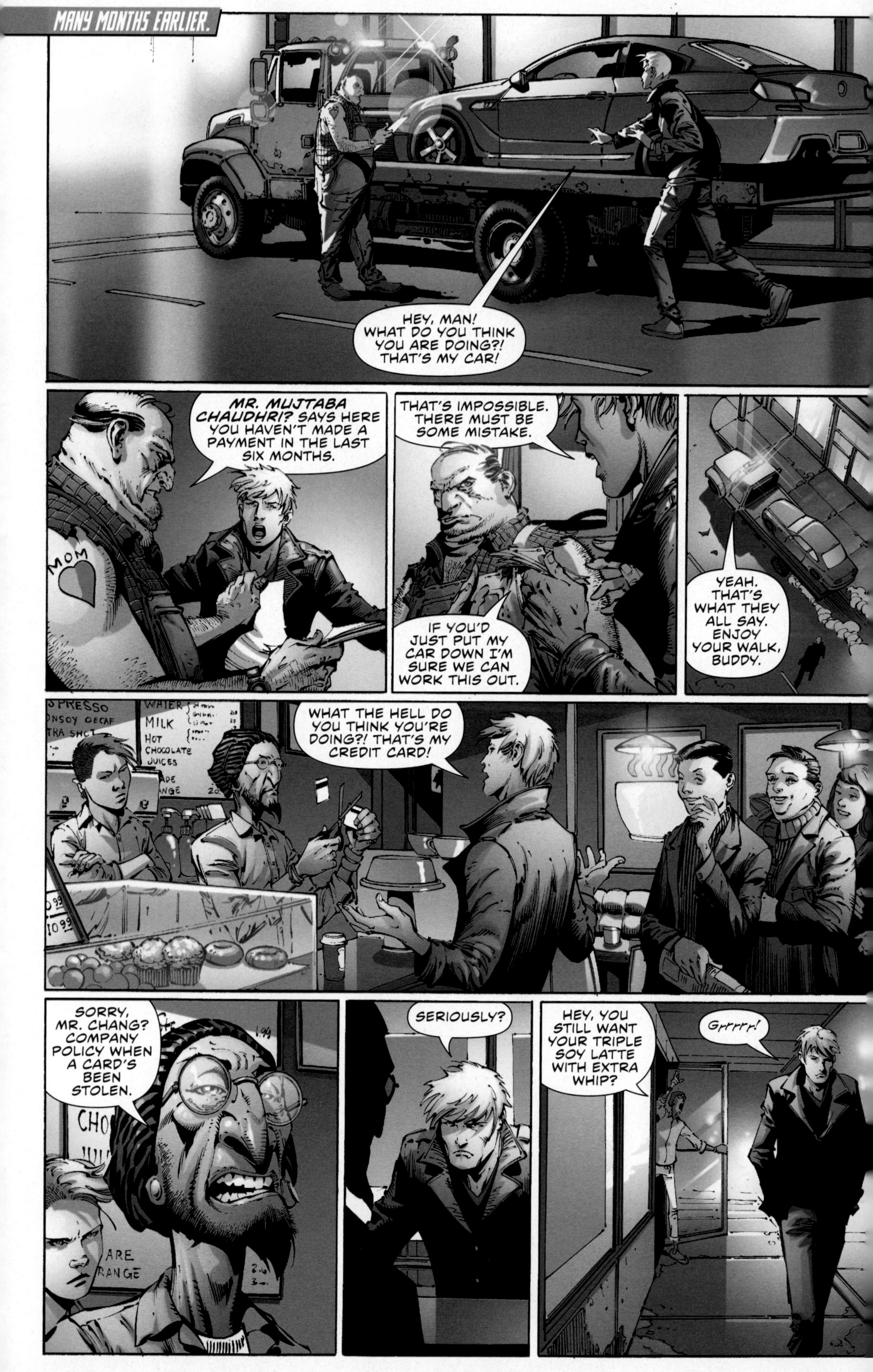
MANY MONTHS EARLIER.
HEY, MAN! WHAT DO YOU THINK YOU ARE DOING?! THAT'S MY CAR!
MR. MUJTABA CHAUDHRI? SAYS HERE YOU HAVEN'T MADE A PAYMENT IN THE LAST SIX MONTHS.
MOM
THAT'S IMPOSSIBLE. THERE MUST BE SOME MISTAKE.
IF YOU'D JUST PUT MY CAR DOWN I'M SURE WE CAN WORK THIS OUT.
YEAH. THAT'S WHAT THEY ALL SAY. ENJOY YOUR WALK, BUDDY.
WHAT THE HELL DO YOU THINK YOU'RE DOING?! THAT'S MY CREDIT CARD!
SORRY, MR. CHANG? COMPANY POLICY WHEN A CARD'S BEEN STOLEN.
SERIOUSLY?
HEY, YOU STILL WANT YOUR TRIPLE SOY LATTE WITH EXTRA WHIP?
Grrrrr!

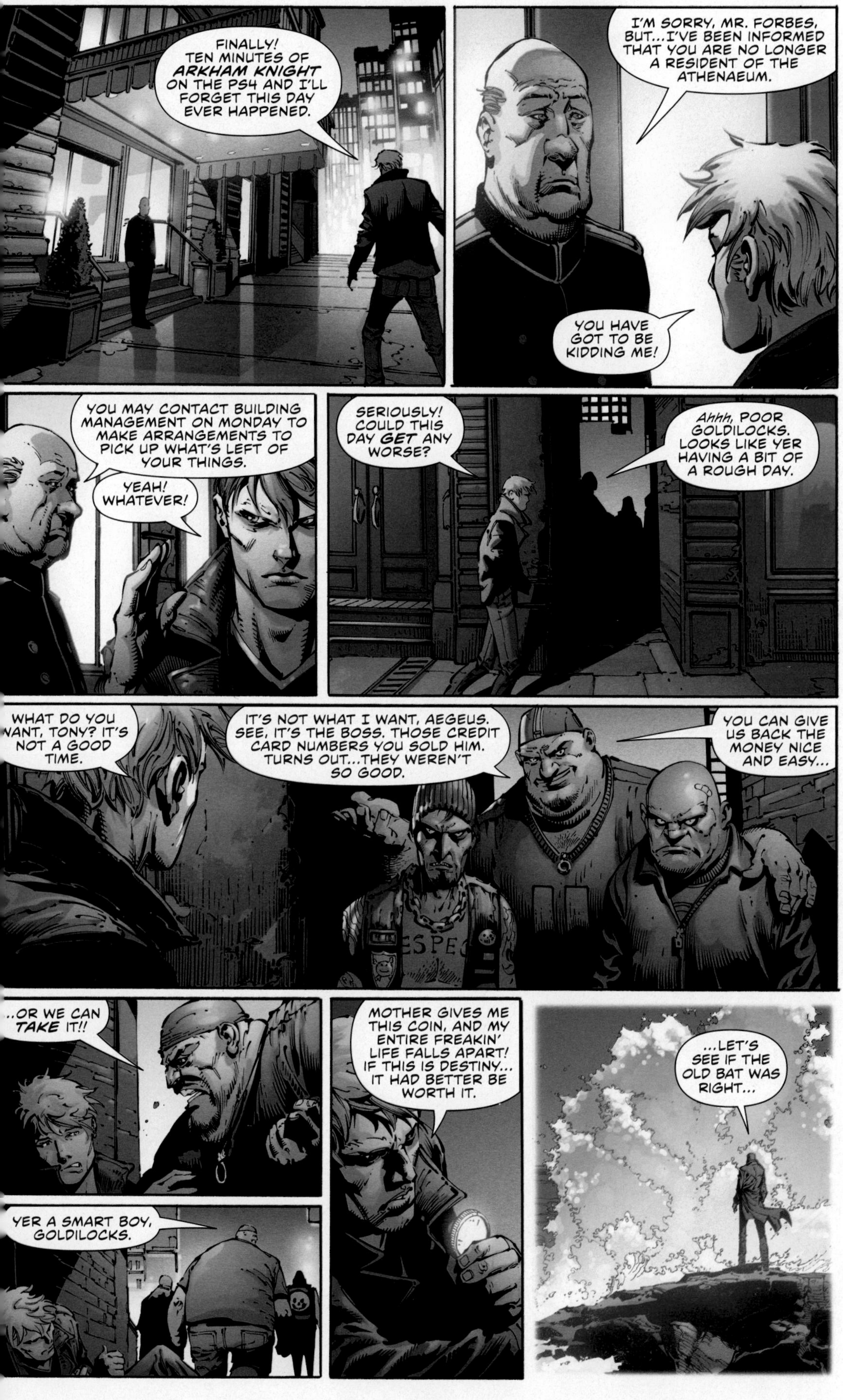
FINALLY! TEN MINUTES OF ARKHAM KNIGHT ON THE PS4 AND I'LL FORGET THIS DAY EVER HAPPENED.
I'M SORRY, MR. FORBES, BUT...I'VE BEEN INFORMED THAT YOU ARE NO LONGER A RESIDENT OF THE ATHENAEUM.
YOU HAVE GOT TO BE KIDDING ME!
YOU MAY CONTACT BUILDING MANAGEMENT ON MONDAY TO MAKE ARRANGEMENTS TO PICK UP WHAT'S LEFT OF YOUR THINGS.
YEAH! WHATEVER!
SERIOUSLY! COULD THIS DAY GET ANY WORSE?
Ahhh, POOR GOLDILOCKS. LOOKS LIKE YER HAVING A BIT OF A ROUGH DAY.
WHAT DO YOU WANT, TONY? IT'S NOT A GOOD TIME.
IT'S NOT WHAT I WANT, AEGEUS. SEE, IT'S THE BOSS. THOSE CREDIT CARD NUMBERS YOU SOLD HIM. TURNS OUT...THEY WEREN'T SO GOOD.
YOU CAN GIVE US BACK THE MONEY NICE AND EASY...
...OR WE CAN TAKE IT!!
YER A SMART BOY, GOLDILOCKS.
MOTHER GIVES ME THIS COIN, AND MY ENTIRE FREAKIN' LIFE FALLS APART! IF THIS IS DESTINY... IT HAD BETTER BE WORTH IT.
...LET'S SEE IF THE OLD BAT WAS RIGHT...

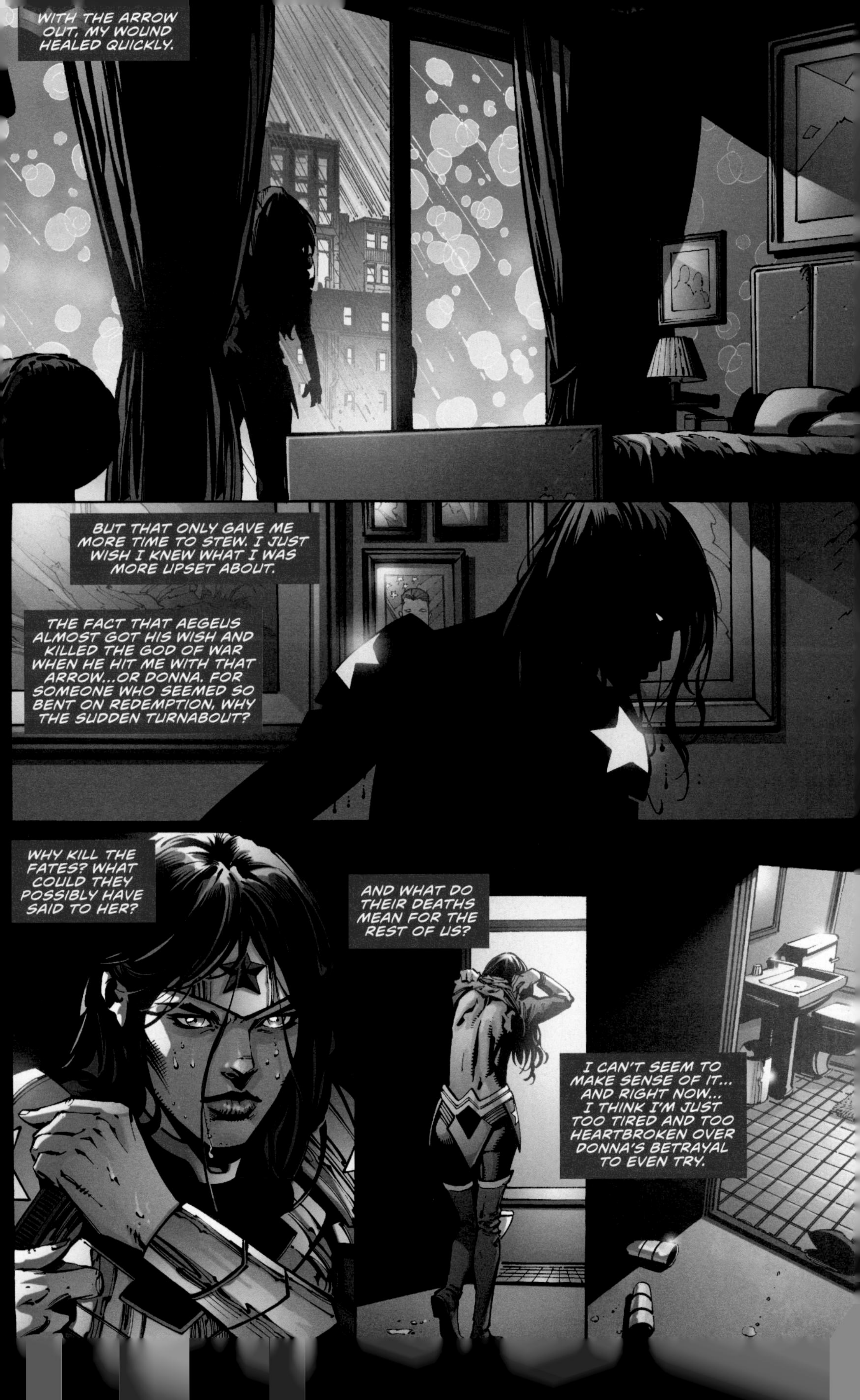
WITH THE ARROW OUT, MY WOUND HEALED QUICKLY.
BUT THAT ONLY GAVE ME MORE TIME TO STEW. I JUST WISH I KNEW WHAT I WAS MORE UPSET ABOUT.
THE FACT THAT AEGEUS ALMOST GOT HIS WISH AND KILLED THE GOD OF WAR WHEN HE HIT ME WITH THAT ARROW...OR DONNA. FOR SOMEONE WHO SEEMED SO BENT ON REDEMPTION, WHY THE SUDDEN TURNABOUT?
WHY KILL THE FATES? WHAT COULD THEY POSSIBLY HAVE SAID TO HER?
AND WHAT DO THEIR DEATHS MEAN FOR THE REST OF US?
I CAN'T SEEM TO MAKE SENSE OF IT... AND RIGHT NOW... I THINK I'M JUST TOO TIRED AND TOO HEARTBROKEN OVER DONNA'S BETRAYAL TO EVEN TRY.

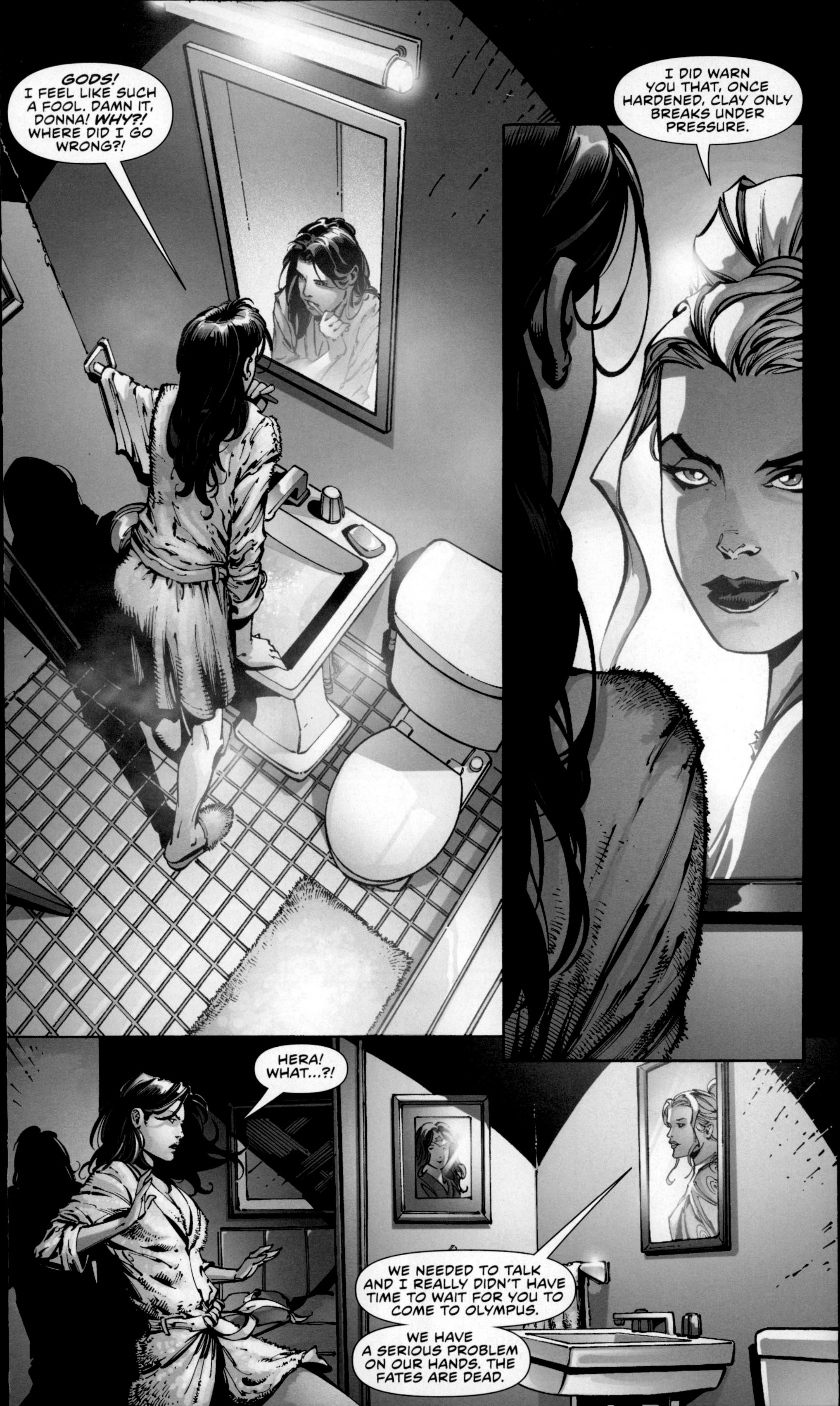

GODS! I FEEL LIKE SUCH A FOOL. DAMN IT, DONNA! WHY?! WHERE DID I GO WRONG?!
I DID WARN YOU THAT, ONCE HARDENED, CLAY ONLY BREAKS UNDER PRESSURE.
HERA! WHAT...?!
WE NEEDED TO TALK AND I REALLY DIDN'T HAVE TIME TO WAIT FOR YOU TO COME TO OLYMPUS.
WE HAVE A SERIOUS PROBLEM ON OUR HANDS. THE FATES ARE DEAD.

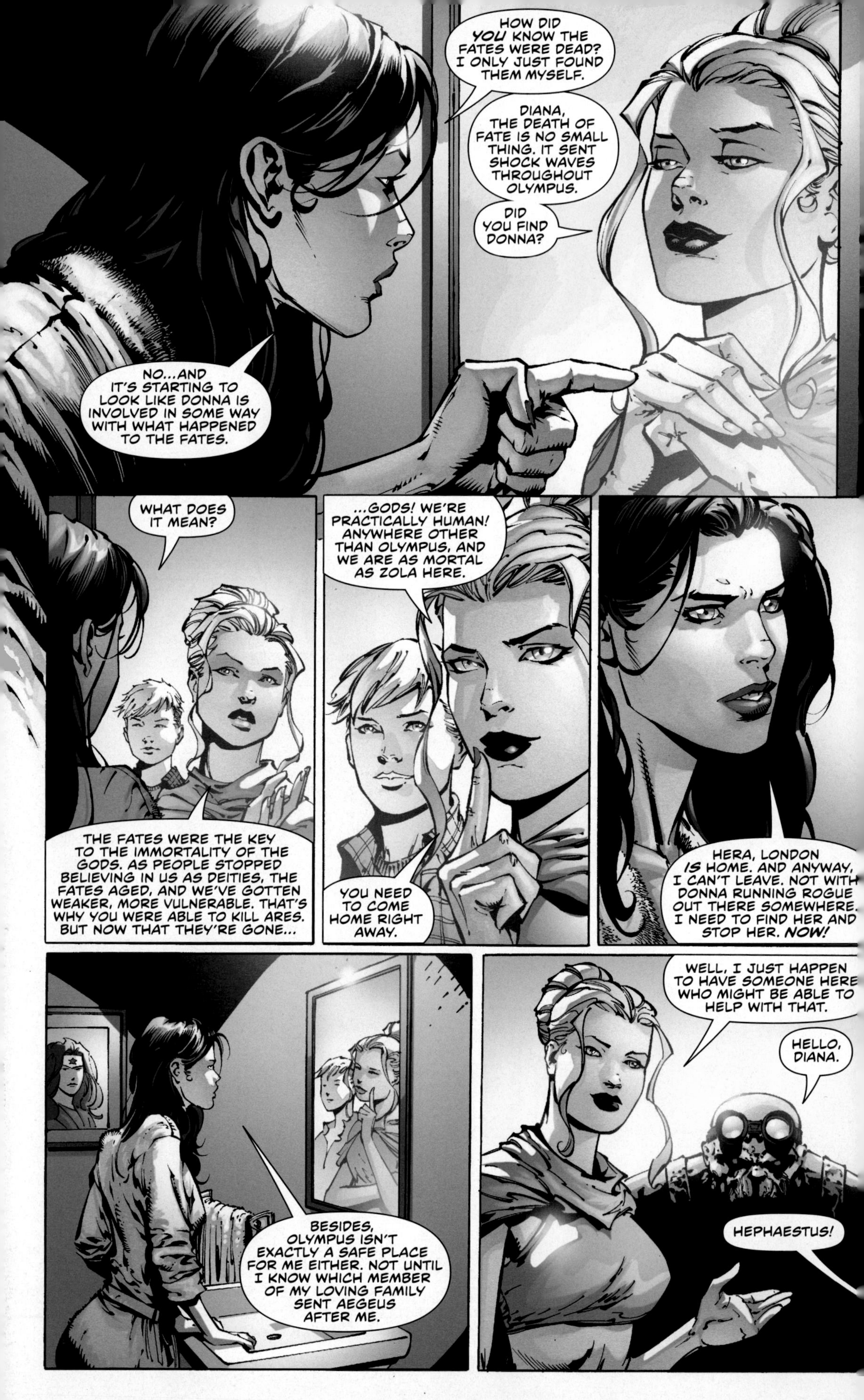
HOW DID YOU KNOW THE FATES WERE DEAD? I ONLY JUST FOUND THEM MYSELF.
DIANA, THE DEATH OF FATE IS NO SMALL THING. IT SENT SHOCK WAVES THROUGHOUT OLYMPUS.
DID YOU FIND DONNA?
NO...AND IT'S STARTING TO LOOK LIKE DONNA IS INVOLVED IN SOME WAY WITH WHAT HAPPENED TO THE FATES.
WHAT DOES IT MEAN?
THE FATES WERE THE KEY TO THE IMMORTALITY OF THE GODS. AS PEOPLE STOPPED BELIEVING IN US AS DEITIES, THE FATES AGED, AND WE'VE GOTTEN WEAKER, MORE VULNERABLE. THAT'S WHY YOU WERE ABLE TO KILL ARES. BUT NOW THAT THEY'RE GONE...
...GODS! WE'RE PRACTICALLY HUMAN! ANYWHERE OTHER THAN OLYMPUS, AND WE ARE AS MORTAL AS ZOLA HERE.
YOU NEED TO COME HOME RIGHT AWAY.
HERA, LONDON IS HOME. AND ANYWAY, I CAN'T LEAVE. NOT WITH DONNA RUNNING ROGUE OUT THERE SOMEWHERE. I NEED TO FIND HER AND STOP HER. NOW!
BESIDES, OLYMPUS ISN'T EXACTLY A SAFE PLACE FOR ME EITHER. NOT UNTIL I KNOW WHICH MEMBER OF MY LOVING FAMILY SENT AEGEUS AFTER ME.
WELL, I JUST HAPPEN TO HAVE SOMEONE HERE WHO MIGHT BE ABLE TO HELP WITH THAT.
HELLO, DIANA.
HEPHAESTUS!

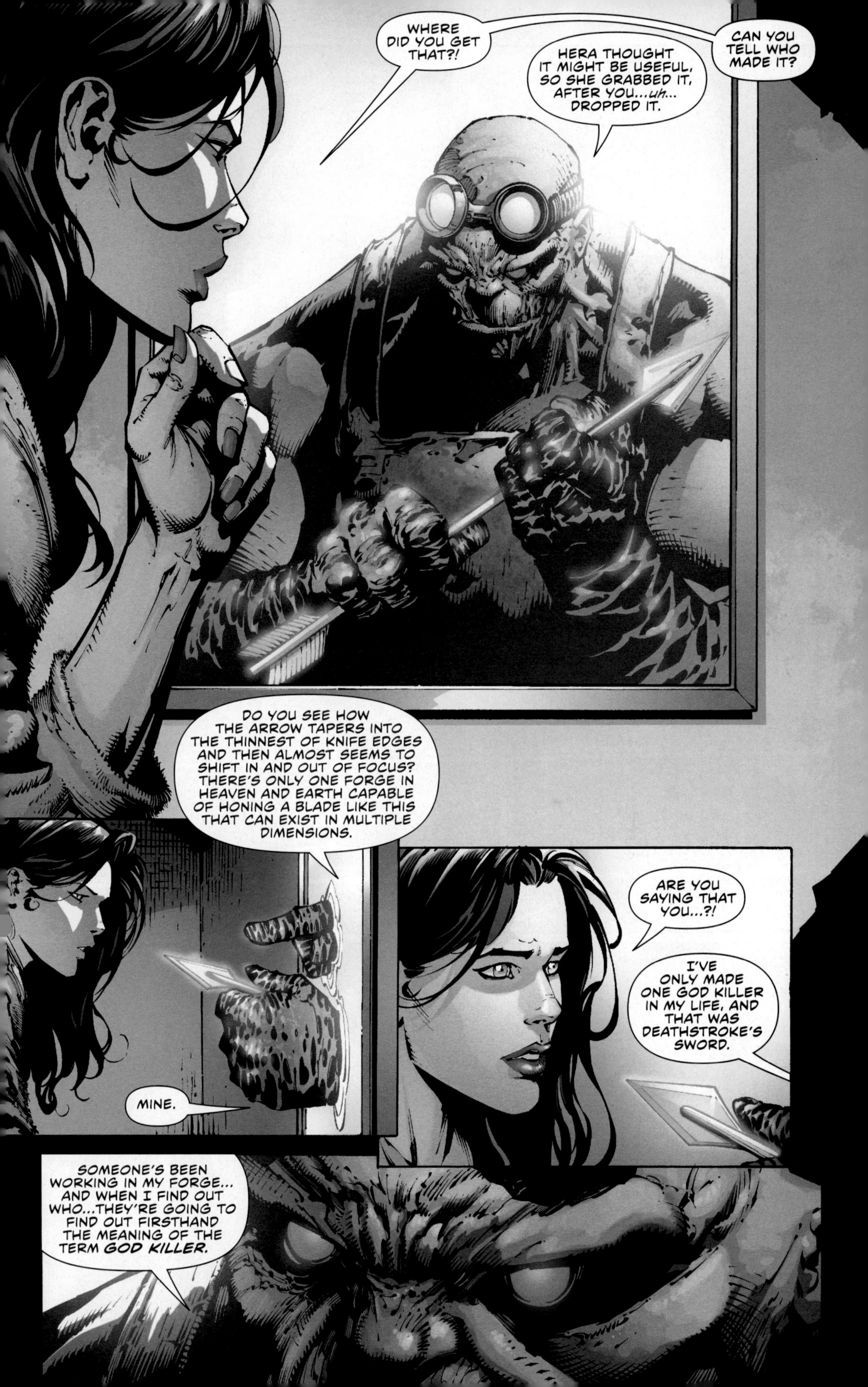
WHERE DID YOU GET THAT?!
CAN YOU TELL WHO MADE IT?
HERA THOUGHT IT MIGHT BE USEFUL, SO SHE GRABBED IT, AFTER YOU...*uh*... DROPPED IT.
DO YOU SEE HOW THE ARROW TAPERS INTO THE THINNEST OF KNIFE EDGES AND THEN ALMOST SEEMS TO SHIFT IN AND OUT OF FOCUS? THERE'S ONLY ONE FORGE IN HEAVEN AND EARTH CAPABLE OF HONING A BLADE LIKE THIS THAT CAN EXIST IN MULTIPLE DIMENSIONS.
MINE.
ARE YOU SAYING THAT YOU...?!
I'VE ONLY MADE ONE GOD KILLER IN MY LIFE, AND THAT WAS DEATHSTROKE'S SWORD.
SOMEONE'S BEEN WORKING IN MY FORGE... AND WHEN I FIND OUT WHO...THEY'RE GOING TO FIND OUT FIRSTHAND THE MEANING OF THE TERM **GOD KILLER**.

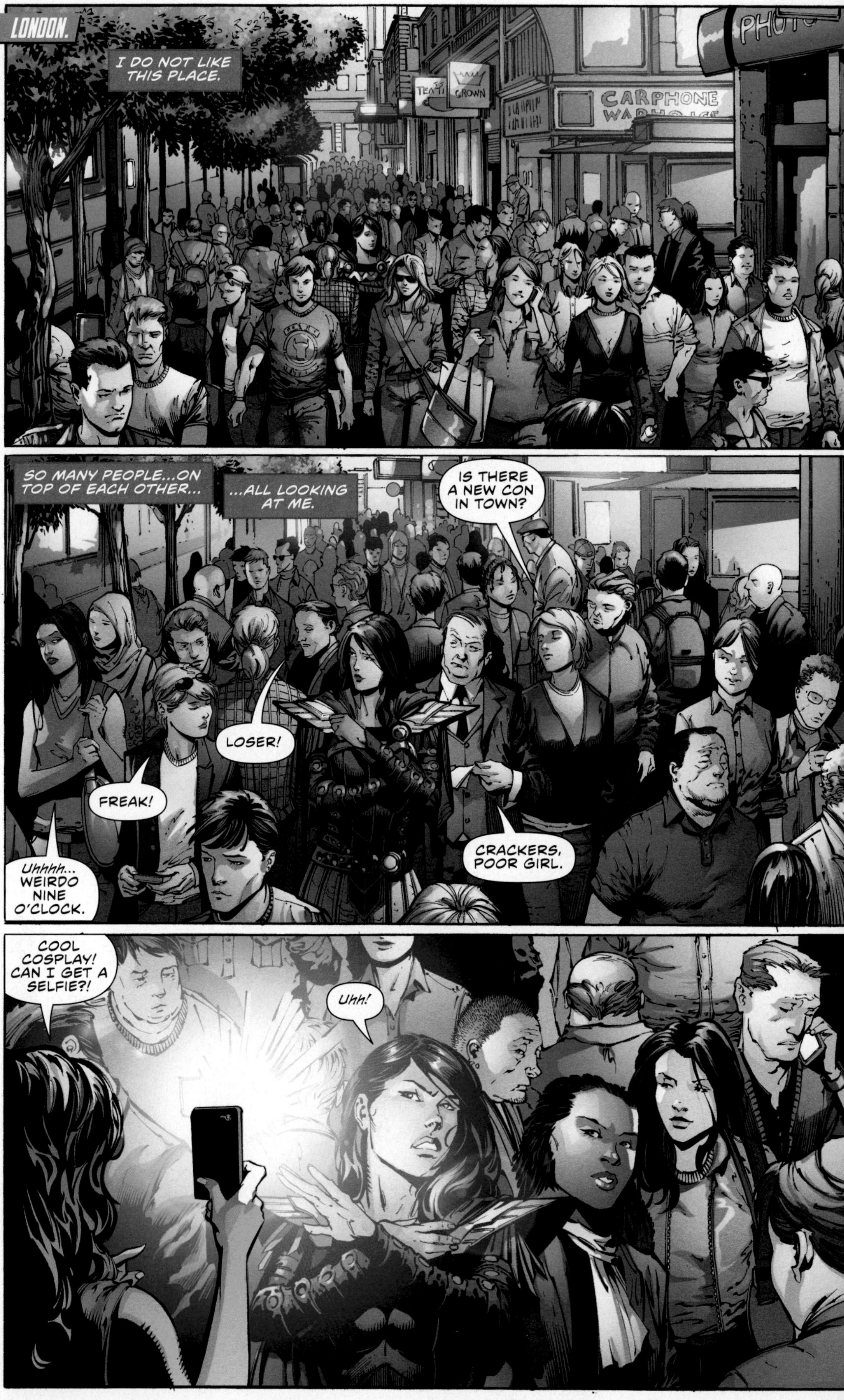

LONDON.
I DO NOT LIKE THIS PLACE.
PHOTO
TEA
CROWN
CARPHONE WAREHOUSE
SO MANY PEOPLE...ON TOP OF EACH OTHER...
...ALL LOOKING AT ME.
IS THERE A NEW CON IN TOWN?
LOSER!
FREAK!
Uhhhh... WEIRDO NINE O'CLOCK.
CRACKERS, POOR GIRL.
COOL COSPLAY! CAN I GET A SELFIE?!
Uhh!

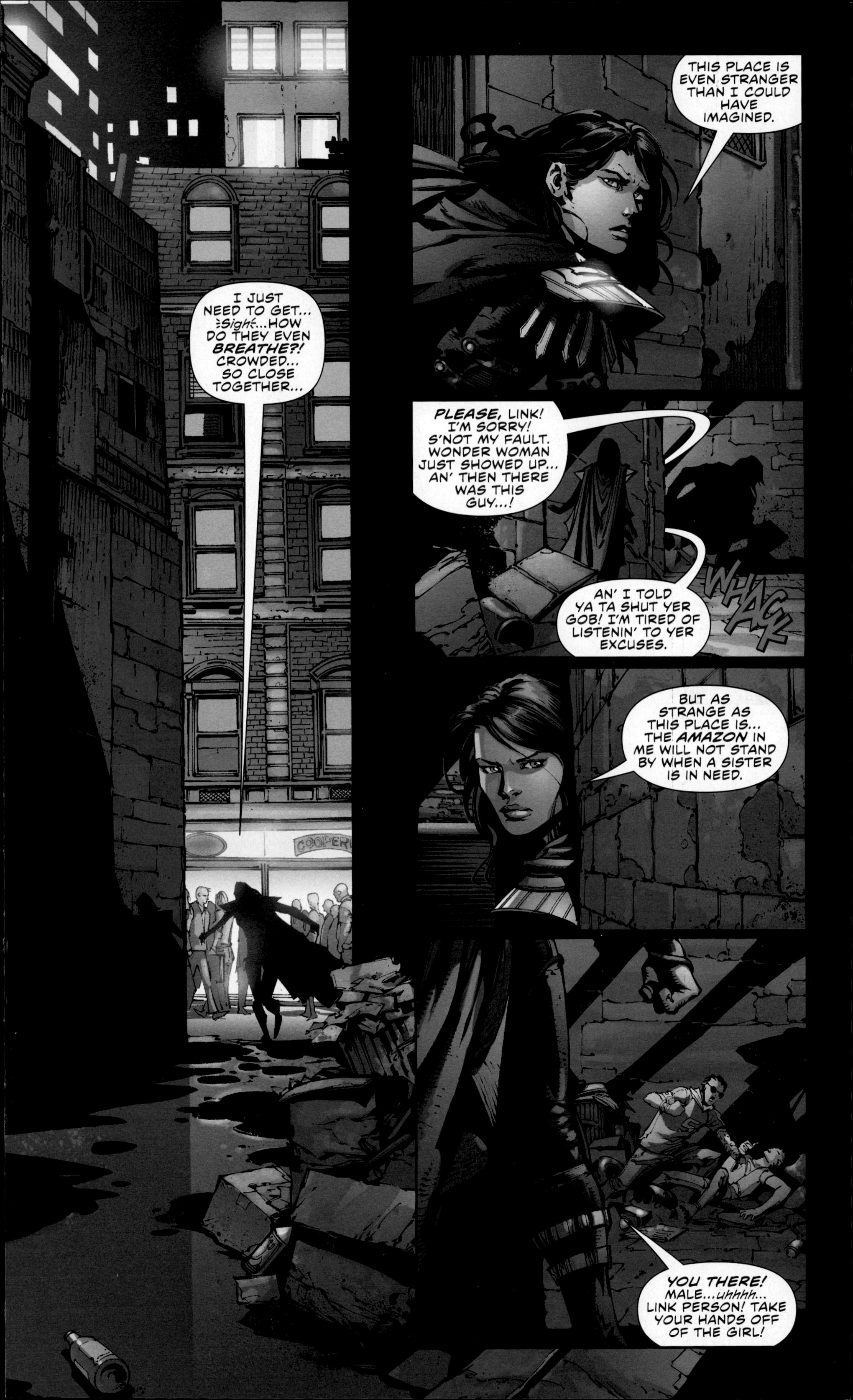
I JUST NEED TO GET... *Sigh*...HOW DO THEY EVEN *BREATHE?!* CROWDED... SO CLOSE TOGETHER...
COOPER
THIS PLACE IS EVEN STRANGER THAN I COULD HAVE IMAGINED.
PLEASE, LINK! I'M SORRY! S'NOT MY FAULT. WONDER WOMAN JUST SHOWED UP... AN' THEN THERE WAS THIS GUY...!
AN' I TOLD YA TA SHUT YER GOB! I'M TIRED OF LISTENIN' TO YER EXCUSES.
WHACK
BUT AS STRANGE AS THIS PLACE IS... THE *AMAZON* IN ME WILL NOT STAND BY WHEN A SISTER IS IN NEED.
YOU THERE! MALE...*uhhhh*... LINK PERSON! TAKE YOUR HANDS OFF OF THE GIRL!

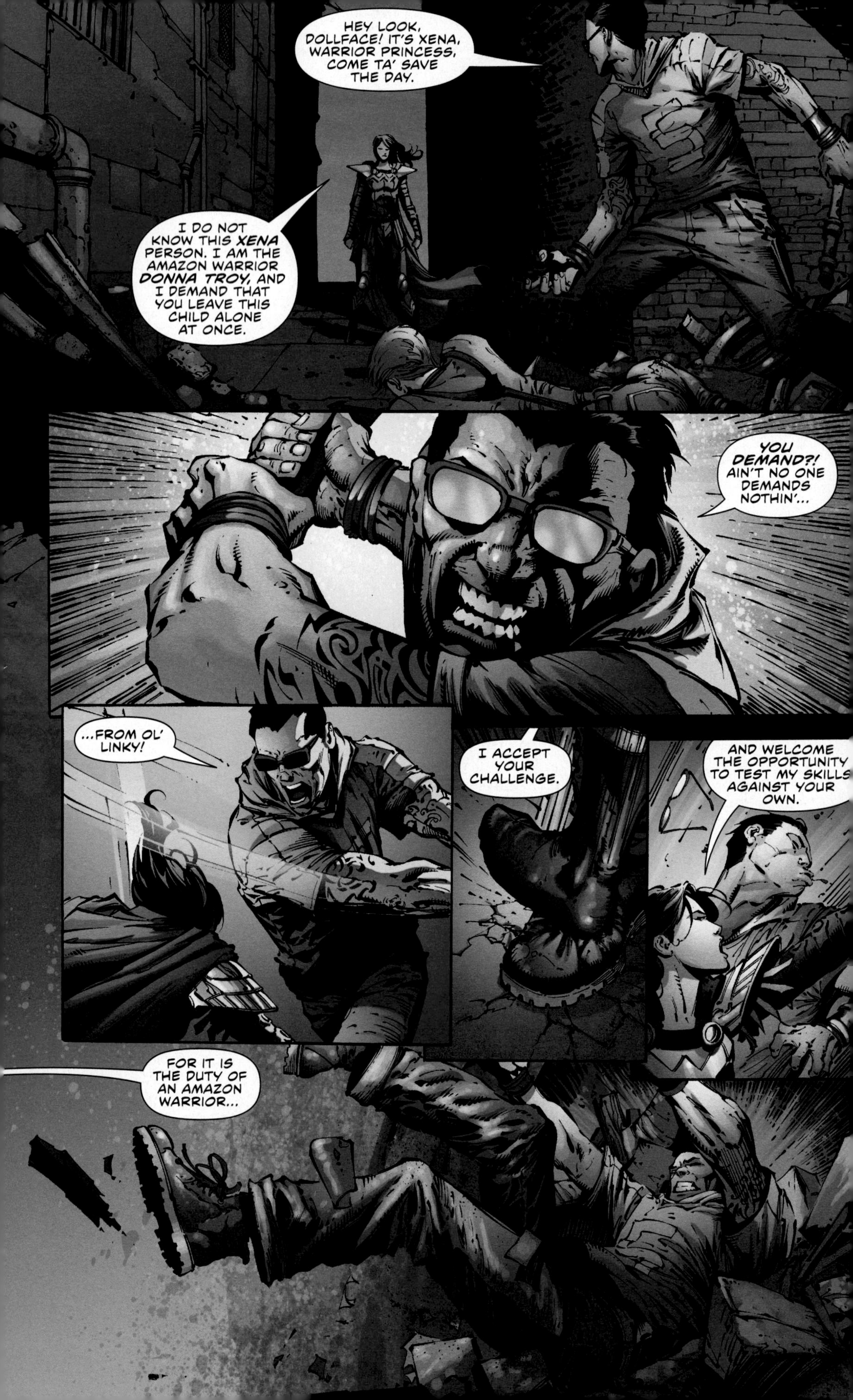
HEY LOOK, DOLLFACE! IT'S XENA, WARRIOR PRINCESS, COME TA' SAVE THE DAY.
I DO NOT KNOW THIS *XENA* PERSON. I AM THE AMAZON WARRIOR ***DONNA TROY***, AND I DEMAND THAT YOU LEAVE THIS CHILD ALONE AT ONCE.
YOU DEMAND?! AIN'T NO ONE DEMANDS NOTHIN'...
...FROM OL' LINKY!
I ACCEPT YOUR CHALLENGE.
AND WELCOME THE OPPORTUNITY TO TEST MY SKILLS AGAINST YOUR OWN.
FOR IT IS THE DUTY OF AN AMAZON WARRIOR...

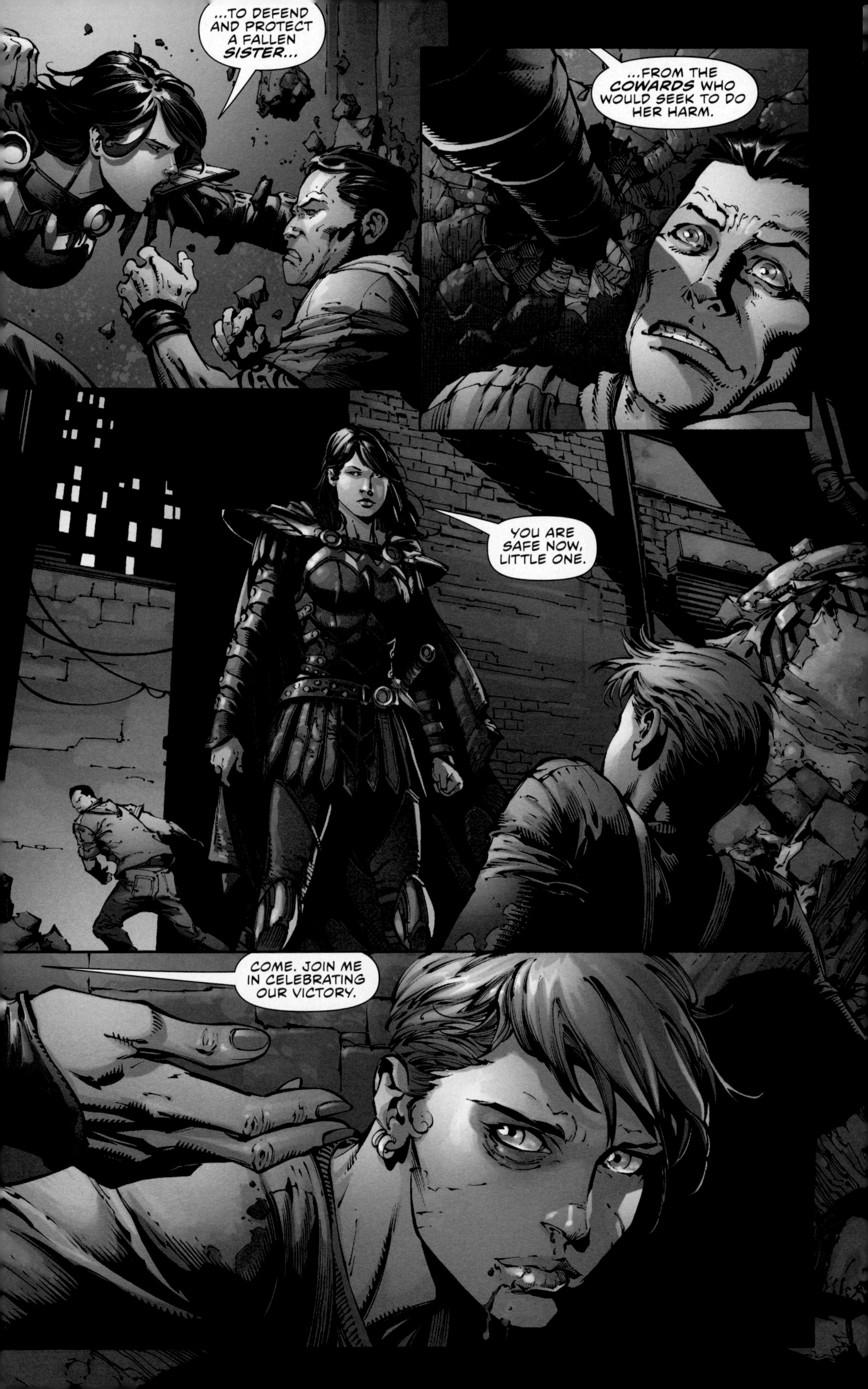
...TO DEFEND AND PROTECT A FALLEN SISTER...
...FROM THE COWARDS WHO WOULD SEEK TO DO HER HARM.
YOU ARE SAFE NOW, LITTLE ONE.
COME. JOIN ME IN CELEBRATING OUR VICTORY.

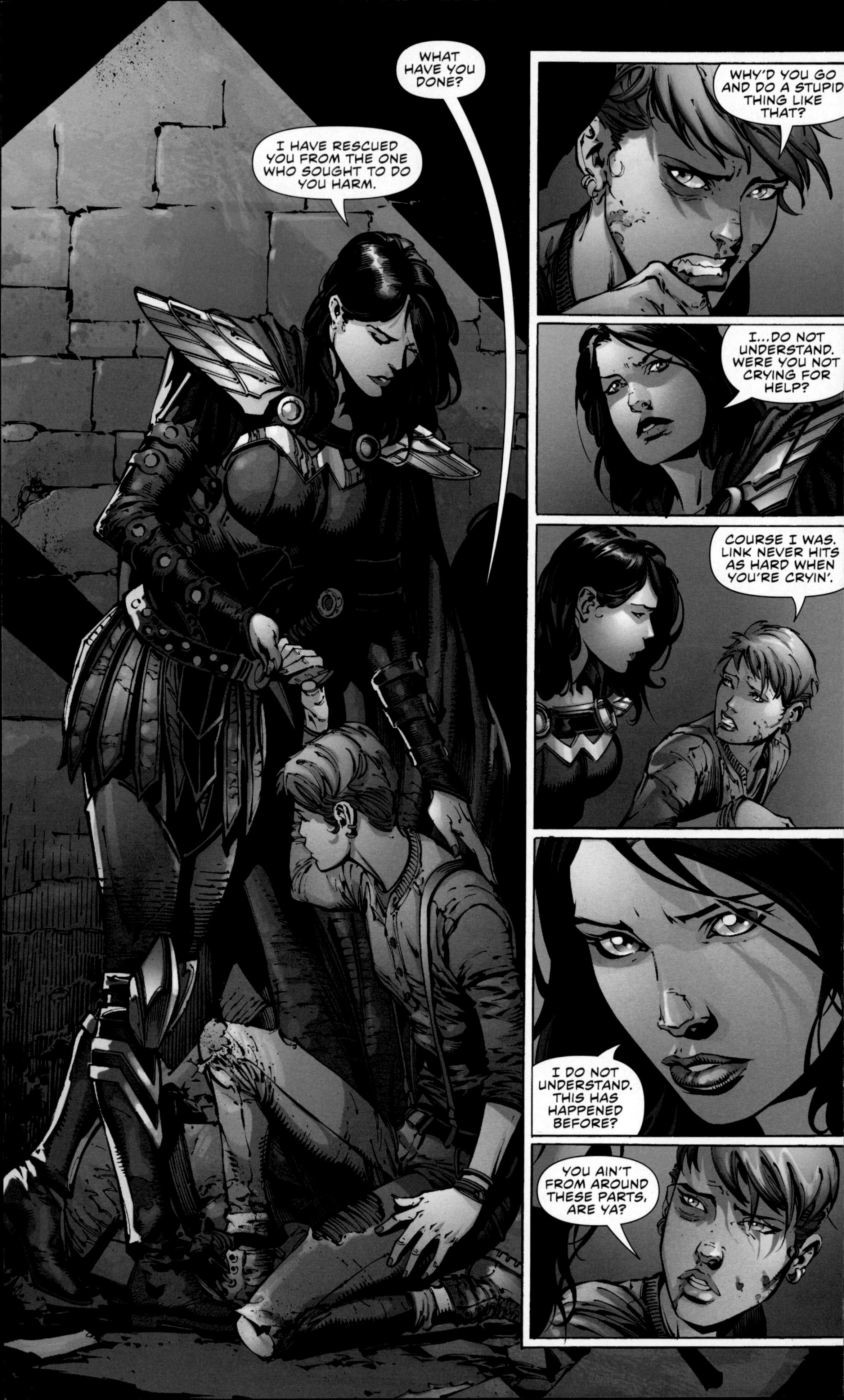

WHAT HAVE YOU DONE?
I HAVE RESCUED YOU FROM THE ONE WHO SOUGHT TO DO YOU HARM.
WHY'D YOU GO AND DO A STUPID THING LIKE THAT?
I...DO NOT UNDERSTAND. WERE YOU NOT CRYING FOR HELP?
COURSE I WAS. LINK NEVER HITS AS HARD WHEN YOU'RE CRYIN'.
I DO NOT UNDERSTAND. THIS HAS HAPPENED BEFORE?
YOU AIN'T FROM AROUND THESE PARTS, ARE YA?

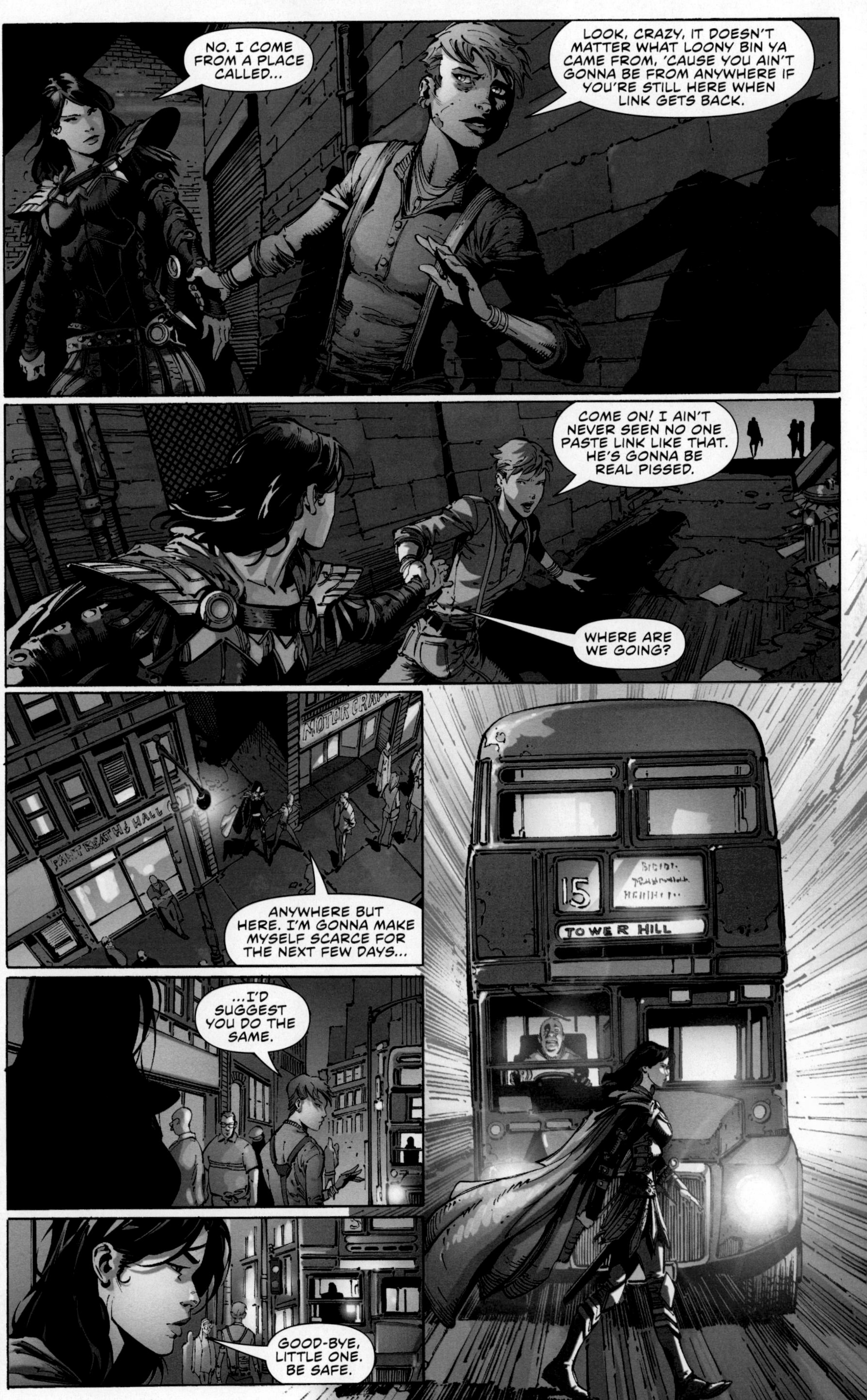
NO. I COME FROM A PLACE CALLED...
LOOK, CRAZY, IT DOESN'T MATTER WHAT LOONY BIN YA CAME FROM, 'CAUSE YOU AIN'T GONNA BE FROM ANYWHERE IF YOU'RE STILL HERE WHEN LINK GETS BACK.
COME ON! I AIN'T NEVER SEEN NO ONE PASTE LINK LIKE THAT. HE'S GONNA BE REAL PISSED.
WHERE ARE WE GOING?
ANYWHERE BUT HERE. I'M GONNA MAKE MYSELF SCARCE FOR THE NEXT FEW DAYS...
...I'D SUGGEST YOU DO THE SAME.
GOOD-BYE, LITTLE ONE. BE SAFE.
15
TOWER HILL

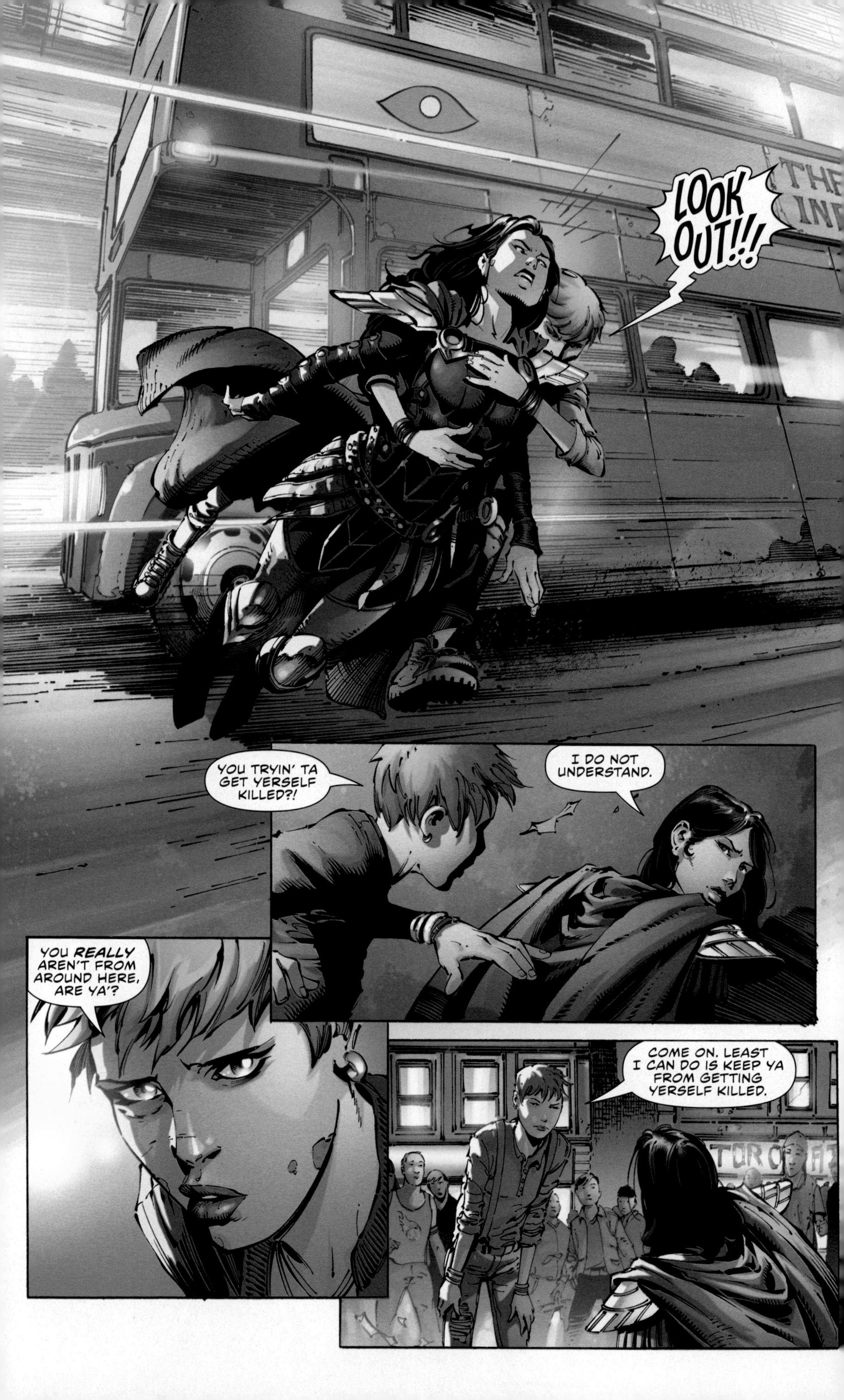
LOOK OUT!!!
YOU TRYIN' TA GET YERSELF KILLED?!
I DO NOT UNDERSTAND.
YOU REALLY AREN'T FROM AROUND HERE, ARE YA'?
COME ON. LEAST I CAN DO IS KEEP YA FROM GETTING YERSELF KILLED.

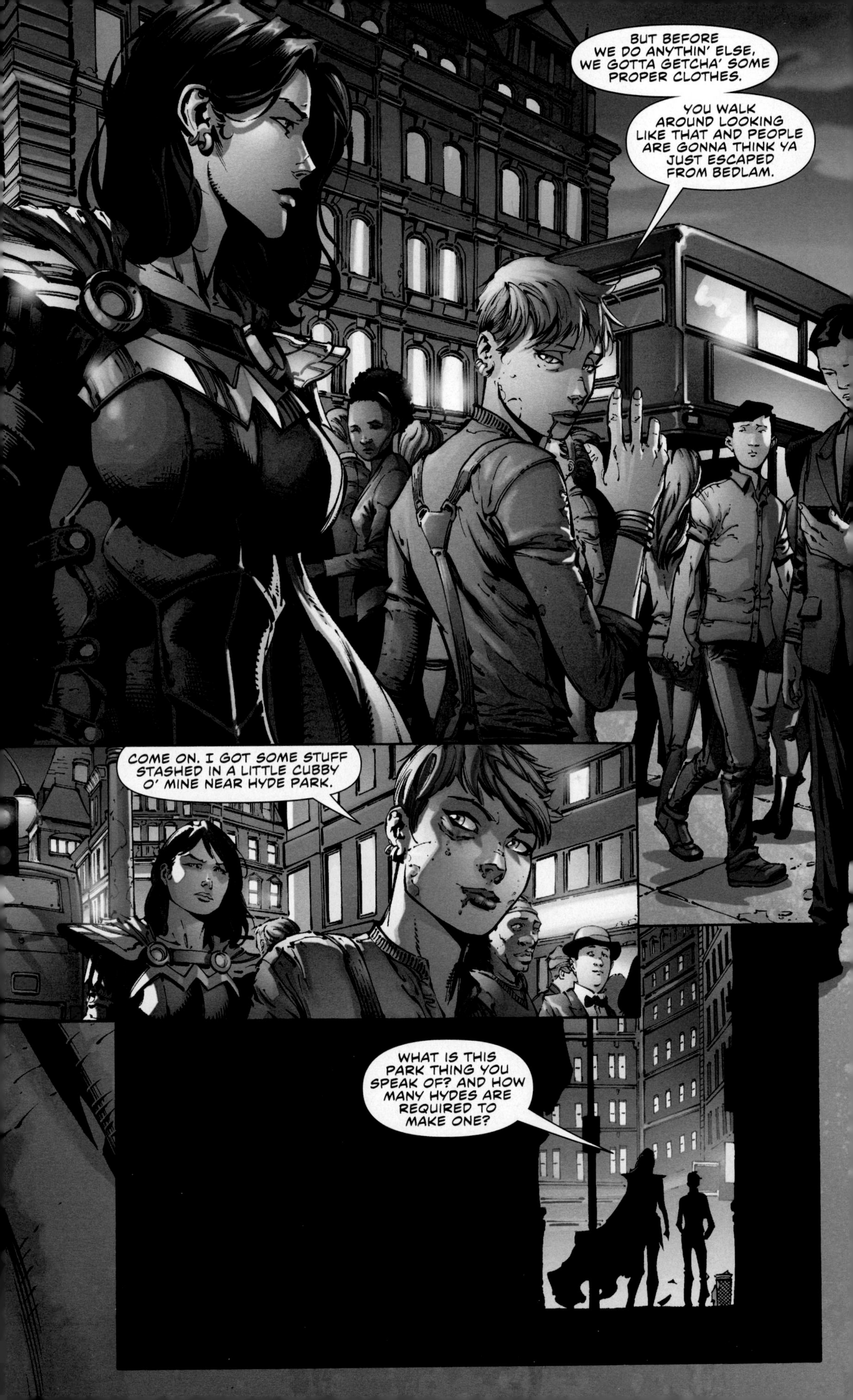

BUT BEFORE WE DO ANYTHIN' ELSE, WE GOTTA GETCHA' SOME PROPER CLOTHES.
YOU WALK AROUND LOOKING LIKE THAT AND PEOPLE ARE GONNA THINK YA JUST ESCAPED FROM BEDLAM.
COME ON. I GOT SOME STUFF STASHED IN A LITTLE CUBBY O' MINE NEAR HYDE PARK.
WHAT IS THIS PARK THING YOU SPEAK OF? AND HOW MANY HYDES ARE REQUIRED TO MAKE ONE?

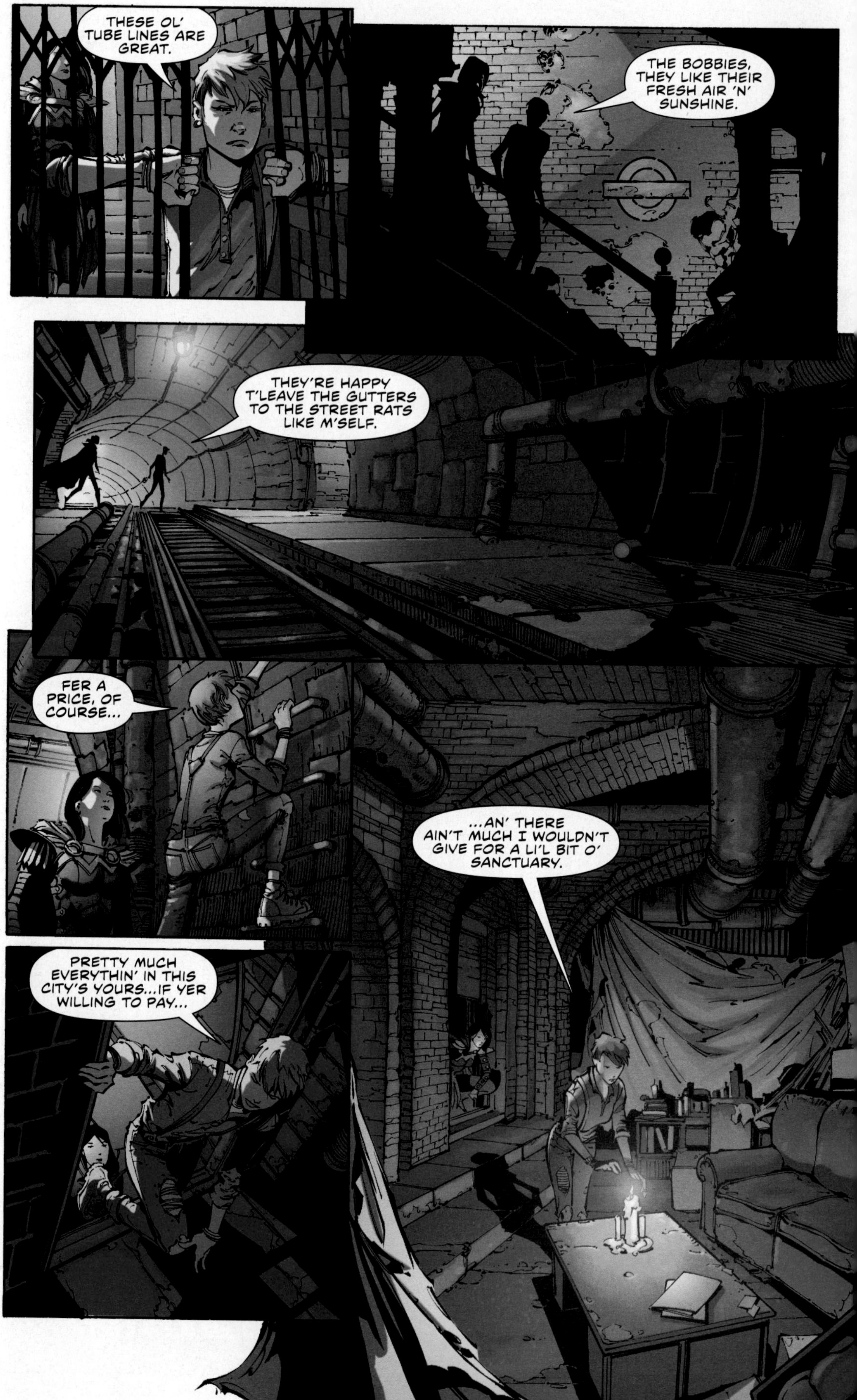
THESE OL' TUBE LINES ARE GREAT.
THE BOBBIES, THEY LIKE THEIR FRESH AIR 'N' SUNSHINE.
THEY'RE HAPPY T'LEAVE THE GUTTERS TO THE STREET RATS LIKE M'SELF.
FER A PRICE, OF COURSE...
...AN' THERE AIN'T MUCH I WOULDN'T GIVE FOR A LI'L BIT O' SANCTUARY.
PRETTY MUCH EVERYTHIN' IN THIS CITY'S YOURS...IF YER WILLING TO PAY...

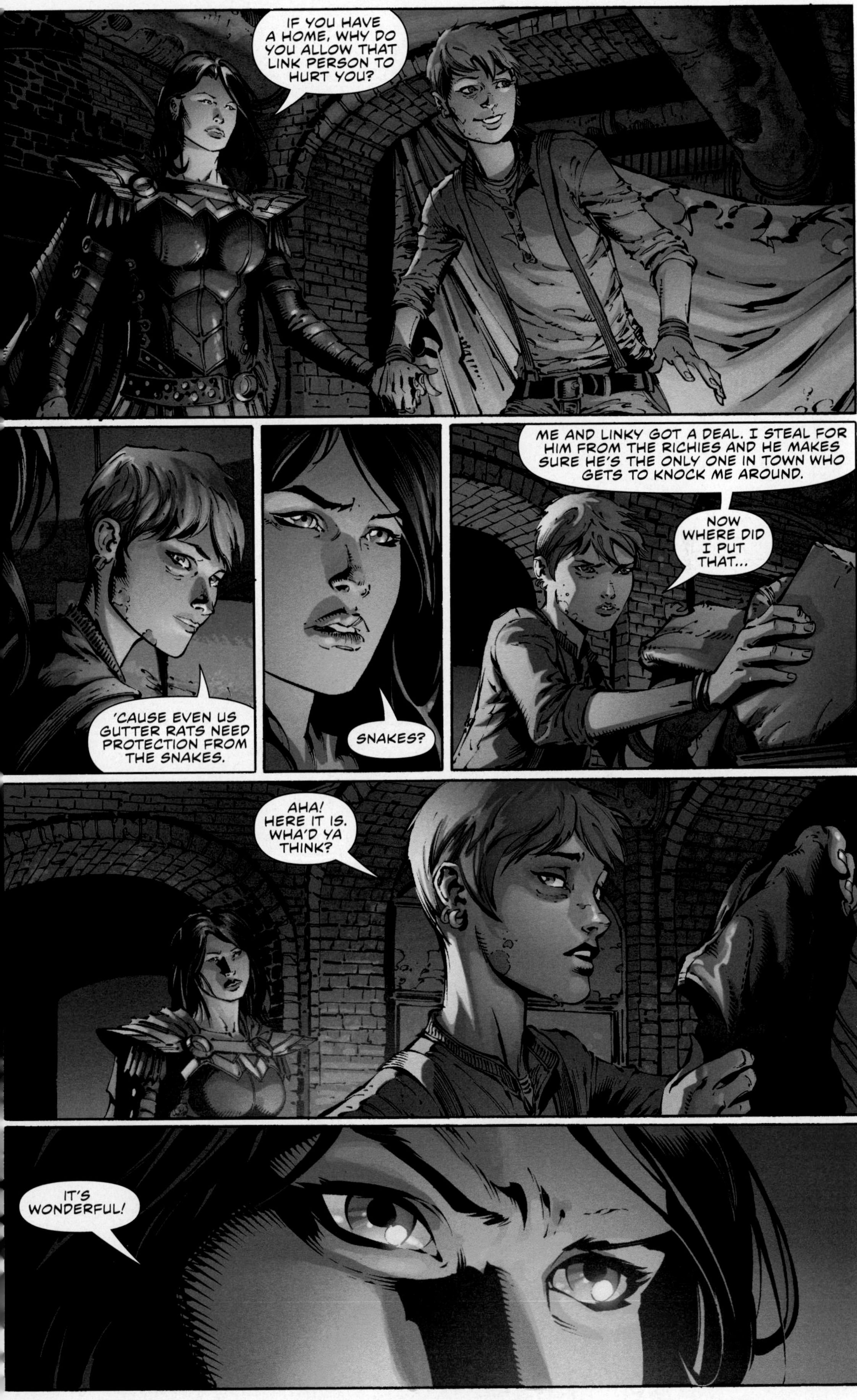
IF YOU HAVE A HOME, WHY DO YOU ALLOW THAT LINK PERSON TO HURT YOU?
'CAUSE EVEN US GUTTER RATS NEED PROTECTION FROM THE SNAKES.
SNAKES?
ME AND LINKY GOT A DEAL. I STEAL FOR HIM FROM THE RICHIES AND HE MAKES SURE HE'S THE ONLY ONE IN TOWN WHO GETS TO KNOCK ME AROUND.
NOW WHERE DID I PUT THAT...
AHA! HERE IT IS. WHA'D YA THINK?
IT'S WONDERFUL!

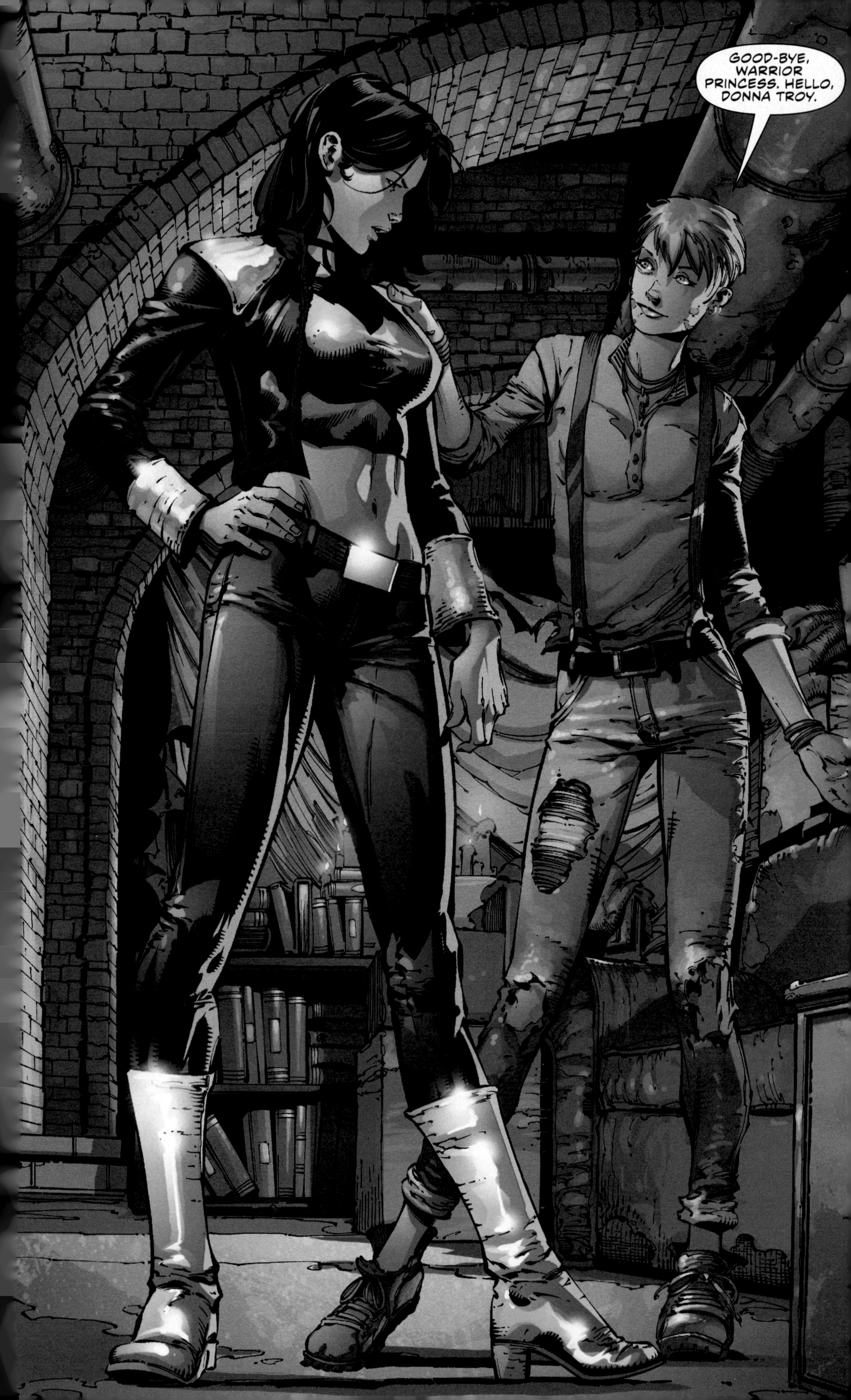
GOOD-BYE, WARRIOR PRINCESS. HELLO, DONNA TROY.

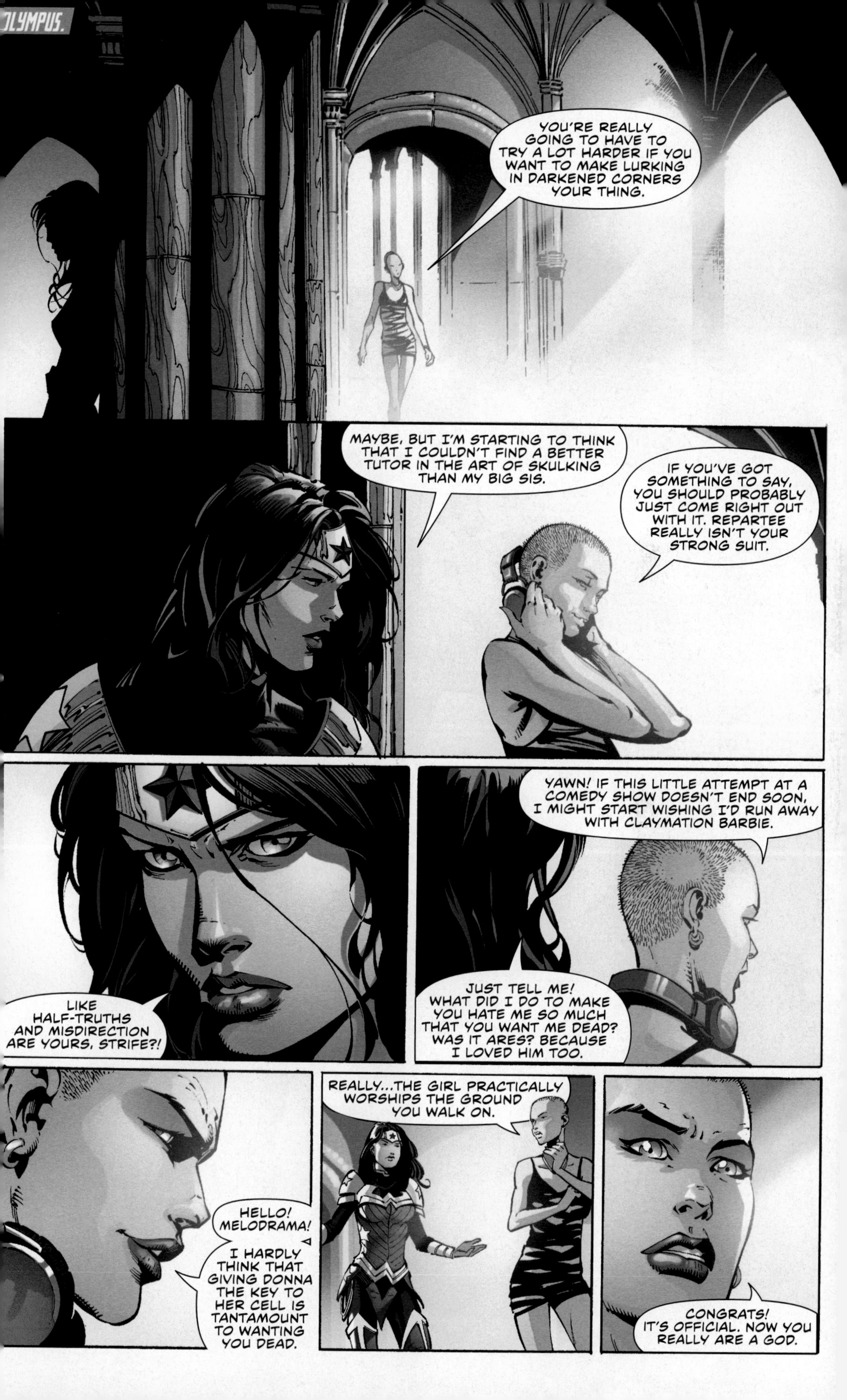
OLYMPUS.
YOU'RE REALLY GOING TO HAVE TO TRY A LOT HARDER IF YOU WANT TO MAKE LURKING IN DARKENED CORNERS YOUR THING.
MAYBE, BUT I'M STARTING TO THINK THAT I COULDN'T FIND A BETTER TUTOR IN THE ART OF SKULKING THAN MY BIG SIS.
IF YOU'VE GOT SOMETHING TO SAY, YOU SHOULD PROBABLY JUST COME RIGHT OUT WITH IT. REPARTEE REALLY ISN'T YOUR STRONG SUIT.
LIKE HALF-TRUTHS AND MISDIRECTION ARE YOURS, STRIFE?!
YAWN! IF THIS LITTLE ATTEMPT AT A COMEDY SHOW DOESN'T END SOON, I MIGHT START WISHING I'D RUN AWAY WITH CLAYMATION BARBIE.
JUST TELL ME! WHAT DID I DO TO MAKE YOU HATE ME SO MUCH THAT YOU WANT ME DEAD? WAS IT ARES? BECAUSE I LOVED HIM TOO.
HELLO! MELODRAMA!
I HARDLY THINK THAT GIVING DONNA THE KEY TO HER CELL IS TANTAMOUNT TO WANTING YOU DEAD.
REALLY...THE GIRL PRACTICALLY WORSHIPS THE GROUND YOU WALK ON.
CONGRATS! IT'S OFFICIAL. NOW YOU REALLY ARE A GOD.

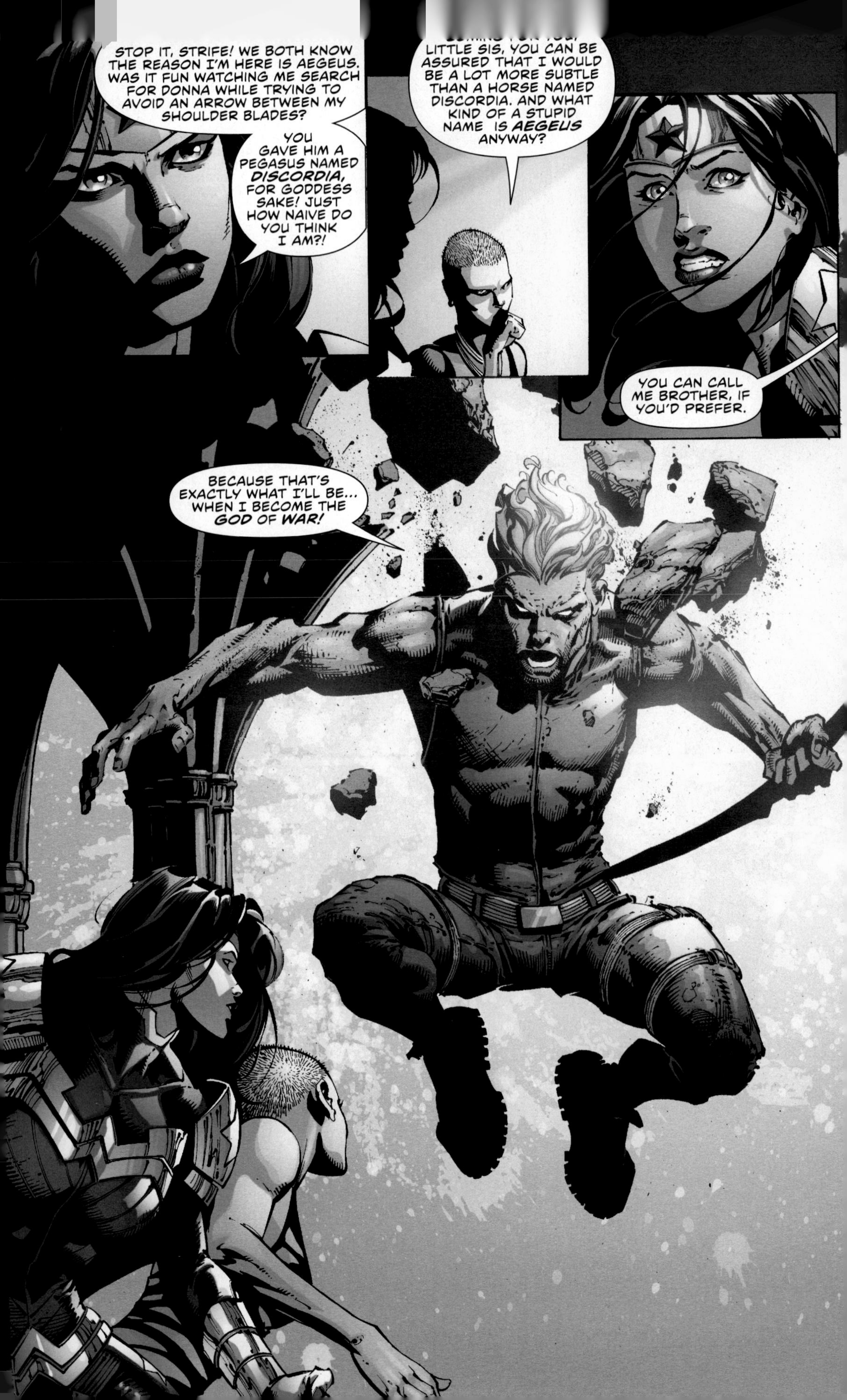
STOP IT, STRIFE! WE BOTH KNOW THE REASON I'M HERE IS AEGEUS. WAS IT FUN WATCHING ME SEARCH FOR DONNA WHILE TRYING TO AVOID AN ARROW BETWEEN MY SHOULDER BLADES?
YOU GAVE HIM A PEGASUS NAMED *DISCORDIA,* FOR GODDESS SAKE! JUST HOW NAIVE DO YOU THINK I AM?!
LITTLE SIS, YOU CAN BE ASSURED THAT I WOULD BE A LOT MORE SUBTLE THAN A HORSE NAMED DISCORDIA. AND WHAT KIND OF A STUPID NAME IS *AEGEUS* ANYWAY?
YOU CAN CALL ME BROTHER, IF YOU'D PREFER.
BECAUSE THAT'S EXACTLY WHAT I'LL BE... WHEN I BECOME THE *GOD* OF *WAR!*

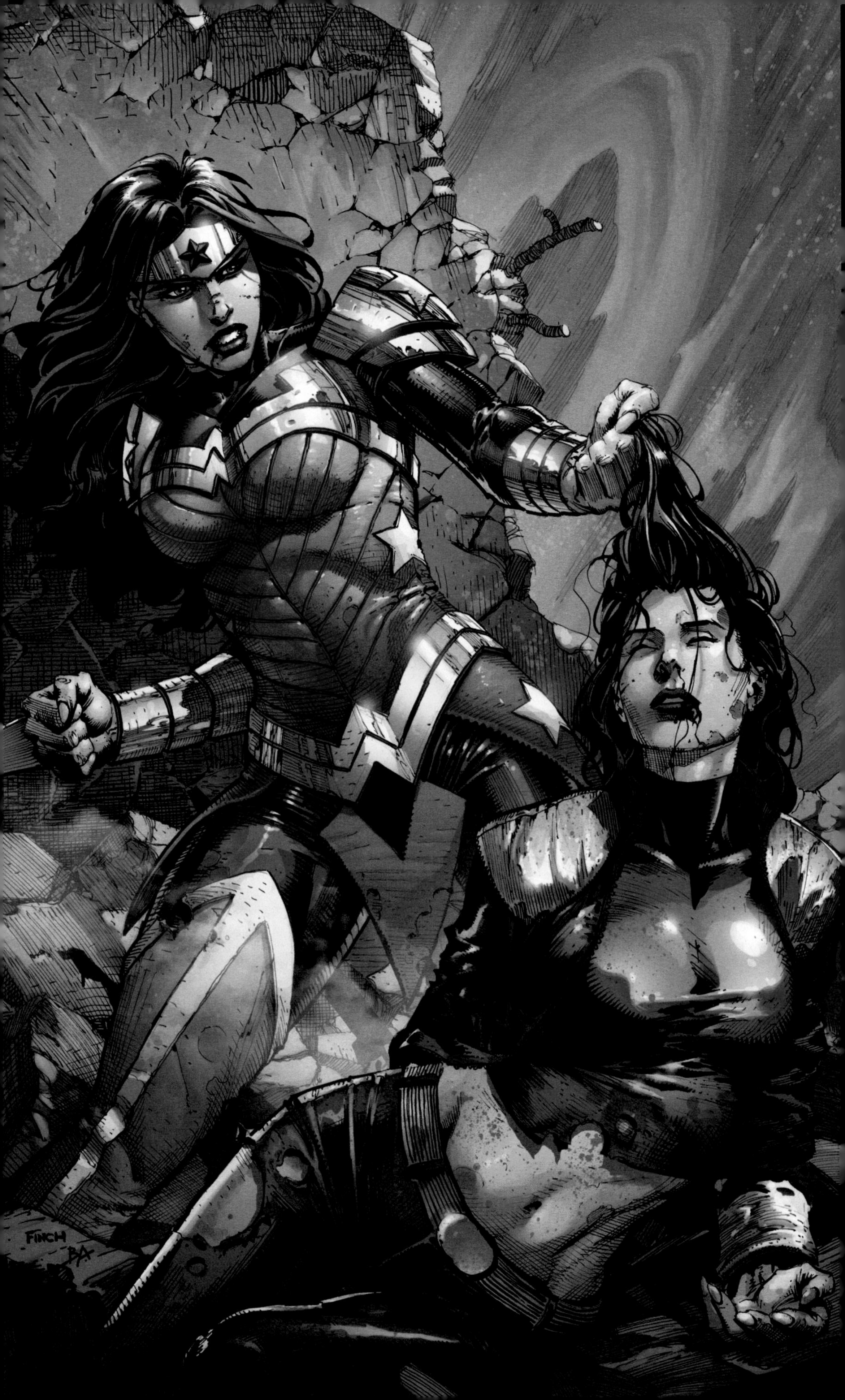
FINCH
BA

CHOICES

MEREDITH FINCH writer **DAVID FINCH** penciller **JONATHAN GLAPION JOHNNY DESJARDINS TREVOR SCOTT** inkers **BRAD ANDERSON** colorist **ROB LEIGH** letterer
cover by **FINCH, GLAPION & ANDERSON**

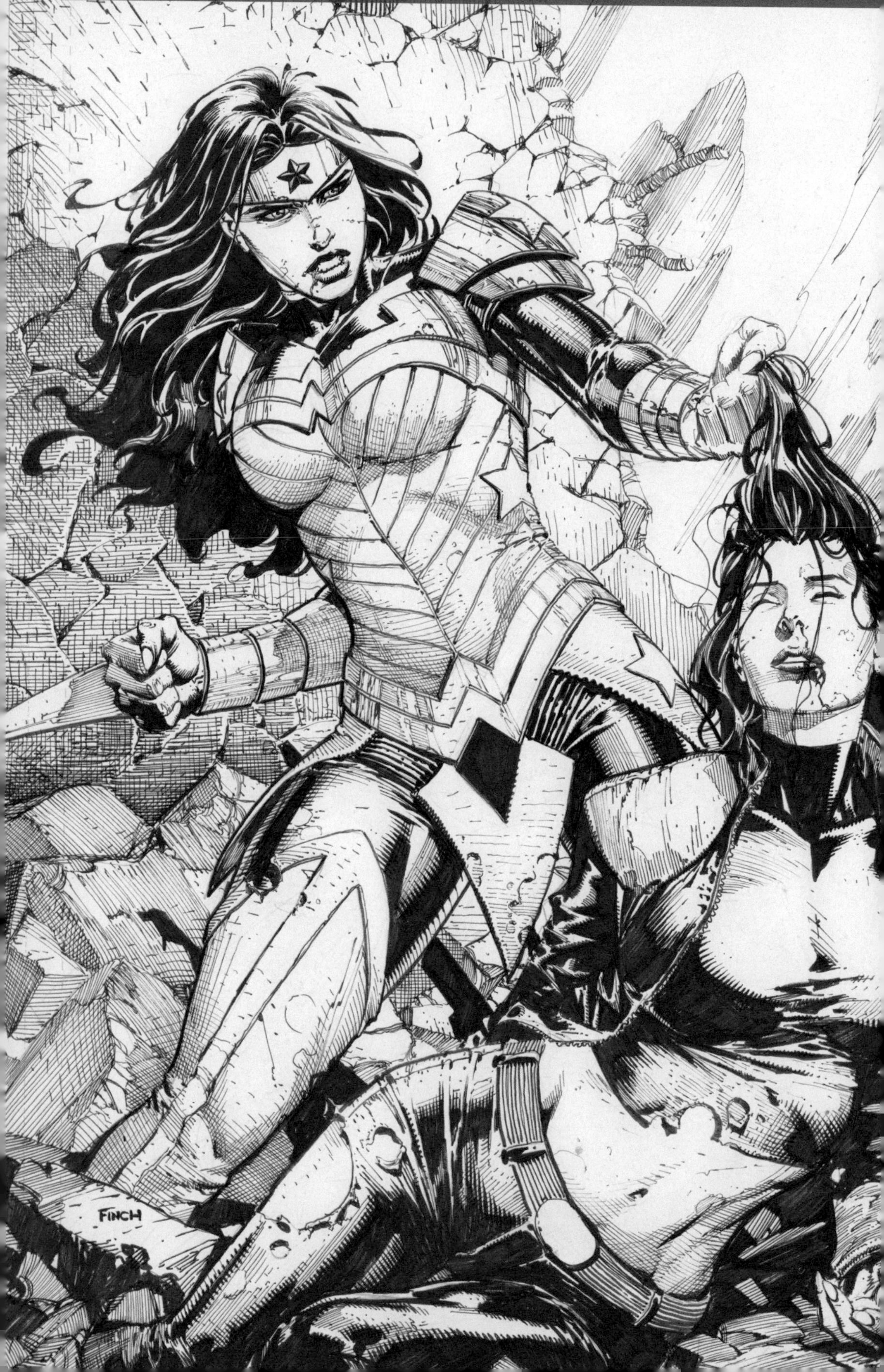
FINCH

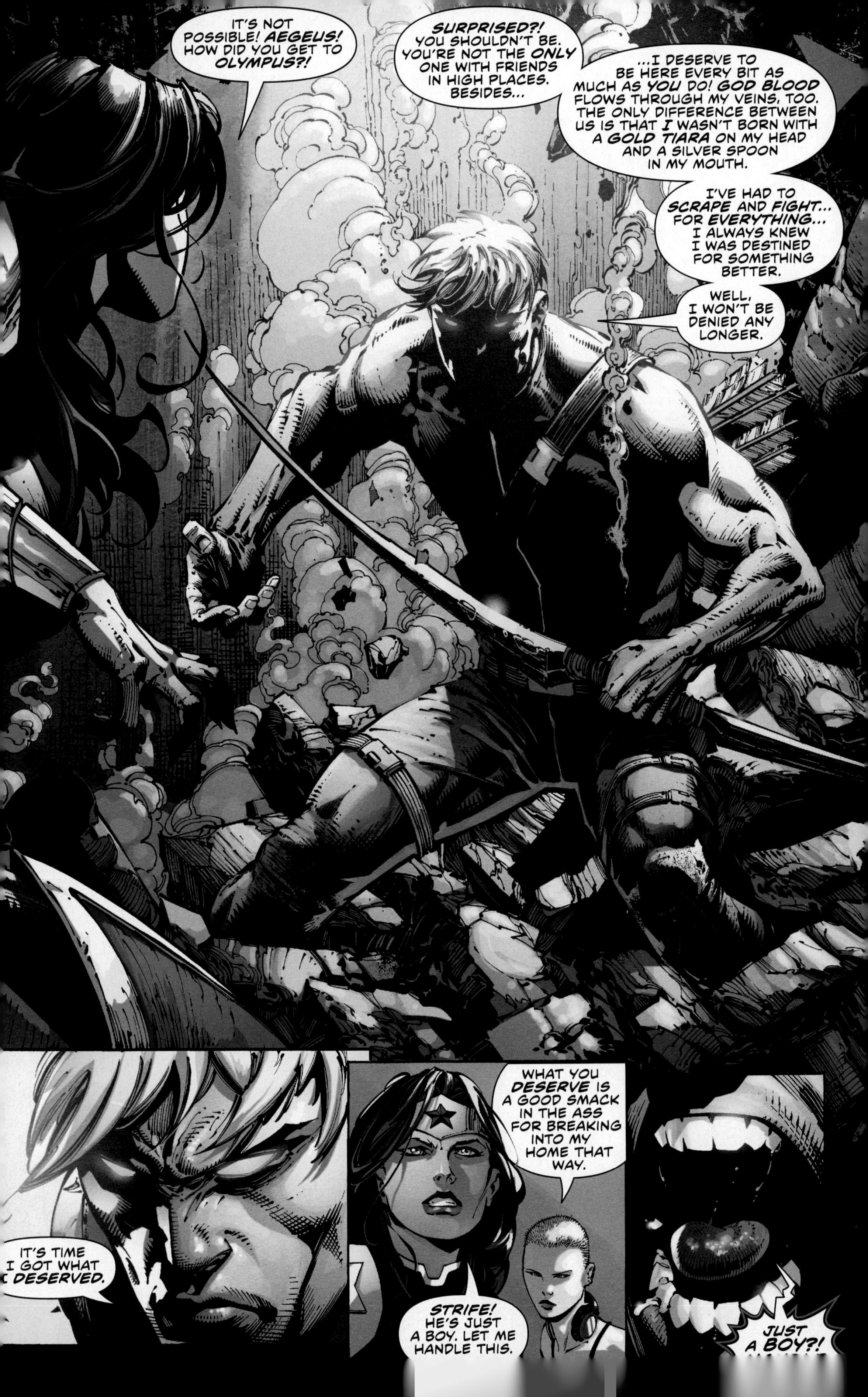
IT'S NOT POSSIBLE! AEGEUS! HOW DID YOU GET TO OLYMPUS?!
SURPRISED?! YOU SHOULDN'T BE. YOU'RE NOT THE ONLY ONE WITH FRIENDS IN HIGH PLACES. BESIDES...
...I DESERVE TO BE HERE EVERY BIT AS MUCH AS YOU DO! GOD BLOOD FLOWS THROUGH MY VEINS, TOO. THE ONLY DIFFERENCE BETWEEN US IS THAT I WASN'T BORN WITH A GOLD TIARA ON MY HEAD AND A SILVER SPOON IN MY MOUTH.
I'VE HAD TO SCRAPE AND FIGHT... FOR EVERYTHING... I ALWAYS KNEW I WAS DESTINED FOR SOMETHING BETTER.
WELL, I WON'T BE DENIED ANY LONGER.
IT'S TIME I GOT WHAT DESERVED.
WHAT YOU DESERVE IS A GOOD SMACK IN THE ASS FOR BREAKING INTO MY HOME THAT WAY.
STRIFE! HE'S JUST A BOY. LET ME HANDLE THIS.
JUST A BOY?!

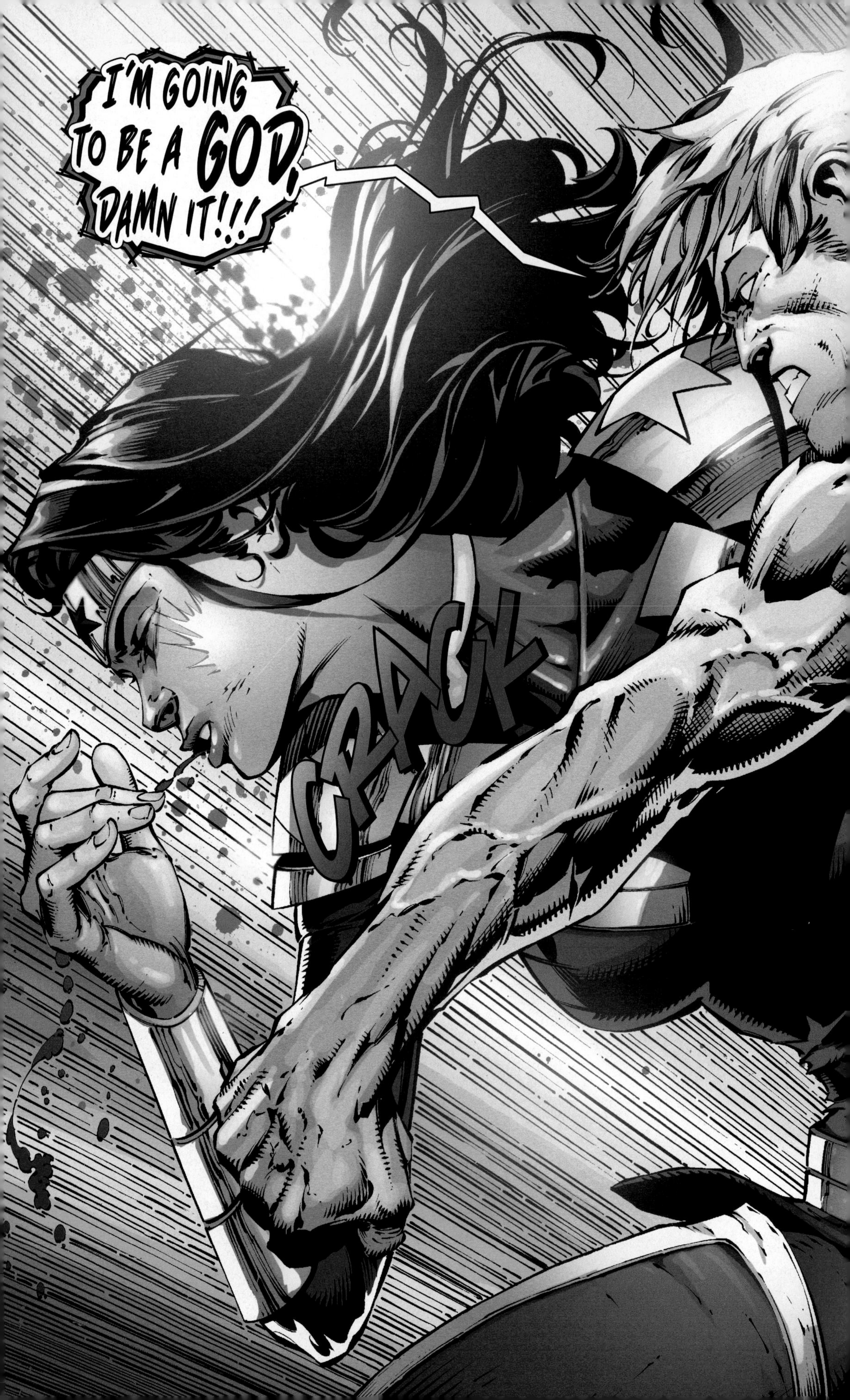
I'M GOING TO BE A GOD, DAMN IT!!!
CRACK

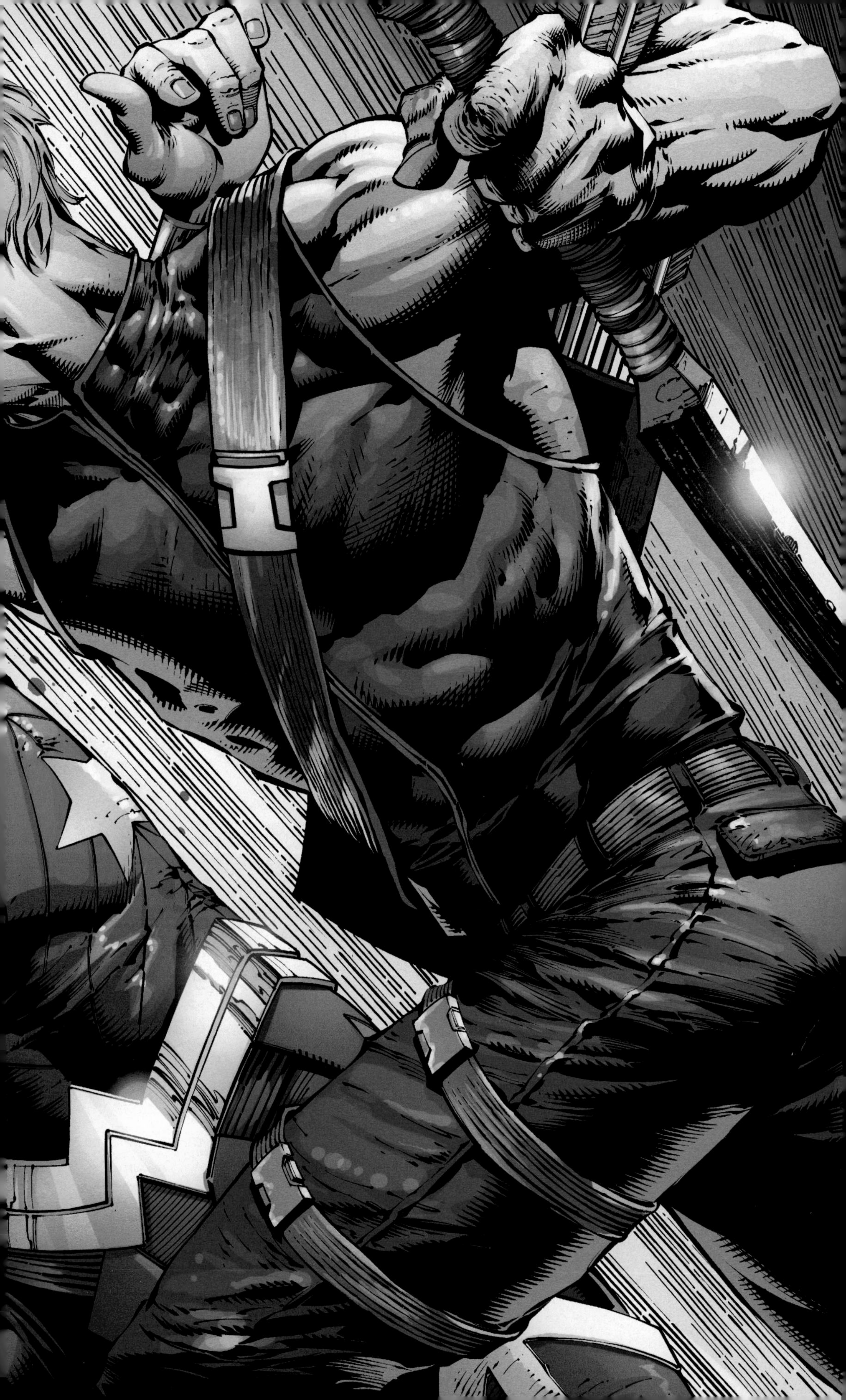

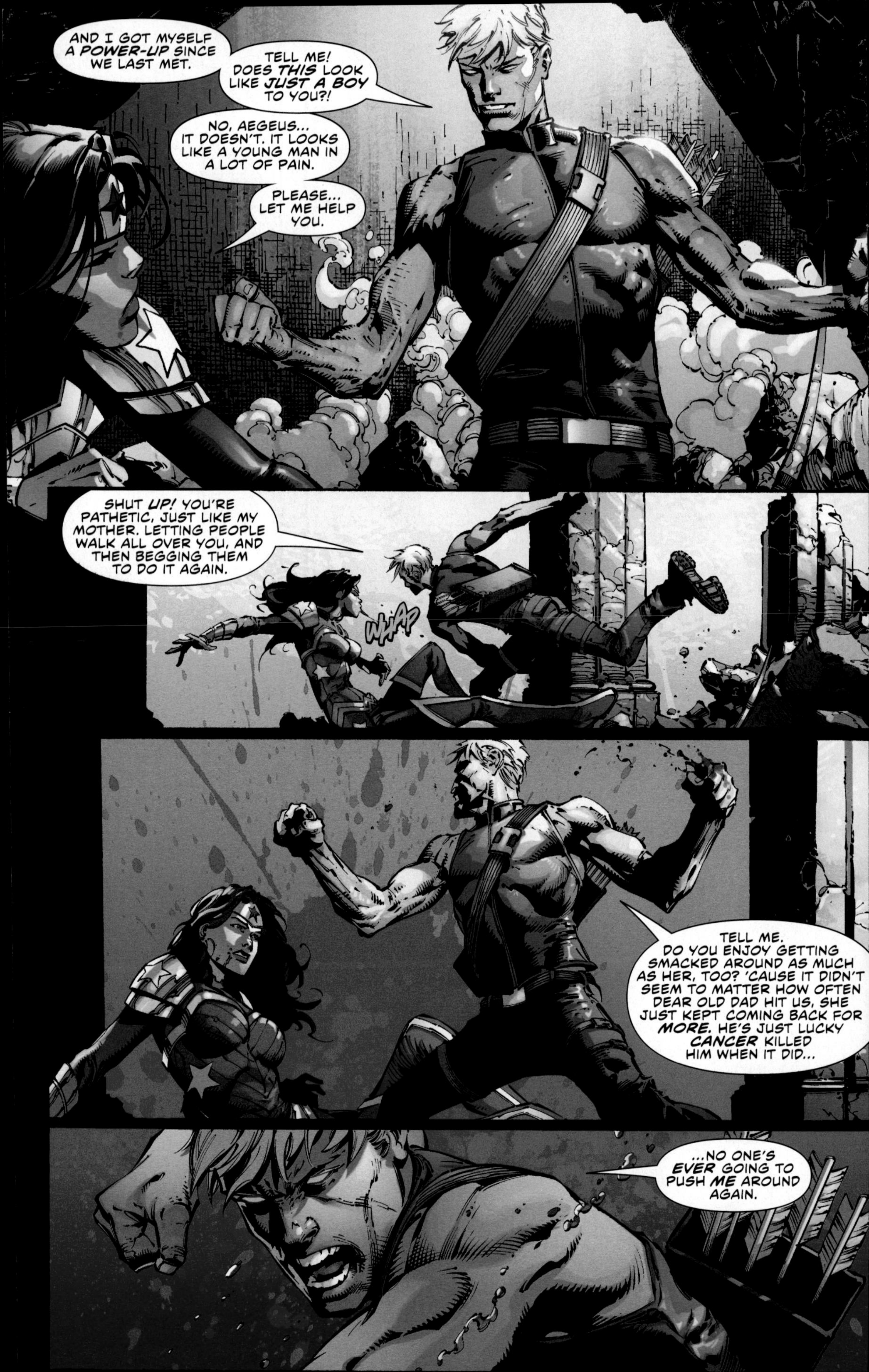
AND I GOT MYSELF A POWER-UP SINCE WE LAST MET.
TELL ME! DOES THIS LOOK LIKE JUST A BOY TO YOU?!
NO, AEGEUS... IT DOESN'T. IT LOOKS LIKE A YOUNG MAN IN A LOT OF PAIN.
PLEASE... LET ME HELP YOU.
SHUT UP! YOU'RE PATHETIC, JUST LIKE MY MOTHER. LETTING PEOPLE WALK ALL OVER YOU, AND THEN BEGGING THEM TO DO IT AGAIN.
WHAP
TELL ME. DO YOU ENJOY GETTING SMACKED AROUND AS MUCH AS HER, TOO? 'CAUSE IT DIDN'T SEEM TO MATTER HOW OFTEN DEAR OLD DAD HIT US, SHE JUST KEPT COMING BACK FOR MORE. HE'S JUST LUCKY CANCER KILLED HIM WHEN IT DID...
...NO ONE'S EVER GOING TO PUSH ME AROUND AGAIN.

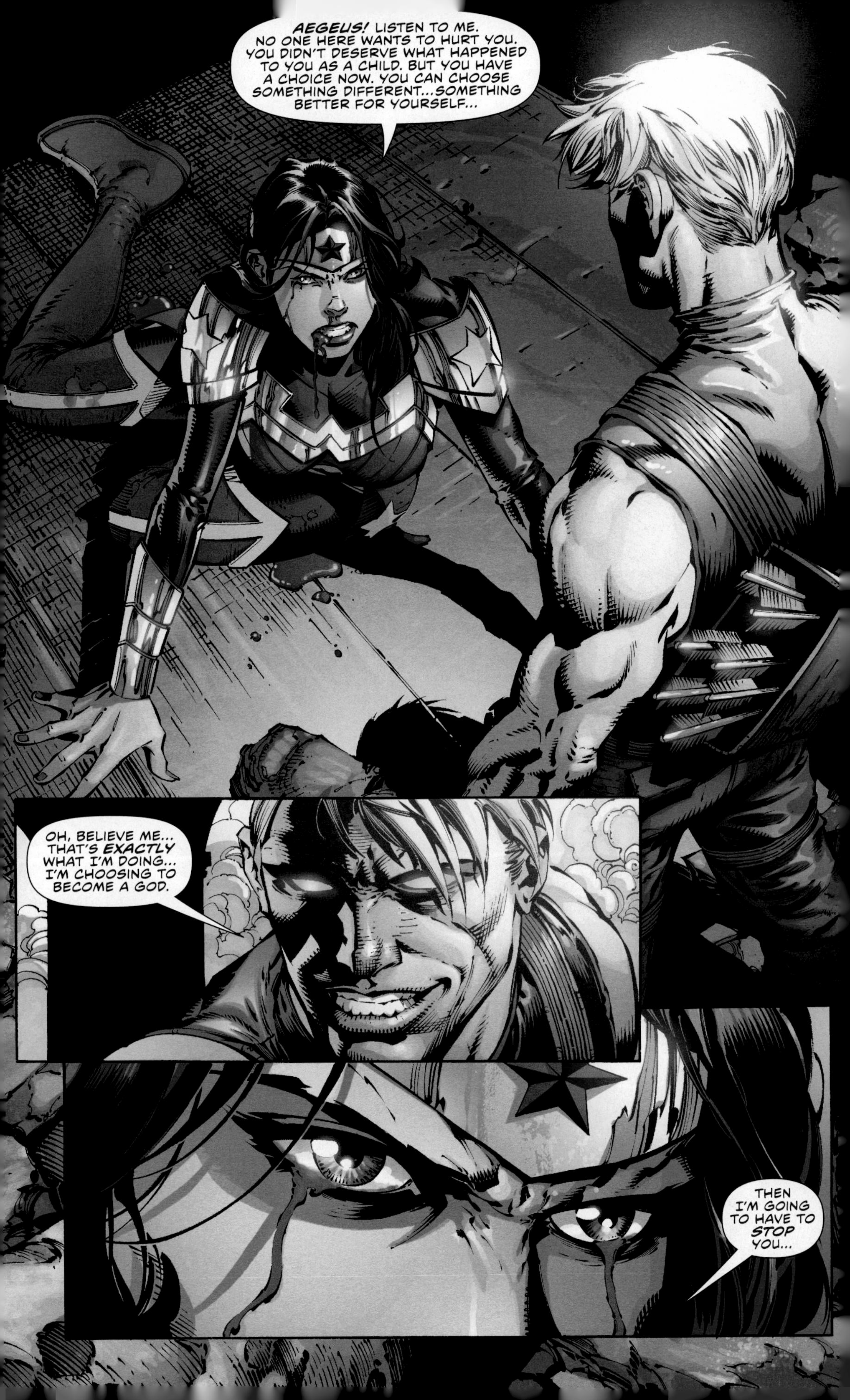

AEGEUS! LISTEN TO ME. NO ONE HERE WANTS TO HURT YOU. YOU DIDN'T DESERVE WHAT HAPPENED TO YOU AS A CHILD. BUT YOU HAVE A CHOICE NOW. YOU CAN CHOOSE SOMETHING DIFFERENT...SOMETHING BETTER FOR YOURSELF...
OH, BELIEVE ME... THAT'S EXACTLY WHAT I'M DOING... I'M CHOOSING TO BECOME A GOD.
THEN I'M GOING TO HAVE TO STOP YOU...

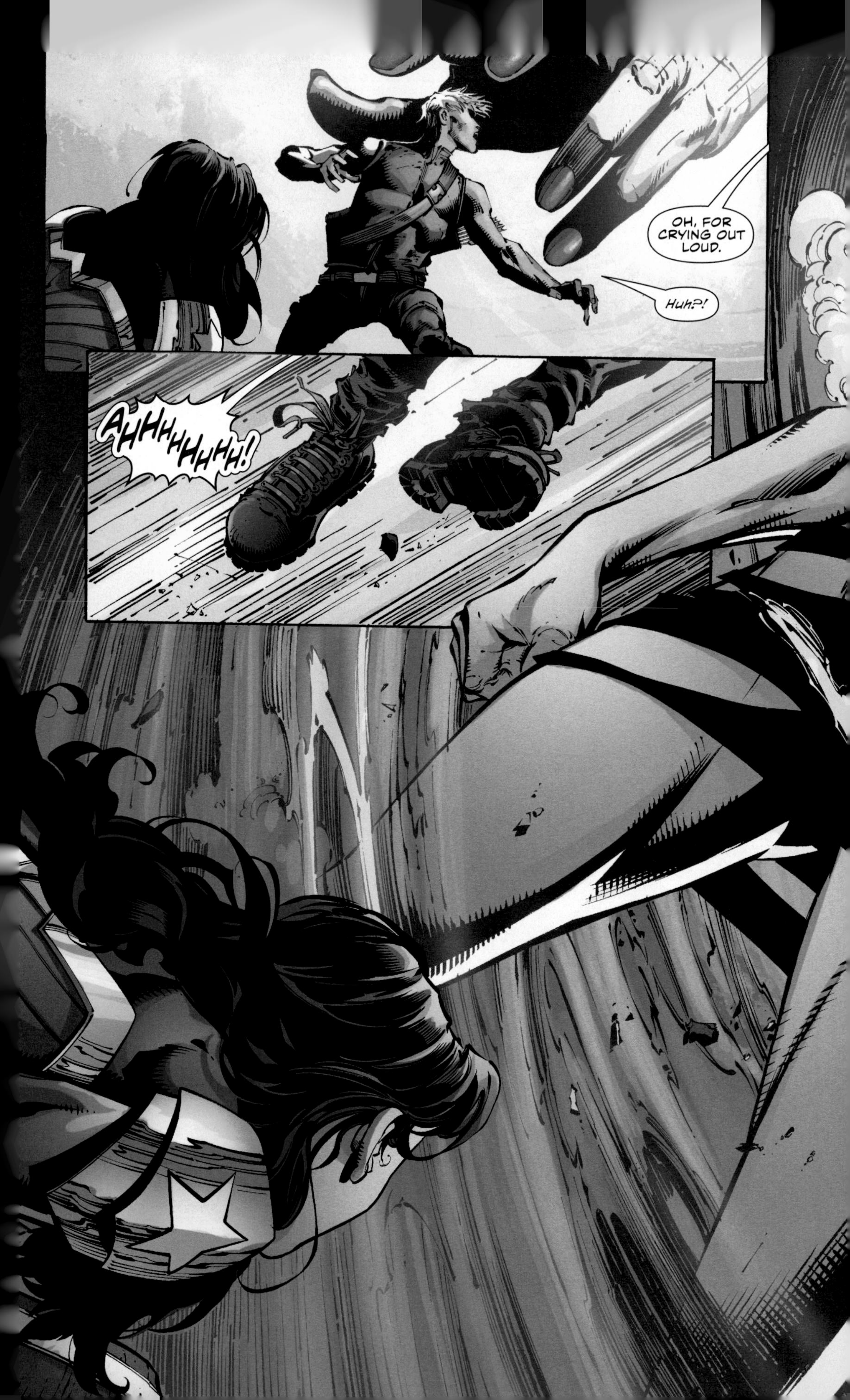
OH, FOR CRYING OUT LOUD.
Huh?!
AHHHHHHHH!

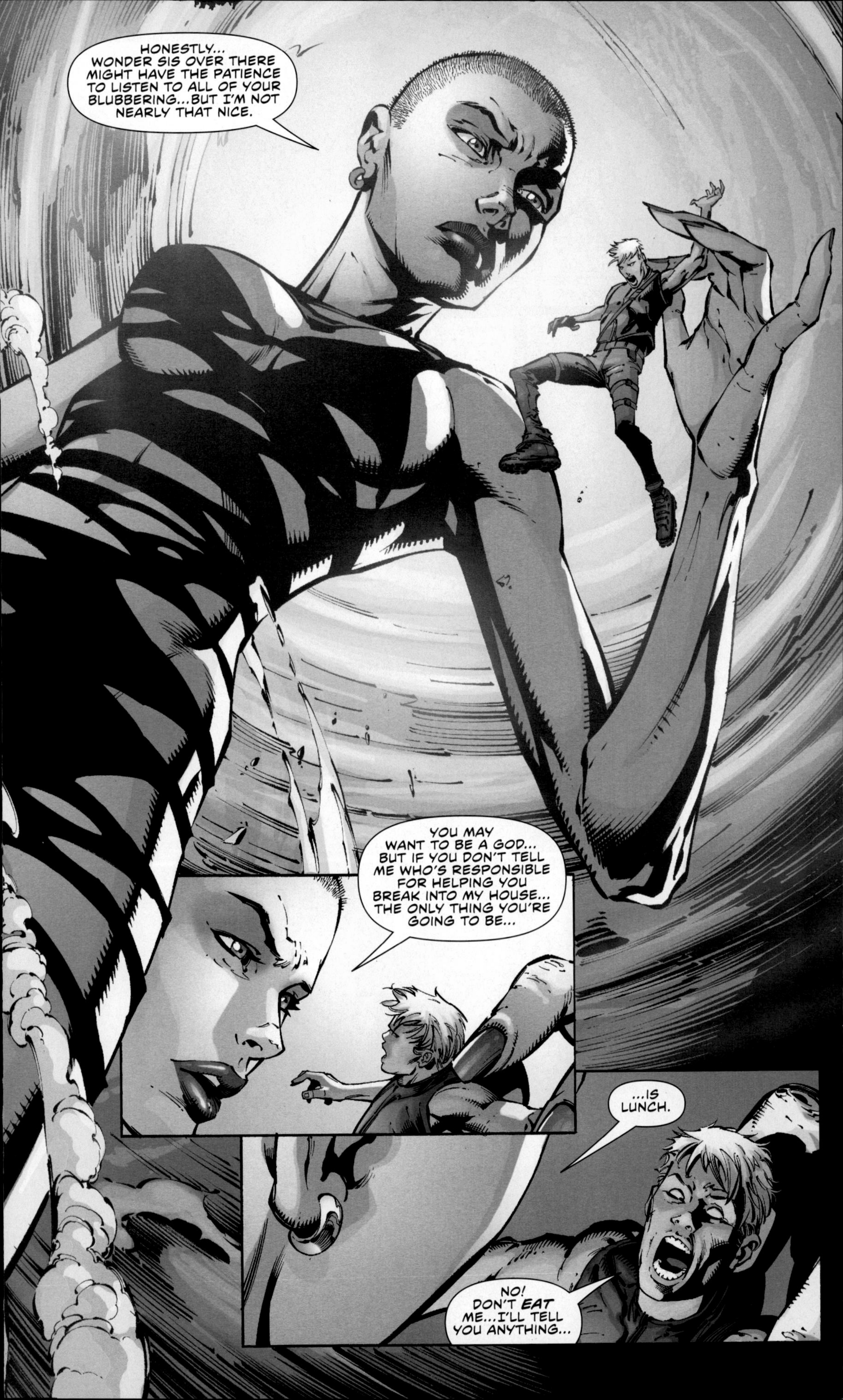
HONESTLY... WONDER SIS OVER THERE MIGHT HAVE THE PATIENCE TO LISTEN TO ALL OF YOUR BLUBBERING...BUT I'M NOT NEARLY THAT NICE.
YOU MAY WANT TO BE A GOD... BUT IF YOU DON'T TELL ME WHO'S RESPONSIBLE FOR HELPING YOU BREAK INTO MY HOUSE... THE ONLY THING YOU'RE GOING TO BE...
...IS LUNCH.
NO! DON'T *EAT* ME...I'LL TELL YOU ANYTHING...

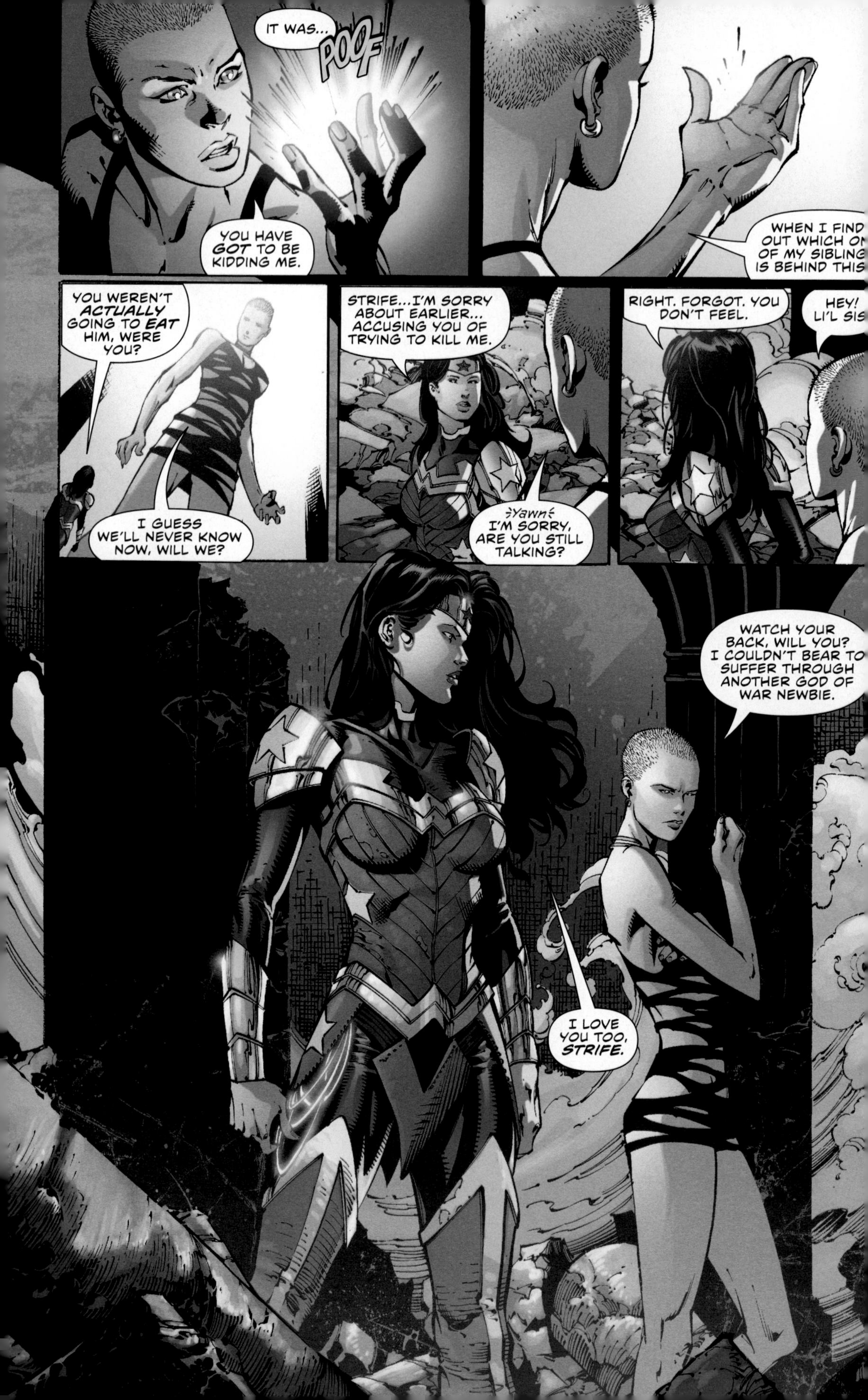
IT WAS...
POOF
YOU HAVE GOT TO BE KIDDING ME.
WHEN I FIND OUT WHICH ON OF MY SIBLING IS BEHIND THIS
YOU WEREN'T ACTUALLY GOING TO EAT HIM, WERE YOU?
I GUESS WE'LL NEVER KNOW NOW, WILL WE?
STRIFE...I'M SORRY ABOUT EARLIER... ACCUSING YOU OF TRYING TO KILL ME.
Yawn
I'M SORRY, ARE YOU STILL TALKING?
RIGHT. FORGOT. YOU DON'T FEEL.
HEY! LI'L SIS
WATCH YOUR BACK, WILL YOU? I COULDN'T BEAR TO SUFFER THROUGH ANOTHER GOD OF WAR NEWBIE.
I LOVE YOU TOO, STRIFE.

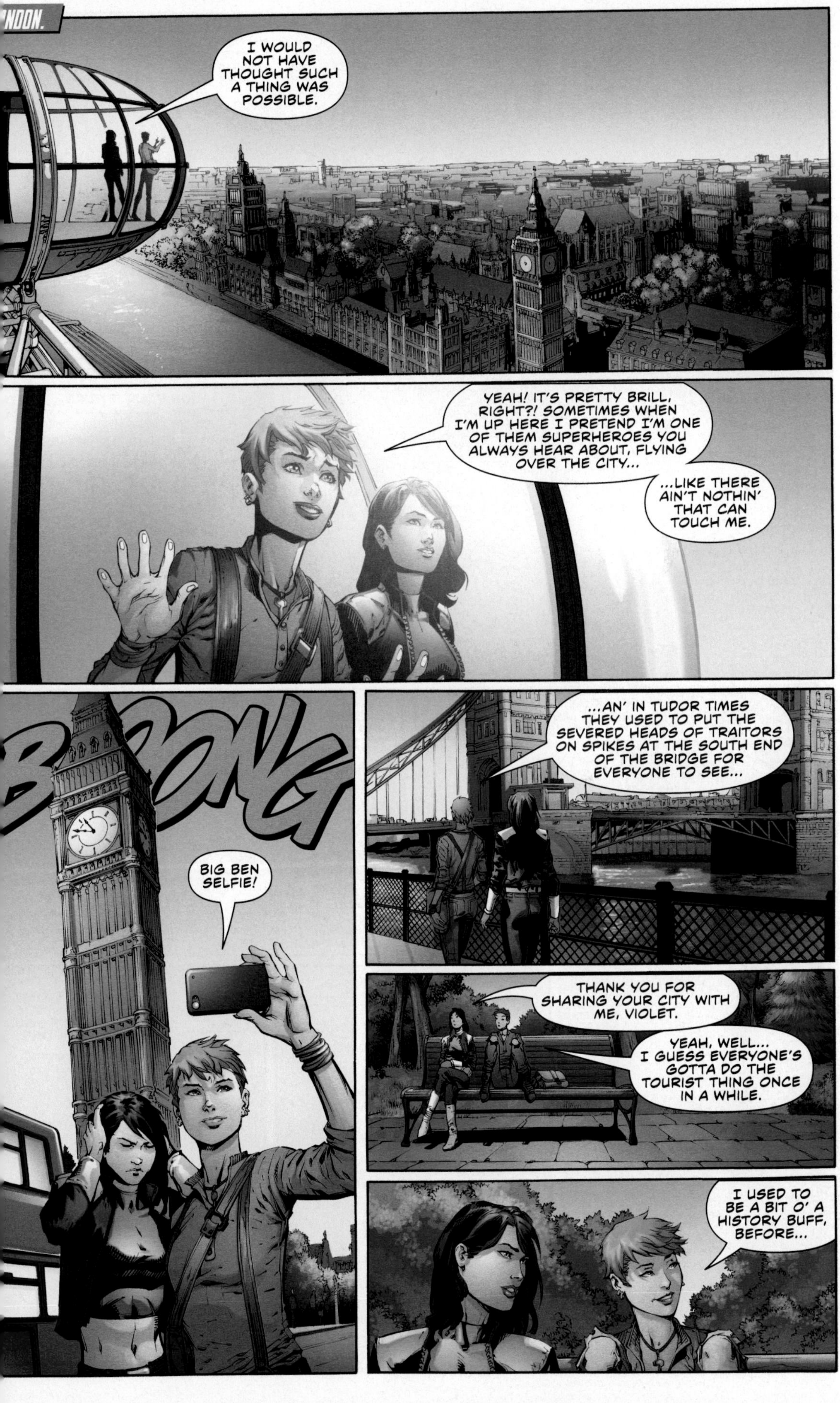

NDON.
I WOULD NOT HAVE THOUGHT SUCH A THING WAS POSSIBLE.
YEAH! IT'S PRETTY BRILL, RIGHT?! SOMETIMES WHEN I'M UP HERE I PRETEND I'M ONE OF THEM SUPERHEROES YOU ALWAYS HEAR ABOUT, FLYING OVER THE CITY...
...LIKE THERE AIN'T NOTHIN' THAT CAN TOUCH ME.
BOONG
BIG BEN SELFIE!
...AN' IN TUDOR TIMES THEY USED TO PUT THE SEVERED HEADS OF TRAITORS ON SPIKES AT THE SOUTH END OF THE BRIDGE FOR EVERYONE TO SEE...
THANK YOU FOR SHARING YOUR CITY WITH ME, VIOLET.
YEAH, WELL... I GUESS EVERYONE'S GOTTA DO THE TOURIST THING ONCE IN A WHILE.
I USED TO BE A BIT O' A HISTORY BUFF, BEFORE...

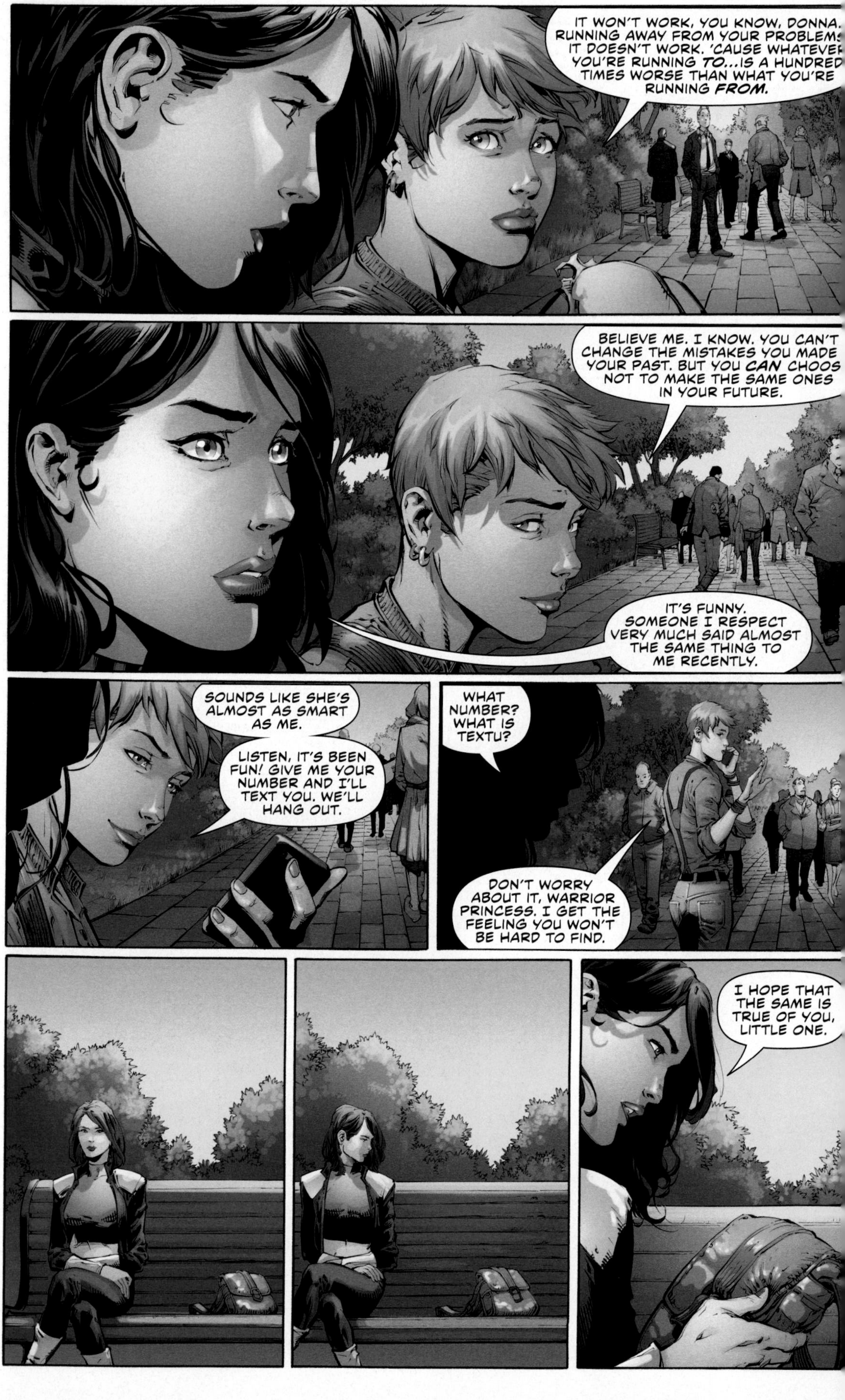

IT WON'T WORK, YOU KNOW, DONNA. RUNNING AWAY FROM YOUR PROBLEMS IT DOESN'T WORK. 'CAUSE WHATEVER YOU'RE RUNNING *TO*...IS A HUNDRED TIMES WORSE THAN WHAT YOU'RE RUNNING *FROM.*
BELIEVE ME. I KNOW. YOU CAN'T CHANGE THE MISTAKES YOU MADE YOUR PAST. BUT YOU *CAN* CHOOS NOT TO MAKE THE SAME ONES IN YOUR FUTURE.
IT'S FUNNY. SOMEONE I RESPECT VERY MUCH SAID ALMOST THE SAME THING TO ME RECENTLY.
SOUNDS LIKE SHE'S ALMOST AS SMART AS ME.
LISTEN, IT'S BEEN FUN! GIVE ME YOUR NUMBER AND I'LL TEXT YOU. WE'LL HANG OUT.
WHAT NUMBER? WHAT IS TEXTU?
DON'T WORRY ABOUT IT, WARRIOR PRINCESS. I GET THE FEELING YOU WON'T BE HARD TO FIND.
I HOPE THAT THE SAME IS TRUE OF YOU, LITTLE ONE.

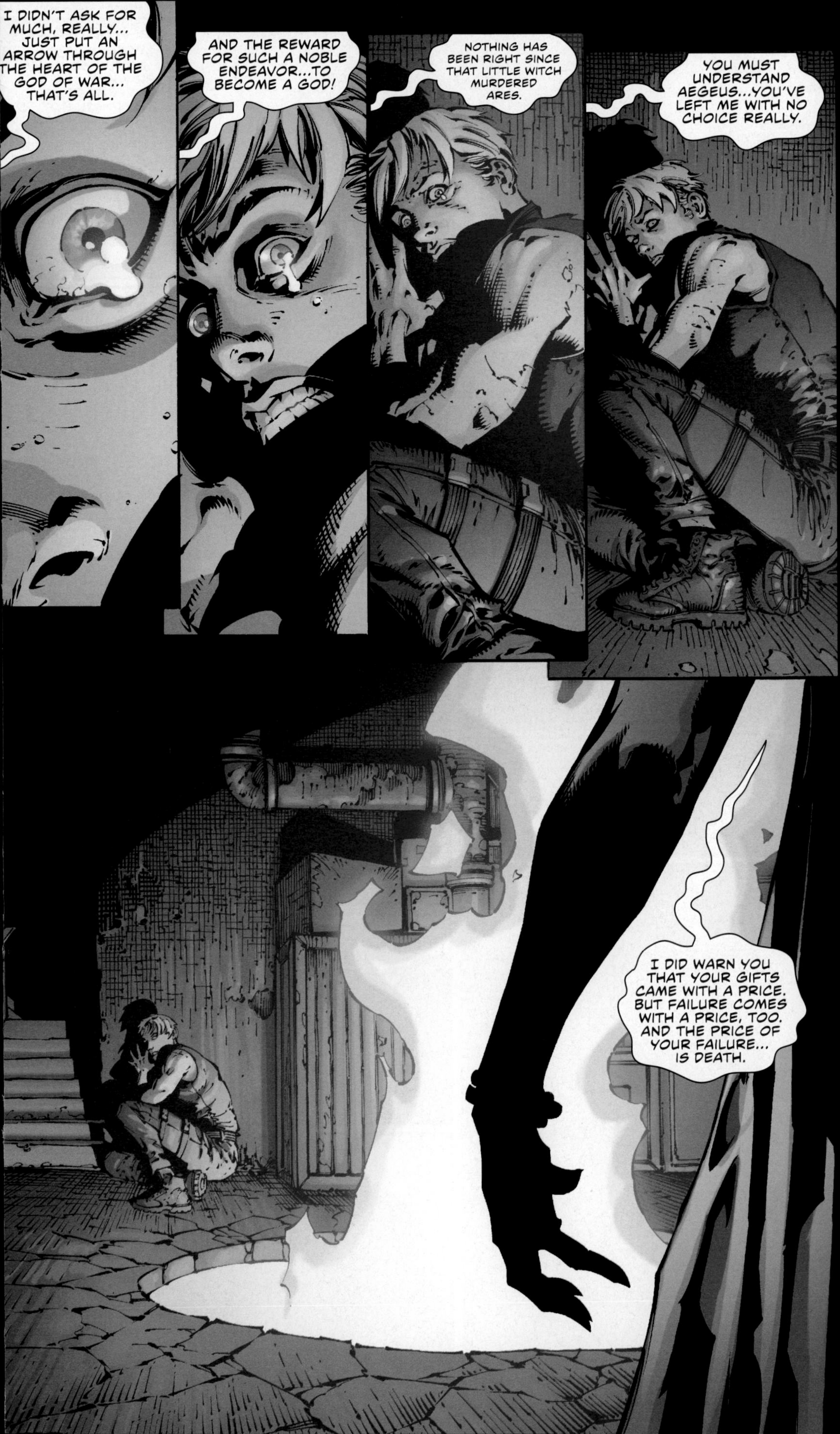
I DIDN'T ASK FOR MUCH, REALLY... JUST PUT AN ARROW THROUGH THE HEART OF THE GOD OF WAR... THAT'S ALL.
AND THE REWARD FOR SUCH A NOBLE ENDEAVOR...TO BECOME A GOD!
NOTHING HAS BEEN RIGHT SINCE THAT LITTLE WITCH MURDERED ARES.
YOU MUST UNDERSTAND AEGEUS...YOU'VE LEFT ME WITH NO CHOICE REALLY.
I DID WARN YOU THAT YOUR GIFTS CAME WITH A PRICE. BUT FAILURE COMES WITH A PRICE, TOO. AND THE PRICE OF YOUR FAILURE... IS DEATH.

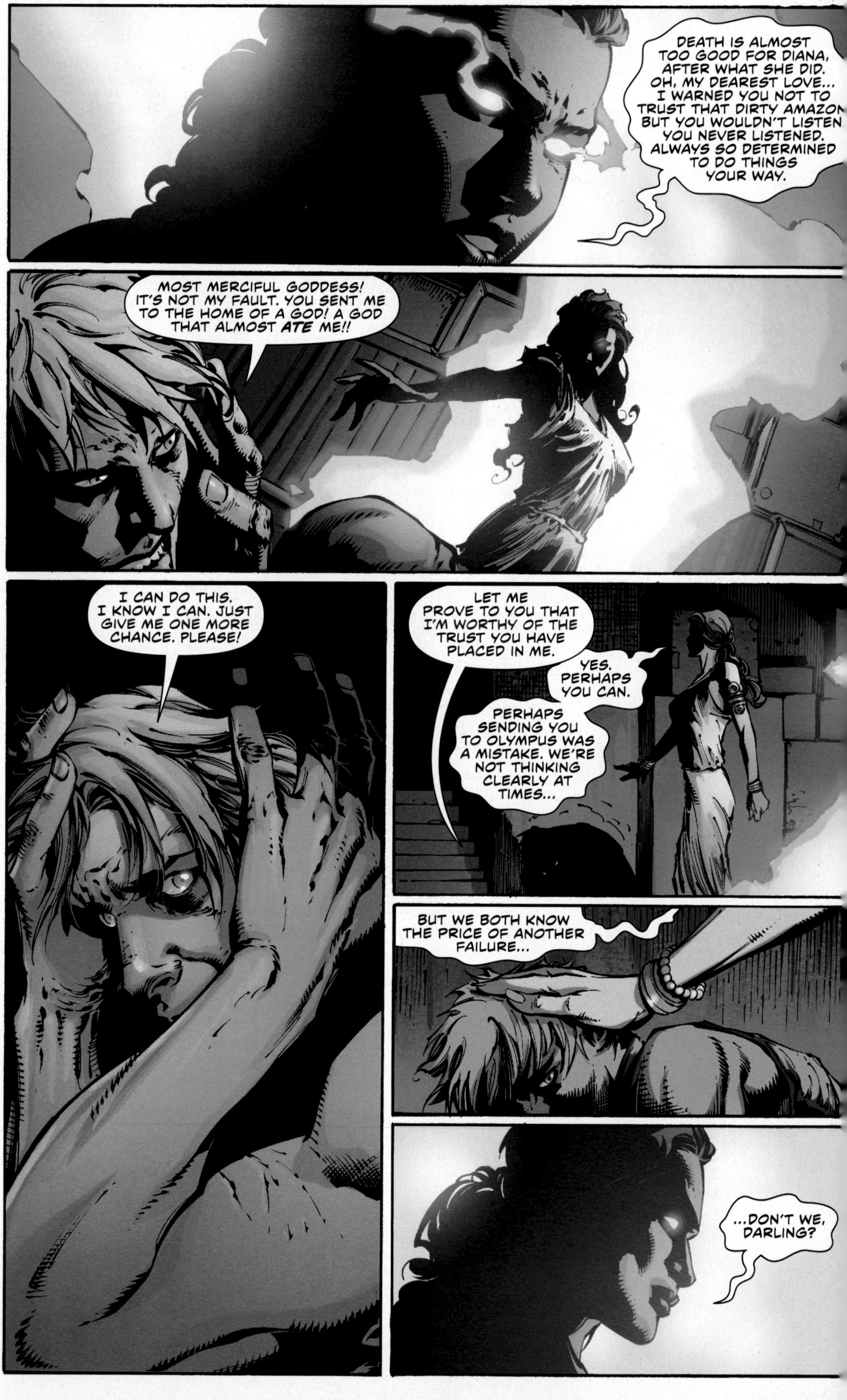
DEATH IS ALMOST TOO GOOD FOR DIANA, AFTER WHAT SHE DID. OH, MY DEAREST LOVE... I WARNED YOU NOT TO TRUST THAT DIRTY AMAZON BUT YOU WOULDN'T LISTEN YOU NEVER LISTENED. ALWAYS SO DETERMINED TO DO THINGS YOUR WAY.
MOST MERCIFUL GODDESS! IT'S NOT MY FAULT. YOU SENT ME TO THE HOME OF A GOD! A GOD THAT ALMOST *ATE* ME!!
I CAN DO THIS. I KNOW I CAN. JUST GIVE ME ONE MORE CHANCE. PLEASE!
LET ME PROVE TO YOU THAT I'M WORTHY OF THE TRUST YOU HAVE PLACED IN ME.
YES. PERHAPS YOU CAN.
PERHAPS SENDING YOU TO OLYMPUS WAS A MISTAKE. WE'RE NOT THINKING CLEARLY AT TIMES...
BUT WE BOTH KNOW THE PRICE OF ANOTHER FAILURE...
...DON'T WE, DARLING?

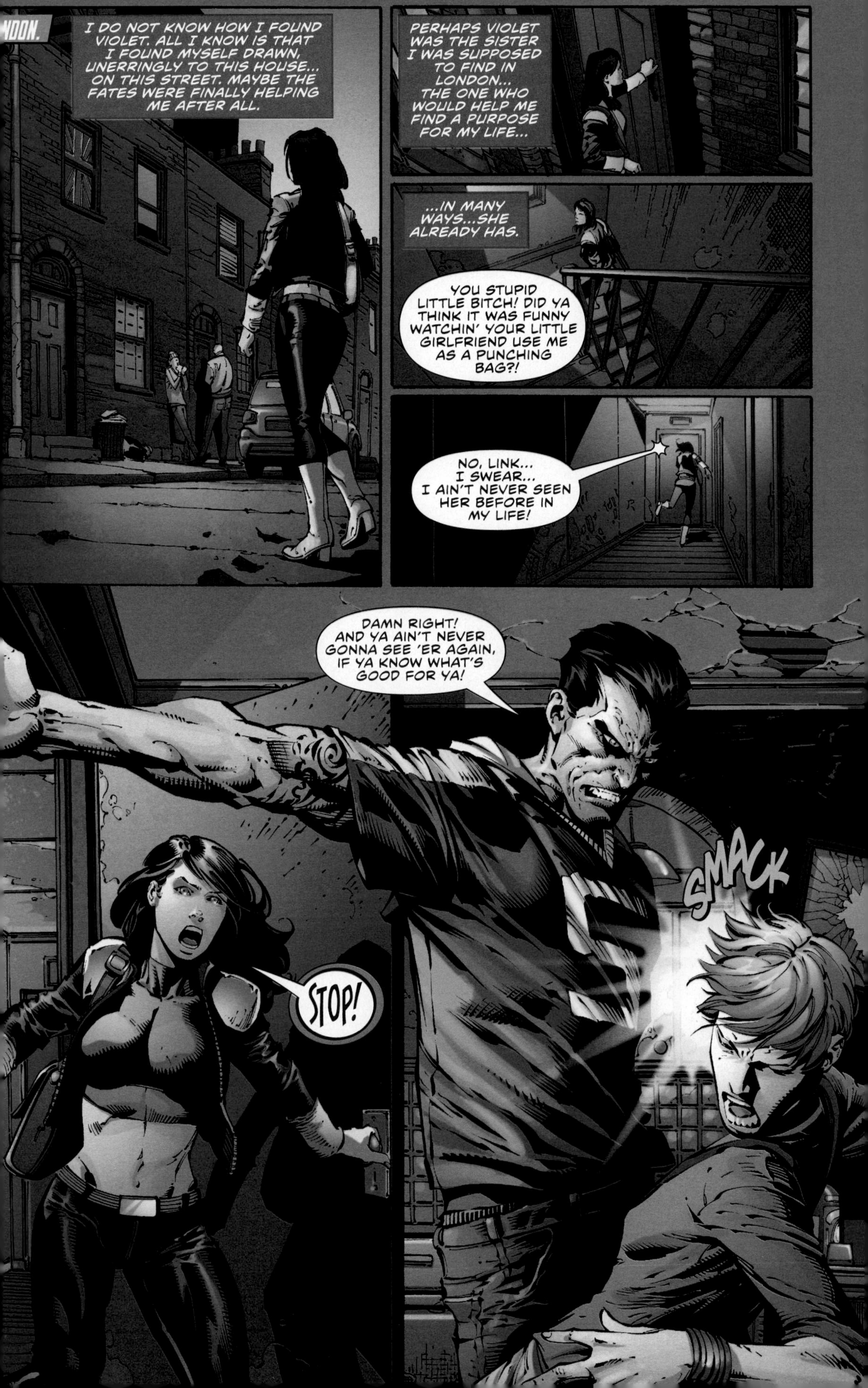
...NDON.
I DO NOT KNOW HOW I FOUND VIOLET. ALL I KNOW IS THAT I FOUND MYSELF DRAWN, UNERRINGLY TO THIS HOUSE... ON THIS STREET. MAYBE THE FATES WERE FINALLY HELPING ME AFTER ALL.
PERHAPS VIOLET WAS THE SISTER I WAS SUPPOSED TO FIND IN LONDON... THE ONE WHO WOULD HELP ME FIND A PURPOSE FOR MY LIFE...
...IN MANY WAYS...SHE ALREADY HAS.
YOU STUPID LITTLE BITCH! DID YA THINK IT WAS FUNNY WATCHIN' YOUR LITTLE GIRLFRIEND USE ME AS A PUNCHING BAG?!
NO, LINK... I SWEAR... I AIN'T NEVER SEEN HER BEFORE IN MY LIFE!
DAMN RIGHT! AND YA AIN'T NEVER GONNA SEE 'ER AGAIN, IF YA KNOW WHAT'S GOOD FOR YA!
STOP!
SMACK

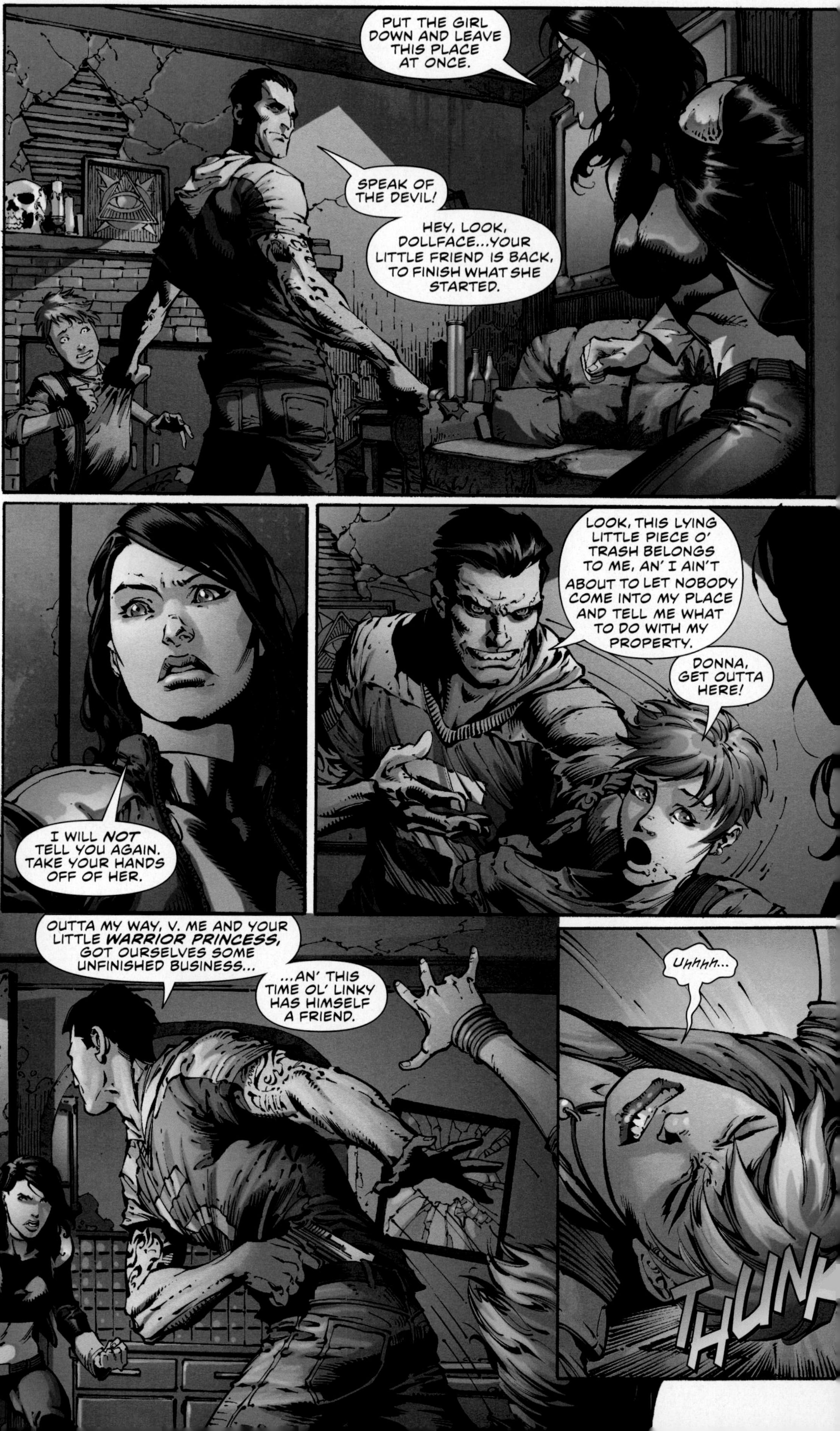
PUT THE GIRL DOWN AND LEAVE THIS PLACE AT ONCE.
SPEAK OF THE DEVIL!
HEY, LOOK, DOLLFACE...YOUR LITTLE FRIEND IS BACK, TO FINISH WHAT SHE STARTED.
I WILL *NOT* TELL YOU AGAIN. TAKE YOUR HANDS OFF OF HER.
LOOK, THIS LYING LITTLE PIECE O' TRASH BELONGS TO ME, AN' I AIN'T ABOUT TO LET NOBODY COME INTO MY PLACE AND TELL ME WHAT TO DO WITH MY PROPERTY.
DONNA, GET OUTTA HERE!
OUTTA MY WAY, V. ME AND YOUR LITTLE ***WARRIOR PRINCESS***, GOT OURSELVES SOME UNFINISHED BUSINESS...
...AN' THIS TIME OL' LINKY HAS HIMSELF A FRIEND.
Uhhhh...
THUNK

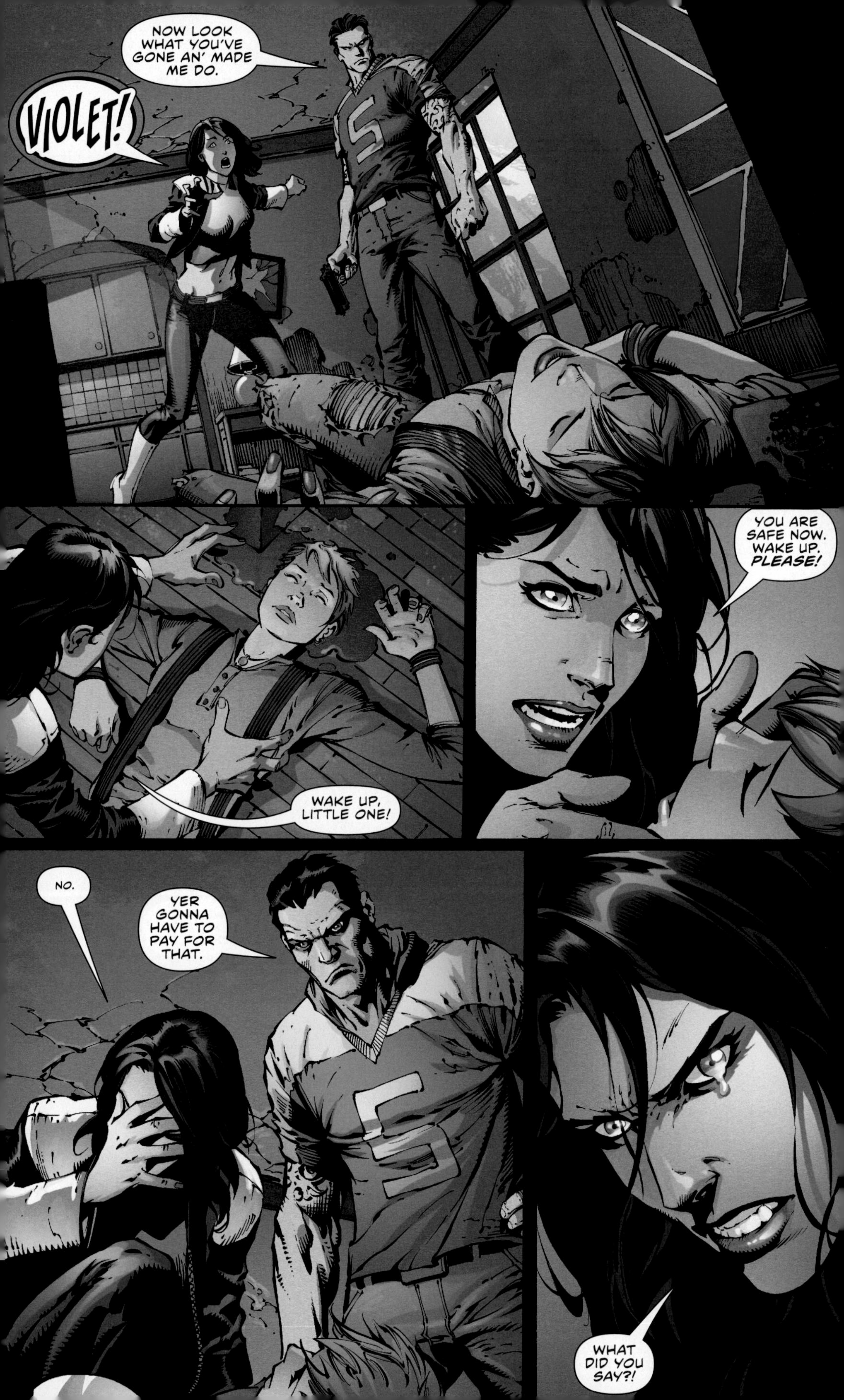
NOW LOOK WHAT YOU'VE GONE AN' MADE ME DO.
VIOLET!
YOU ARE SAFE NOW. WAKE UP. PLEASE!
WAKE UP, LITTLE ONE!
NO.
YER GONNA HAVE TO PAY FOR THAT.
WHAT DID YOU SAY?!

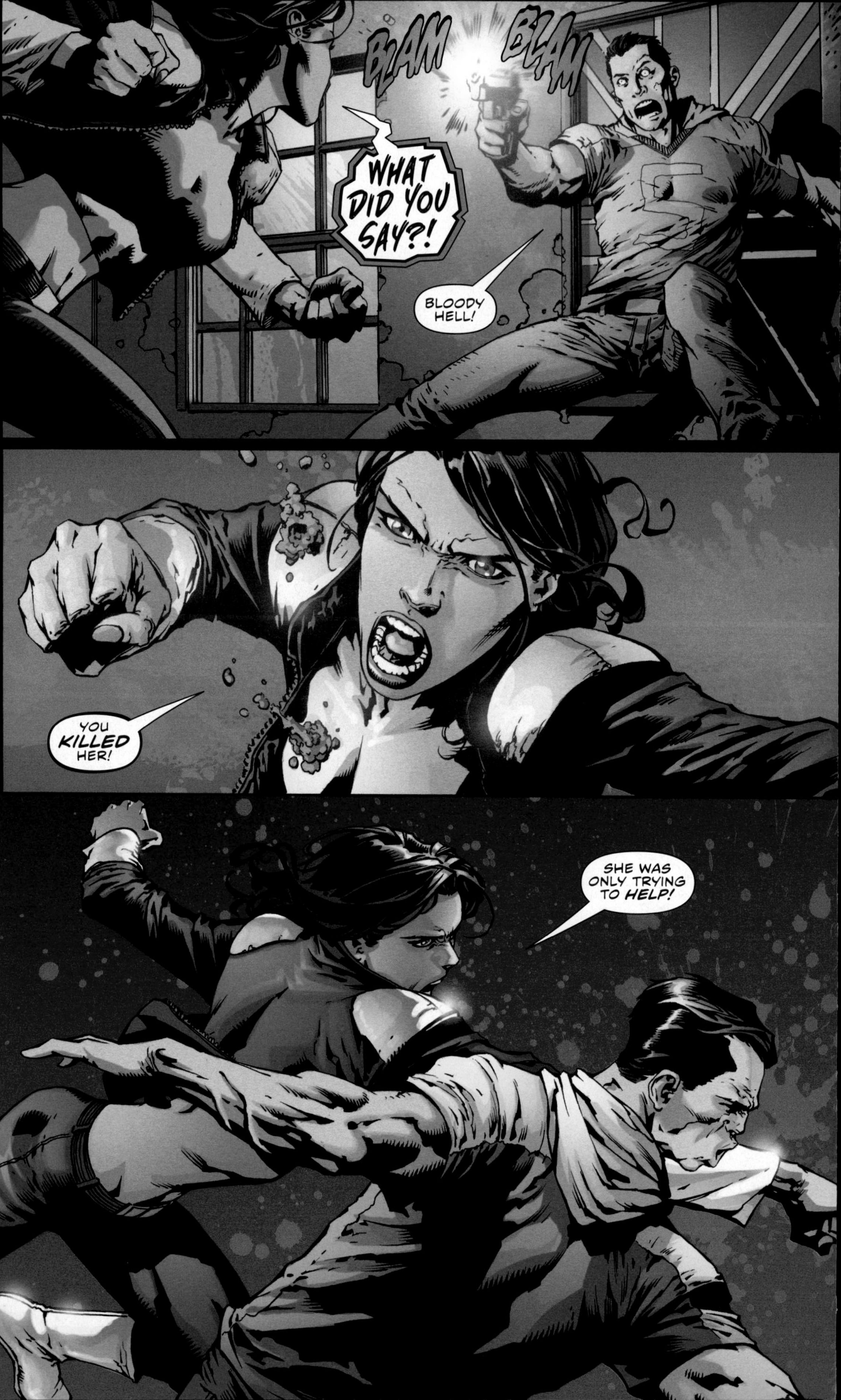
BLAM BLAM
WHAT DID YOU SAY?!
BLOODY HELL!
YOU KILLED HER!
SHE WAS ONLY TRYING TO HELP!

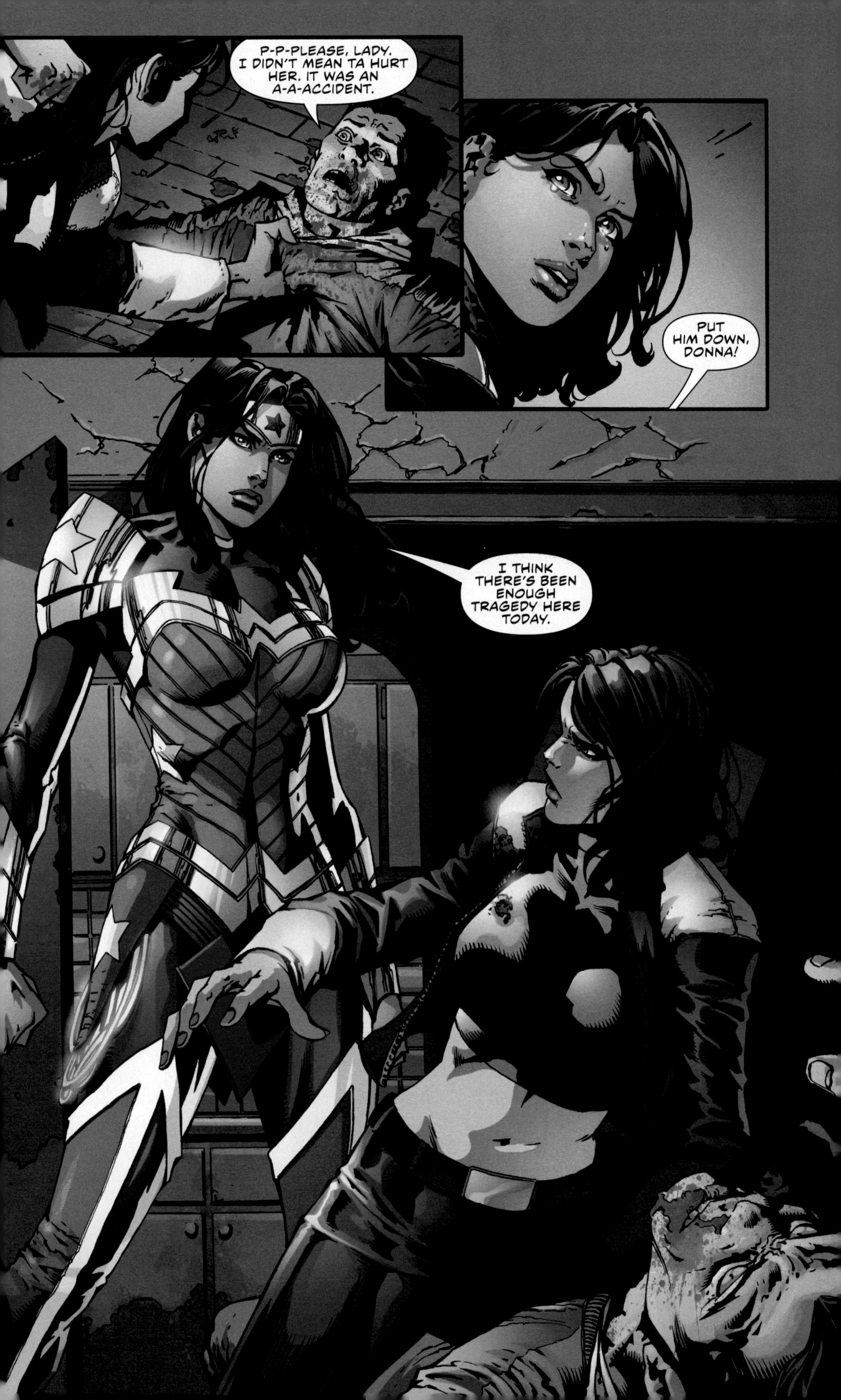
P-P-PLEASE, LADY. I DIDN'T MEAN TA HURT HER. IT WAS AN A-A-ACCIDENT.
PUT HIM DOWN, DONNA!
I THINK THERE'S BEEN ENOUGH TRAGEDY HERE TODAY.

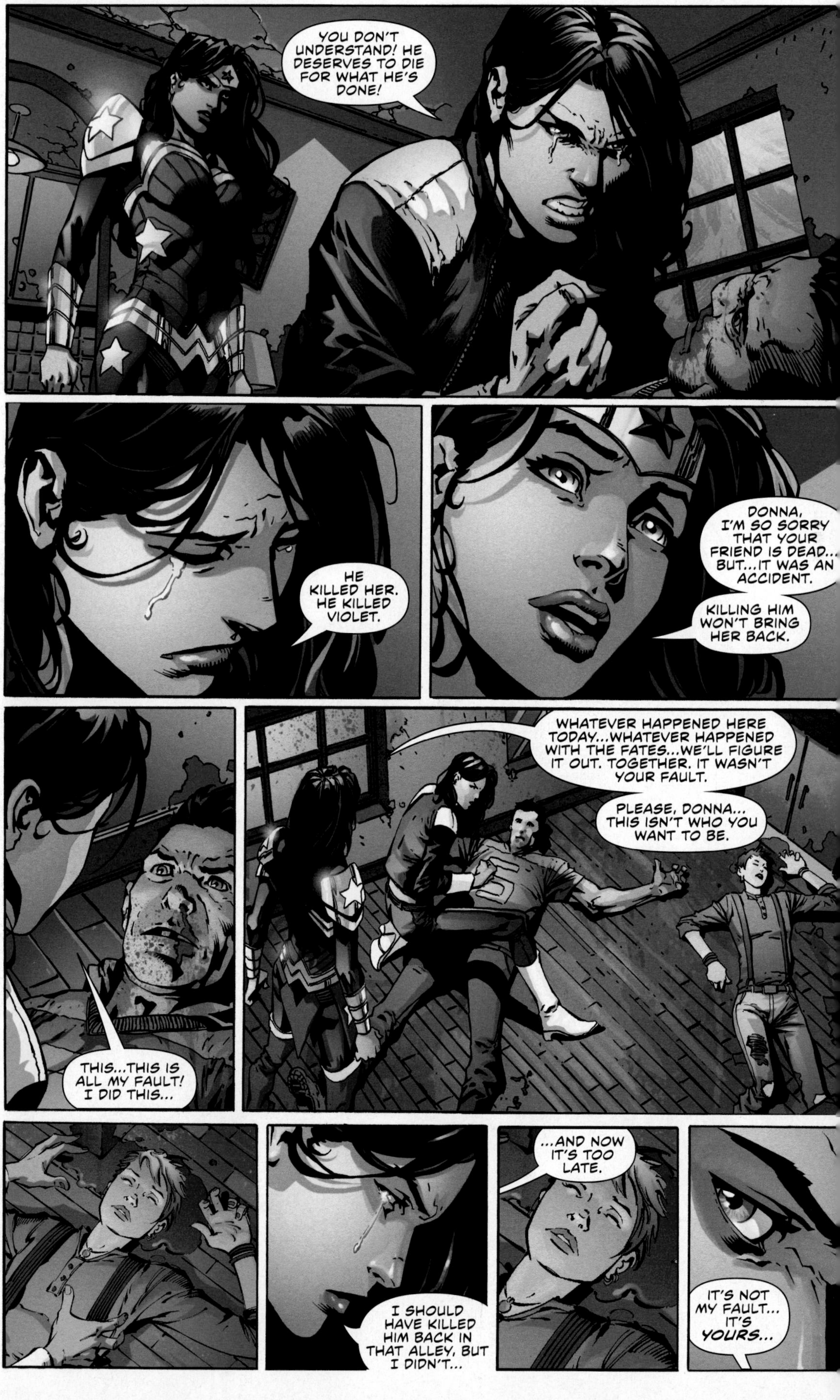
YOU DON'T UNDERSTAND! HE DESERVES TO DIE FOR WHAT HE'S DONE!
HE KILLED HER. HE KILLED VIOLET.
DONNA, I'M SO SORRY THAT YOUR FRIEND IS DEAD... BUT...IT WAS AN ACCIDENT.
KILLING HIM WON'T BRING HER BACK.
THIS...THIS IS ALL MY FAULT! I DID THIS...
WHATEVER HAPPENED HERE TODAY...WHATEVER HAPPENED WITH THE FATES...WE'LL FIGURE IT OUT. TOGETHER. IT WASN'T YOUR FAULT.
PLEASE, DONNA... THIS ISN'T WHO YOU WANT TO BE.
I SHOULD HAVE KILLED HIM BACK IN THAT ALLEY, BUT I DIDN'T...
...AND NOW IT'S TOO LATE.
IT'S NOT MY FAULT... IT'S *YOURS...*

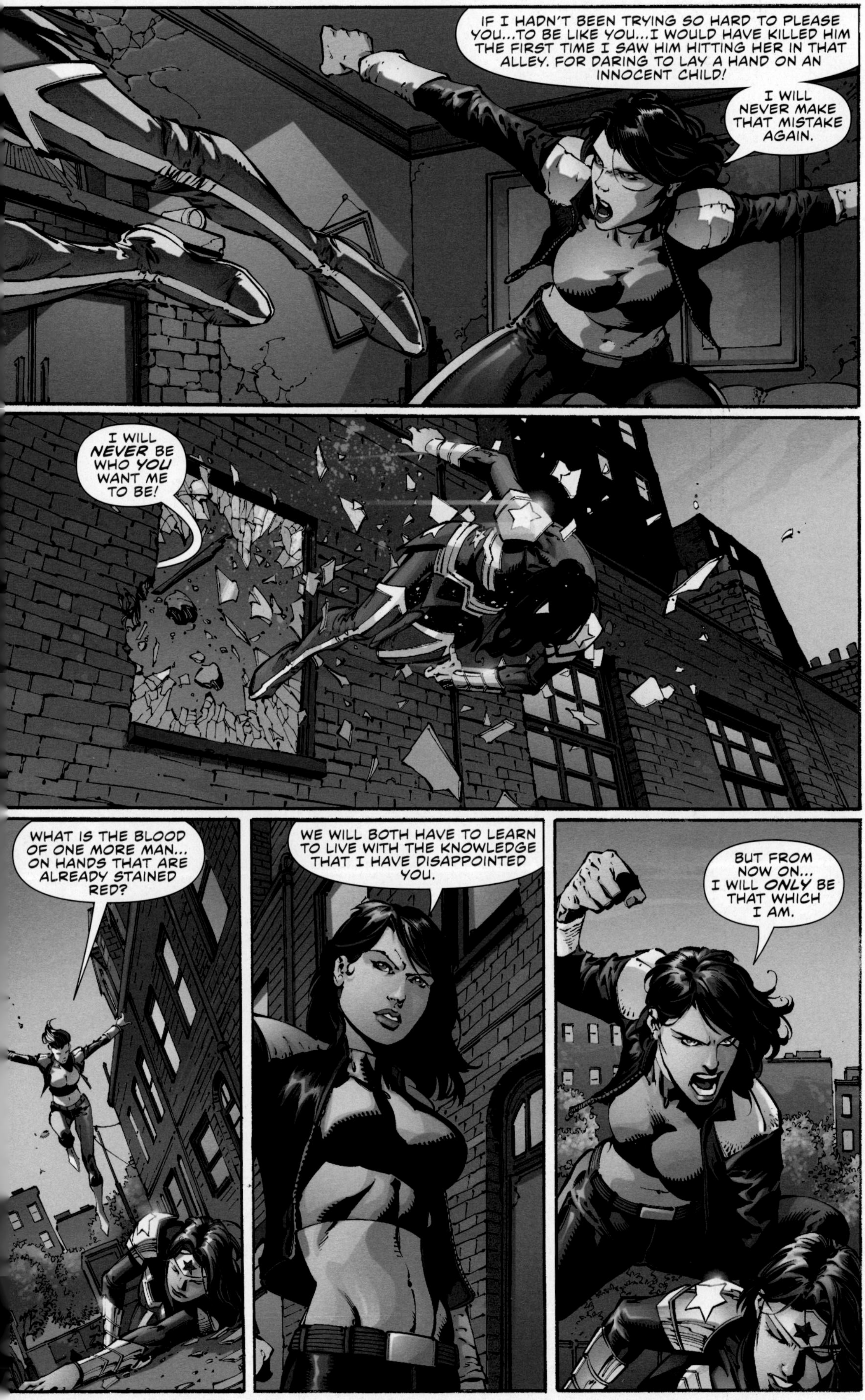
IF I HADN'T BEEN TRYING SO HARD TO PLEASE YOU...TO BE LIKE YOU...I WOULD HAVE KILLED HIM THE FIRST TIME I SAW HIM HITTING HER IN THAT ALLEY. FOR DARING TO LAY A HAND ON AN INNOCENT CHILD!
I WILL NEVER MAKE THAT MISTAKE AGAIN.
I WILL NEVER BE WHO YOU WANT ME TO BE!
WHAT IS THE BLOOD OF ONE MORE MAN... ON HANDS THAT ARE ALREADY STAINED RED?
WE WILL BOTH HAVE TO LEARN TO LIVE WITH THE KNOWLEDGE THAT I HAVE DISAPPOINTED YOU.
BUT FROM NOW ON... I WILL ONLY BE THAT WHICH I AM.

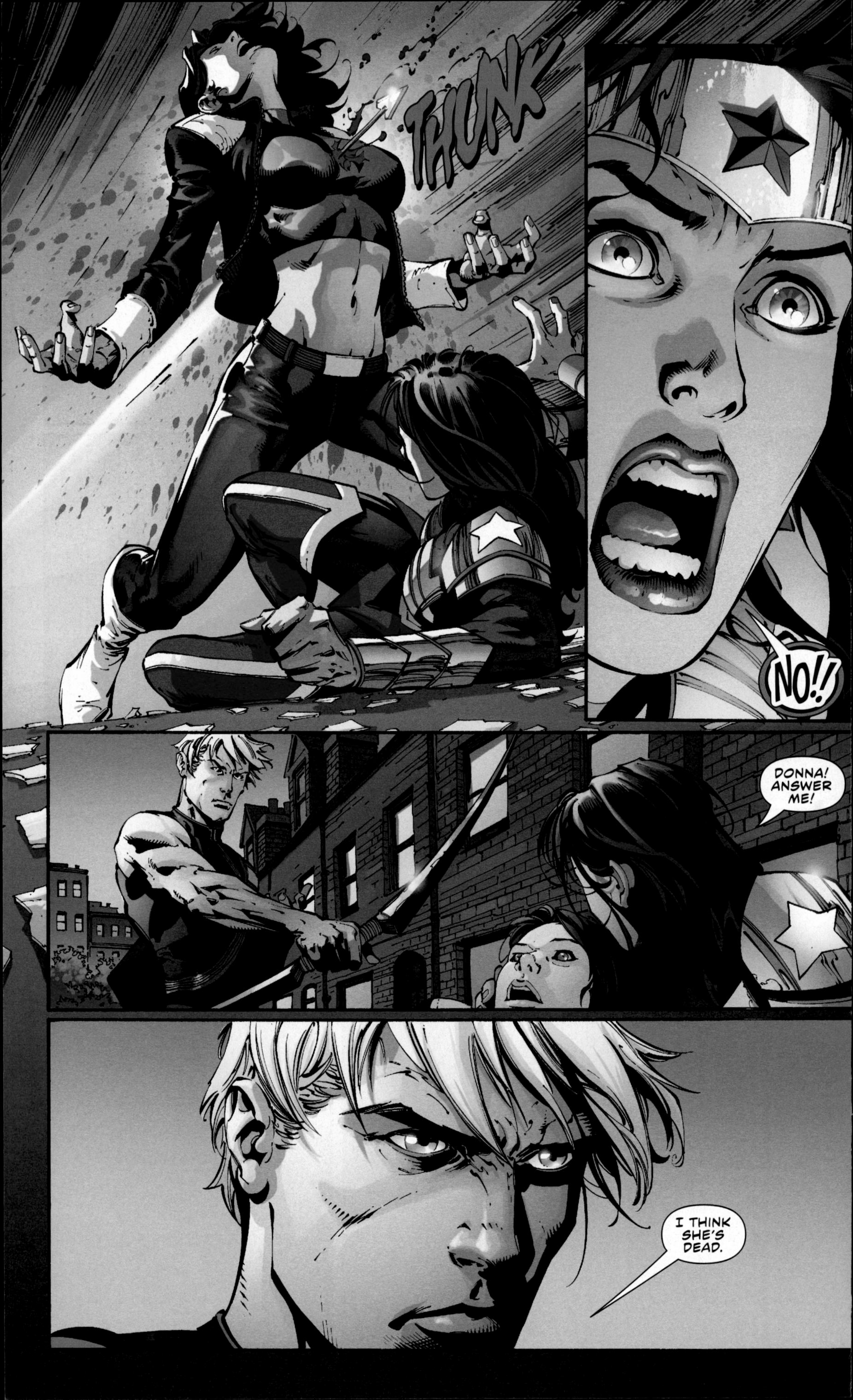
THUNK
NO!!
DONNA! ANSWER ME!
I THINK SHE'S DEAD.

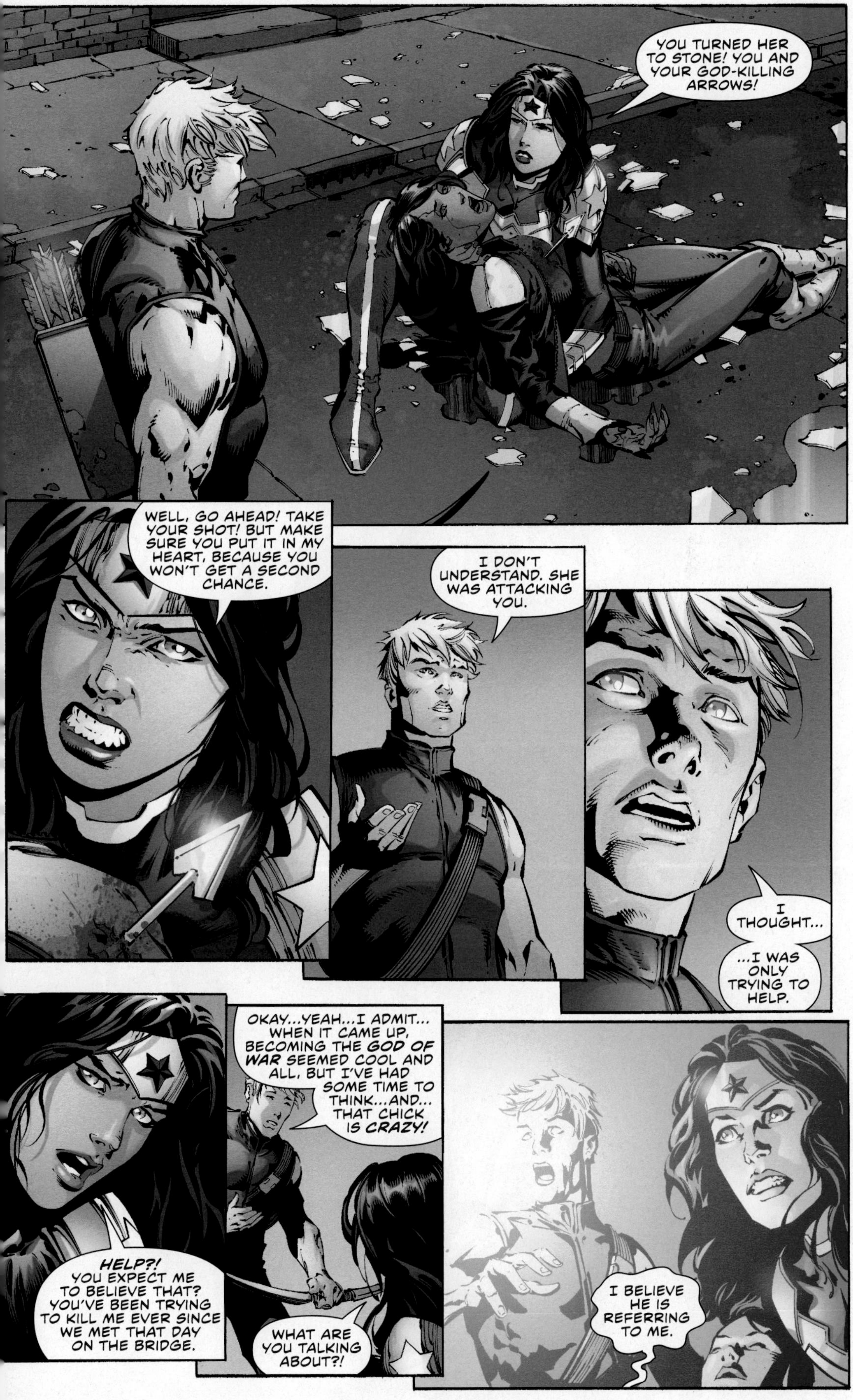
YOU TURNED HER TO STONE! YOU AND YOUR GOD-KILLING ARROWS!
WELL, GO AHEAD! TAKE YOUR SHOT! BUT MAKE SURE YOU PUT IT IN MY HEART, BECAUSE YOU WON'T GET A SECOND CHANCE.
I DON'T UNDERSTAND. SHE WAS ATTACKING YOU.
I THOUGHT...
...I WAS ONLY TRYING TO HELP.
HELP?! YOU EXPECT ME TO BELIEVE THAT? YOU'VE BEEN TRYING TO KILL ME EVER SINCE WE MET THAT DAY ON THE BRIDGE.
OKAY...YEAH...I ADMIT... WHEN IT CAME UP, BECOMING THE GOD OF WAR SEEMED COOL AND ALL, BUT I'VE HAD SOME TIME TO THINK...AND... THAT CHICK IS CRAZY!
WHAT ARE YOU TALKING ABOUT?!
I BELIEVE HE IS REFERRING TO ME.

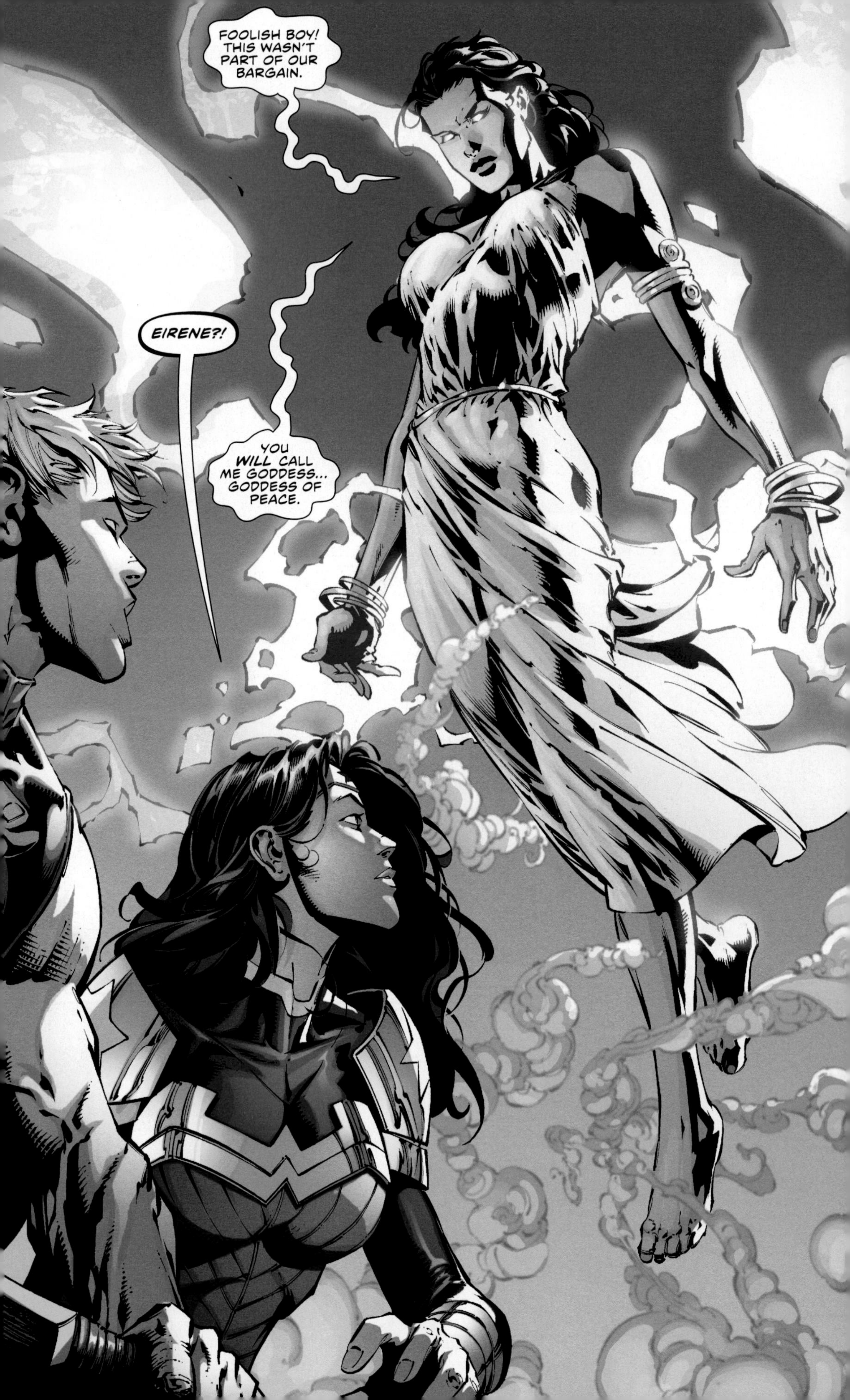
FOOLISH BOY! THIS WASN'T PART OF OUR BARGAIN.
EIRENE?!
YOU WILL CALL ME GODDESS... GODDESS OF PEACE.

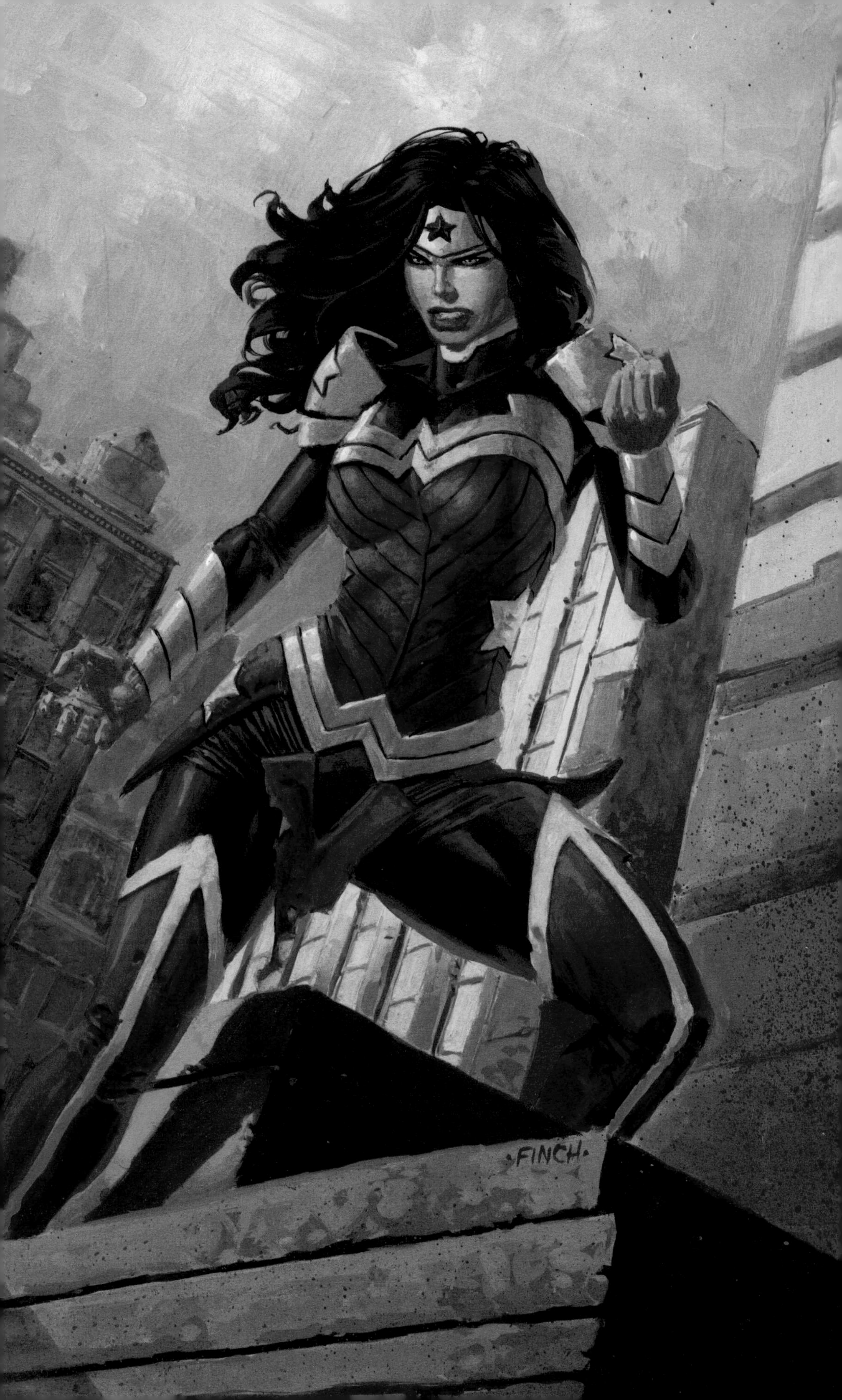
FINCH

WAR & PEACE

MEREDITH FINCH writer **DAVID FINCH** penciller **SCOTT HANNA** inker **BRAD ANDERSON** colorist **ROB LEIGH** letterer cover by **DAVID FINCH**

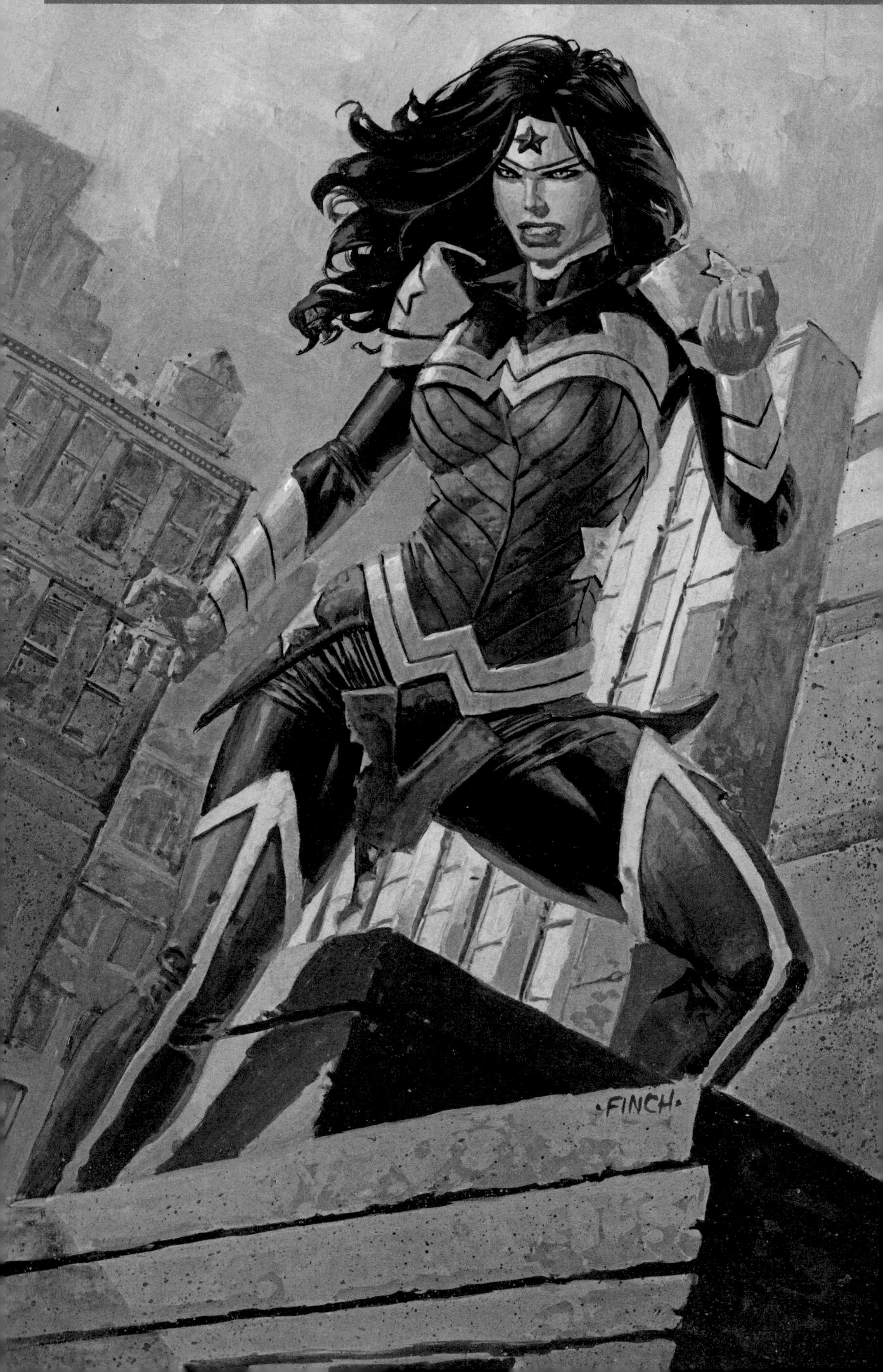

FINCH

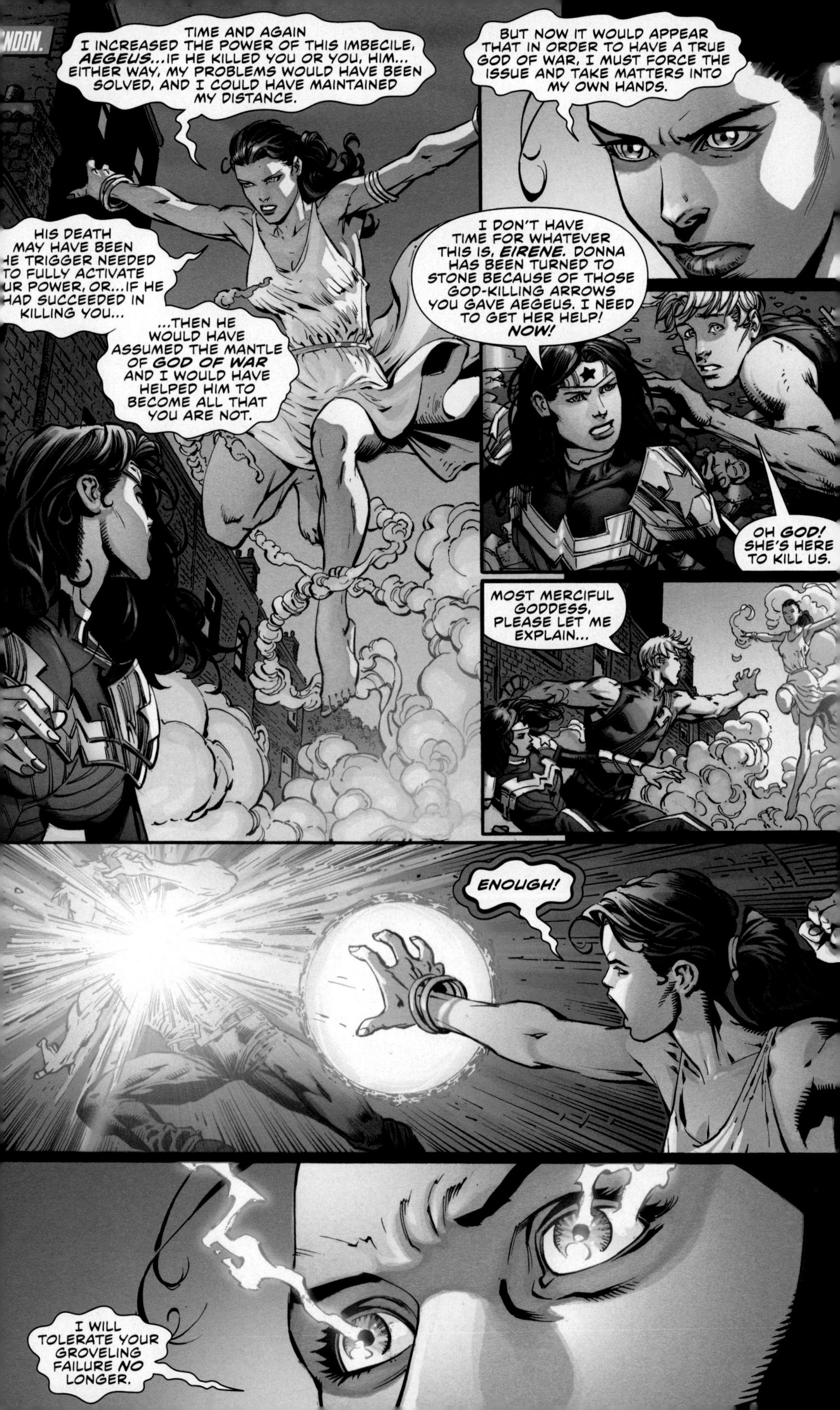
NDON.
TIME AND AGAIN I INCREASED THE POWER OF THIS IMBECILE, AEGEUS...IF HE KILLED YOU OR YOU, HIM... EITHER WAY, MY PROBLEMS WOULD HAVE BEEN SOLVED, AND I COULD HAVE MAINTAINED MY DISTANCE.
HIS DEATH MAY HAVE BEEN HE TRIGGER NEEDED TO FULLY ACTIVATE UR POWER, OR...IF HE HAD SUCCEEDED IN KILLING YOU...
...THEN HE WOULD HAVE ASSUMED THE MANTLE OF GOD OF WAR AND I WOULD HAVE HELPED HIM TO BECOME ALL THAT YOU ARE NOT.
BUT NOW IT WOULD APPEAR THAT IN ORDER TO HAVE A TRUE GOD OF WAR, I MUST FORCE THE ISSUE AND TAKE MATTERS INTO MY OWN HANDS.
I DON'T HAVE TIME FOR WHATEVER THIS IS, EIRENE. DONNA HAS BEEN TURNED TO STONE BECAUSE OF THOSE GOD-KILLING ARROWS YOU GAVE AEGEUS. I NEED TO GET HER HELP! NOW!
OH GOD! SHE'S HERE TO KILL US.
MOST MERCIFUL GODDESS, PLEASE LET ME EXPLAIN...
ENOUGH!
I WILL TOLERATE YOUR GROVELING FAILURE NO LONGER.

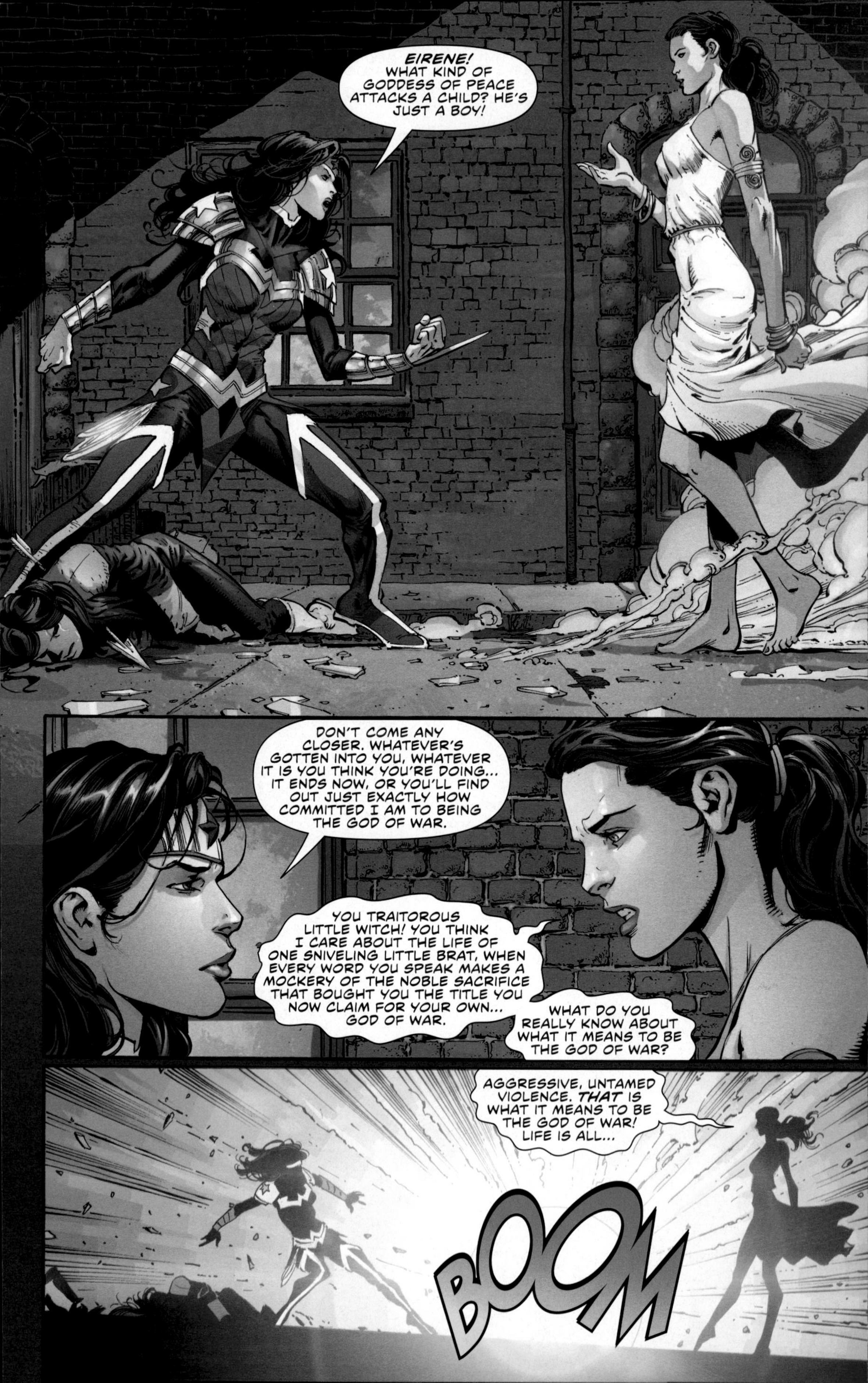
EIRENE! WHAT KIND OF GODDESS OF PEACE ATTACKS A CHILD? HE'S JUST A BOY!
DON'T COME ANY CLOSER. WHATEVER'S GOTTEN INTO YOU, WHATEVER IT IS YOU THINK YOU'RE DOING... IT ENDS NOW, OR YOU'LL FIND OUT JUST EXACTLY HOW COMMITTED I AM TO BEING THE GOD OF WAR.
YOU TRAITOROUS LITTLE WITCH! YOU THINK I CARE ABOUT THE LIFE OF ONE SNIVELING LITTLE BRAT, WHEN EVERY WORD YOU SPEAK MAKES A MOCKERY OF THE NOBLE SACRIFICE THAT BOUGHT YOU THE TITLE YOU NOW CLAIM FOR YOUR OWN... GOD OF WAR.
WHAT DO YOU REALLY KNOW ABOUT WHAT IT MEANS TO BE THE GOD OF WAR?
AGGRESSIVE, UNTAMED VIOLENCE. THAT IS WHAT IT MEANS TO BE THE GOD OF WAR! LIFE IS ALL...
BOOM

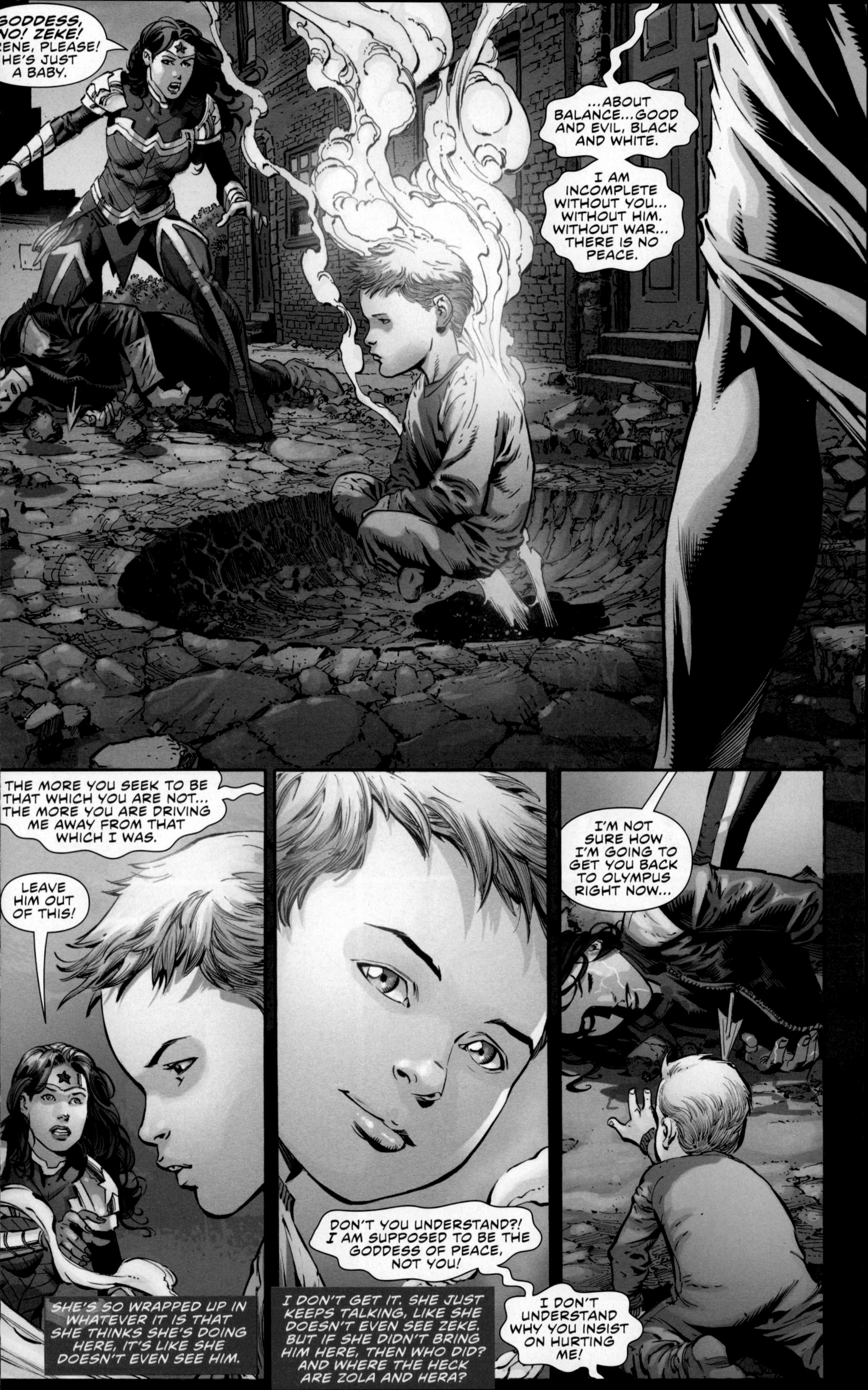
GODDESS, NO! ZEKE! RENE, PLEASE! HE'S JUST A BABY.
...ABOUT BALANCE...GOOD AND EVIL, BLACK AND WHITE.
I AM INCOMPLETE WITHOUT YOU... WITHOUT HIM. WITHOUT WAR... THERE IS NO PEACE.
THE MORE YOU SEEK TO BE THAT WHICH YOU ARE NOT... THE MORE YOU ARE DRIVING ME AWAY FROM THAT WHICH I WAS.
LEAVE HIM OUT OF THIS!
SHE'S SO WRAPPED UP IN WHATEVER IT IS THAT SHE THINKS SHE'S DOING HERE, IT'S LIKE SHE DOESN'T EVEN SEE HIM.
DON'T YOU UNDERSTAND?! I AM SUPPOSED TO BE THE GODDESS OF PEACE, NOT YOU!
I DON'T GET IT. SHE JUST KEEPS TALKING, LIKE SHE DOESN'T EVEN SEE ZEKE. BUT IF SHE DIDN'T BRING HIM HERE, THEN WHO DID? AND WHERE THE HECK ARE ZOLA AND HERA?
I'M NOT SURE HOW I'M GOING TO GET YOU BACK TO OLYMPUS RIGHT NOW...
I DON'T UNDERSTAND WHY YOU INSIST ON HURTING ME!

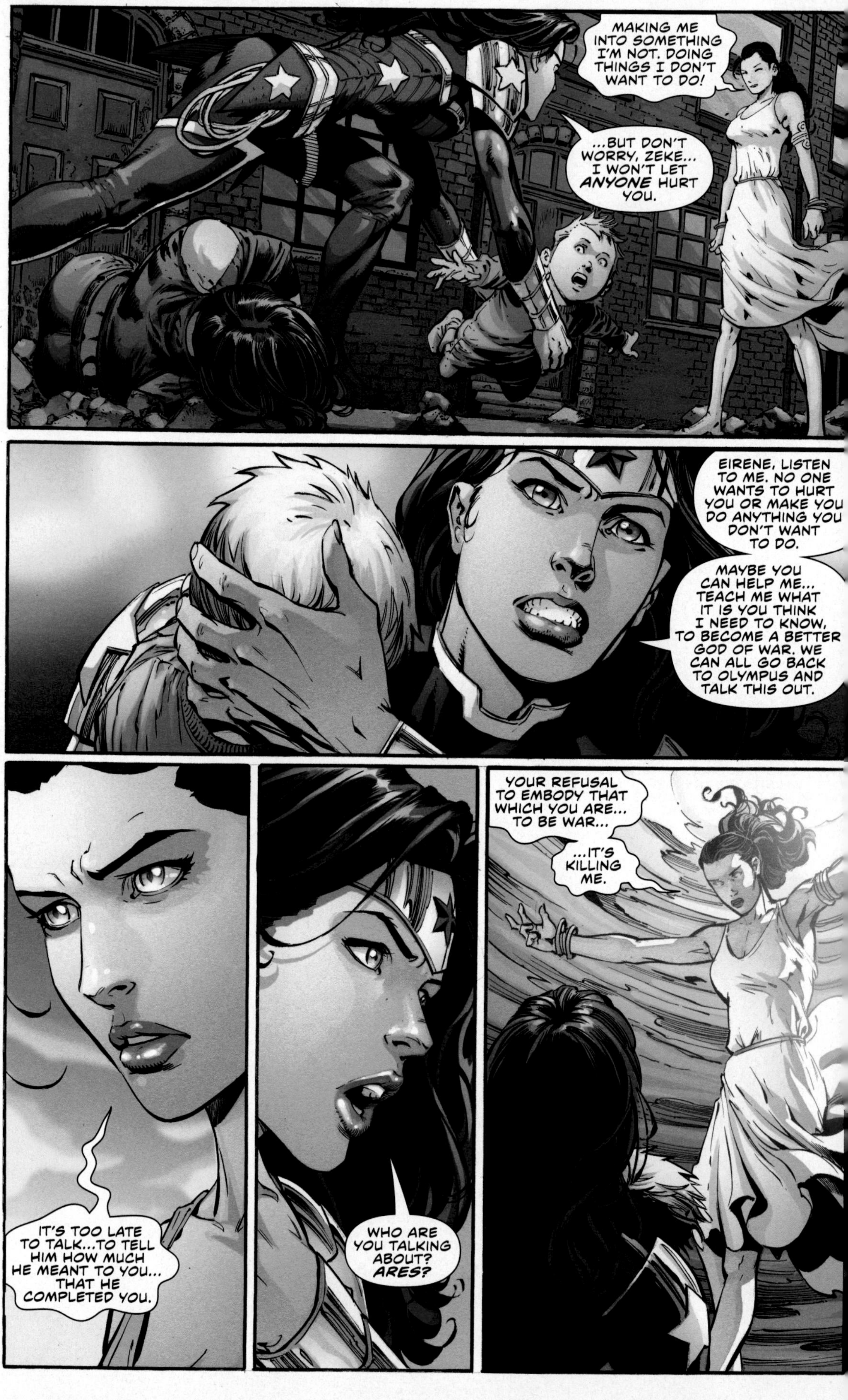
MAKING ME INTO SOMETHING I'M NOT. DOING THINGS I DON'T WANT TO DO!
...BUT DON'T WORRY, ZEKE... I WON'T LET ANYONE HURT YOU.
EIRENE, LISTEN TO ME. NO ONE WANTS TO HURT YOU OR MAKE YOU DO ANYTHING YOU DON'T WANT TO DO.
MAYBE YOU CAN HELP ME... TEACH ME WHAT IT IS YOU THINK I NEED TO KNOW, TO BECOME A BETTER GOD OF WAR. WE CAN ALL GO BACK TO OLYMPUS AND TALK THIS OUT.
IT'S TOO LATE TO TALK...TO TELL HIM HOW MUCH HE MEANT TO YOU... THAT HE COMPLETED YOU.
WHO ARE YOU TALKING ABOUT? ARES?
YOUR REFUSAL TO EMBODY THAT WHICH YOU ARE... TO BE WAR...
...IT'S KILLING ME.

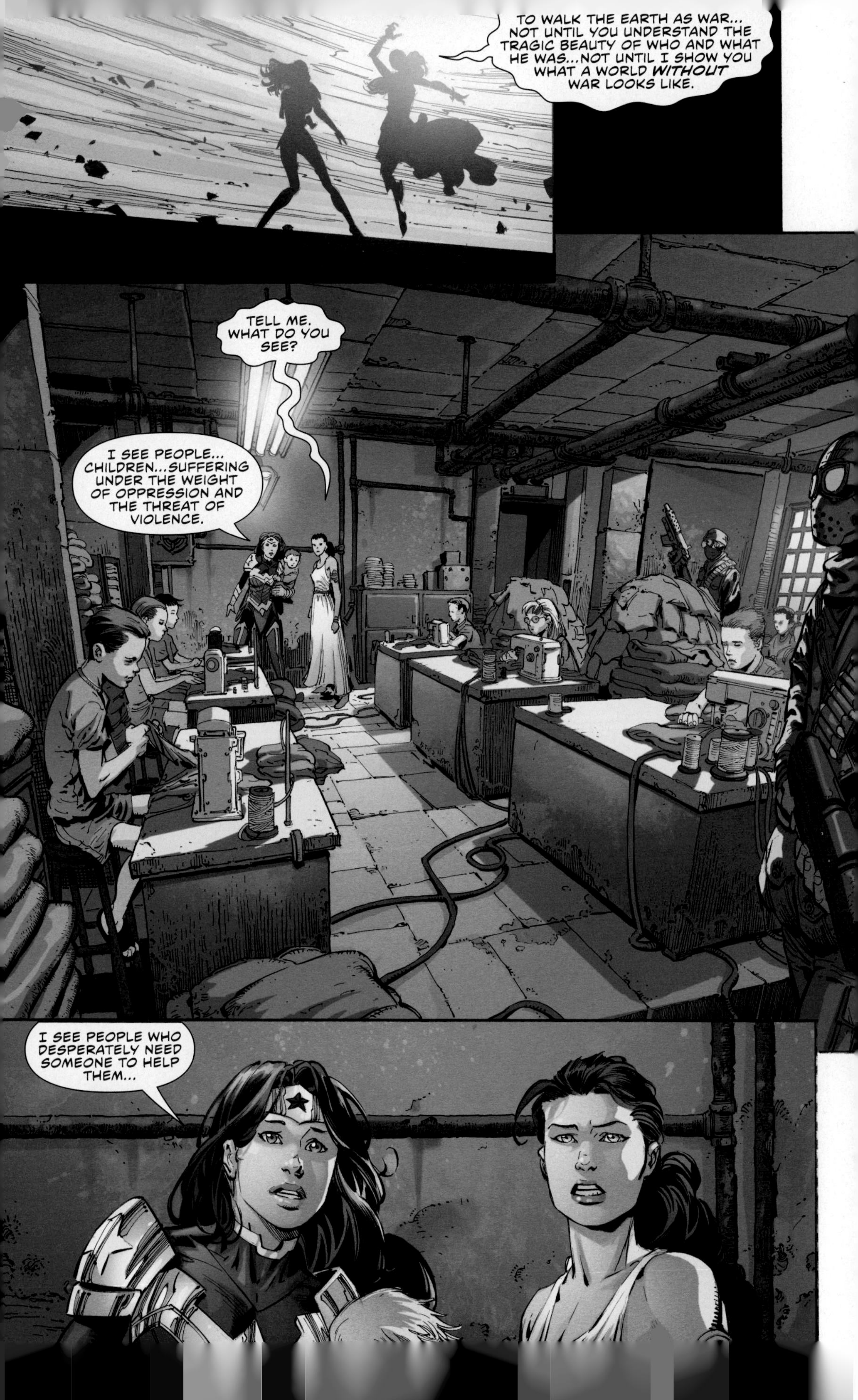
TO WALK THE EARTH AS WAR... NOT UNTIL YOU UNDERSTAND THE TRAGIC BEAUTY OF WHO AND WHAT HE WAS...NOT UNTIL I SHOW YOU WHAT A WORLD *WITHOUT* WAR LOOKS LIKE.
TELL ME. WHAT DO YOU SEE?
I SEE PEOPLE... CHILDREN...SUFFERING UNDER THE WEIGHT OF OPPRESSION AND THE THREAT OF VIOLENCE.
I SEE PEOPLE WHO DESPERATELY NEED SOMEONE TO HELP THEM...

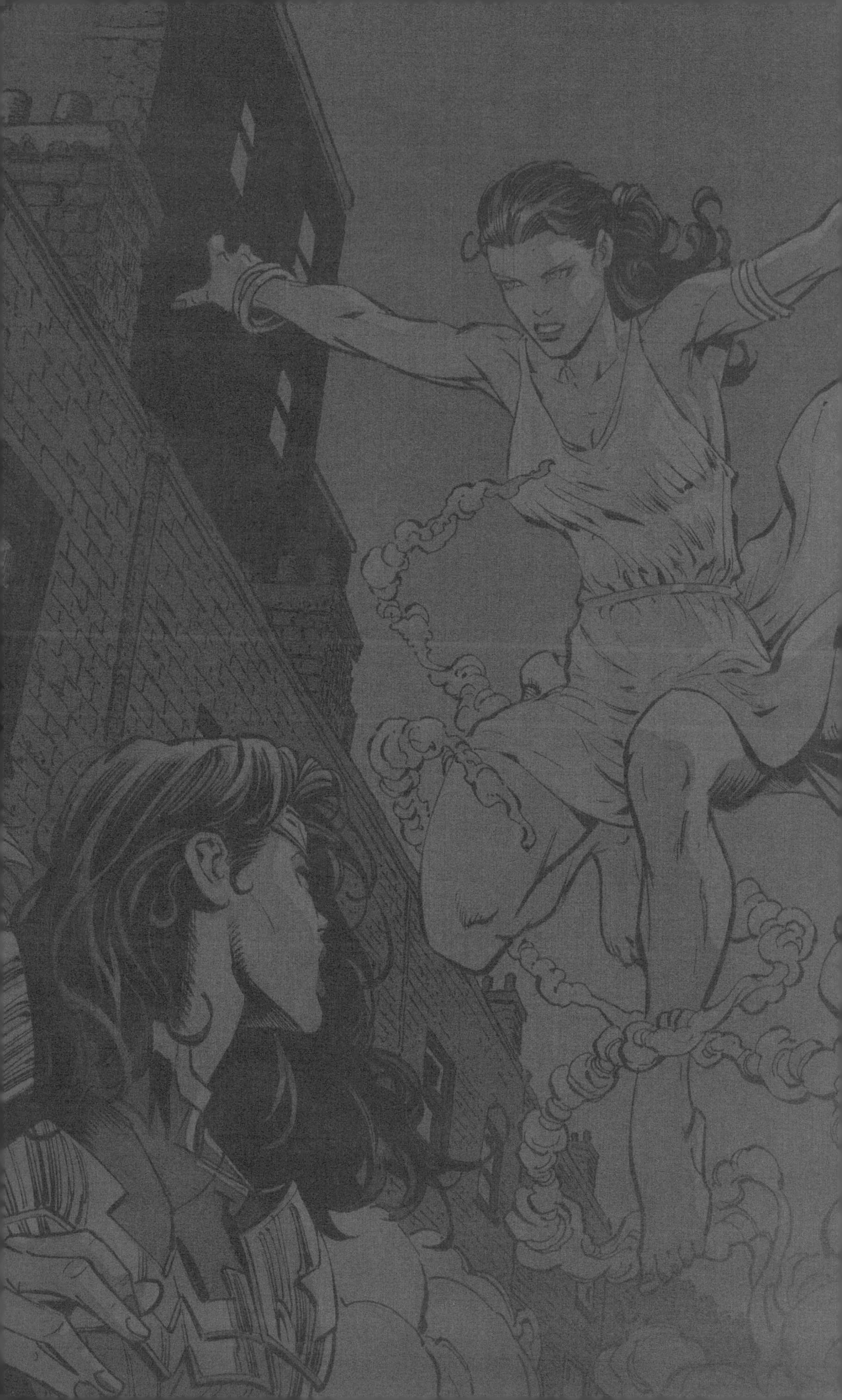

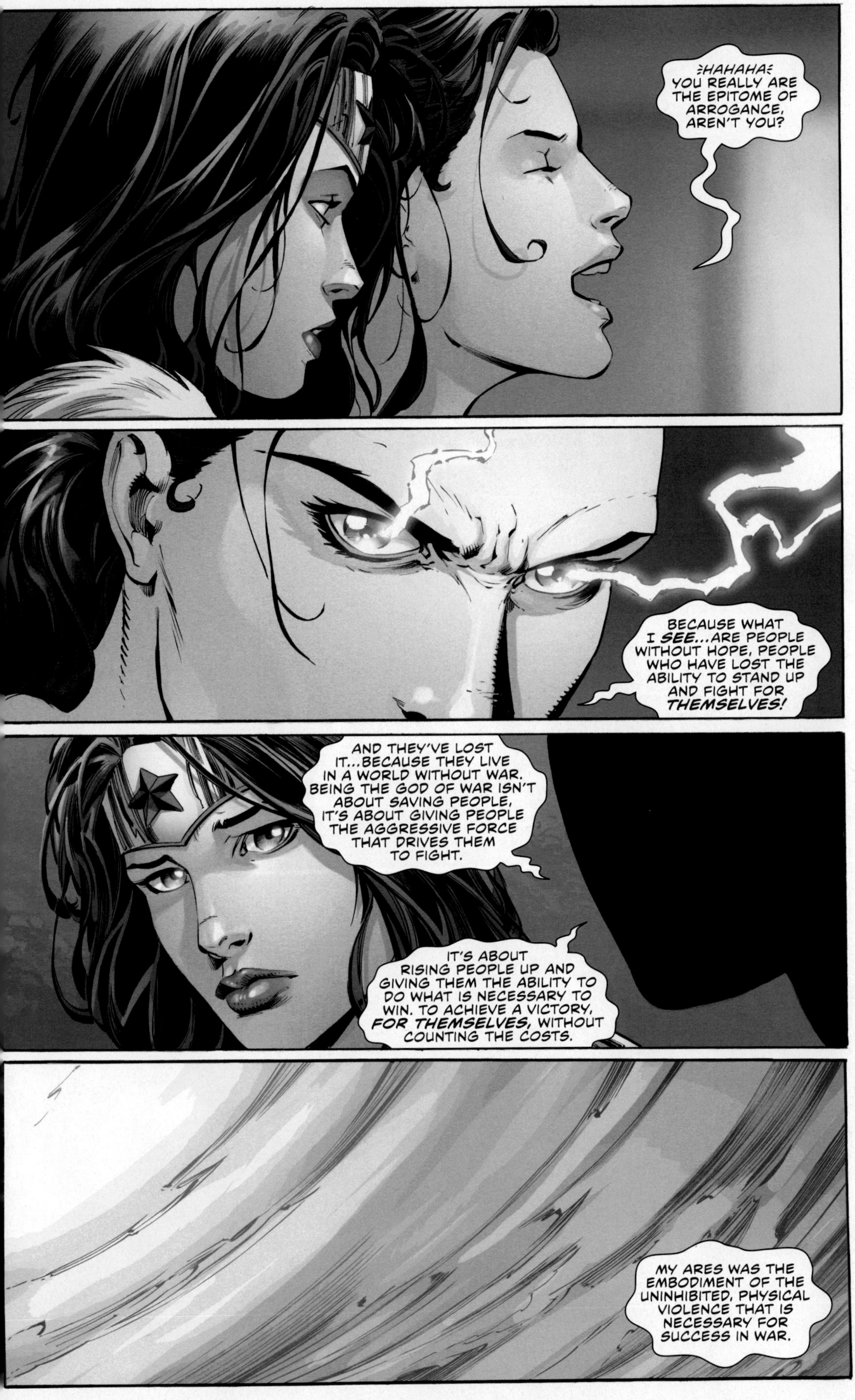
HAHAHA YOU REALLY ARE THE EPITOME OF ARROGANCE, AREN'T YOU?
BECAUSE WHAT I SEE...ARE PEOPLE WITHOUT HOPE, PEOPLE WHO HAVE LOST THE ABILITY TO STAND UP AND FIGHT FOR THEMSELVES!
AND THEY'VE LOST IT...BECAUSE THEY LIVE IN A WORLD WITHOUT WAR. BEING THE GOD OF WAR ISN'T ABOUT SAVING PEOPLE, IT'S ABOUT GIVING PEOPLE THE AGGRESSIVE FORCE THAT DRIVES THEM TO FIGHT.
IT'S ABOUT RISING PEOPLE UP AND GIVING THEM THE ABILITY TO DO WHAT IS NECESSARY TO WIN. TO ACHIEVE A VICTORY, FOR THEMSELVES, WITHOUT COUNTING THE COSTS.
MY ARES WAS THE EMBODIMENT OF THE UNINHIBITED, PHYSICAL VIOLENCE THAT IS NECESSARY FOR SUCCESS IN WAR.

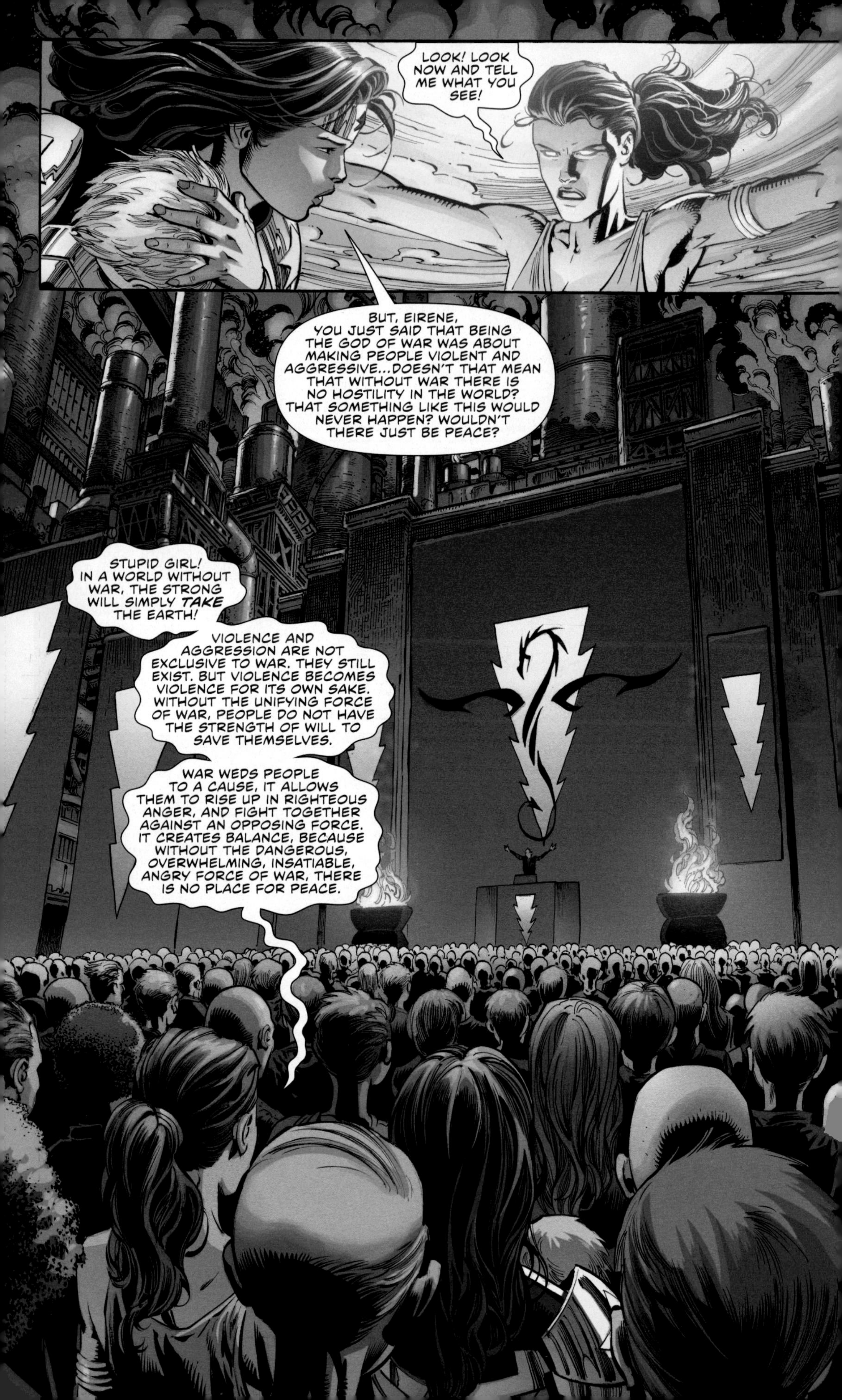
LOOK! LOOK NOW AND TELL ME WHAT YOU SEE!
BUT, EIRENE, YOU JUST SAID THAT BEING THE GOD OF WAR WAS ABOUT MAKING PEOPLE VIOLENT AND AGGRESSIVE...DOESN'T THAT MEAN THAT WITHOUT WAR THERE IS NO HOSTILITY IN THE WORLD? THAT SOMETHING LIKE THIS WOULD NEVER HAPPEN? WOULDN'T THERE JUST BE PEACE?
STUPID GIRL! IN A WORLD WITHOUT WAR, THE STRONG WILL SIMPLY *TAKE* THE EARTH!
VIOLENCE AND AGGRESSION ARE NOT EXCLUSIVE TO WAR. THEY STILL EXIST. BUT VIOLENCE BECOMES VIOLENCE FOR ITS OWN SAKE. WITHOUT THE UNIFYING FORCE OF WAR, PEOPLE DO NOT HAVE THE STRENGTH OF WILL TO SAVE THEMSELVES.
WAR WEDS PEOPLE TO A CAUSE, IT ALLOWS THEM TO RISE UP IN RIGHTEOUS ANGER, AND FIGHT TOGETHER AGAINST AN OPPOSING FORCE. IT CREATES BALANCE, BECAUSE WITHOUT THE DANGEROUS, OVERWHELMING, INSATIABLE, ANGRY FORCE OF WAR, THERE IS NO PLACE FOR PEACE.

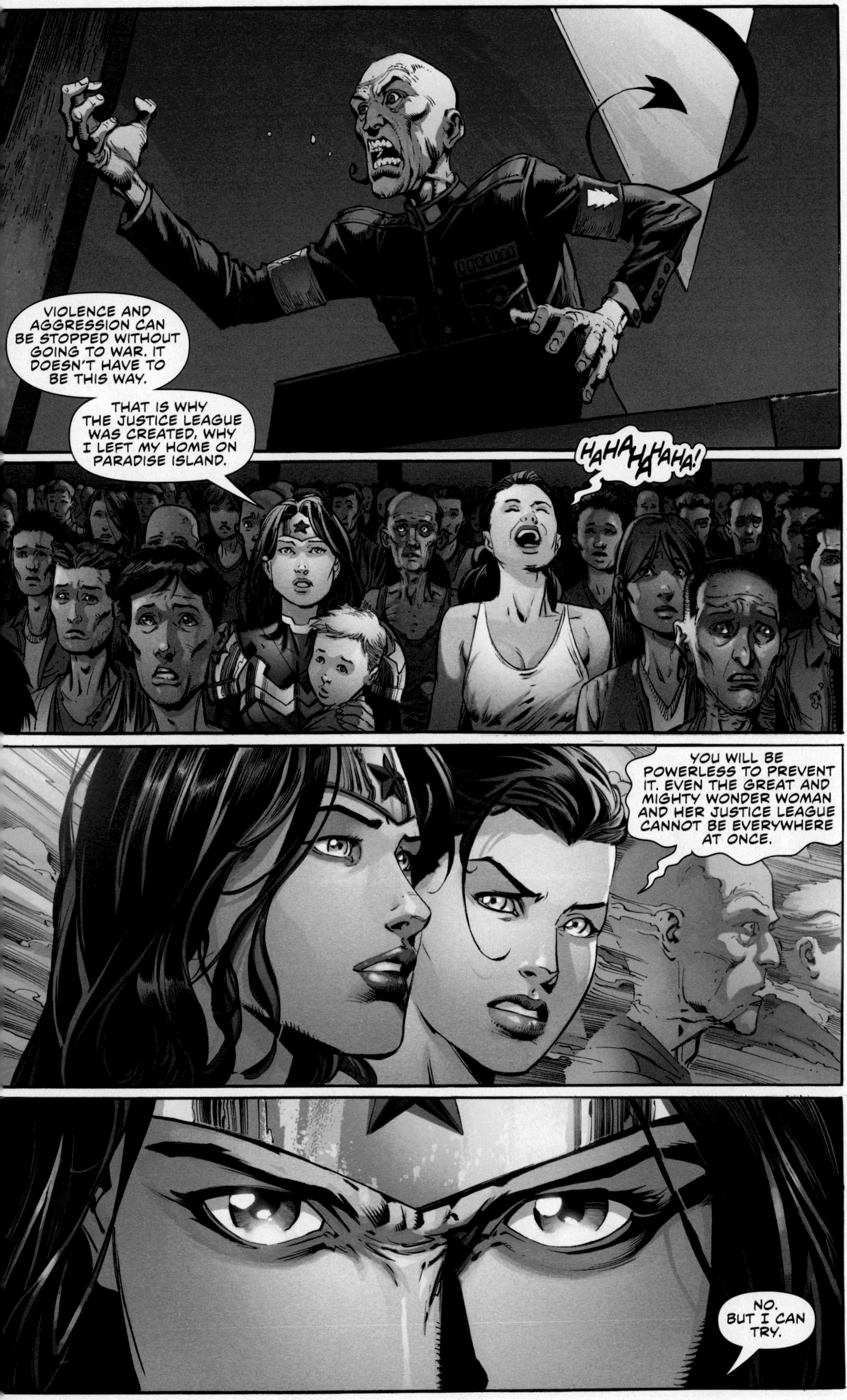

VIOLENCE AND AGGRESSION CAN BE STOPPED WITHOUT GOING TO WAR. IT DOESN'T HAVE TO BE THIS WAY.
THAT IS WHY THE JUSTICE LEAGUE WAS CREATED, WHY I LEFT MY HOME ON PARADISE ISLAND.
HAHAHAHAHA!
YOU WILL BE POWERLESS TO PREVENT IT. EVEN THE GREAT AND MIGHTY WONDER WOMAN AND HER JUSTICE LEAGUE CANNOT BE EVERYWHERE AT ONCE.
NO. BUT I CAN TRY.

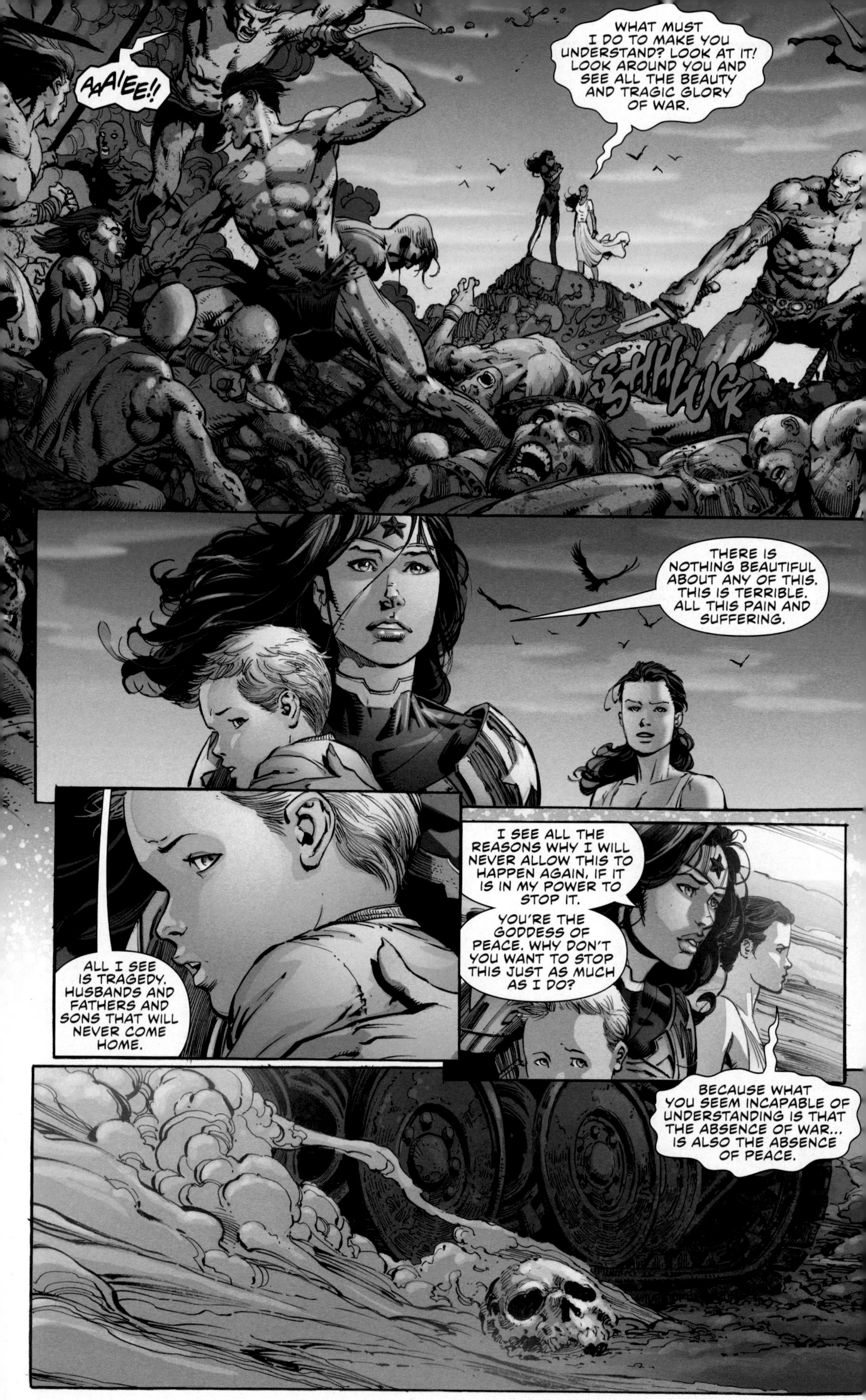
AAAIEE!!
WHAT MUST I DO TO MAKE YOU UNDERSTAND? LOOK AT IT! LOOK AROUND YOU AND SEE ALL THE BEAUTY AND TRAGIC GLORY OF WAR.
SSHHLUGK
THERE IS NOTHING BEAUTIFUL ABOUT ANY OF THIS. THIS IS TERRIBLE. ALL THIS PAIN AND SUFFERING.
ALL I SEE IS TRAGEDY. HUSBANDS AND FATHERS AND SONS THAT WILL NEVER COME HOME.
I SEE ALL THE REASONS WHY I WILL NEVER ALLOW THIS TO HAPPEN AGAIN, IF IT IS IN MY POWER TO STOP IT.
YOU'RE THE GODDESS OF PEACE. WHY DON'T YOU WANT TO STOP THIS JUST AS MUCH AS I DO?
BECAUSE WHAT YOU SEEM INCAPABLE OF UNDERSTANDING IS THAT THE ABSENCE OF WAR... IS ALSO THE ABSENCE OF PEACE.

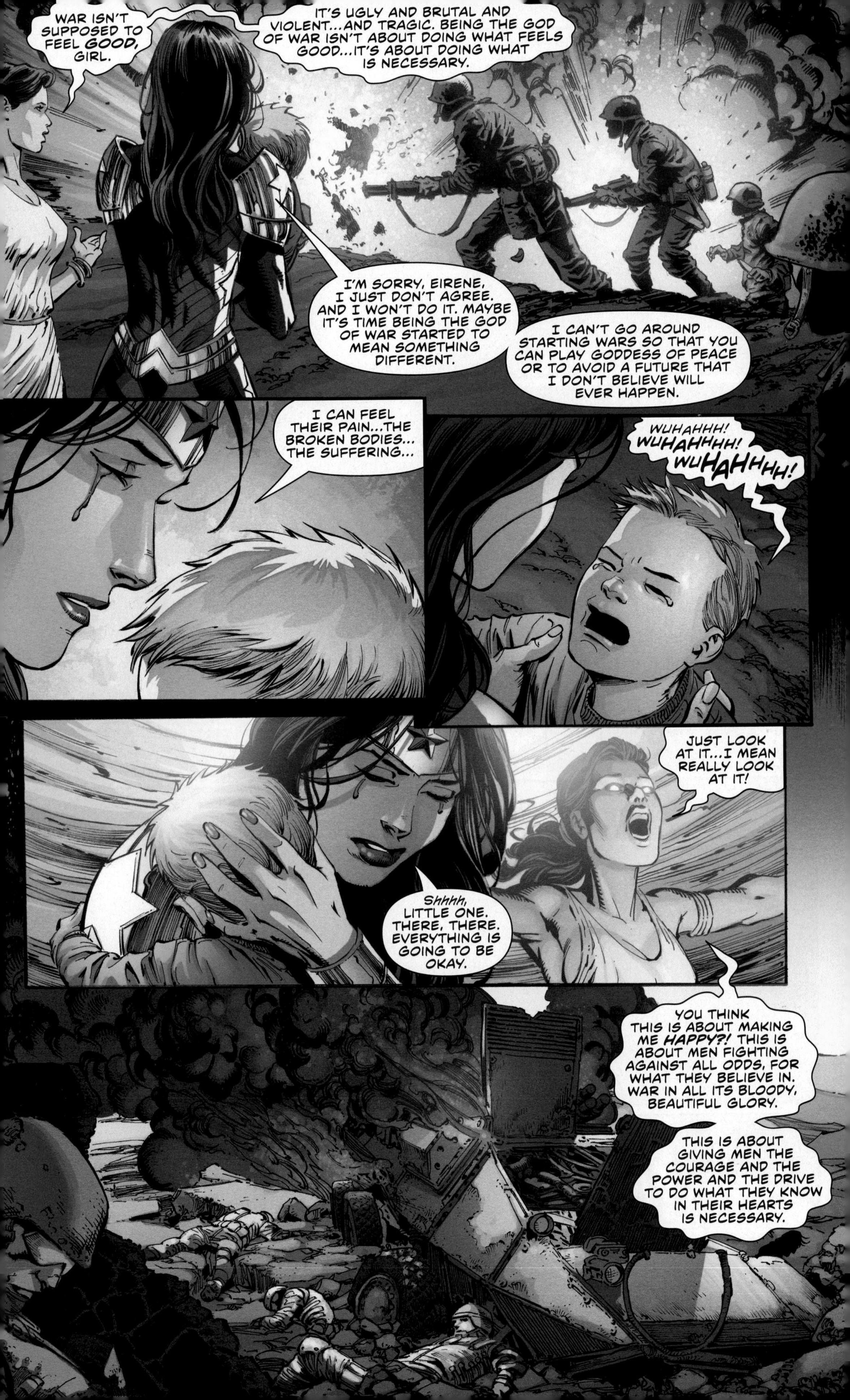
WAR ISN'T SUPPOSED TO FEEL GOOD, GIRL.
IT'S UGLY AND BRUTAL AND VIOLENT...AND TRAGIC. BEING THE GOD OF WAR ISN'T ABOUT DOING WHAT FEELS GOOD...IT'S ABOUT DOING WHAT IS NECESSARY.
I'M SORRY, EIRENE, I JUST DON'T AGREE. AND I WON'T DO IT. MAYBE IT'S TIME BEING THE GOD OF WAR STARTED TO MEAN SOMETHING DIFFERENT.
I CAN'T GO AROUND STARTING WARS SO THAT YOU CAN PLAY GODDESS OF PEACE OR TO AVOID A FUTURE THAT I DON'T BELIEVE WILL EVER HAPPEN.
I CAN FEEL THEIR PAIN...THE BROKEN BODIES... THE SUFFERING...
WUHAHHH! WUHAHHHH! WUHAHHHH!
JUST LOOK AT IT...I MEAN REALLY LOOK AT IT!
Shhhh, LITTLE ONE. THERE, THERE. EVERYTHING IS GOING TO BE OKAY.
YOU THINK THIS IS ABOUT MAKING ME HAPPY?! THIS IS ABOUT MEN FIGHTING AGAINST ALL ODDS, FOR WHAT THEY BELIEVE IN. WAR IN ALL ITS BLOODY, BEAUTIFUL GLORY.
THIS IS ABOUT GIVING MEN THE COURAGE AND THE POWER AND THE DRIVE TO DO WHAT THEY KNOW IN THEIR HEARTS IS NECESSARY.

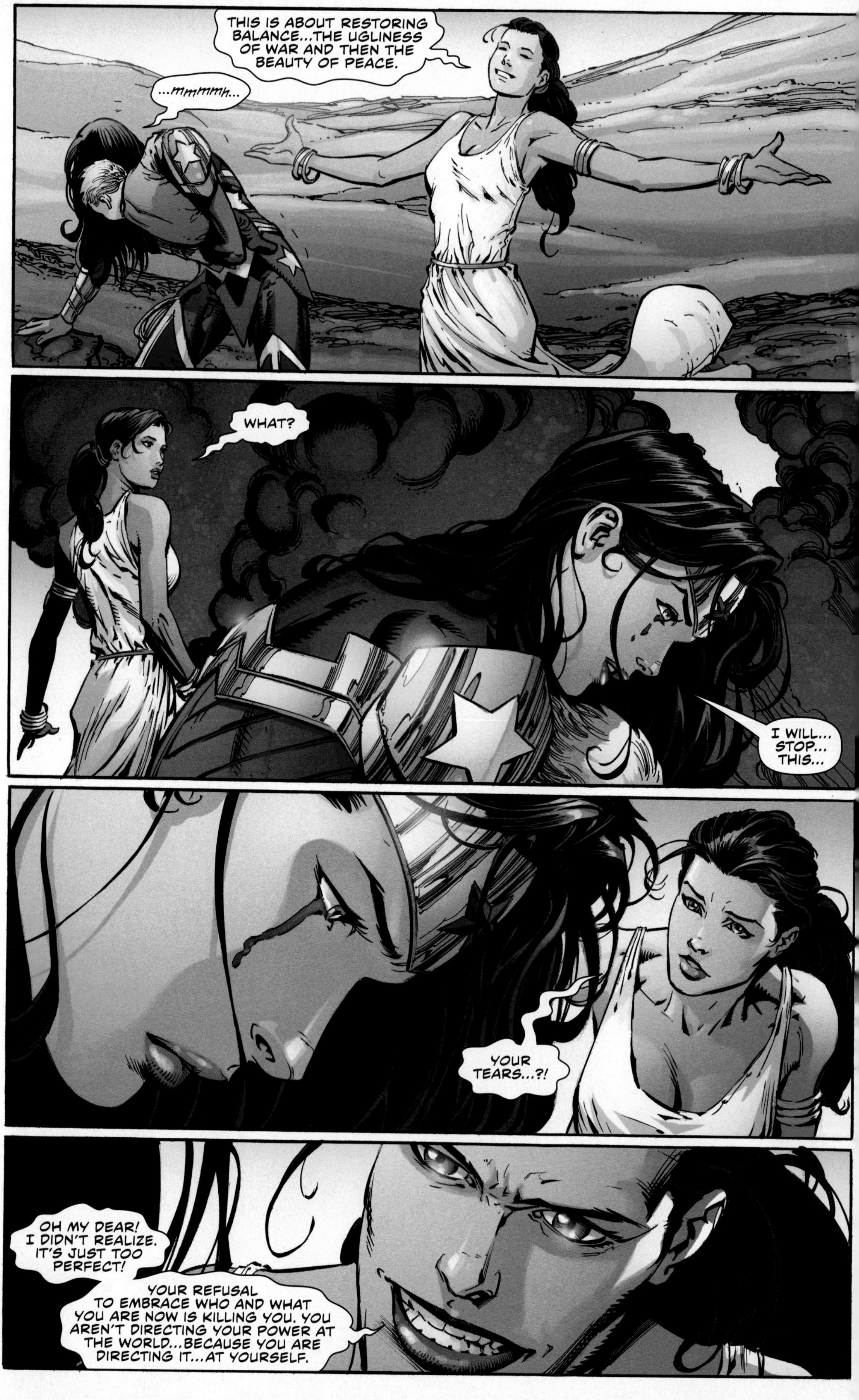

THIS IS ABOUT RESTORING BALANCE...THE UGLINESS OF WAR AND THEN THE BEAUTY OF PEACE.
...mmmmmh...
WHAT?
I WILL... STOP... THIS...
YOUR TEARS...?!
OH MY DEAR! I DIDN'T REALIZE. IT'S JUST TOO PERFECT!
YOUR REFUSAL TO EMBRACE WHO AND WHAT YOU ARE NOW IS KILLING YOU. YOU AREN'T DIRECTING YOUR POWER AT THE WORLD...BECAUSE YOU ARE DIRECTING IT...AT YOURSELF.

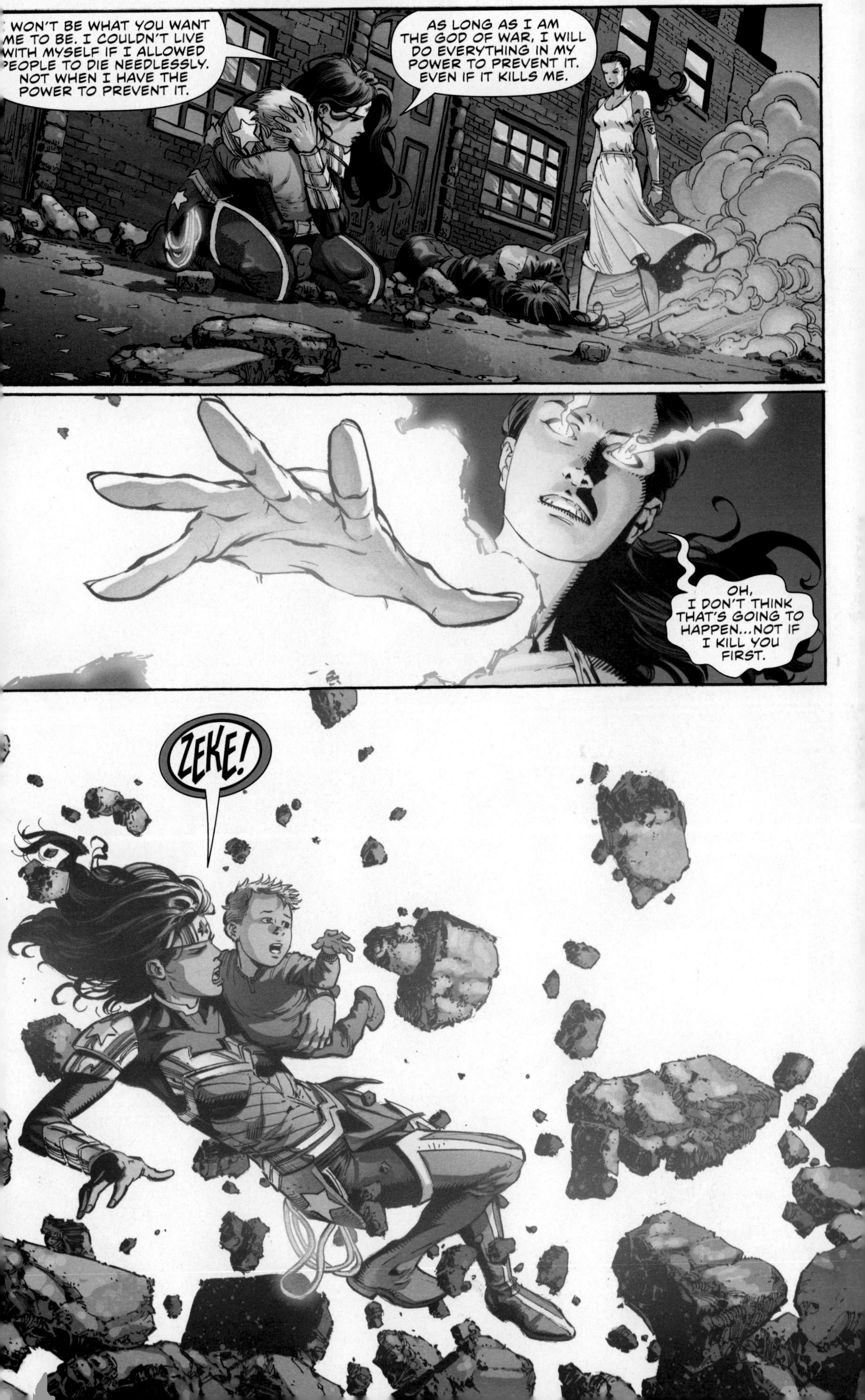
I WON'T BE WHAT YOU WANT ME TO BE. I COULDN'T LIVE WITH MYSELF IF I ALLOWED PEOPLE TO DIE NEEDLESSLY. NOT WHEN I HAVE THE POWER TO PREVENT IT.
AS LONG AS I AM THE GOD OF WAR, I WILL DO EVERYTHING IN MY POWER TO PREVENT IT. EVEN IF IT KILLS ME.
OH, I DON'T THINK THAT'S GOING TO HAPPEN...NOT IF I KILL YOU FIRST.
ZEKE!

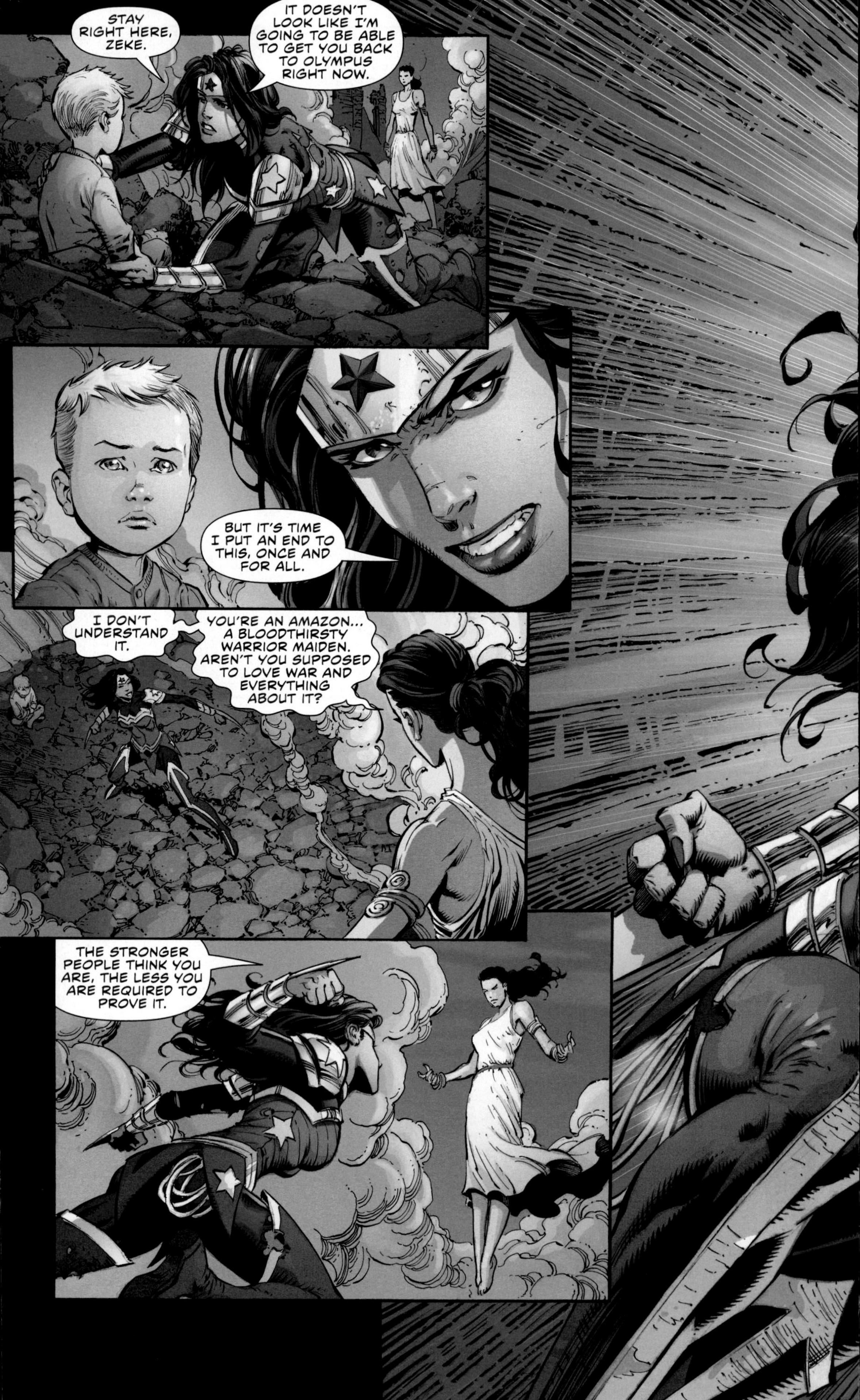
STAY RIGHT HERE, ZEKE.
IT DOESN'T LOOK LIKE I'M GOING TO BE ABLE TO GET YOU BACK TO OLYMPUS RIGHT NOW.
BUT IT'S TIME I PUT AN END TO THIS, ONCE AND FOR ALL.
I DON'T UNDERSTAND IT.
YOU'RE AN AMAZON... A BLOODTHIRSTY WARRIOR MAIDEN. AREN'T YOU SUPPOSED TO LOVE WAR AND EVERYTHING ABOUT IT?
THE STRONGER PEOPLE THINK YOU ARE, THE LESS YOU ARE REQUIRED TO PROVE IT.

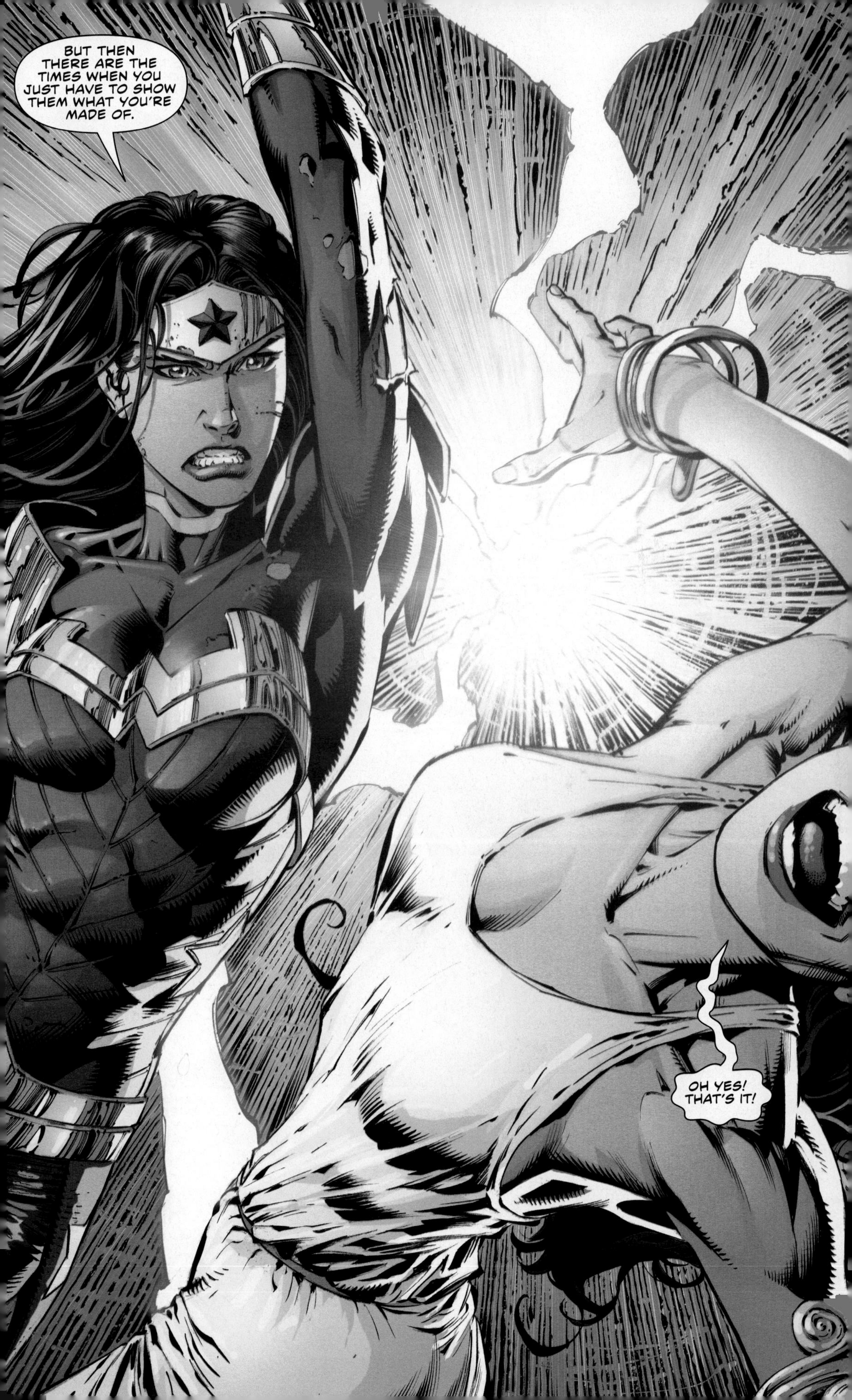
BUT THEN THERE ARE THE TIMES WHEN YOU JUST HAVE TO SHOW THEM WHAT YOU'RE MADE OF.
OH YES! THAT'S IT!

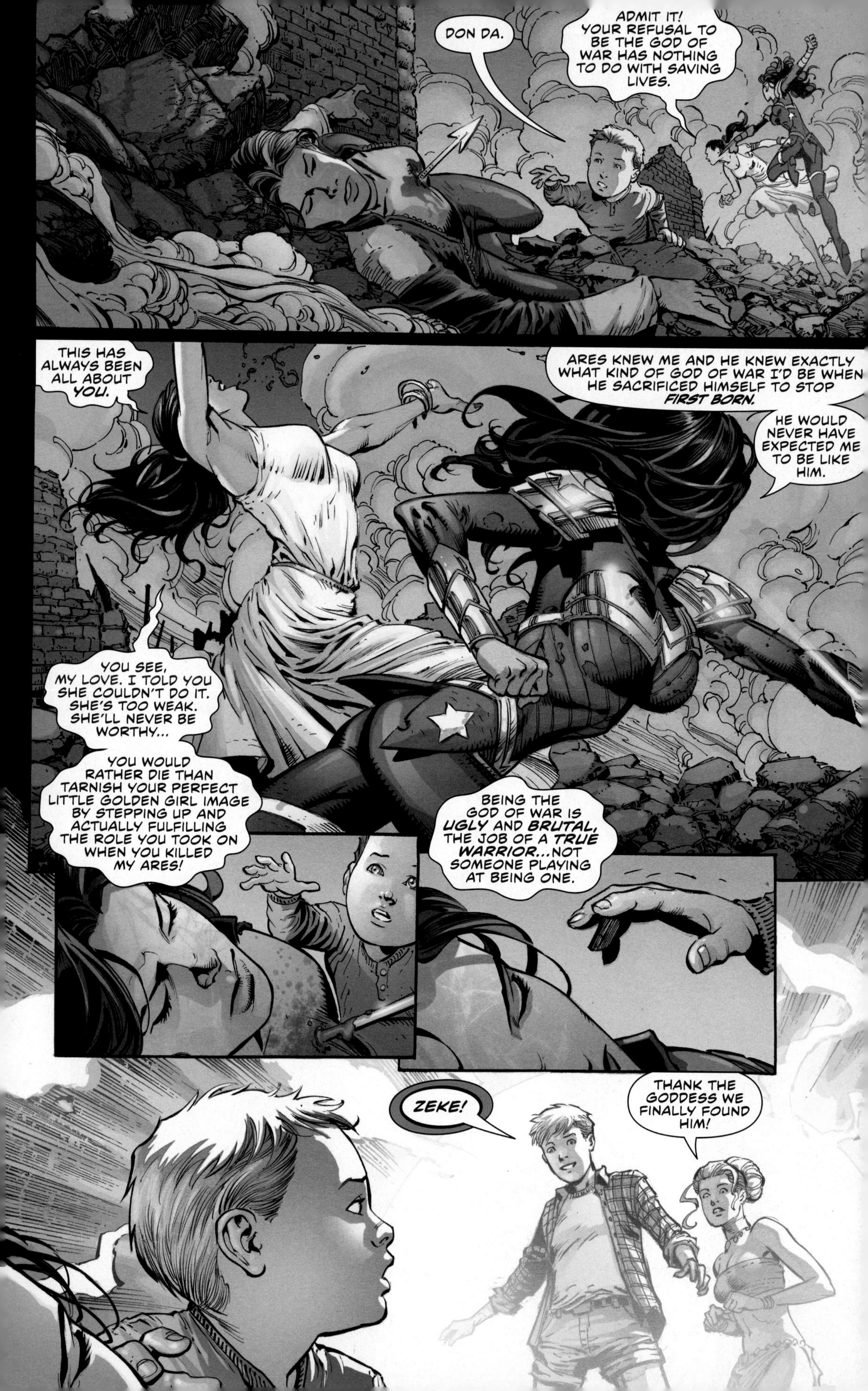
DON DA.
ADMIT IT! YOUR REFUSAL TO BE THE GOD OF WAR HAS NOTHING TO DO WITH SAVING LIVES.
THIS HAS ALWAYS BEEN ALL ABOUT *YOU.*
ARES KNEW ME AND HE KNEW EXACTLY WHAT KIND OF GOD OF WAR I'D BE WHEN HE SACRIFICED HIMSELF TO STOP *FIRST BORN.*
HE WOULD NEVER HAVE EXPECTED ME TO BE LIKE HIM.
YOU SEE, MY LOVE. I TOLD YOU SHE COULDN'T DO IT. SHE'S TOO WEAK. SHE'LL NEVER BE WORTHY...
YOU WOULD RATHER DIE THAN TARNISH YOUR PERFECT LITTLE GOLDEN GIRL IMAGE BY STEPPING UP AND ACTUALLY FULFILLING THE ROLE YOU TOOK ON WHEN YOU KILLED MY ARES!
BEING THE GOD OF WAR IS *UGLY* AND *BRUTAL,* THE JOB OF A *TRUE WARRIOR*...NOT SOMEONE PLAYING AT BEING ONE.
ZEKE!
THANK THE GODDESS WE FINALLY FOUND HIM!

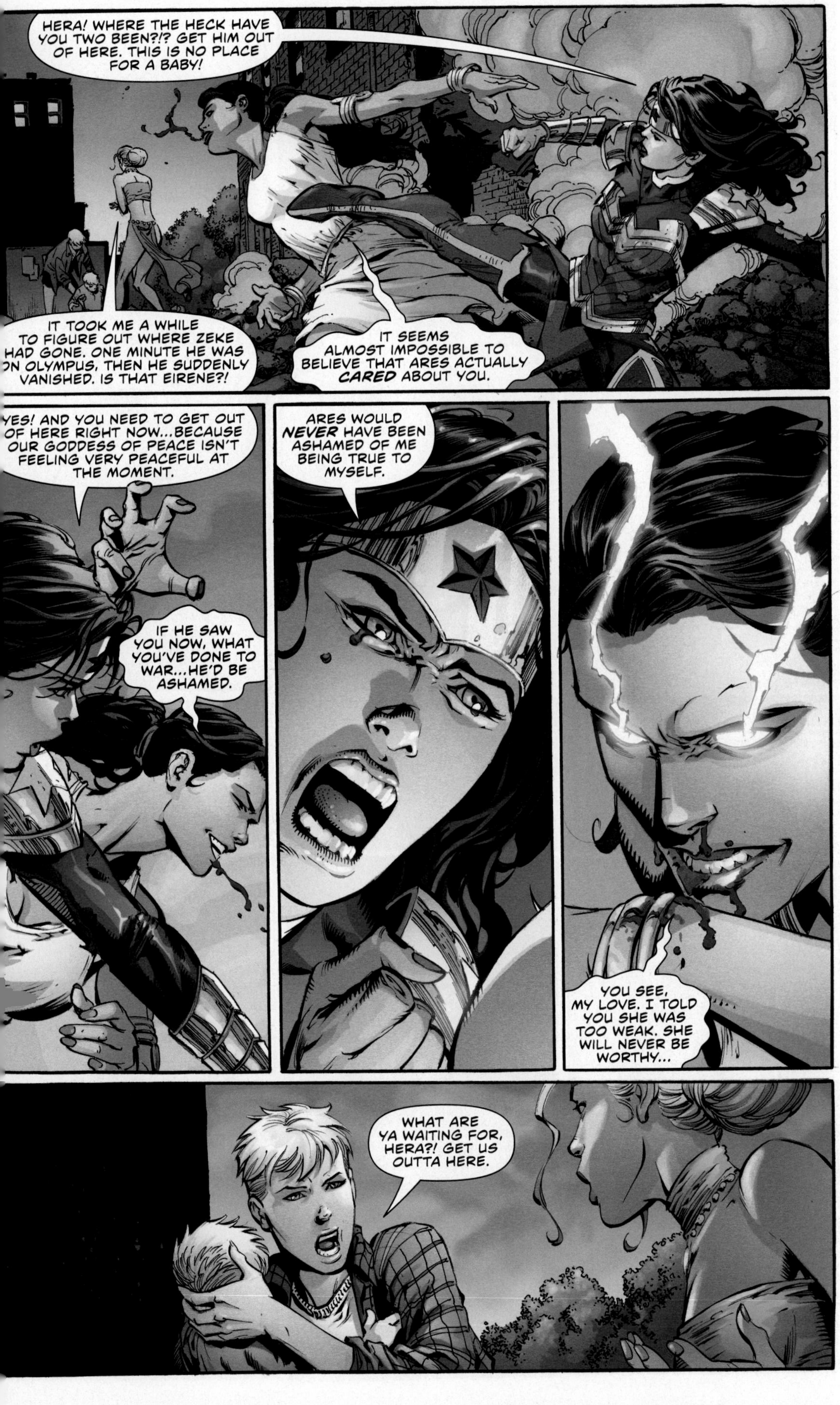
HERA! WHERE THE HECK HAVE YOU TWO BEEN?!? GET HIM OUT OF HERE. THIS IS NO PLACE FOR A BABY!
IT TOOK ME A WHILE TO FIGURE OUT WHERE ZEKE HAD GONE. ONE MINUTE HE WAS ON OLYMPUS, THEN HE SUDDENLY VANISHED. IS THAT EIRENE?!
IT SEEMS ALMOST IMPOSSIBLE TO BELIEVE THAT ARES ACTUALLY CARED ABOUT YOU.
YES! AND YOU NEED TO GET OUT OF HERE RIGHT NOW...BECAUSE OUR GODDESS OF PEACE ISN'T FEELING VERY PEACEFUL AT THE MOMENT.
IF HE SAW YOU NOW, WHAT YOU'VE DONE TO WAR...HE'D BE ASHAMED.
ARES WOULD NEVER HAVE BEEN ASHAMED OF ME BEING TRUE TO MYSELF.
YOU SEE, MY LOVE. I TOLD YOU SHE WAS TOO WEAK. SHE WILL NEVER BE WORTHY...
WHAT ARE YA WAITING FOR, HERA?! GET US OUTTA HERE.

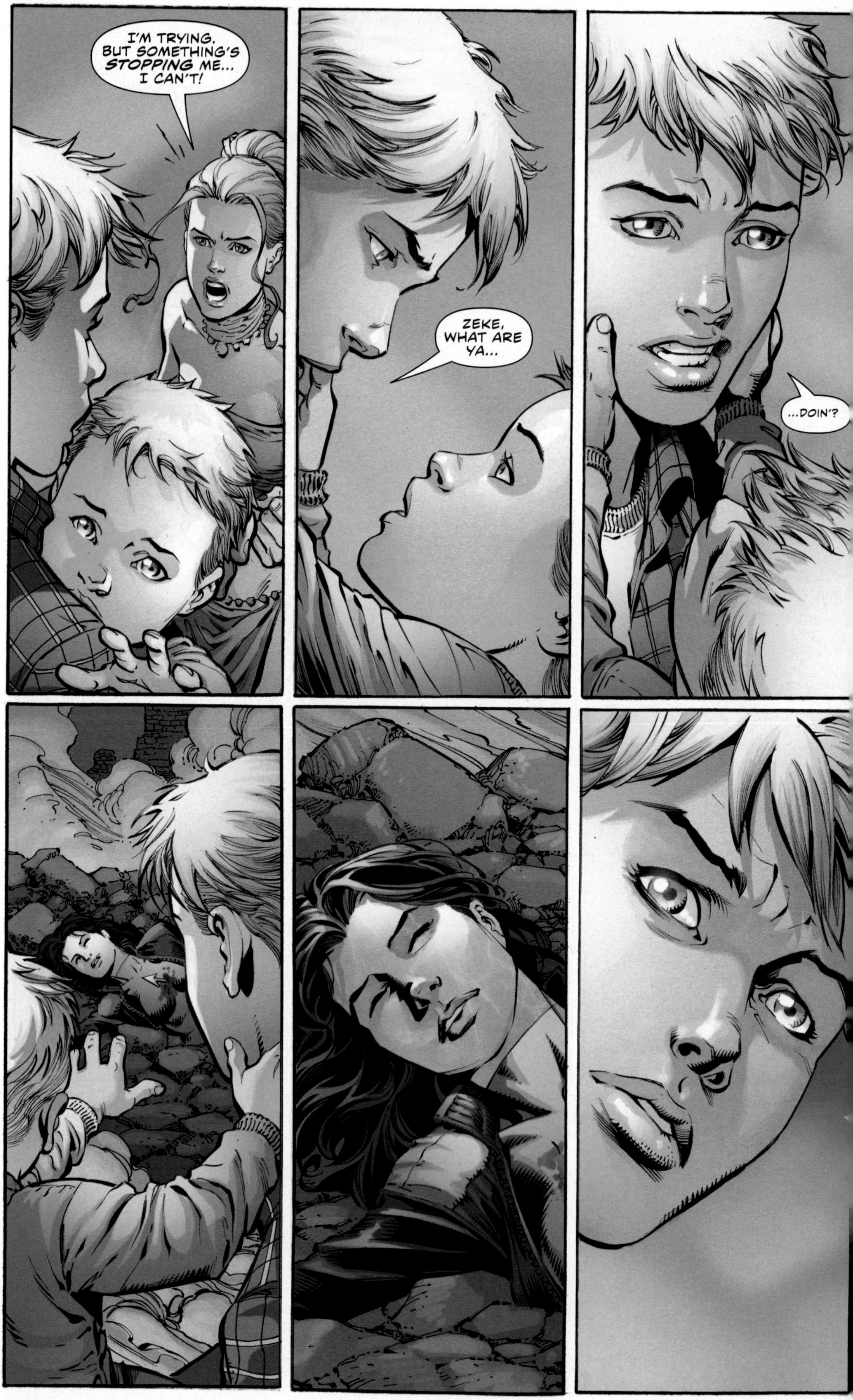
I'M TRYING. BUT SOMETHING'S STOPPING ME... I CAN'T!
ZEKE, WHAT ARE YA...
...DOIN'?

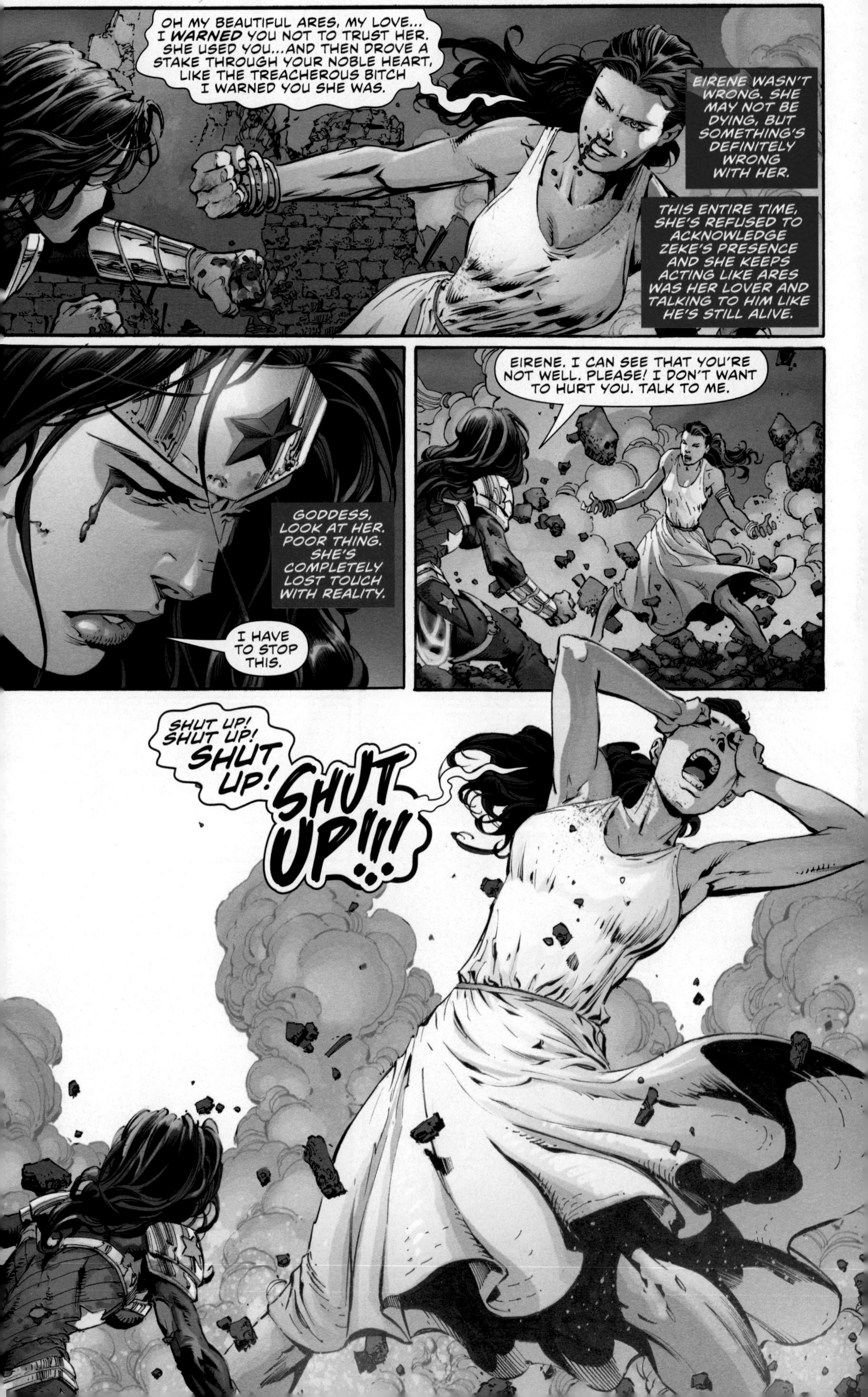
OH MY BEAUTIFUL ARES, MY LOVE... I WARNED YOU NOT TO TRUST HER. SHE USED YOU...AND THEN DROVE A STAKE THROUGH YOUR NOBLE HEART, LIKE THE TREACHEROUS BITCH I WARNED YOU SHE WAS.
EIRENE WASN'T WRONG. SHE MAY NOT BE DYING, BUT SOMETHING'S DEFINITELY WRONG WITH HER.
THIS ENTIRE TIME, SHE'S REFUSED TO ACKNOWLEDGE ZEKE'S PRESENCE AND SHE KEEPS ACTING LIKE ARES WAS HER LOVER AND TALKING TO HIM LIKE HE'S STILL ALIVE.
GODDESS, LOOK AT HER. POOR THING. SHE'S COMPLETELY LOST TOUCH WITH REALITY.
I HAVE TO STOP THIS.
EIRENE. I CAN SEE THAT YOU'RE NOT WELL. PLEASE! I DON'T WANT TO HURT YOU. TALK TO ME.
SHUT UP! SHUT UP! SHUT UP! SHUT UP!!!

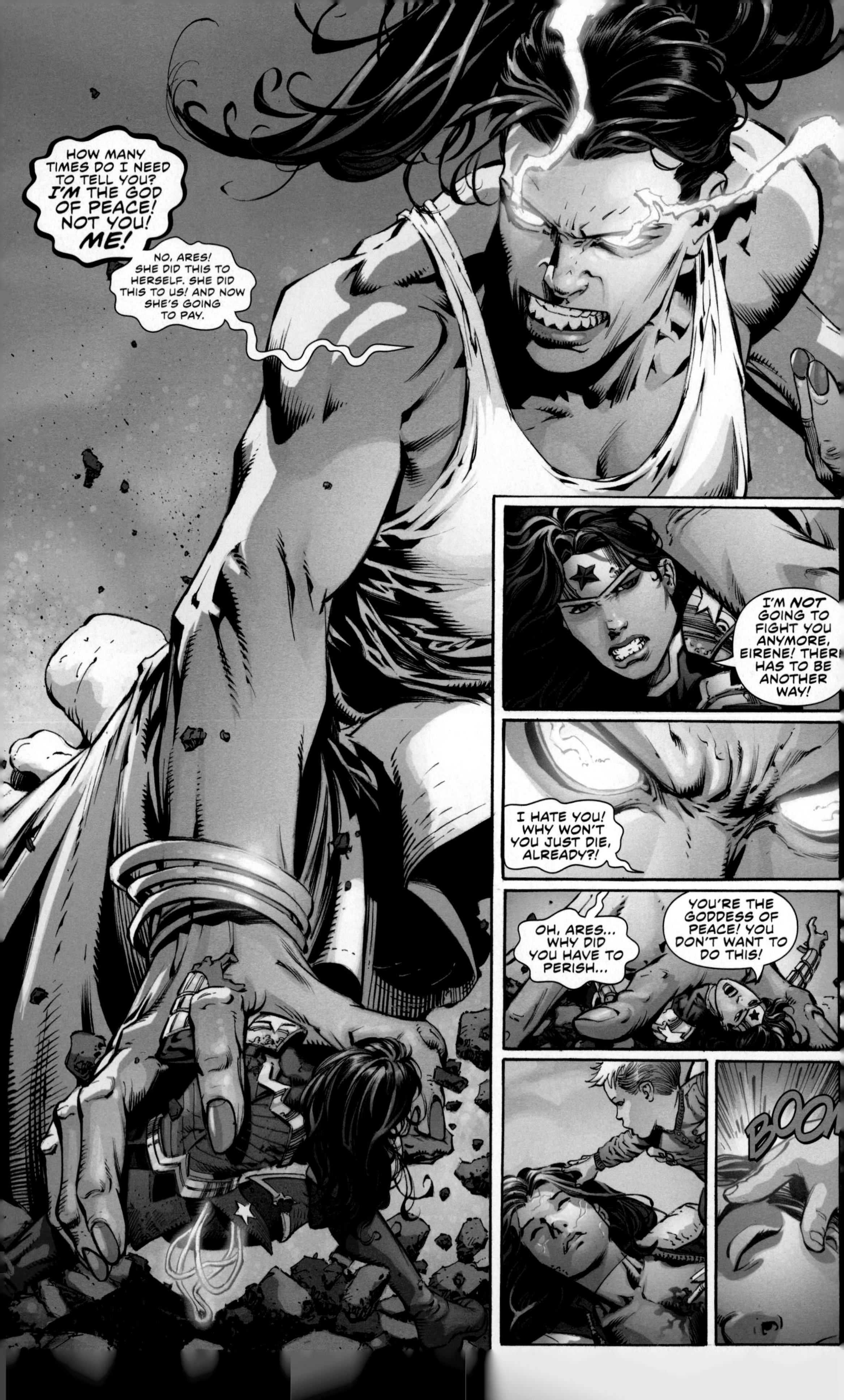

HOW MANY TIMES DO I NEED TO TELL YOU? *I'M* THE GOD OF PEACE! NOT YOU! **ME!**
NO, ARES! SHE DID THIS TO HERSELF. SHE DID THIS TO US! AND NOW SHE'S GOING TO PAY.
I'M **NOT** GOING TO FIGHT YOU ANYMORE, EIRENE! THER HAS TO BE ANOTHER WAY!
I HATE YOU! WHY WON'T YOU JUST DIE, ALREADY?!
YOU'RE THE GODDESS OF PEACE! YOU DON'T WANT TO DO THIS!
OH, ARES... WHY DID YOU HAVE TO PERISH...
BOO

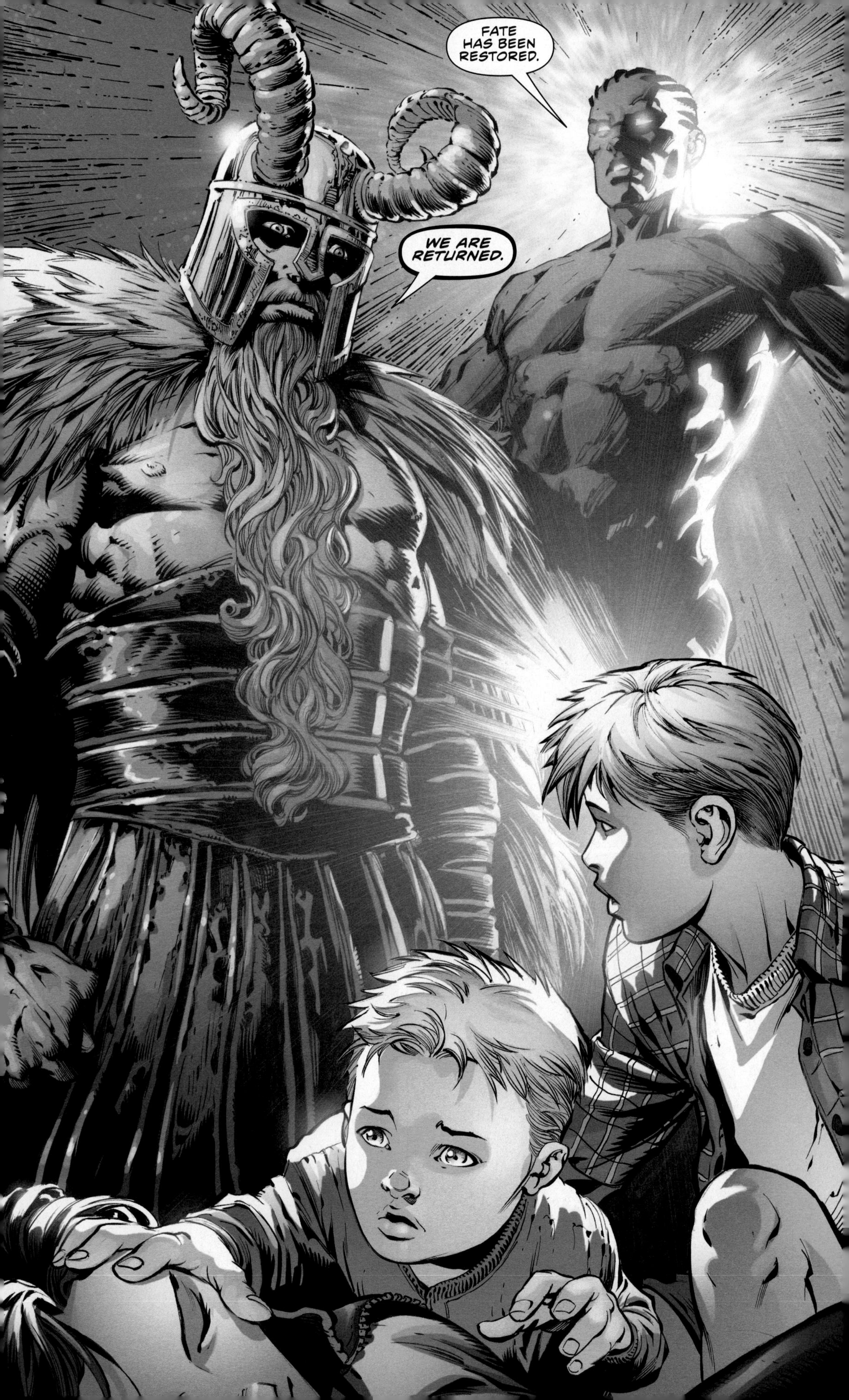
FATE HAS BEEN RESTORED.
WE ARE RETURNED.

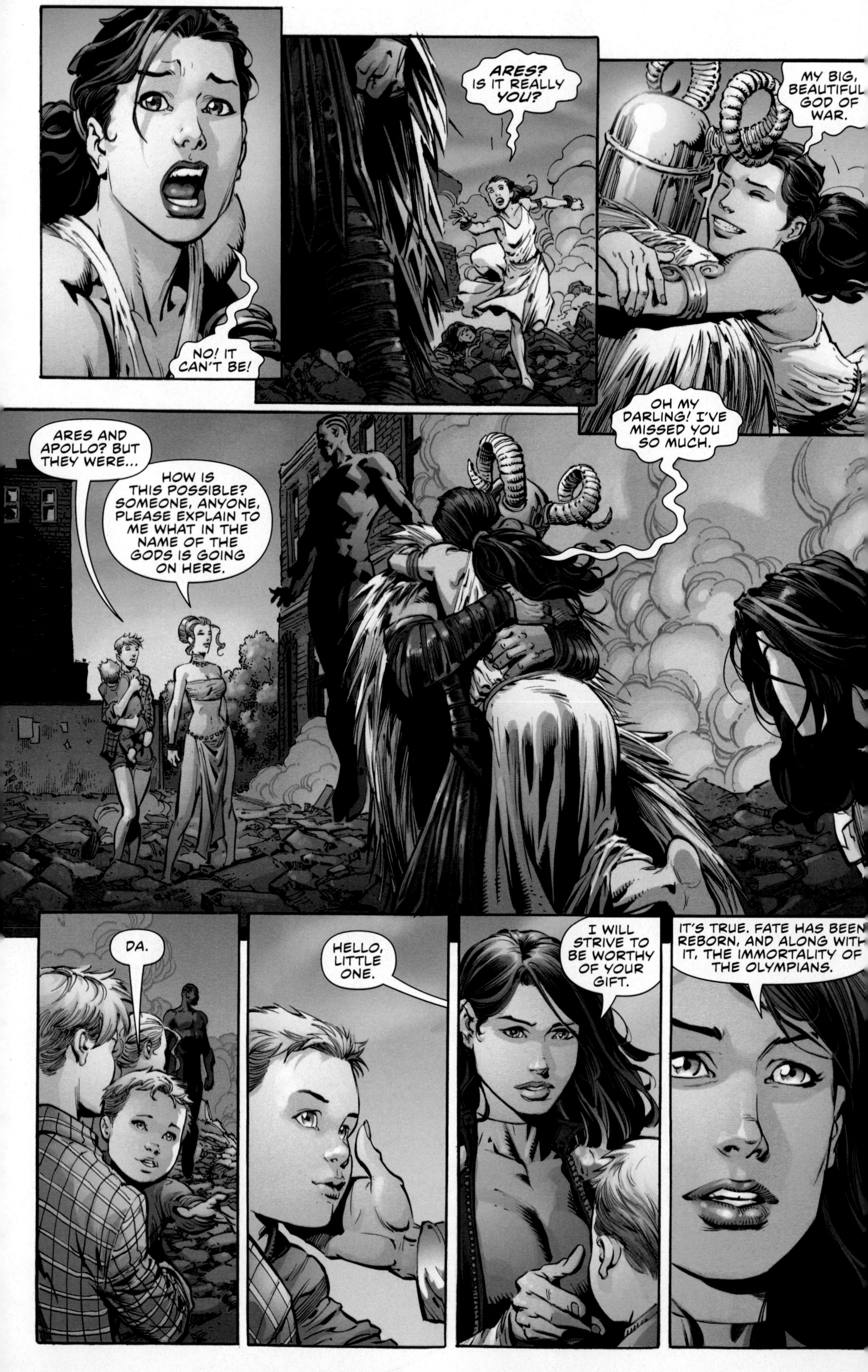
NO! IT CAN'T BE!
ARES? IS IT REALLY YOU?
MY BIG, BEAUTIFUL GOD OF WAR.
OH MY DARLING! I'VE MISSED YOU SO MUCH.
ARES AND APOLLO? BUT THEY WERE...
HOW IS THIS POSSIBLE? SOMEONE, ANYONE, PLEASE EXPLAIN TO ME WHAT IN THE NAME OF THE GODS IS GOING ON HERE.
DA.
HELLO, LITTLE ONE.
I WILL STRIVE TO BE WORTHY OF YOUR GIFT.
IT'S TRUE. FATE HAS BEEN REBORN, AND ALONG WITH IT, THE IMMORTALITY OF THE OLYMPIANS.

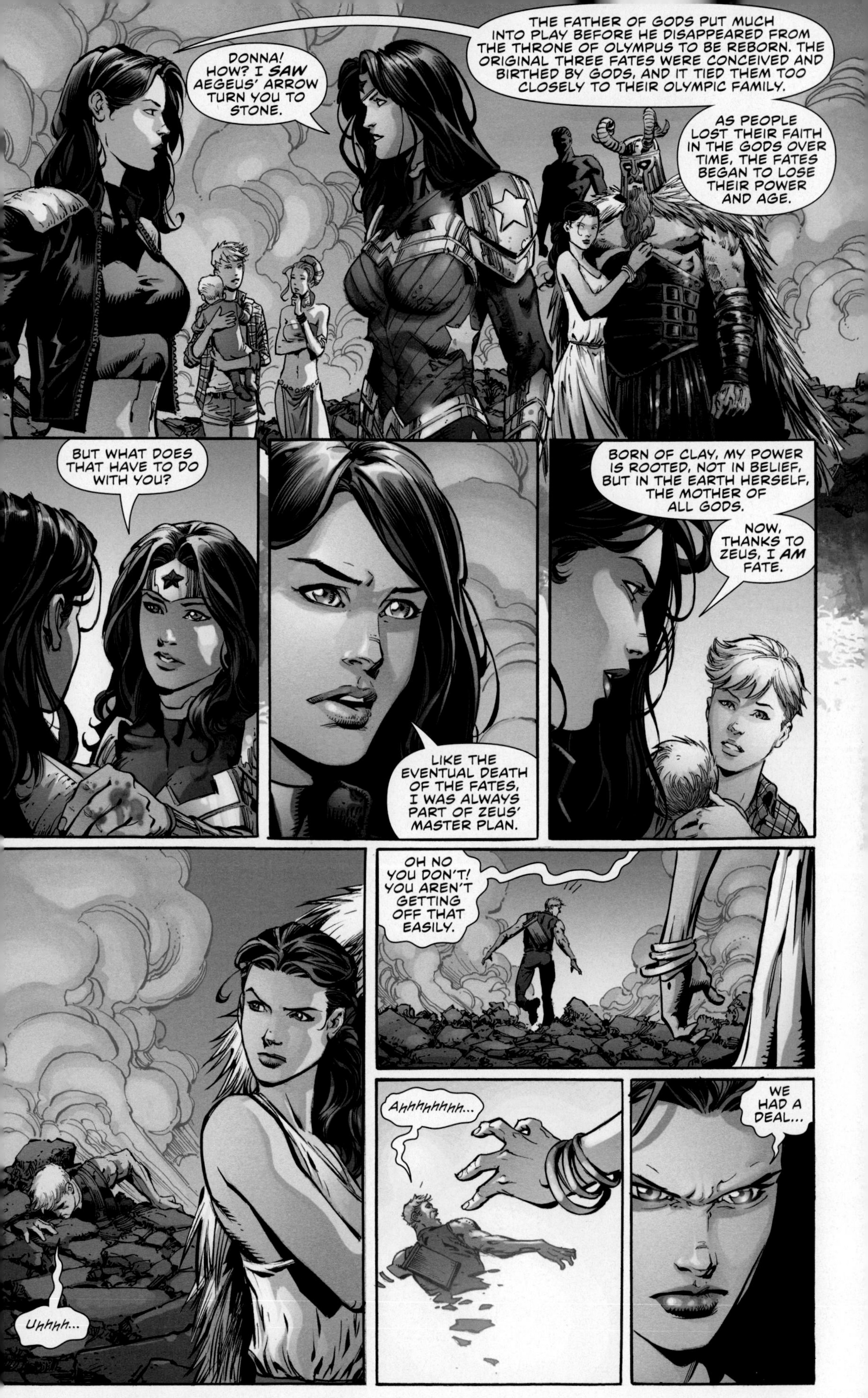
DONNA! HOW? I SAW AEGEUS' ARROW TURN YOU TO STONE.
THE FATHER OF GODS PUT MUCH INTO PLAY BEFORE HE DISAPPEARED FROM THE THRONE OF OLYMPUS TO BE REBORN. THE ORIGINAL THREE FATES WERE CONCEIVED AND BIRTHED BY GODS, AND IT TIED THEM TOO CLOSELY TO THEIR OLYMPIC FAMILY.
AS PEOPLE LOST THEIR FAITH IN THE GODS OVER TIME, THE FATES BEGAN TO LOSE THEIR POWER AND AGE.
BUT WHAT DOES THAT HAVE TO DO WITH YOU?
LIKE THE EVENTUAL DEATH OF THE FATES, I WAS ALWAYS PART OF ZEUS' MASTER PLAN.
BORN OF CLAY, MY POWER IS ROOTED, NOT IN BELIEF, BUT IN THE EARTH HERSELF, THE MOTHER OF ALL GODS.
NOW, THANKS TO ZEUS, I AM FATE.
Uhhhh...
OH NO YOU DON'T! YOU AREN'T GETTING OFF THAT EASILY.
Ahhhhhhhh...
WE HAD A DEAL...

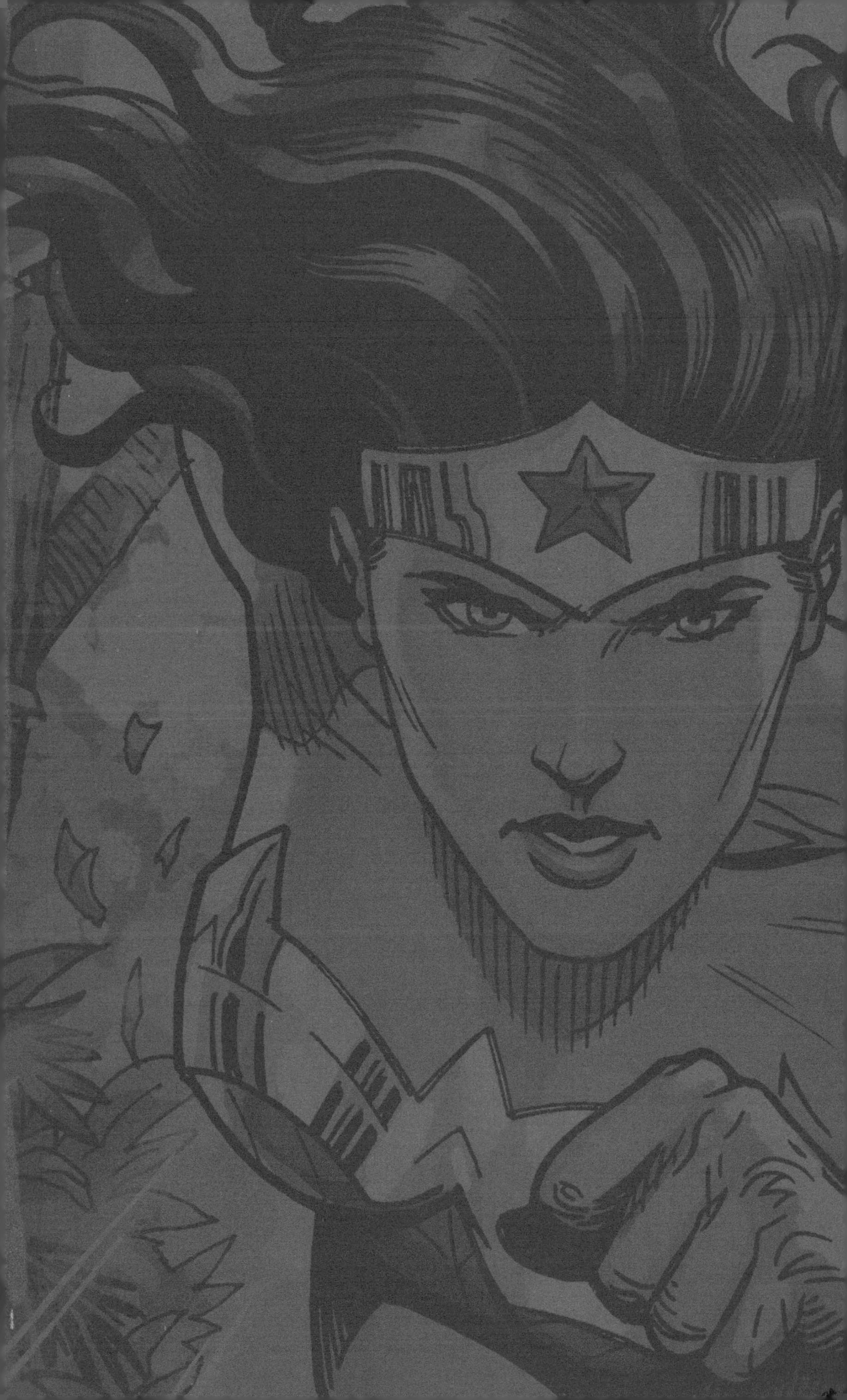

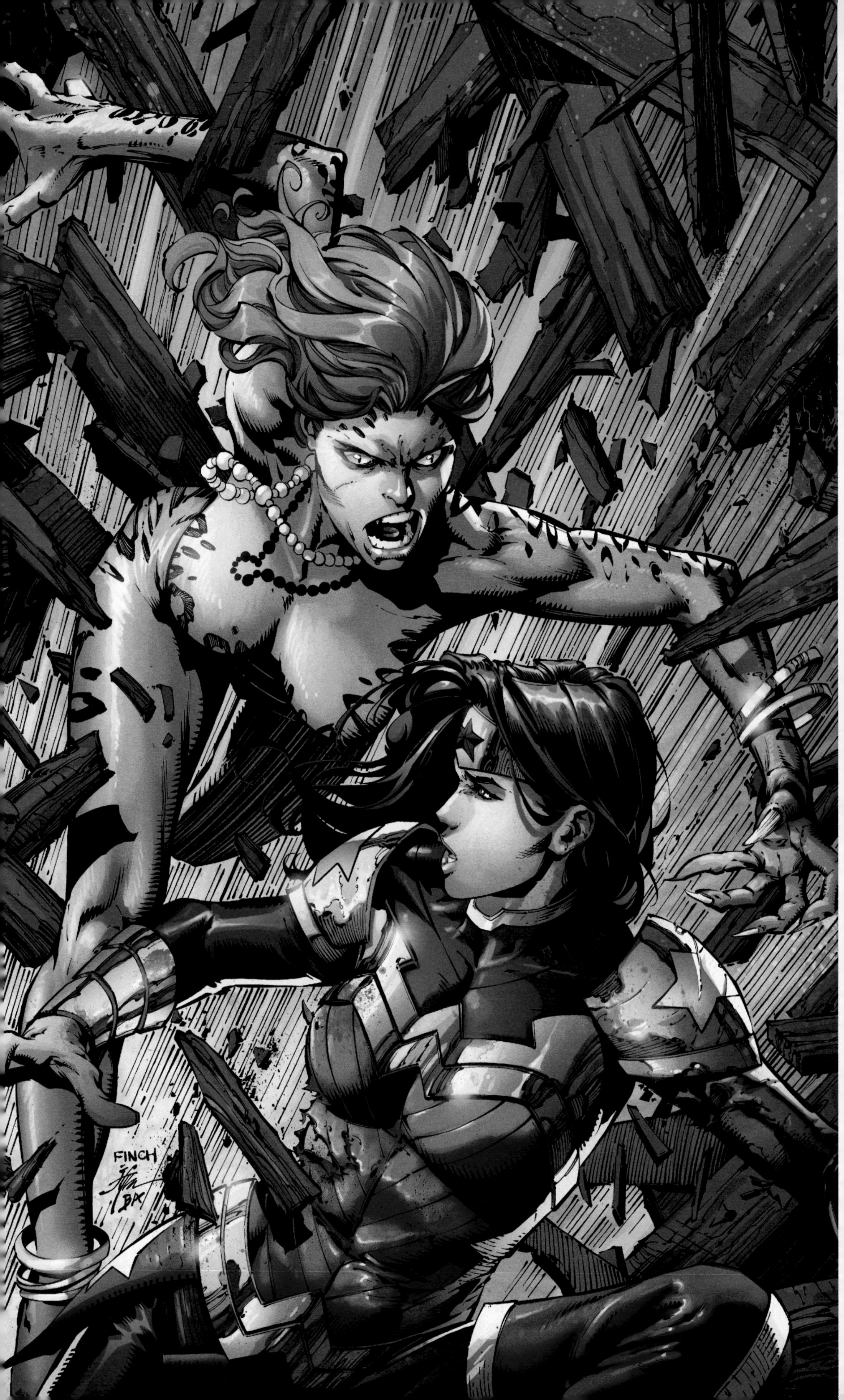
FINCH

INTO THE EYE

MEREDITH FINCH writer MIGUEL MENDONÇA penciller DEXTER VINES inker BETH SOTELO colorist ROB LEIGH letterer
cover by FINCH, GLAPION & ANDERSON

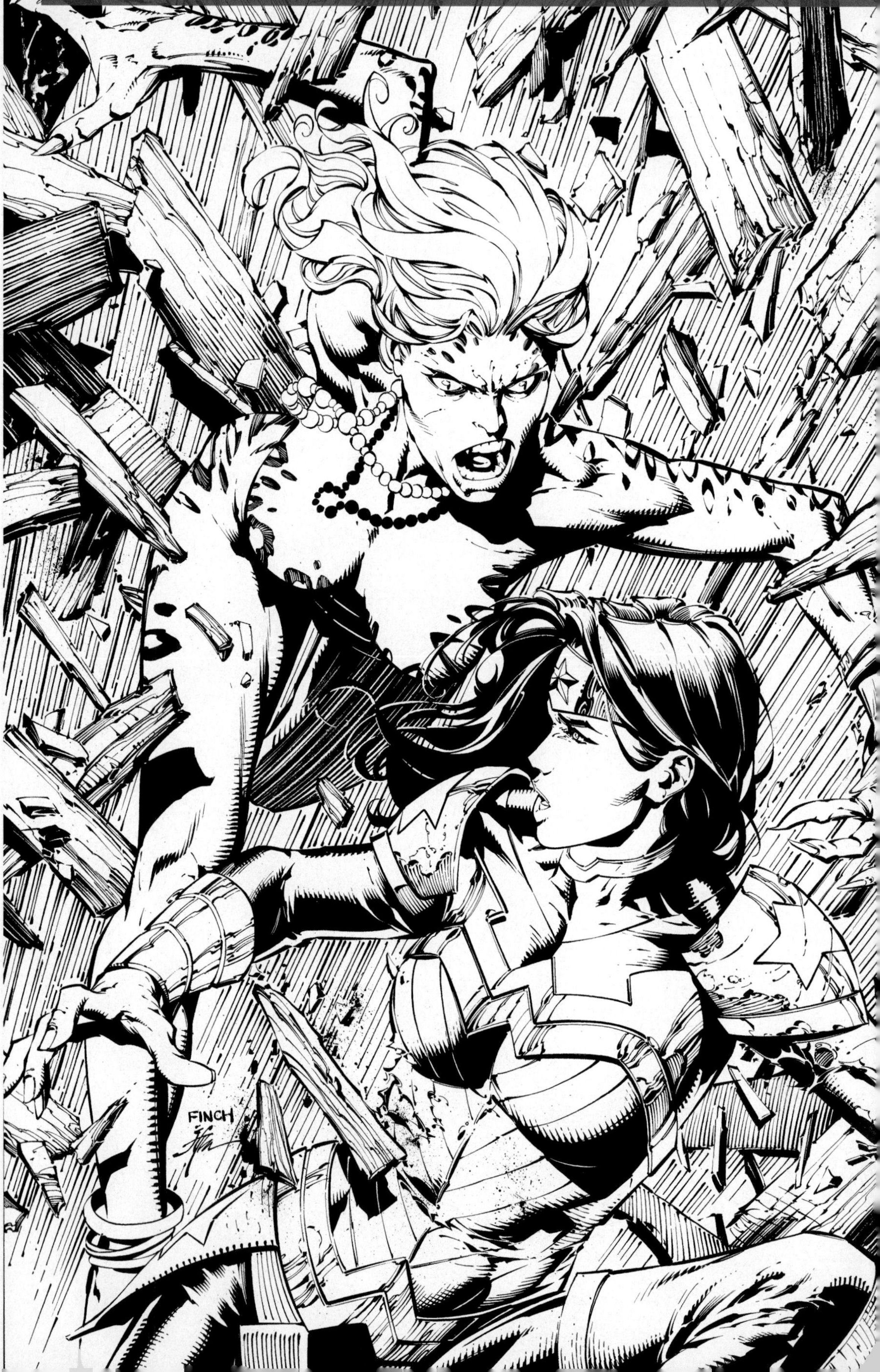
FINCH

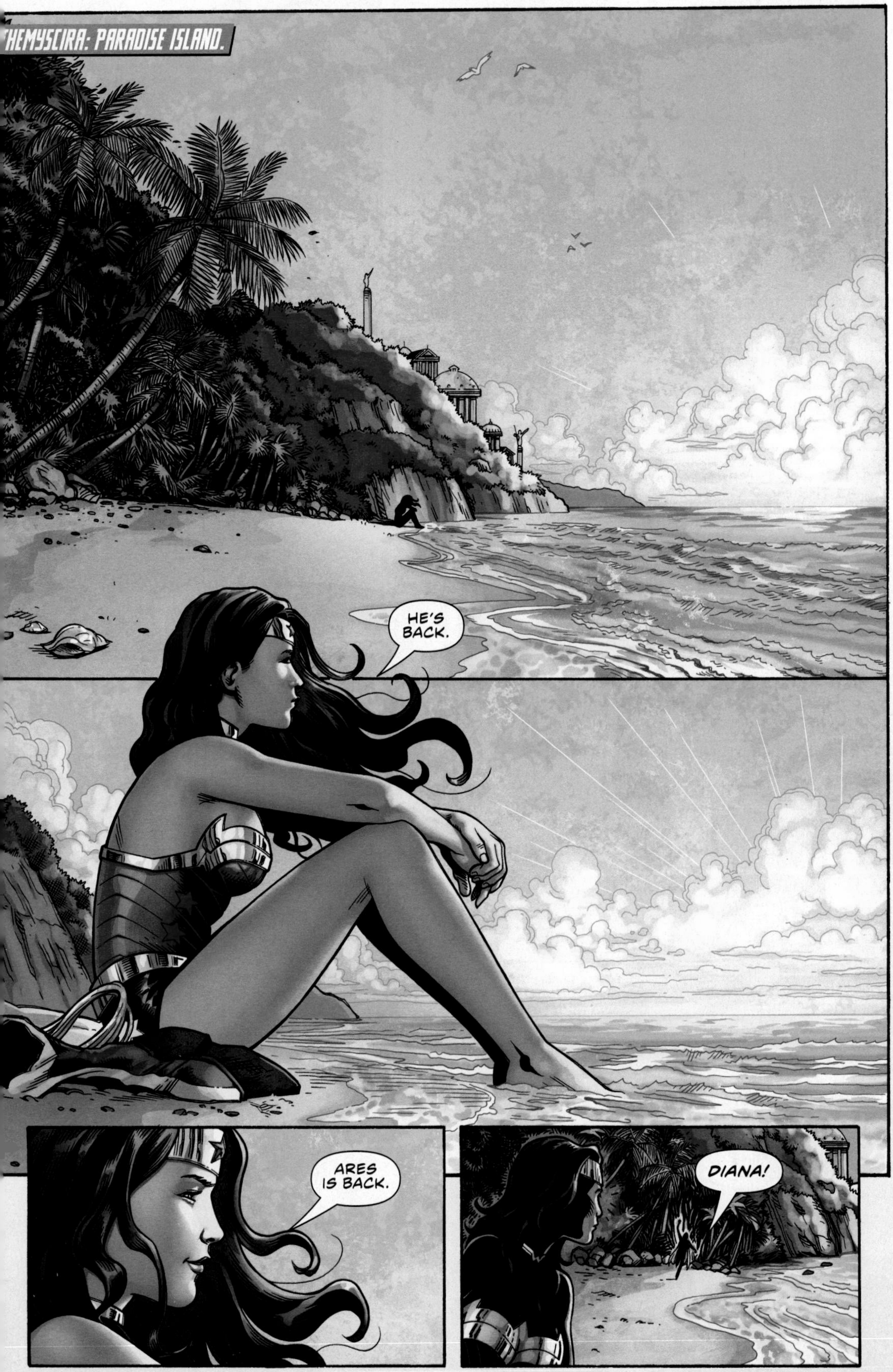
THEMYSCIRA: PARADISE ISLAND.
HE'S BACK.
ARES IS BACK.
DIANA!

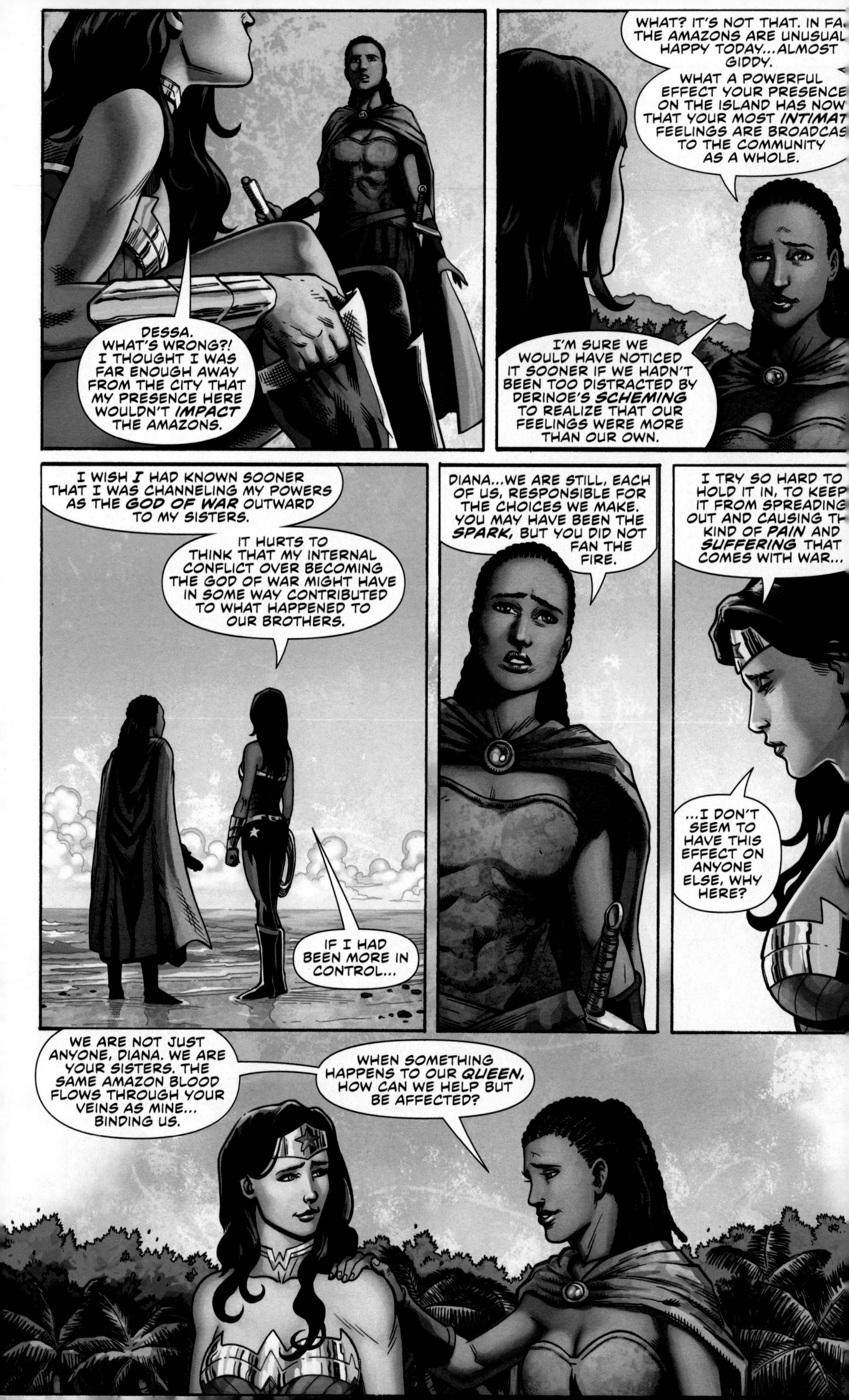
DESSA. WHAT'S WRONG?! I THOUGHT I WAS FAR ENOUGH AWAY FROM THE CITY THAT MY PRESENCE HERE WOULDN'T *IMPACT* THE AMAZONS.
WHAT? IT'S NOT THAT. IN FA THE AMAZONS ARE UNUSUAL HAPPY TODAY...ALMOST GIDDY.
WHAT A POWERFUL EFFECT YOUR PRESENCE ON THE ISLAND HAS NOW THAT YOUR MOST *INTIMAT* FEELINGS ARE BROADCAS TO THE COMMUNITY AS A WHOLE.
I'M SURE WE WOULD HAVE NOTICED IT SOONER IF WE HADN'T BEEN TOO DISTRACTED BY DERINOE'S *SCHEMING* TO REALIZE THAT OUR FEELINGS WERE MORE THAN OUR OWN.
I WISH *I* HAD KNOWN SOONER THAT I WAS CHANNELING MY POWERS AS THE *GOD OF WAR* OUTWARD TO MY SISTERS.
IT HURTS TO THINK THAT MY INTERNAL CONFLICT OVER BECOMING THE GOD OF WAR MIGHT HAVE IN SOME WAY CONTRIBUTED TO WHAT HAPPENED TO OUR BROTHERS.
IF I HAD BEEN MORE IN CONTROL...
DIANA...WE ARE STILL, EACH OF US, RESPONSIBLE FOR THE CHOICES WE MAKE. YOU MAY HAVE BEEN THE *SPARK,* BUT YOU DID NOT FAN THE FIRE.
I TRY SO HARD TO HOLD IT IN, TO KEEP IT FROM SPREADING OUT AND CAUSING TH KIND OF *PAIN* AND *SUFFERING* THAT COMES WITH WAR...
...I DON'T SEEM TO HAVE THIS EFFECT ON ANYONE ELSE, WHY HERE?
WE ARE NOT JUST ANYONE, DIANA. WE ARE YOUR SISTERS. THE SAME AMAZON BLOOD FLOWS THROUGH YOUR VEINS AS MINE... BINDING US.
WHEN SOMETHING HAPPENS TO OUR *QUEEN,* HOW CAN WE HELP BUT BE AFFECTED?

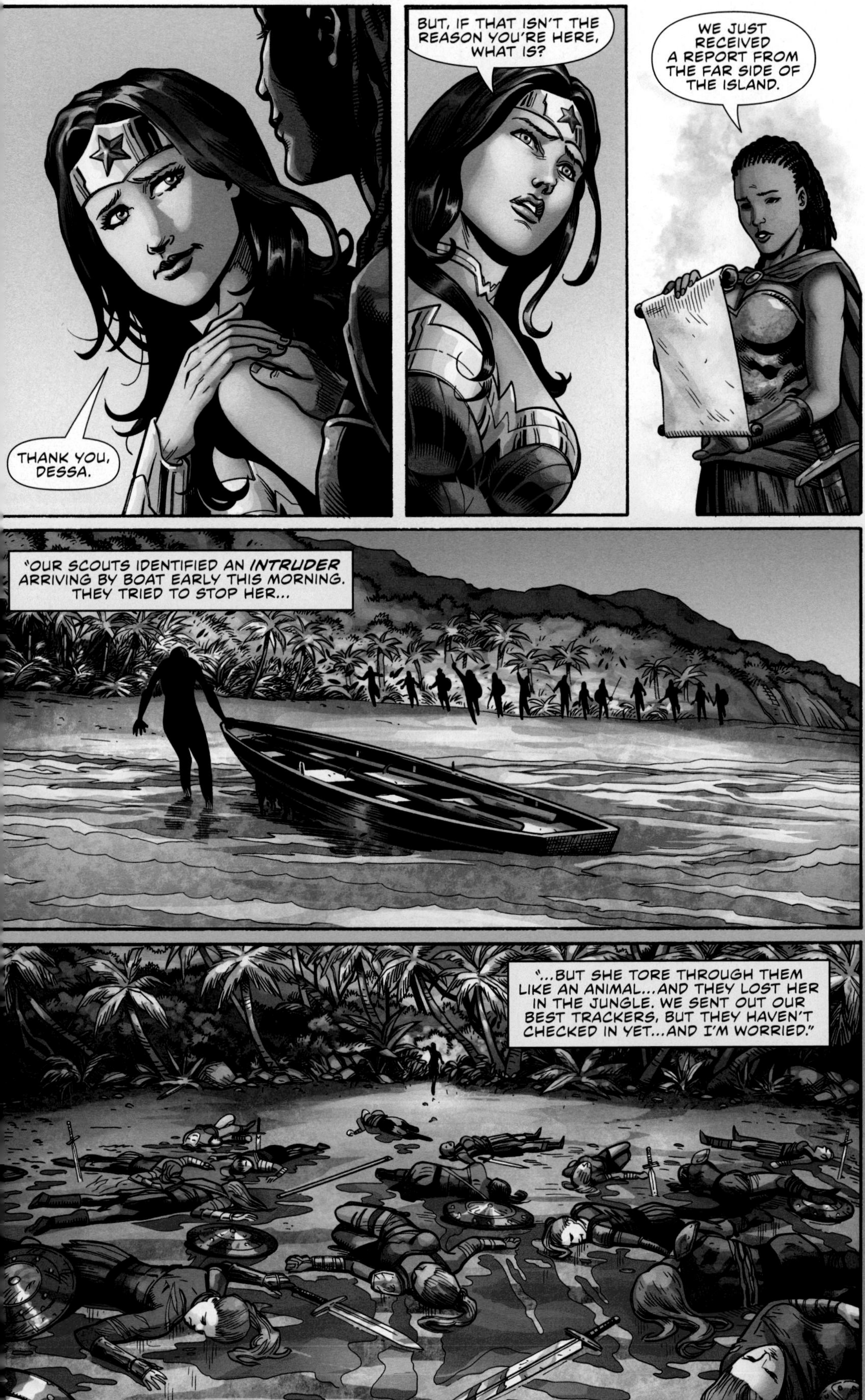
THANK YOU, DESSA.
BUT, IF THAT ISN'T THE REASON YOU'RE HERE, WHAT IS?
WE JUST RECEIVED A REPORT FROM THE FAR SIDE OF THE ISLAND.
"OUR SCOUTS IDENTIFIED AN *INTRUDER* ARRIVING BY BOAT EARLY THIS MORNING. THEY TRIED TO STOP HER...
"...BUT SHE TORE THROUGH THEM LIKE AN ANIMAL...AND THEY LOST HER IN THE JUNGLE. WE SENT OUT OUR BEST TRACKERS, BUT THEY HAVEN'T CHECKED IN YET...AND I'M WORRIED."

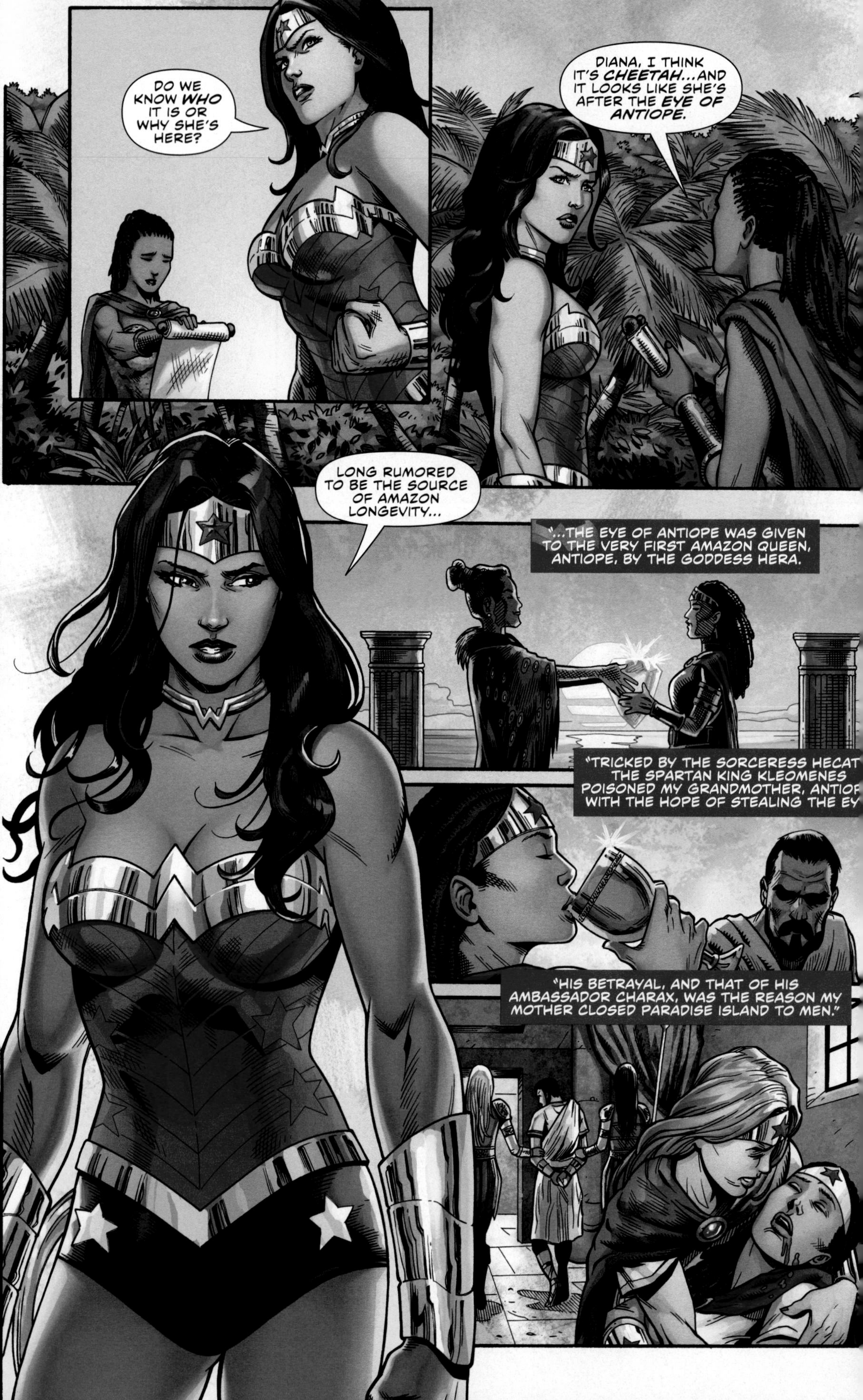

DO WE KNOW WHO IT IS OR WHY SHE'S HERE?
DIANA, I THINK IT'S CHEETAH...AND IT LOOKS LIKE SHE'S AFTER THE EYE OF ANTIOPE.
LONG RUMORED TO BE THE SOURCE OF AMAZON LONGEVITY...
"...THE EYE OF ANTIOPE WAS GIVEN TO THE VERY FIRST AMAZON QUEEN, ANTIOPE, BY THE GODDESS HERA.
"TRICKED BY THE SORCERESS HECAT THE SPARTAN KING KLEOMENES POISONED MY GRANDMOTHER, ANTIOP WITH THE HOPE OF STEALING THE EY
"HIS BETRAYAL, AND THAT OF HIS AMBASSADOR CHARAX, WAS THE REASON MY MOTHER CLOSED PARADISE ISLAND TO MEN."

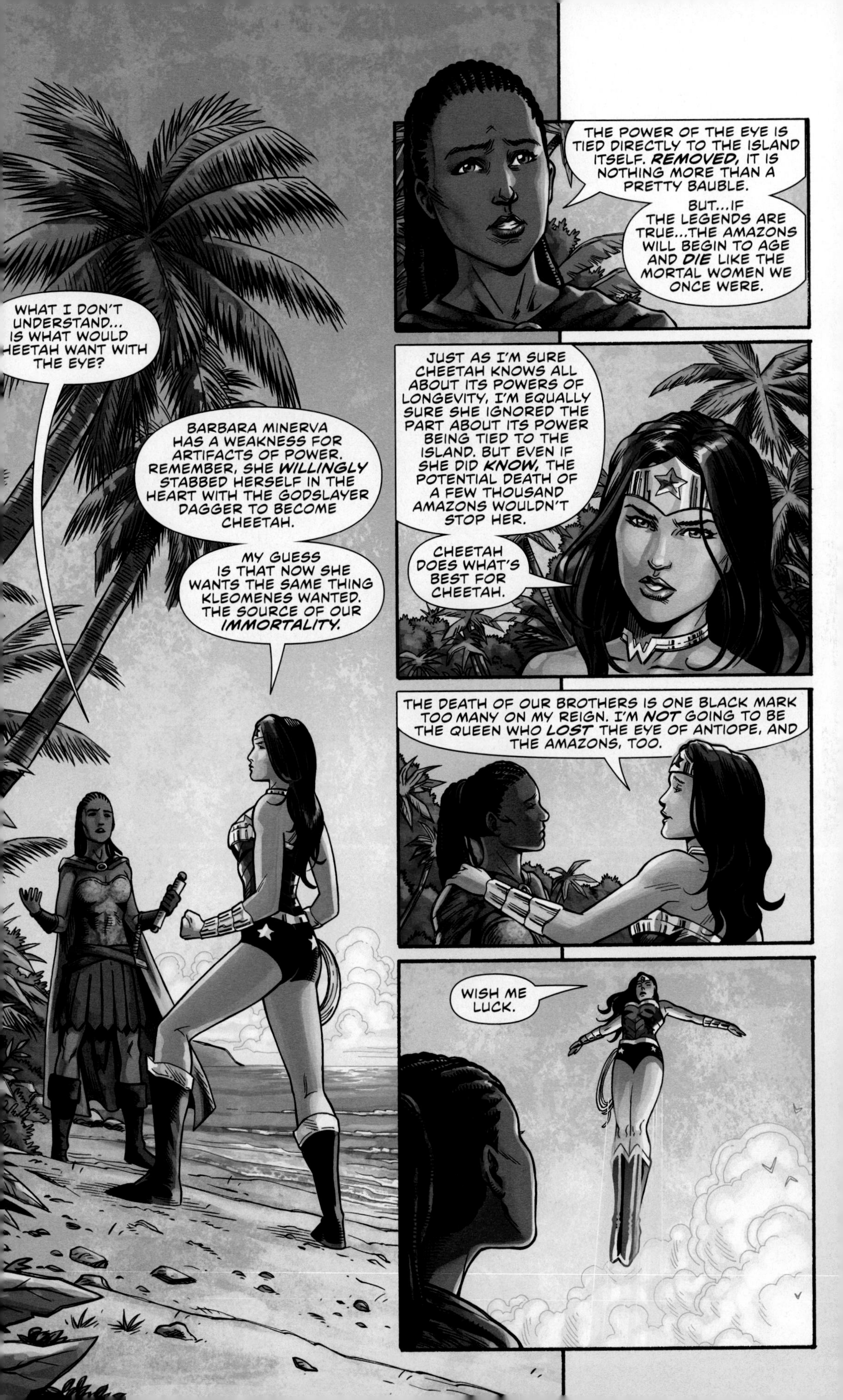
WHAT I DON'T UNDERSTAND... IS WHAT WOULD CHEETAH WANT WITH THE EYE?
BARBARA MINERVA HAS A WEAKNESS FOR ARTIFACTS OF POWER. REMEMBER, SHE WILLINGLY STABBED HERSELF IN THE HEART WITH THE GODSLAYER DAGGER TO BECOME CHEETAH.
MY GUESS IS THAT NOW SHE WANTS THE SAME THING KLEOMENES WANTED. THE SOURCE OF OUR IMMORTALITY.
THE POWER OF THE EYE IS TIED DIRECTLY TO THE ISLAND ITSELF. REMOVED, IT IS NOTHING MORE THAN A PRETTY BAUBLE.
BUT...IF THE LEGENDS ARE TRUE...THE AMAZONS WILL BEGIN TO AGE AND DIE LIKE THE MORTAL WOMEN WE ONCE WERE.
JUST AS I'M SURE CHEETAH KNOWS ALL ABOUT ITS POWERS OF LONGEVITY, I'M EQUALLY SURE SHE IGNORED THE PART ABOUT ITS POWER BEING TIED TO THE ISLAND. BUT EVEN IF SHE DID KNOW, THE POTENTIAL DEATH OF A FEW THOUSAND AMAZONS WOULDN'T STOP HER.
CHEETAH DOES WHAT'S BEST FOR CHEETAH.
THE DEATH OF OUR BROTHERS IS ONE BLACK MARK TOO MANY ON MY REIGN. I'M NOT GOING TO BE THE QUEEN WHO LOST THE EYE OF ANTIOPE, AND THE AMAZONS, TOO.
WISH ME LUCK.

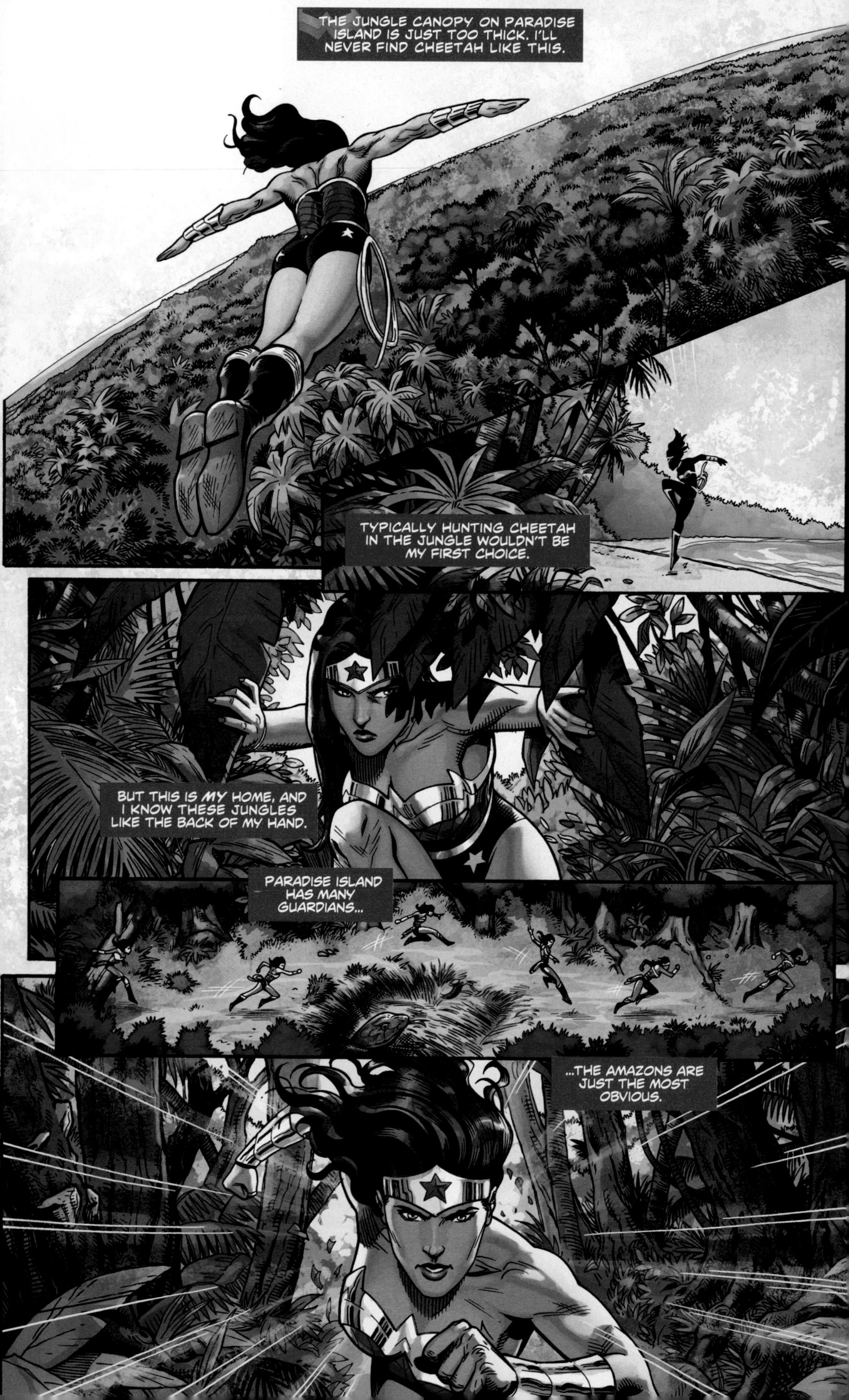

THE JUNGLE CANOPY ON PARADISE ISLAND IS JUST TOO THICK. I'LL NEVER FIND CHEETAH LIKE THIS.
TYPICALLY HUNTING CHEETAH IN THE JUNGLE WOULDN'T BE MY FIRST CHOICE.
BUT THIS IS *MY* HOME, AND I KNOW THESE JUNGLES LIKE THE BACK OF MY HAND.
PARADISE ISLAND HAS MANY GUARDIANS...
...THE AMAZONS ARE JUST THE MOST OBVIOUS.

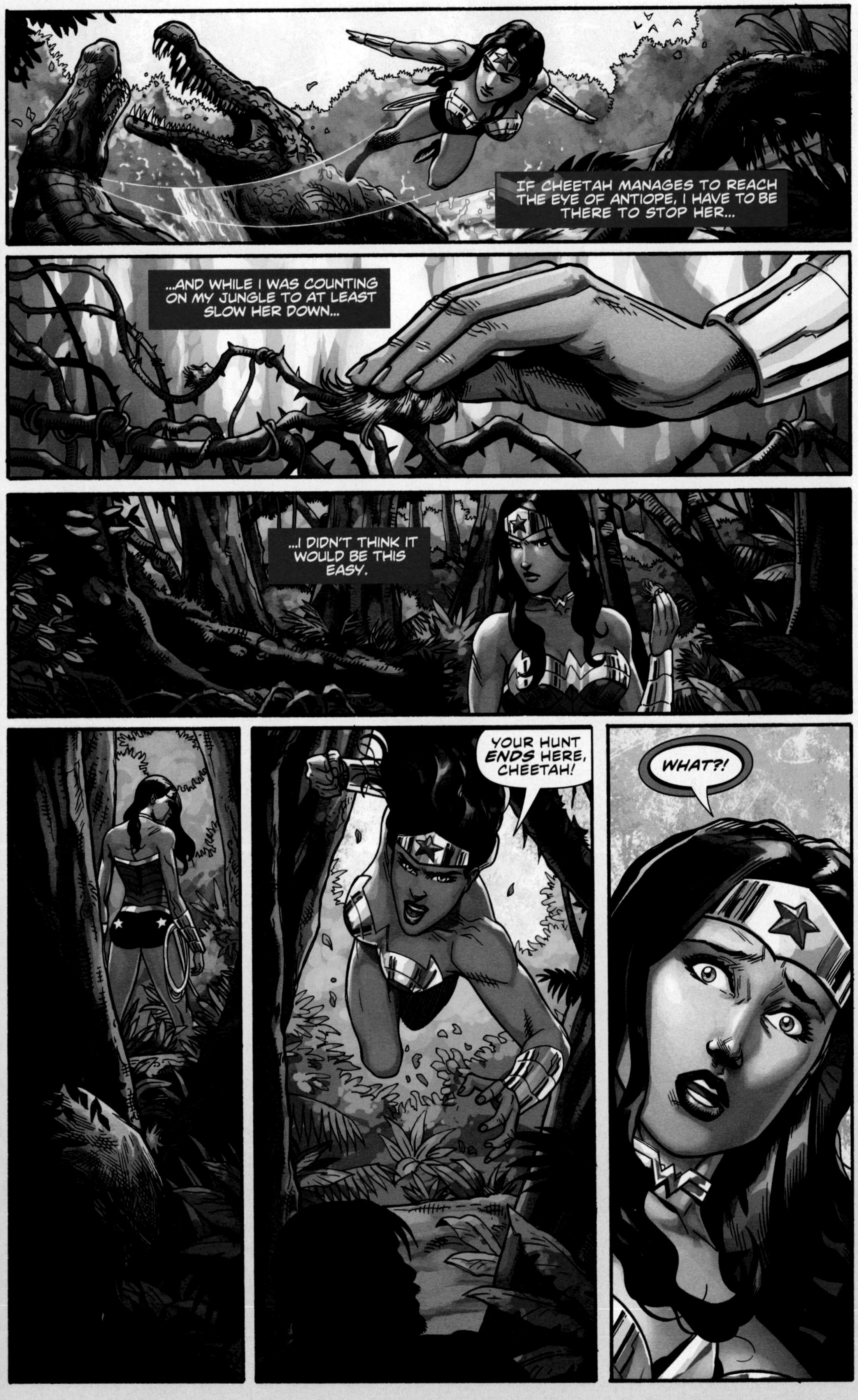
IF CHEETAH MANAGES TO REACH THE EYE OF ANTIOPE, I HAVE TO BE THERE TO STOP HER...
...AND WHILE I WAS COUNTING ON MY JUNGLE TO AT LEAST SLOW HER DOWN...
...I DIDN'T THINK IT WOULD BE THIS EASY.
YOUR HUNT ENDS HERE, CHEETAH!
WHAT?!

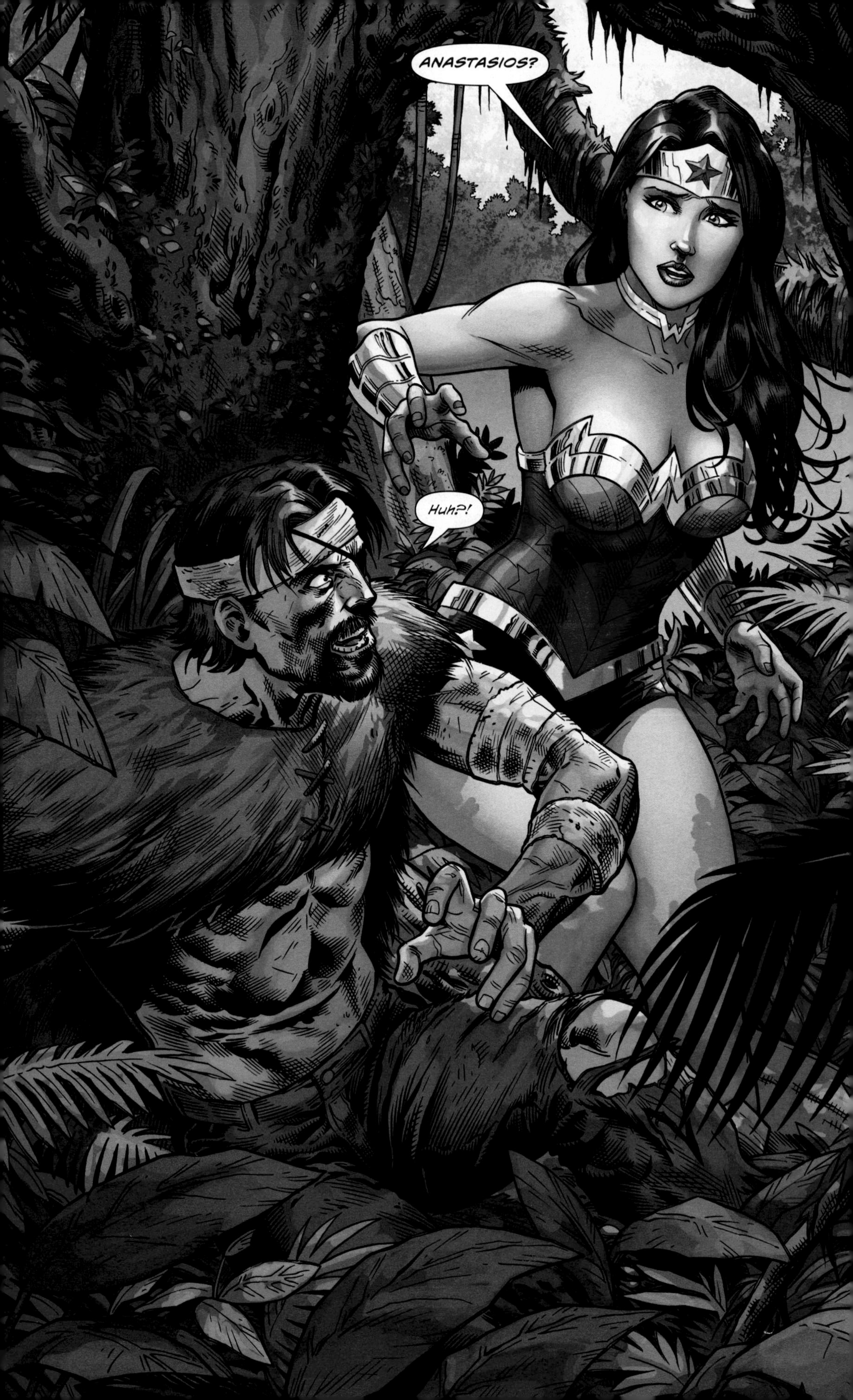
ANASTASIOS?
Huh?!

ANASTASIOS! *WAIT!*

I'M NOT GOING TO HURT YOU!

IT'S ME. DIANA!

DIANA?! DIANA THE GOD OF WAR?! DIANA WHO *PROMISED* US A HOME AND THEN STOOD BY AND ALLOWED HER *BLOOD-THIRSTY SISTERS* TO SLAUGHTER US WHERE WE STOOD? *DIANA?!*

I GOT THERE AS SOON AS I COULD... BUT...

YOU'RE RIGHT. I WAS FOOLISH AND ARROGANT...SO CAUGHT UP IN DOING WHAT I BELIEVED TO BE RIGHT, THAT I COULDN'T *SEE* WHAT WAS HAPPENING AROUND ME...

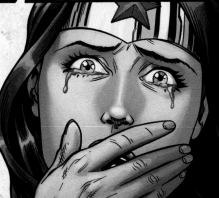

ANASTASIOS! OH NO....!

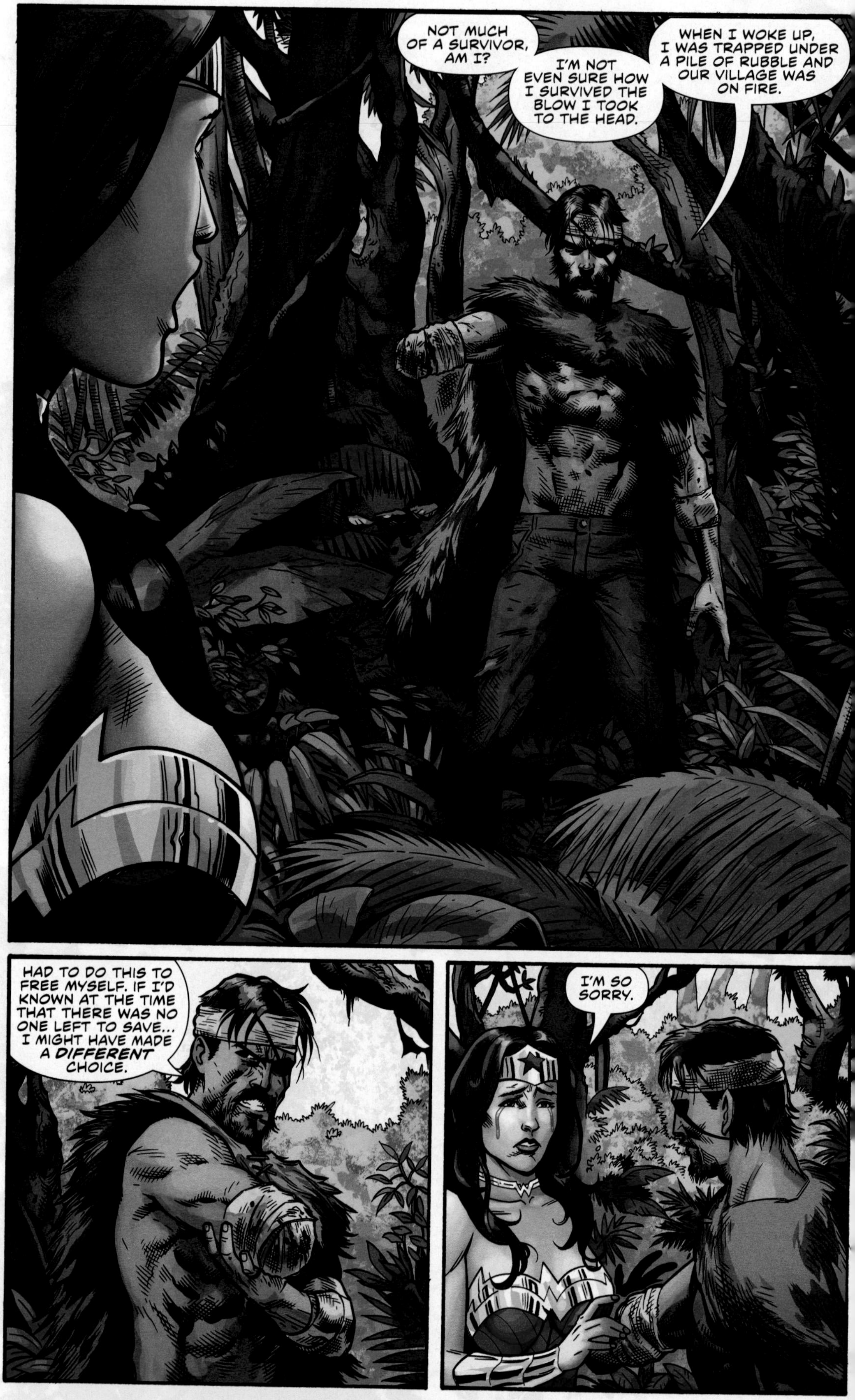
NOT MUCH OF A SURVIVOR, AM I?
I'M NOT EVEN SURE HOW I SURVIVED THE BLOW I TOOK TO THE HEAD.
WHEN I WOKE UP, I WAS TRAPPED UNDER A PILE OF RUBBLE AND OUR VILLAGE WAS ON FIRE.
HAD TO DO THIS TO FREE MYSELF. IF I'D KNOWN AT THE TIME THAT THERE WAS NO ONE LEFT TO SAVE... I MIGHT HAVE MADE A *DIFFERENT* CHOICE.
I'M SO SORRY.

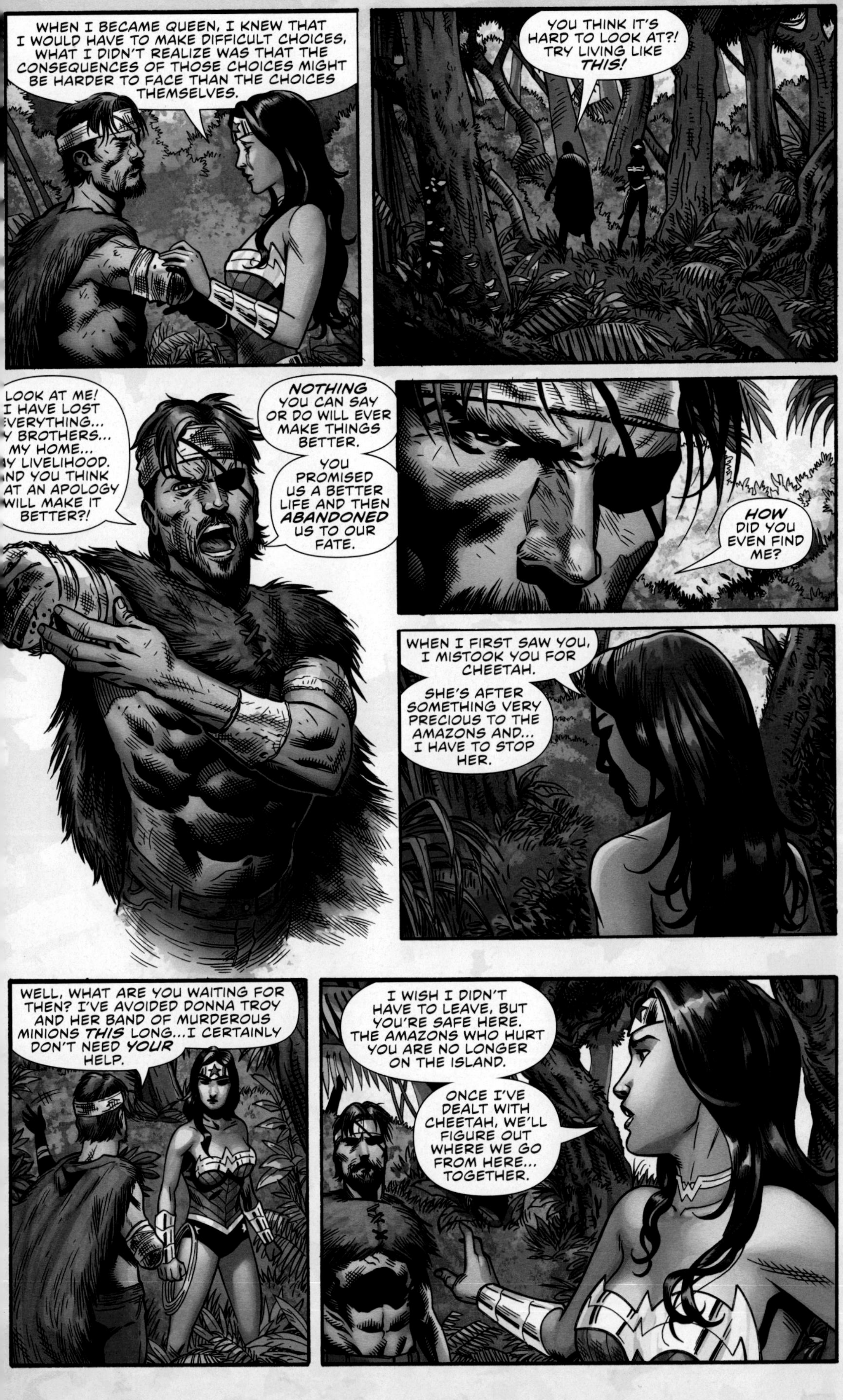

WHEN I BECAME QUEEN, I KNEW THAT I WOULD HAVE TO MAKE DIFFICULT CHOICES. WHAT I DIDN'T REALIZE WAS THAT THE CONSEQUENCES OF THOSE CHOICES MIGHT BE HARDER TO FACE THAN THE CHOICES THEMSELVES.
YOU THINK IT'S HARD TO LOOK AT?! TRY LIVING LIKE *THIS!*
LOOK AT ME! I HAVE LOST VERYTHING... Y BROTHERS... MY HOME... Y LIVELIHOOD. ND YOU THINK AT AN APOLOGY WILL MAKE IT BETTER?!
NOTHING YOU CAN SAY OR DO WILL EVER MAKE THINGS BETTER.
YOU PROMISED US A BETTER LIFE AND THEN *ABANDONED* US TO OUR FATE.
HOW DID YOU EVEN FIND ME?
WHEN I FIRST SAW YOU, I MISTOOK YOU FOR CHEETAH.
SHE'S AFTER SOMETHING VERY PRECIOUS TO THE AMAZONS AND... I HAVE TO STOP HER.
WELL, WHAT ARE YOU WAITING FOR THEN? I'VE AVOIDED DONNA TROY AND HER BAND OF MURDEROUS MINIONS *THIS* LONG...I CERTAINLY DON'T NEED *YOUR* HELP.
I WISH I DIDN'T HAVE TO LEAVE, BUT YOU'RE SAFE HERE. THE AMAZONS WHO HURT YOU ARE NO LONGER ON THE ISLAND.
ONCE I'VE DEALT WITH CHEETAH, WE'LL FIGURE OUT WHERE WE GO FROM HERE... TOGETHER.

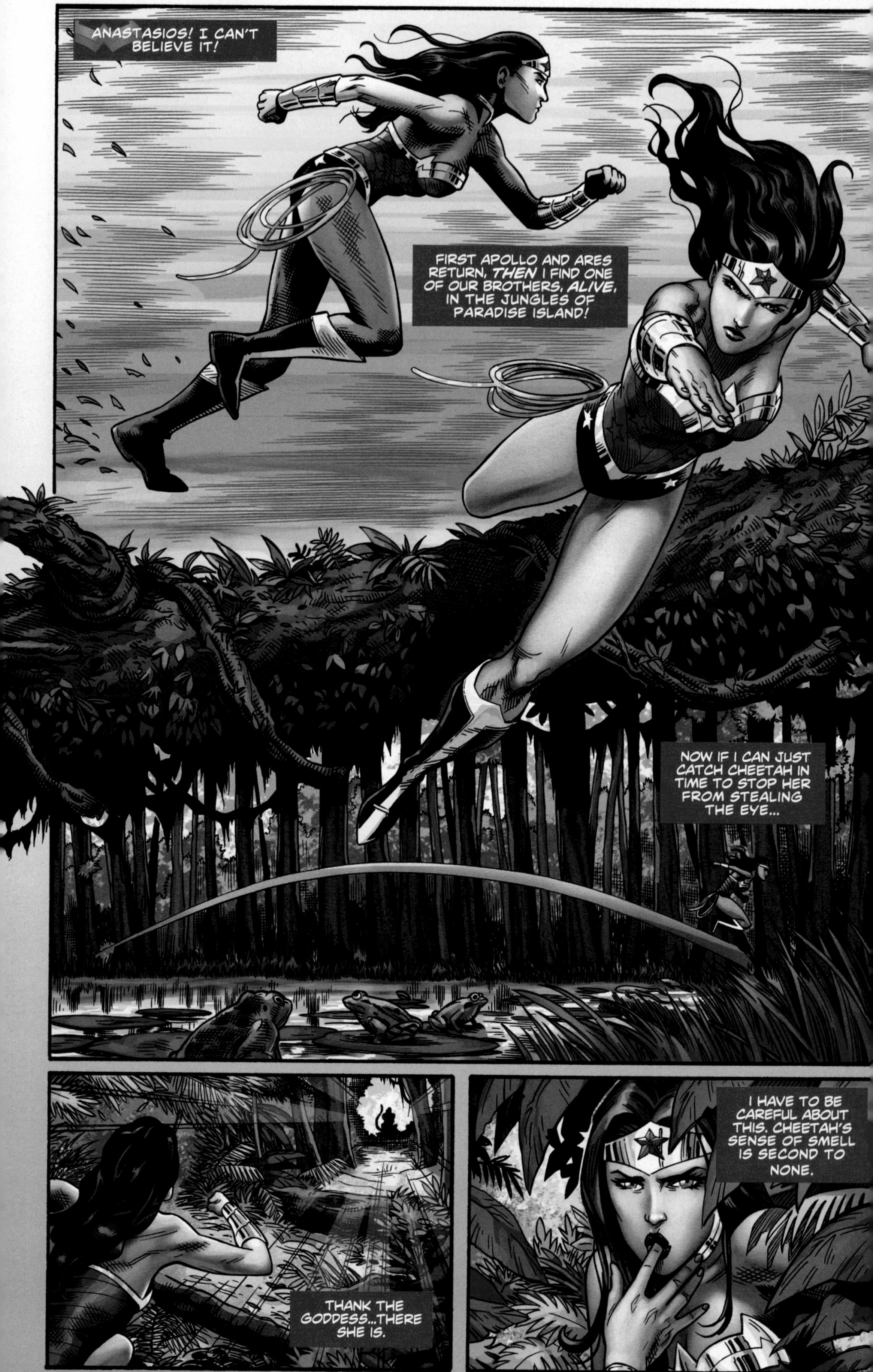
ANASTASIOS! I CAN'T BELIEVE IT!
FIRST APOLLO AND ARES RETURN, THEN I FIND ONE OF OUR BROTHERS, ALIVE, IN THE JUNGLES OF PARADISE ISLAND!
NOW IF I CAN JUST CATCH CHEETAH IN TIME TO STOP HER FROM STEALING THE EYE...
THANK THE GODDESS...THERE SHE IS.
I HAVE TO BE CAREFUL ABOUT THIS. CHEETAH'S SENSE OF SMELL IS SECOND TO NONE.

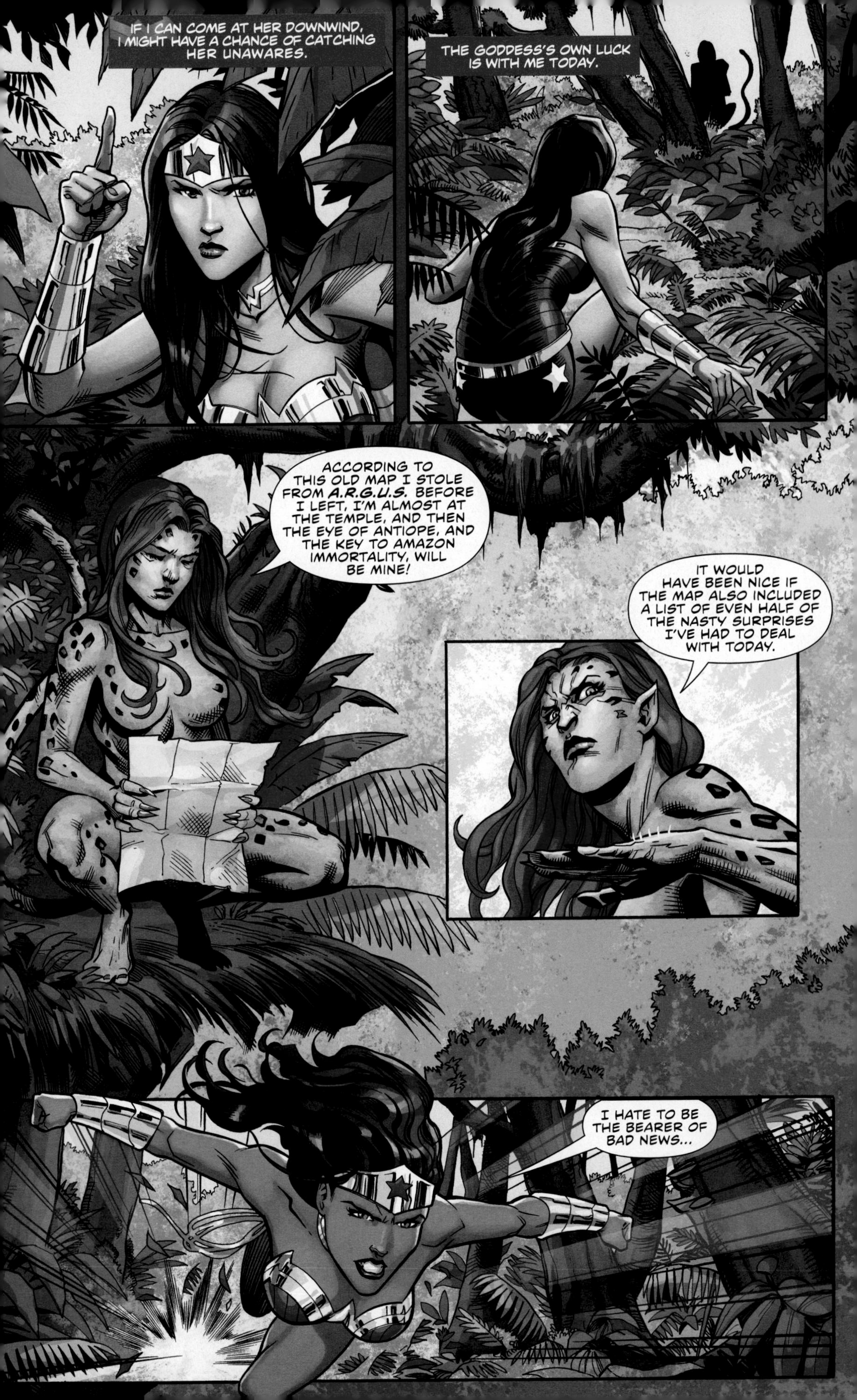
IF I CAN COME AT HER DOWNWIND, I MIGHT HAVE A CHANCE OF CATCHING HER UNAWARES.
THE GODDESS'S OWN LUCK IS WITH ME TODAY.
ACCORDING TO THIS OLD MAP I STOLE FROM A.R.G.U.S. BEFORE I LEFT, I'M ALMOST AT THE TEMPLE, AND THEN THE EYE OF ANTIOPE, AND THE KEY TO AMAZON IMMORTALITY, WILL BE MINE!
IT WOULD HAVE BEEN NICE IF THE MAP ALSO INCLUDED A LIST OF EVEN HALF OF THE NASTY SURPRISES I'VE HAD TO DEAL WITH TODAY.
I HATE TO BE THE BEARER OF BAD NEWS...

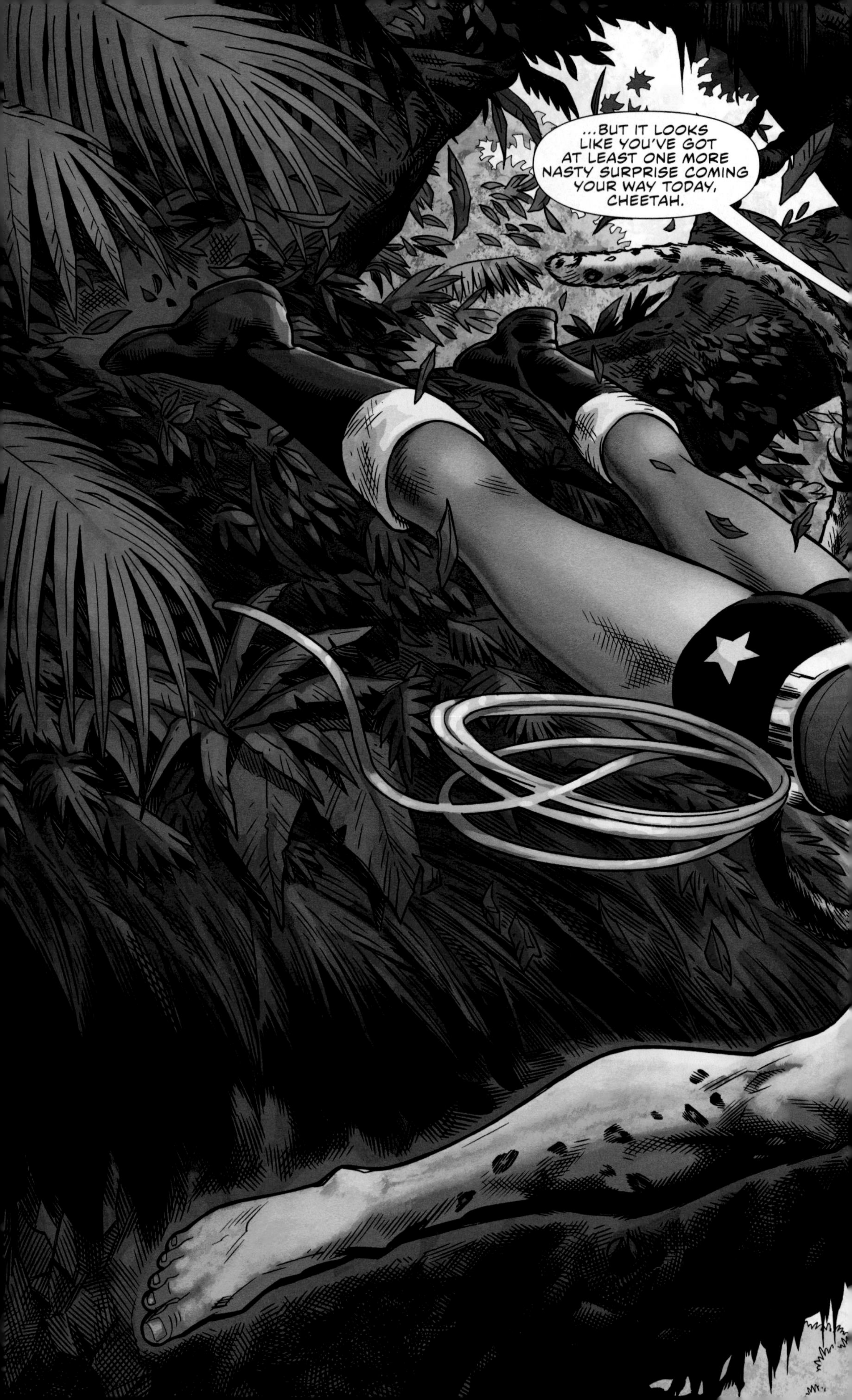
...BUT IT LOOKS LIKE YOU'VE GOT AT LEAST ONE MORE NASTY SURPRISE COMING YOUR WAY TODAY, CHEETAH.

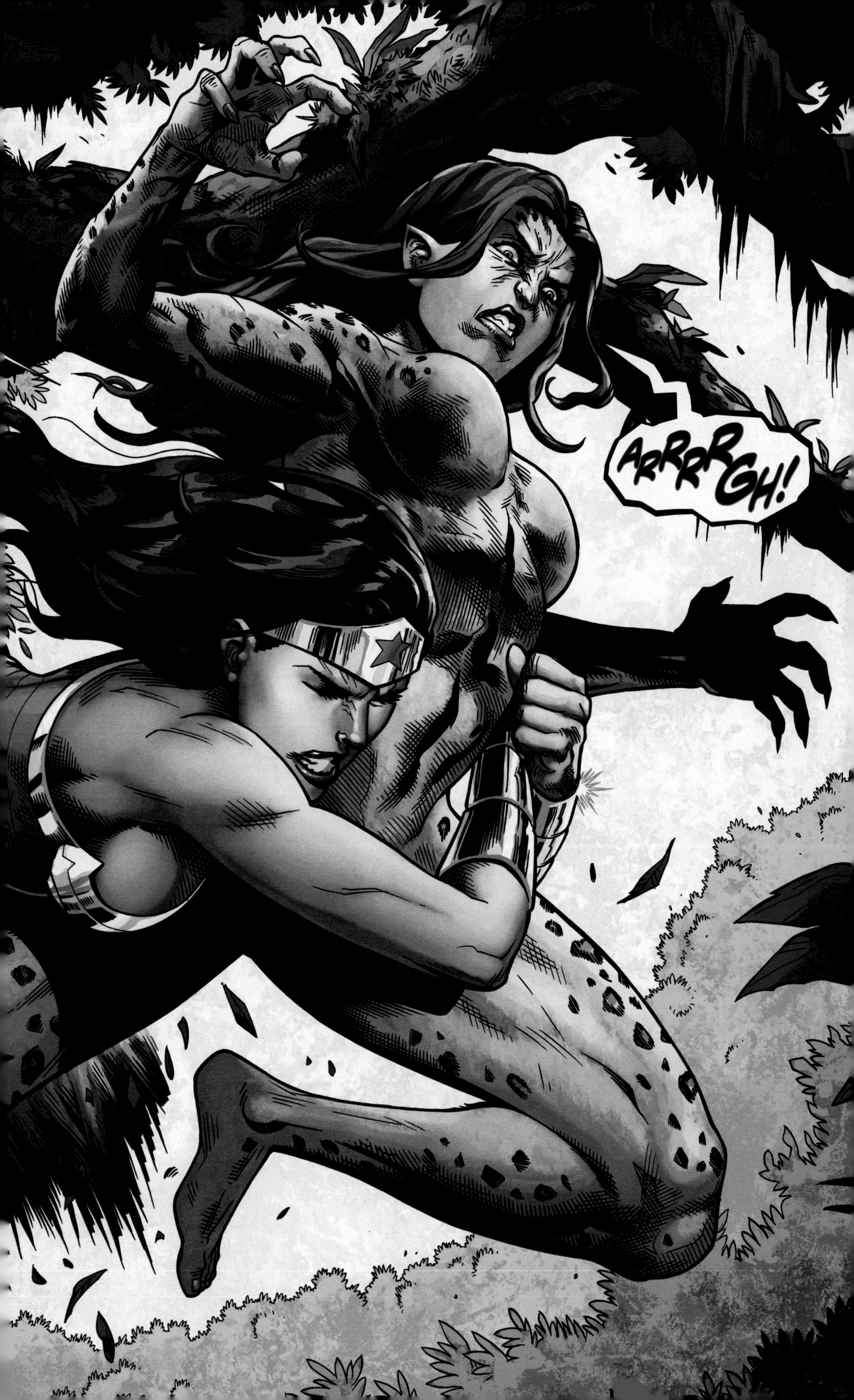
ARRRRGH!

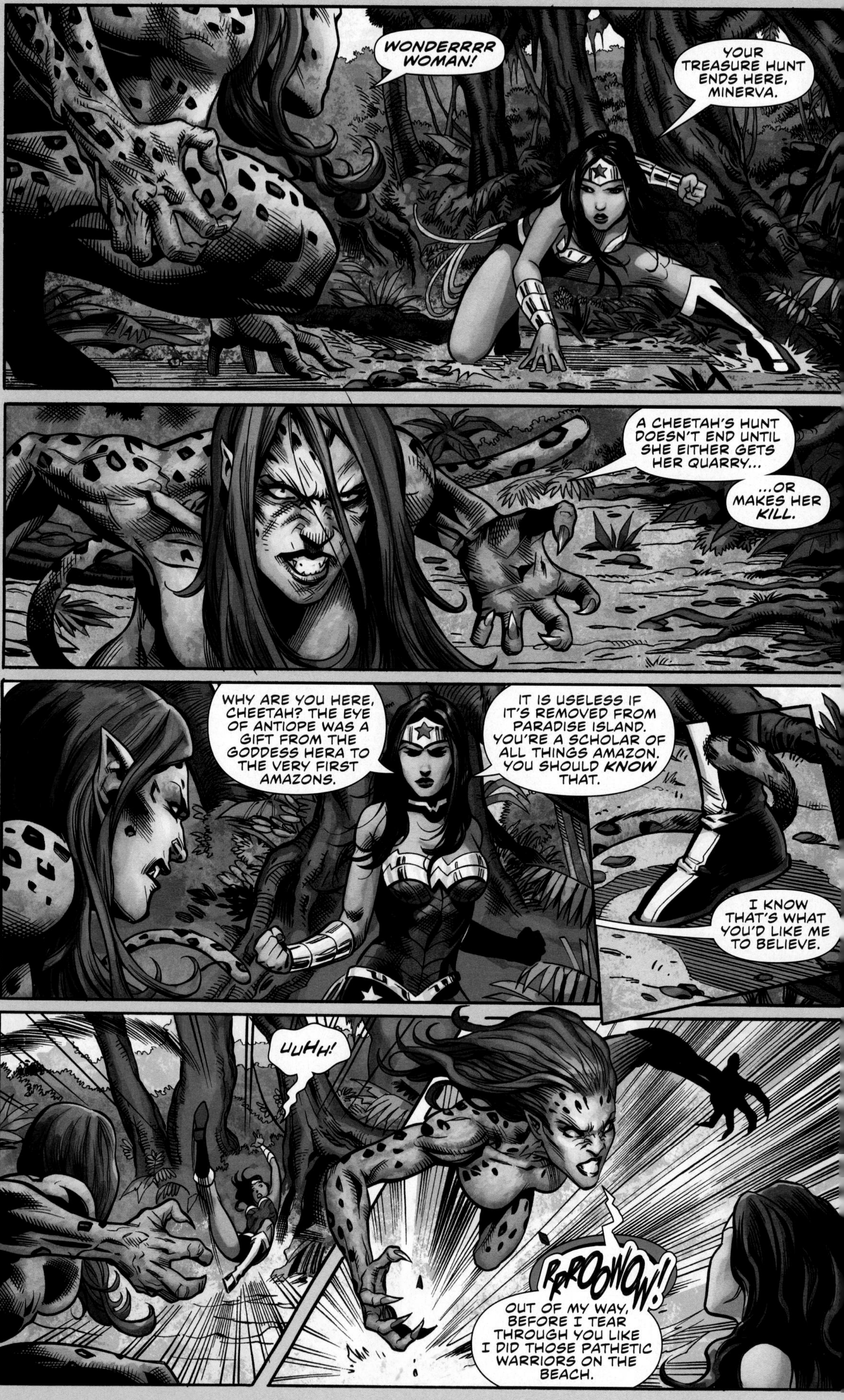

WONDERRRR WOMAN!
YOUR TREASURE HUNT ENDS HERE, MINERVA.
A CHEETAH'S HUNT DOESN'T END UNTIL SHE EITHER GETS HER QUARRY...
...OR MAKES HER KILL.
WHY ARE YOU HERE, CHEETAH? THE EYE OF ANTIOPE WAS A GIFT FROM THE GODDESS HERA TO THE VERY FIRST AMAZONS.
IT IS USELESS IF IT'S REMOVED FROM PARADISE ISLAND. YOU'RE A SCHOLAR OF ALL THINGS AMAZON. YOU SHOULD KNOW THAT.
I KNOW THAT'S WHAT YOU'D LIKE ME TO BELIEVE.
UUHH!
RRROOWOW!
OUT OF MY WAY, BEFORE I TEAR THROUGH YOU LIKE I DID THOSE PATHETIC WARRIORS ON THE BEACH.

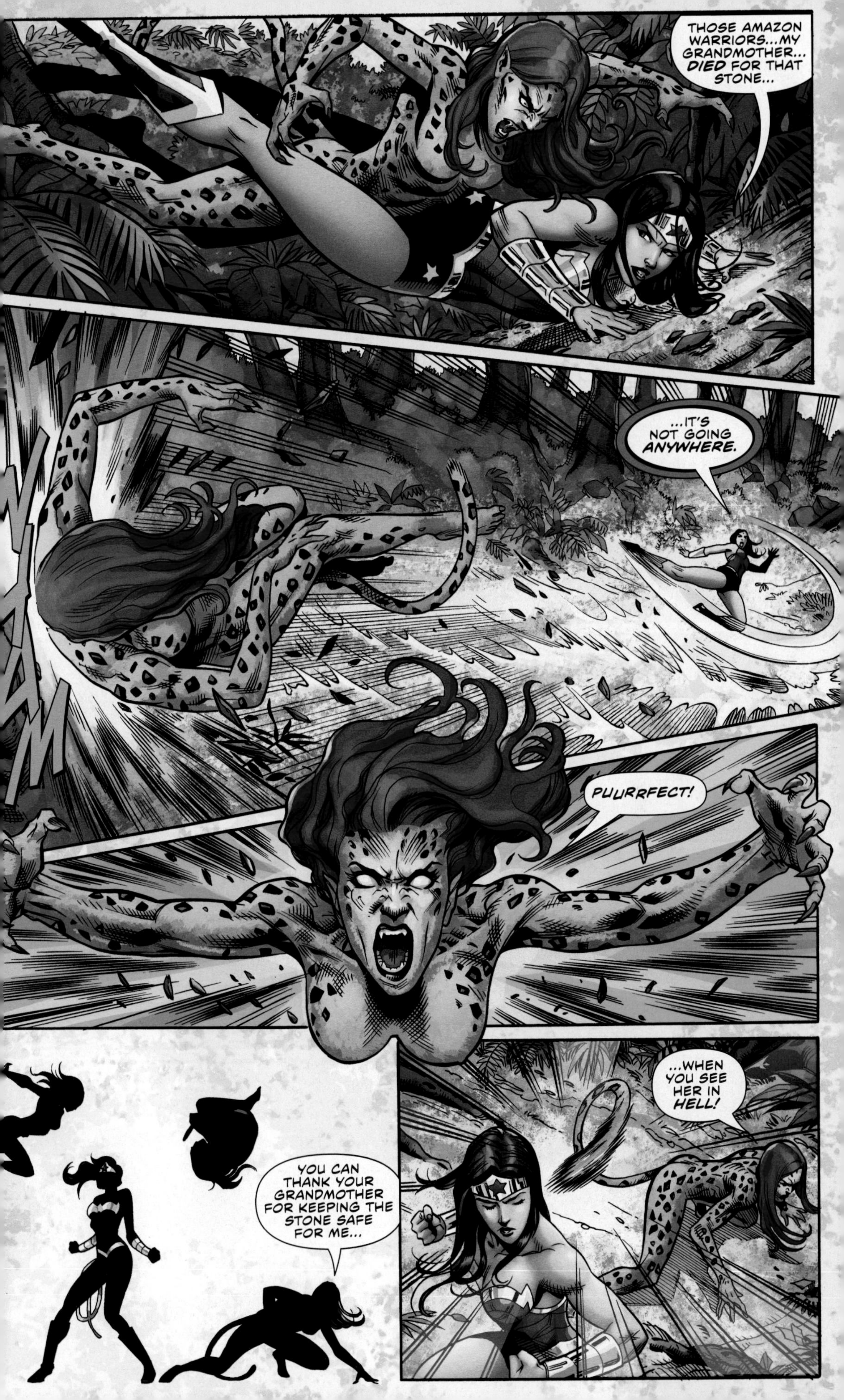
THOSE AMAZON WARRIORS...MY GRANDMOTHER... DIED FOR THAT STONE...
...IT'S NOT GOING ANYWHERE.
PUURRFECT!
YOU CAN THANK YOUR GRANDMOTHER FOR KEEPING THE STONE SAFE FOR ME...
...WHEN YOU SEE HER IN HELL!

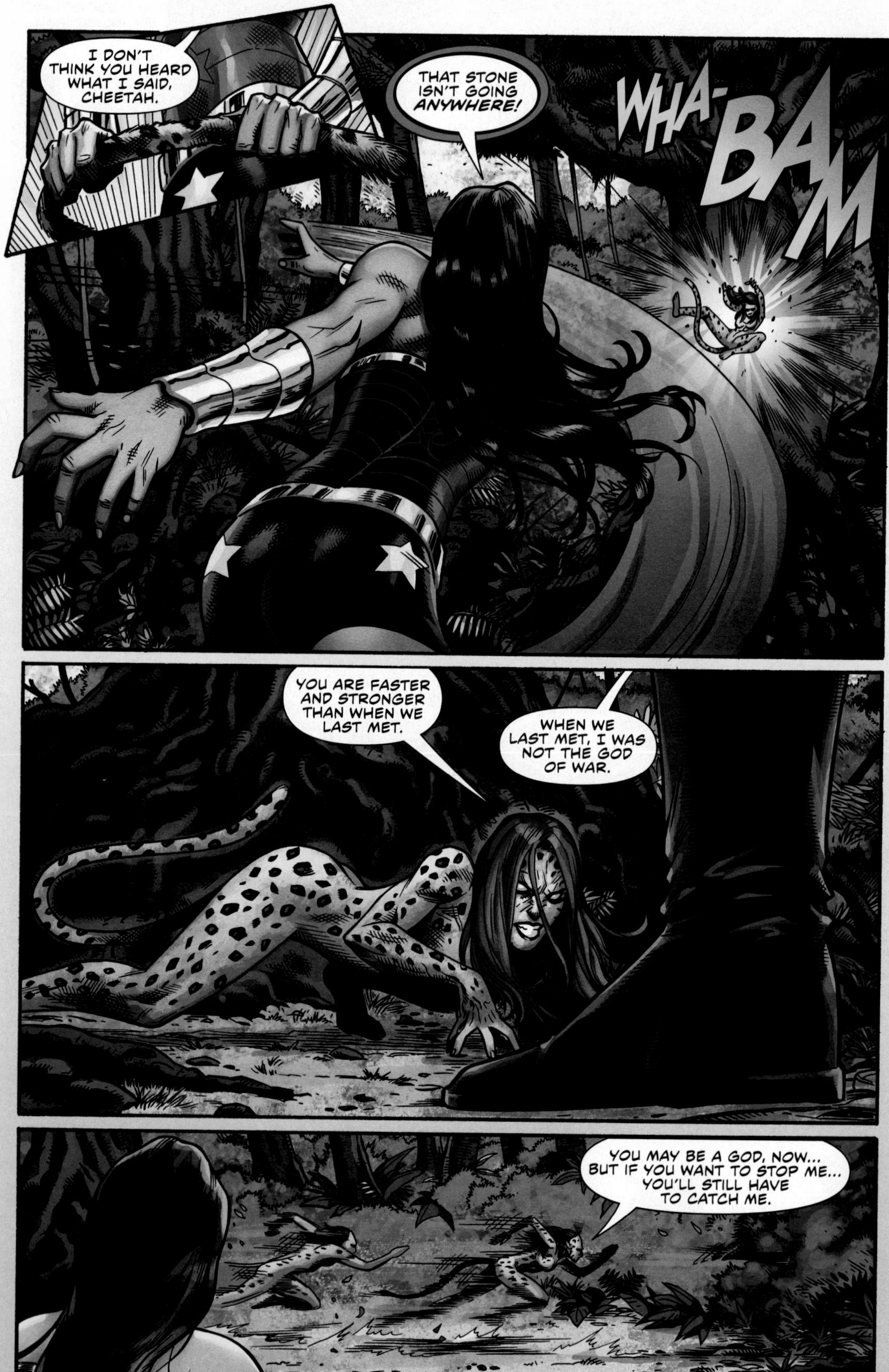
I DON'T THINK YOU HEARD WHAT I SAID, CHEETAH.
THAT STONE ISN'T GOING ANYWHERE!
WHA-BAM
YOU ARE FASTER AND STRONGER THAN WHEN WE LAST MET.
WHEN WE LAST MET, I WAS NOT THE GOD OF WAR.
YOU MAY BE A GOD, NOW... BUT IF YOU WANT TO STOP ME... YOU'LL STILL HAVE TO CATCH ME.

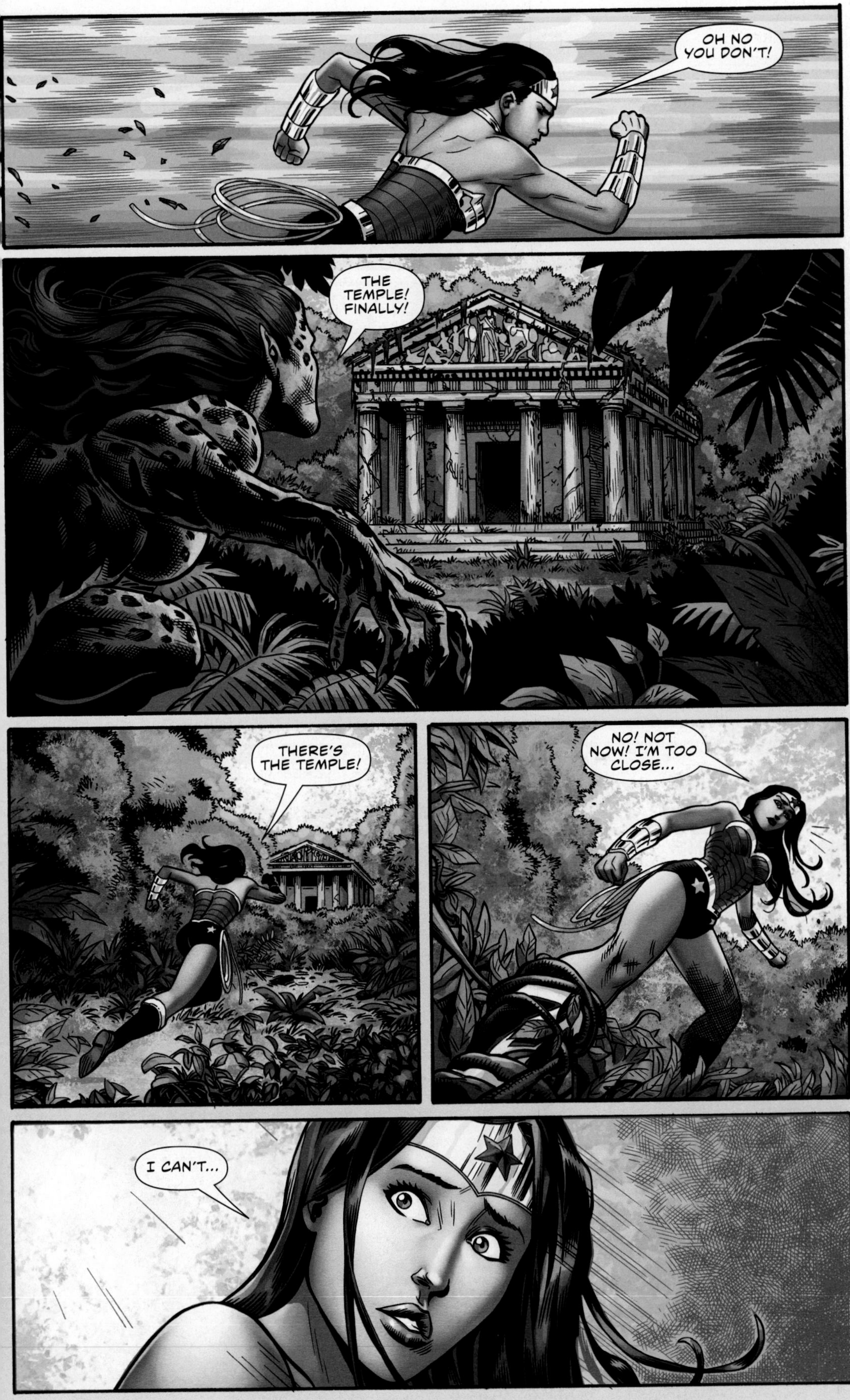
OH NO YOU DON'T!
THE TEMPLE! FINALLY!
THERE'S THE TEMPLE!
NO! NOT NOW! I'M TOO CLOSE...
I CAN'T...

MOTHER?

GREETINGS, DAUGHTER.

BUT THE EYE OF ANTIOPE! THE AMAZONS?!

I KNOW THIS MUST BE DIFFICULT TO UNDERSTAND, AND I AM SORRY, BUT I CANNOT ALLOW YOU TO *FOLLOW* CHEETAH INTO THE TEMPLE.

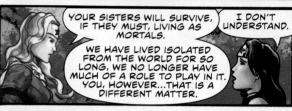

YOUR SISTERS WILL SURVIVE, IF THEY MUST, LIVING AS MORTALS.

WE HAVE LIVED ISOLATED FROM THE WORLD FOR SO LONG, WE NO LONGER HAVE MUCH OF A ROLE TO PLAY IN IT. YOU, HOWEVER...THAT IS A DIFFERENT MATTER.

I DON'T UNDERSTAND.

YOU MAY BE A GOD NOW, DIANA, BUT YOU DO NOT KNOW WHAT IT MEANS TO BE BORN A GOD.

TO BE THAT WHICH YOU REPRESENT, DOWN TO YOUR VERY CORE. AND YOU DO NOT YET KNOW OR UNDERSTAND THE JEALOUSY OF GODHOOD. THIS TEMPLE WAS CONSECRATED TO HERA LONG AGO.

SHOULD ANOTHER GOD ENTER, IT WOULD BE CONSTRUED AS AN ACT OF WAR.

HERA WON'T CARE, MOTHER. SHE'S MY FRIEND. SHE WOULD UNDERSTAND THAT I DID WHAT I HAD TO DO TO SAVE THE AMAZONS.

HERA HAS BEEN A GOD FOR EONS, AND YOUR FRIEND FOR ONLY A SHORT WHILE.

HER TEMPLE IS SACRED GROUND AND SHE WILL NOT OVERLOOK YOUR TRESPASS, NOR WILL SHE FORGIVE YOU YOUR IGNORANCE. YOU MUST NOT ENTER.

BUT CHEETAH!

PATIENCE, DAUGHTER... AND WE MAY SEE THAT THE EYE IS NOT EVERYTHING CHEETAH HOPES IT TO BE.

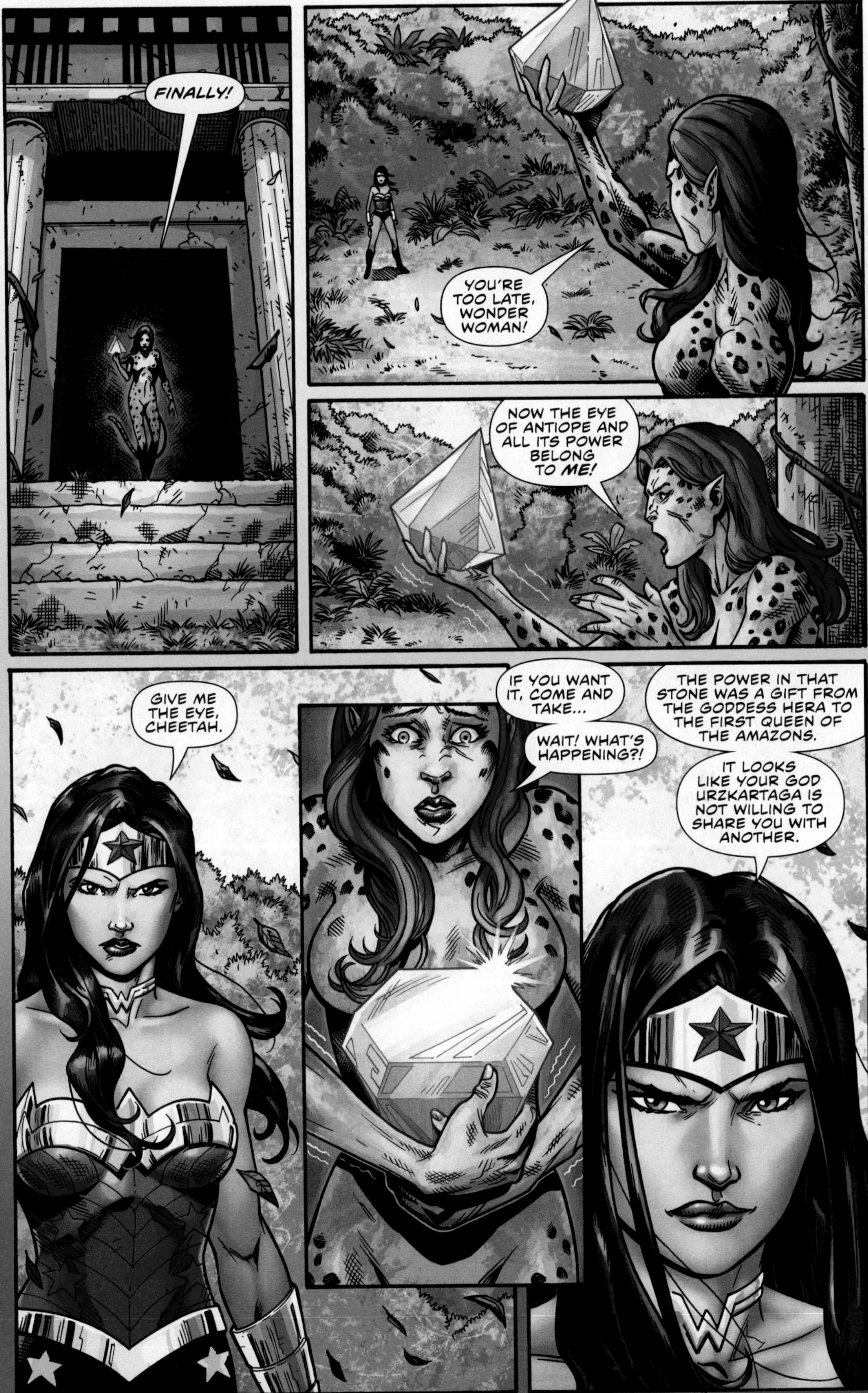
FINALLY!
YOU'RE TOO LATE, WONDER WOMAN!
NOW THE EYE OF ANTIOPE AND ALL ITS POWER BELONG TO ME!
GIVE ME THE EYE, CHEETAH.
IF YOU WANT IT, COME AND TAKE...
WAIT! WHAT'S HAPPENING?!
THE POWER IN THAT STONE WAS A GIFT FROM THE GODDESS HERA TO THE FIRST QUEEN OF THE AMAZONS.
IT LOOKS LIKE YOUR GOD URZKARTAGA IS NOT WILLING TO SHARE YOU WITH ANOTHER.

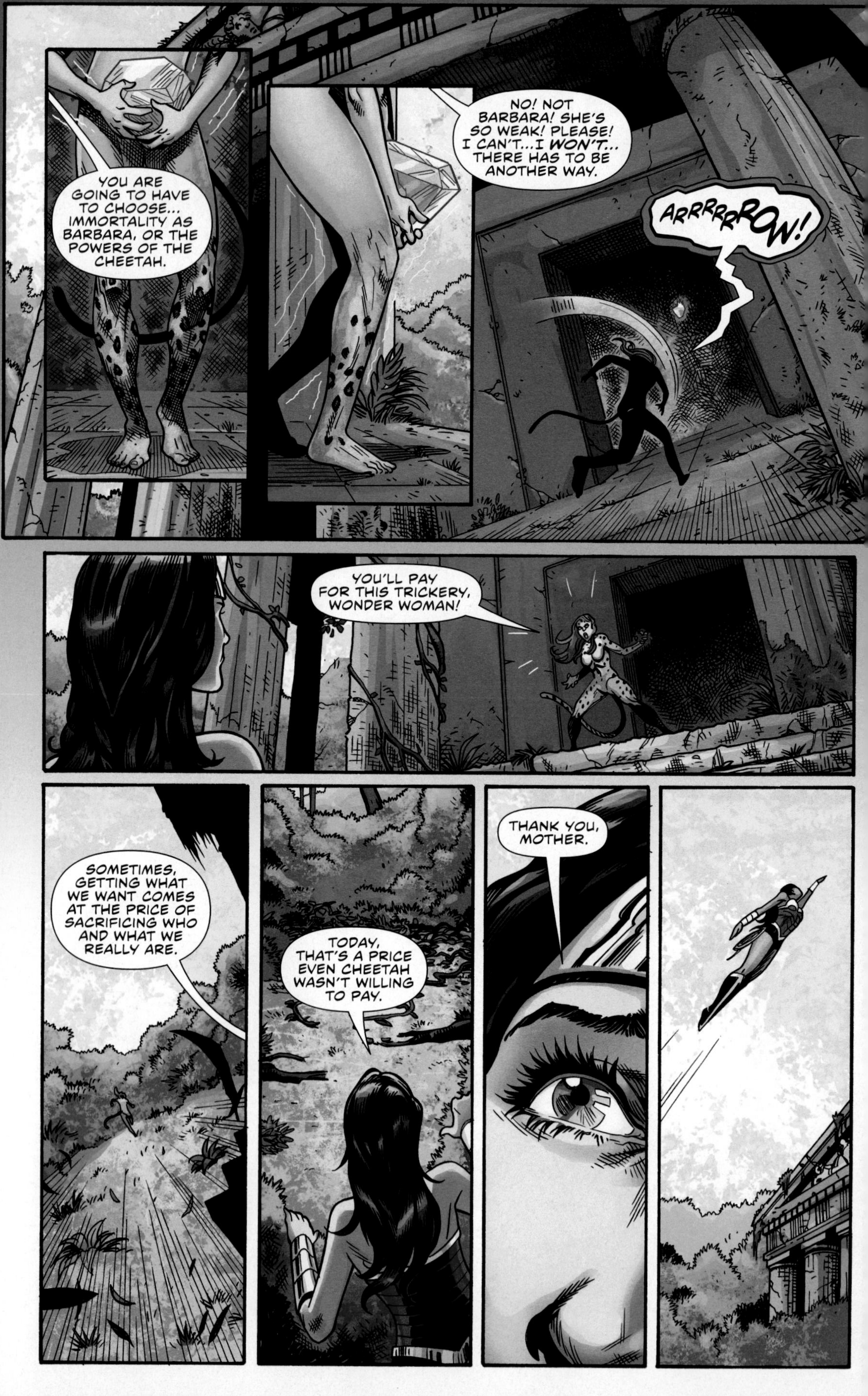
YOU ARE GOING TO HAVE TO CHOOSE... IMMORTALITY AS BARBARA, OR THE POWERS OF THE CHEETAH.
NO! NOT BARBARA! SHE'S SO WEAK! PLEASE! I CAN'T...I WON'T... THERE HAS TO BE ANOTHER WAY.
ARRRRRROW!
YOU'LL PAY FOR THIS TRICKERY, WONDER WOMAN!
SOMETIMES, GETTING WHAT WE WANT COMES AT THE PRICE OF SACRIFICING WHO AND WHAT WE REALLY ARE.
TODAY, THAT'S A PRICE EVEN CHEETAH WASN'T WILLING TO PAY.
THANK YOU, MOTHER.

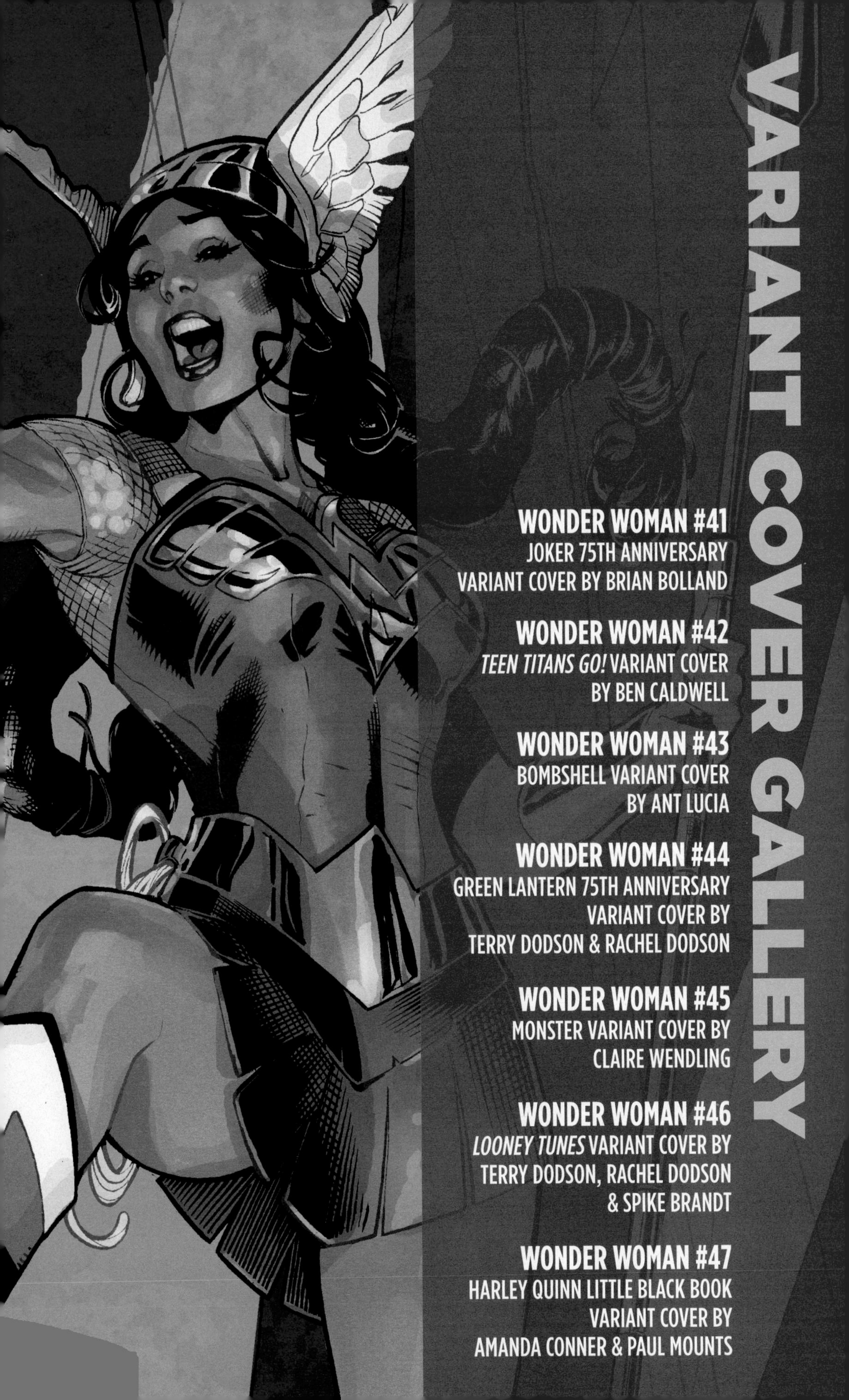

VARIANT COVER GALLERY

WONDER WOMAN #41
JOKER 75TH ANNIVERSARY
VARIANT COVER BY BRIAN BOLLAND

WONDER WOMAN #42
TEEN TITANS GO! VARIANT COVER
BY BEN CALDWELL

WONDER WOMAN #43
BOMBSHELL VARIANT COVER
BY ANT LUCIA

WONDER WOMAN #44
GREEN LANTERN 75TH ANNIVERSARY
VARIANT COVER BY
TERRY DODSON & RACHEL DODSON

WONDER WOMAN #45
MONSTER VARIANT COVER BY
CLAIRE WENDLING

WONDER WOMAN #46
LOONEY TUNES VARIANT COVER BY
TERRY DODSON, RACHEL DODSON
& SPIKE BRANDT

WONDER WOMAN #47
HARLEY QUINN LITTLE BLACK BOOK
VARIANT COVER BY
AMANDA CONNER & PAUL MOUNTS

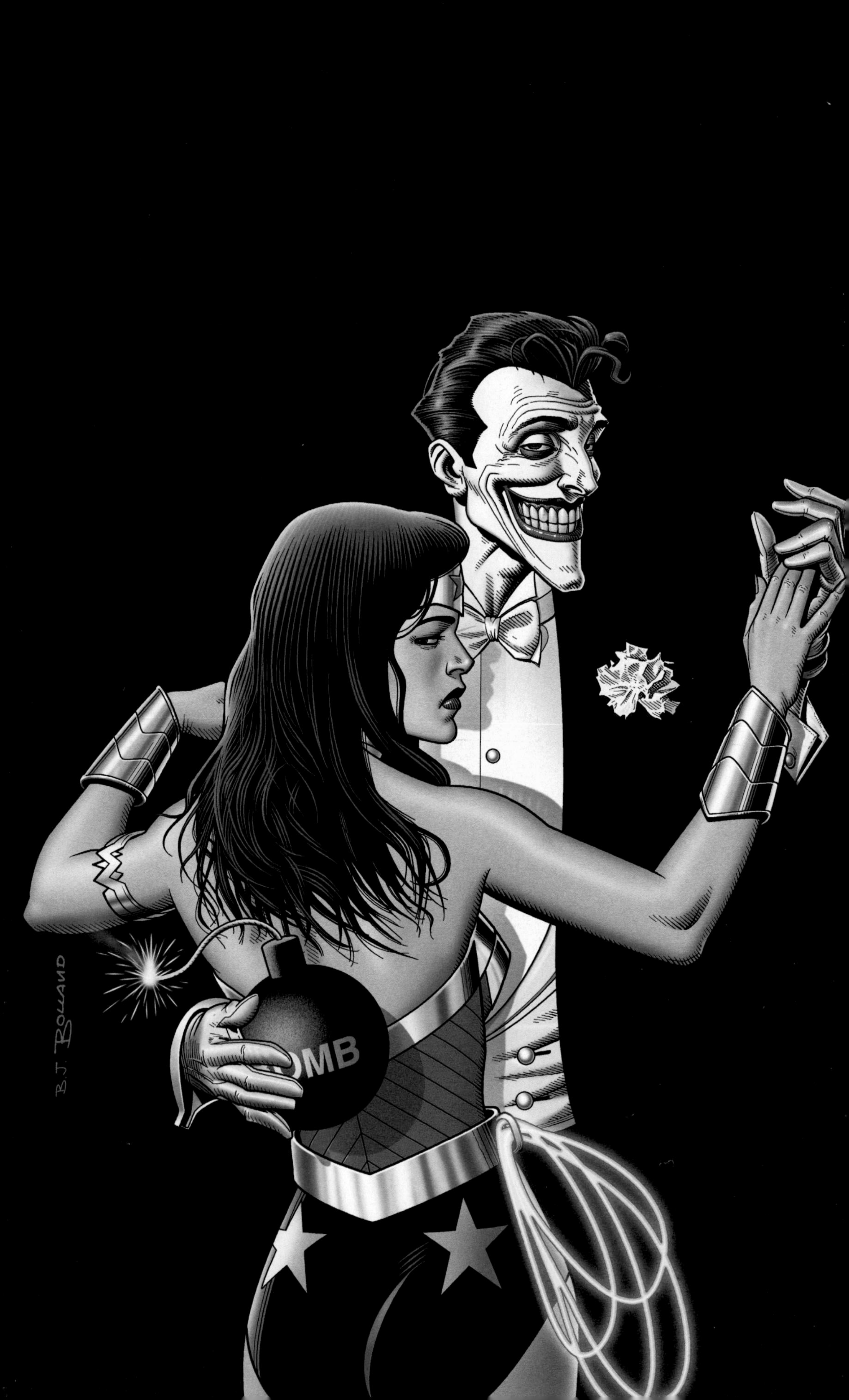
OMB
B.J. BOLLAND

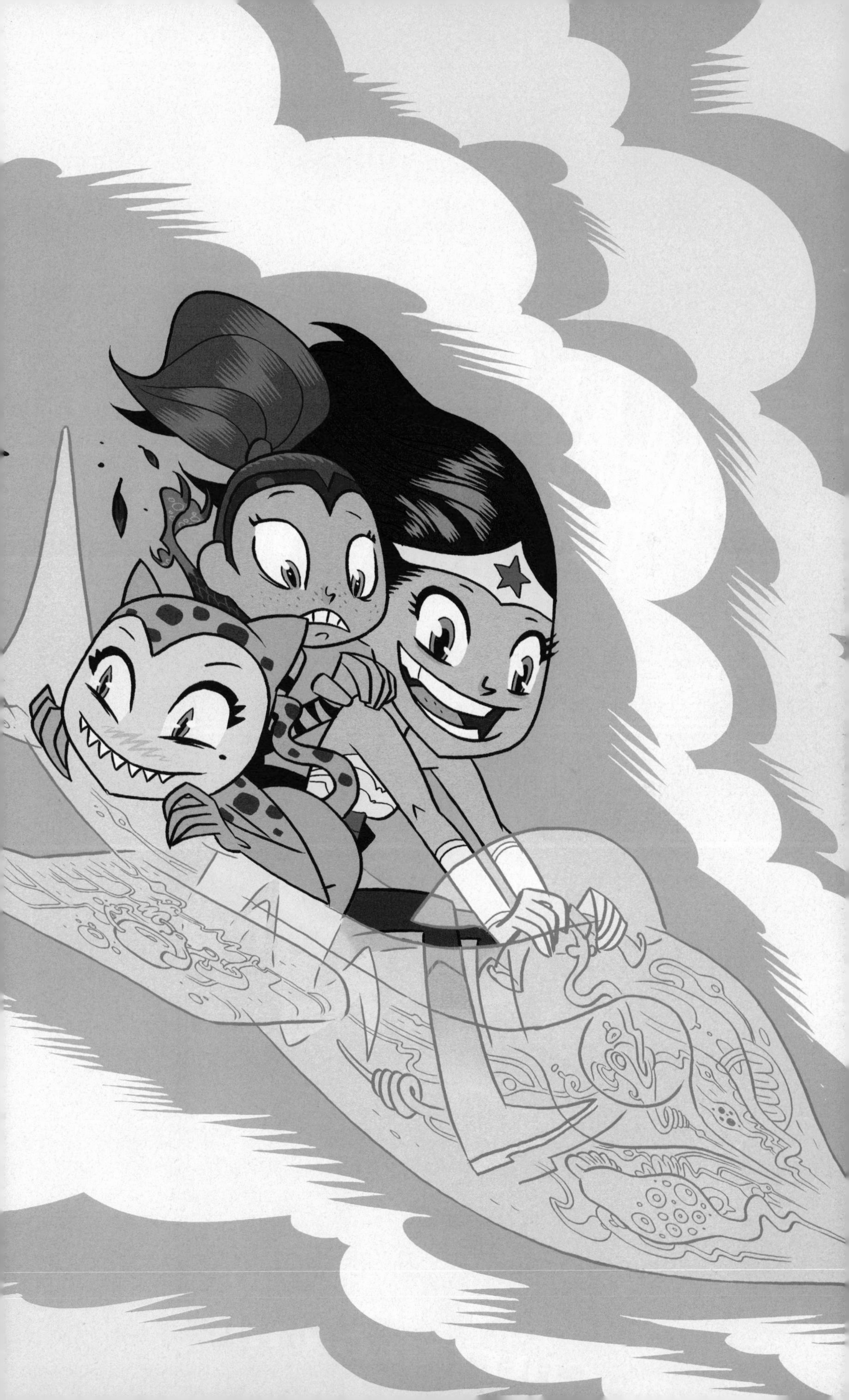

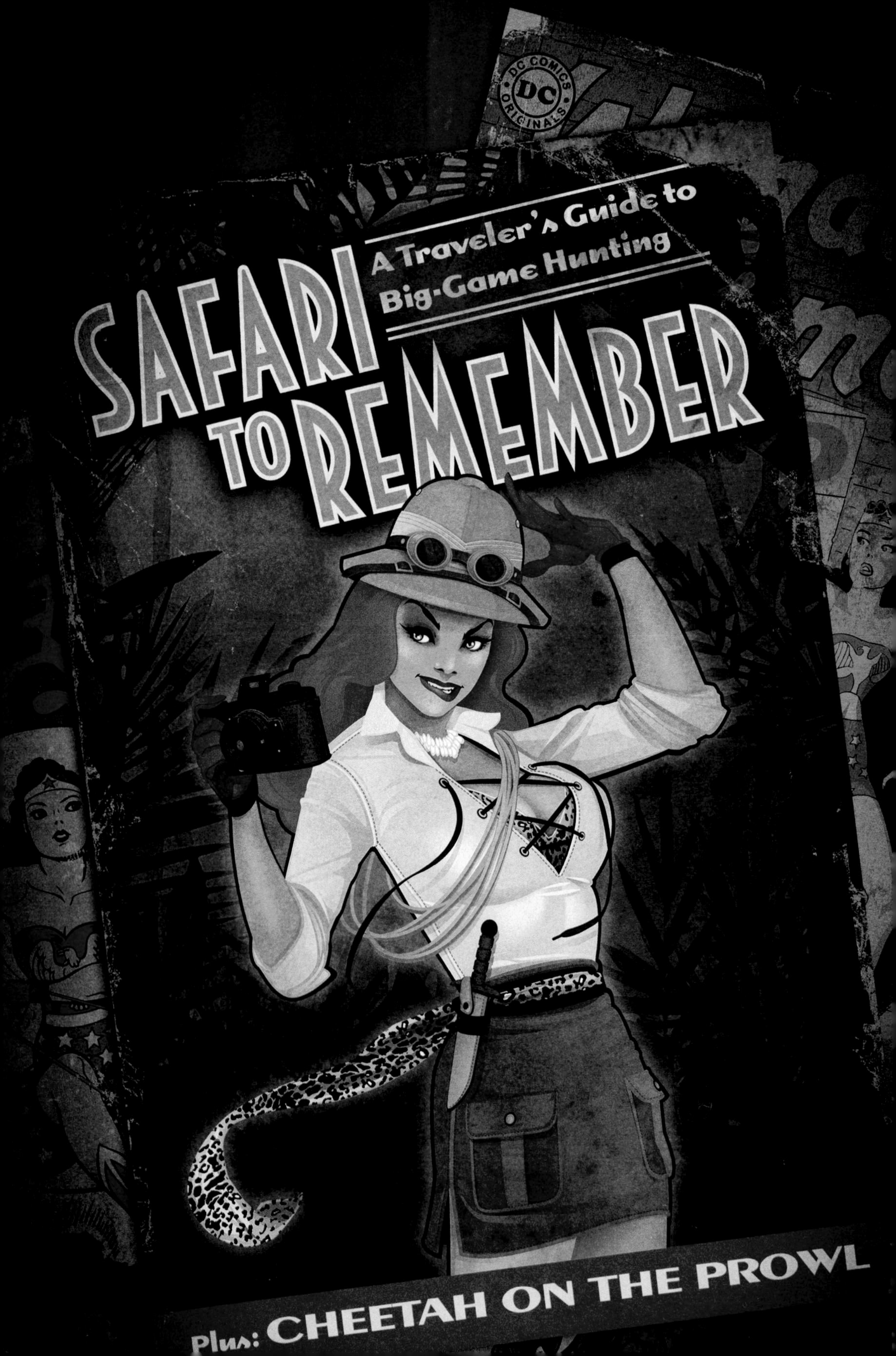

DC COMICS ORIGINALS
DC
A Traveler's Guide to Big-Game Hunting
SAFARI TO REMEMBER
Plus: CHEETAH ON THE PROWL

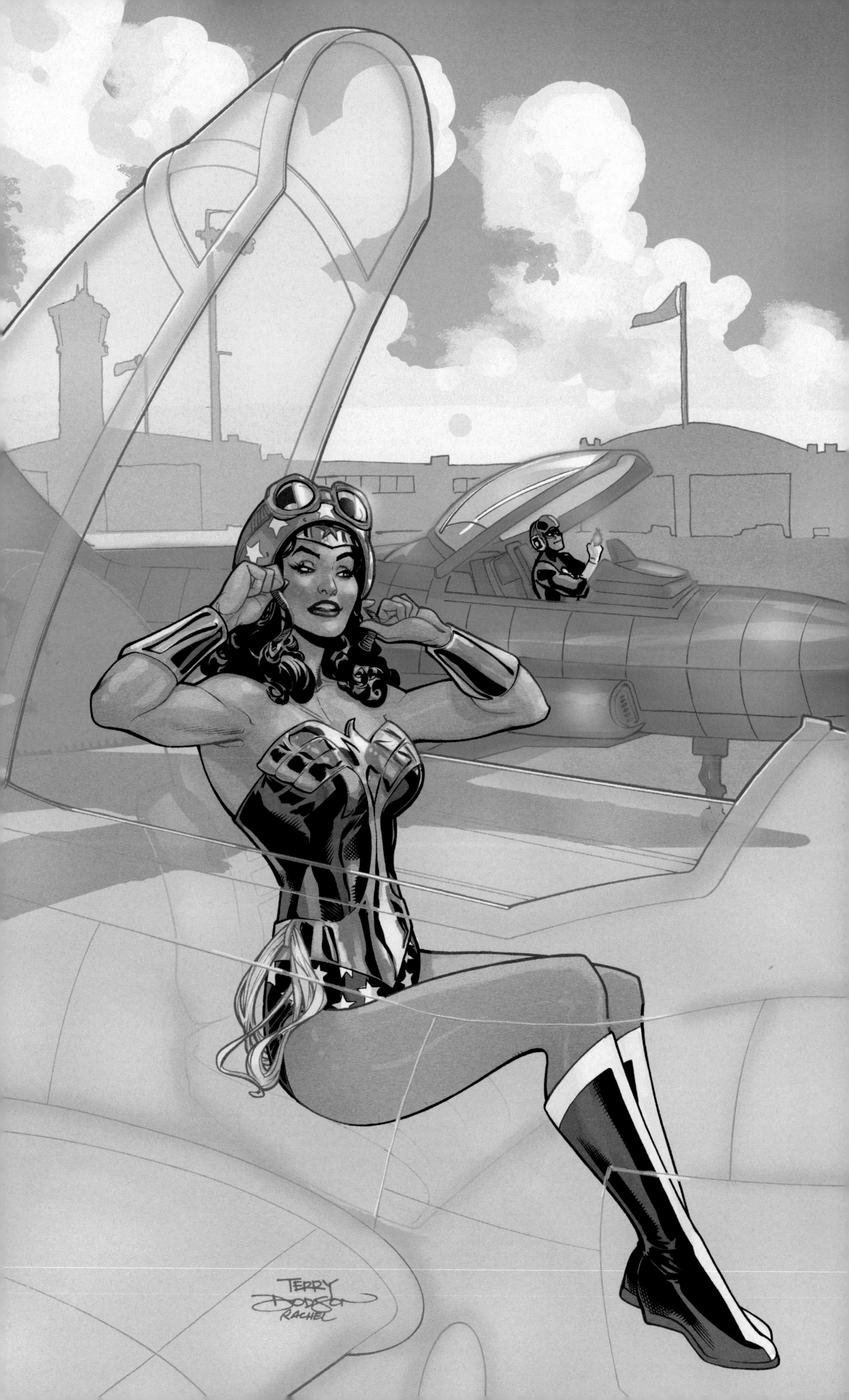
TERRY
DODSON
RACHEL

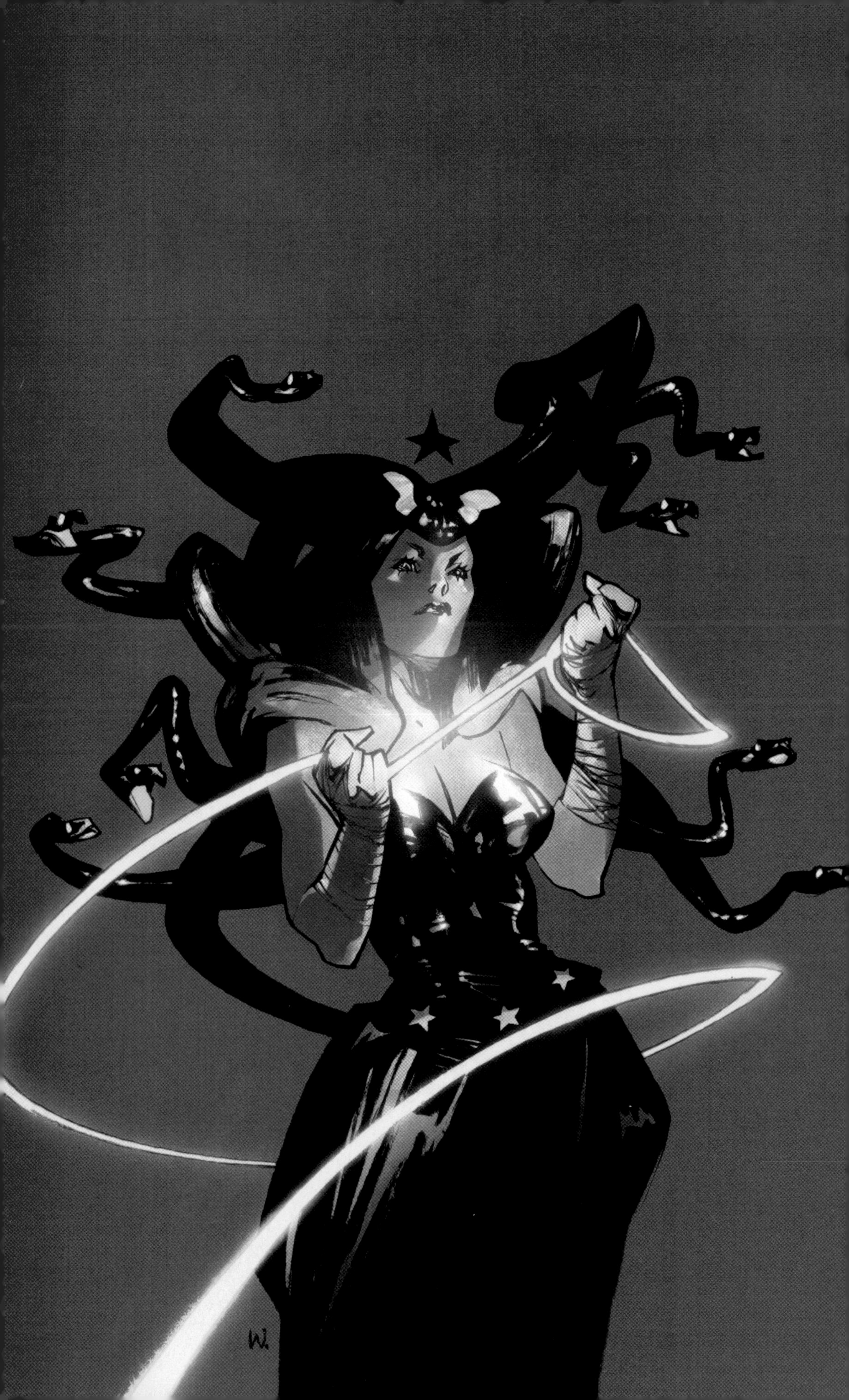

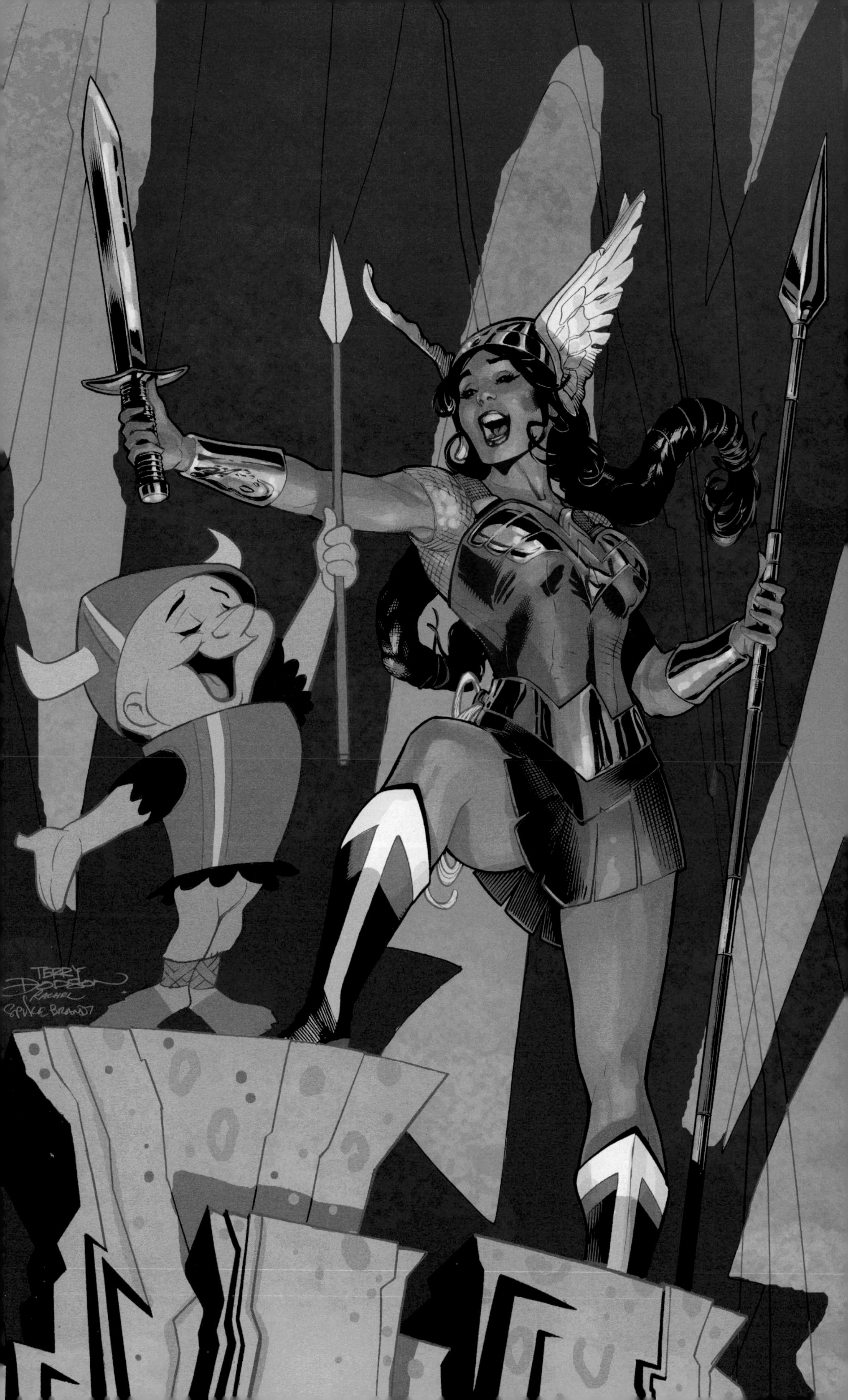
TERRY DODSON
RACHEL
SPIKE BRANDT

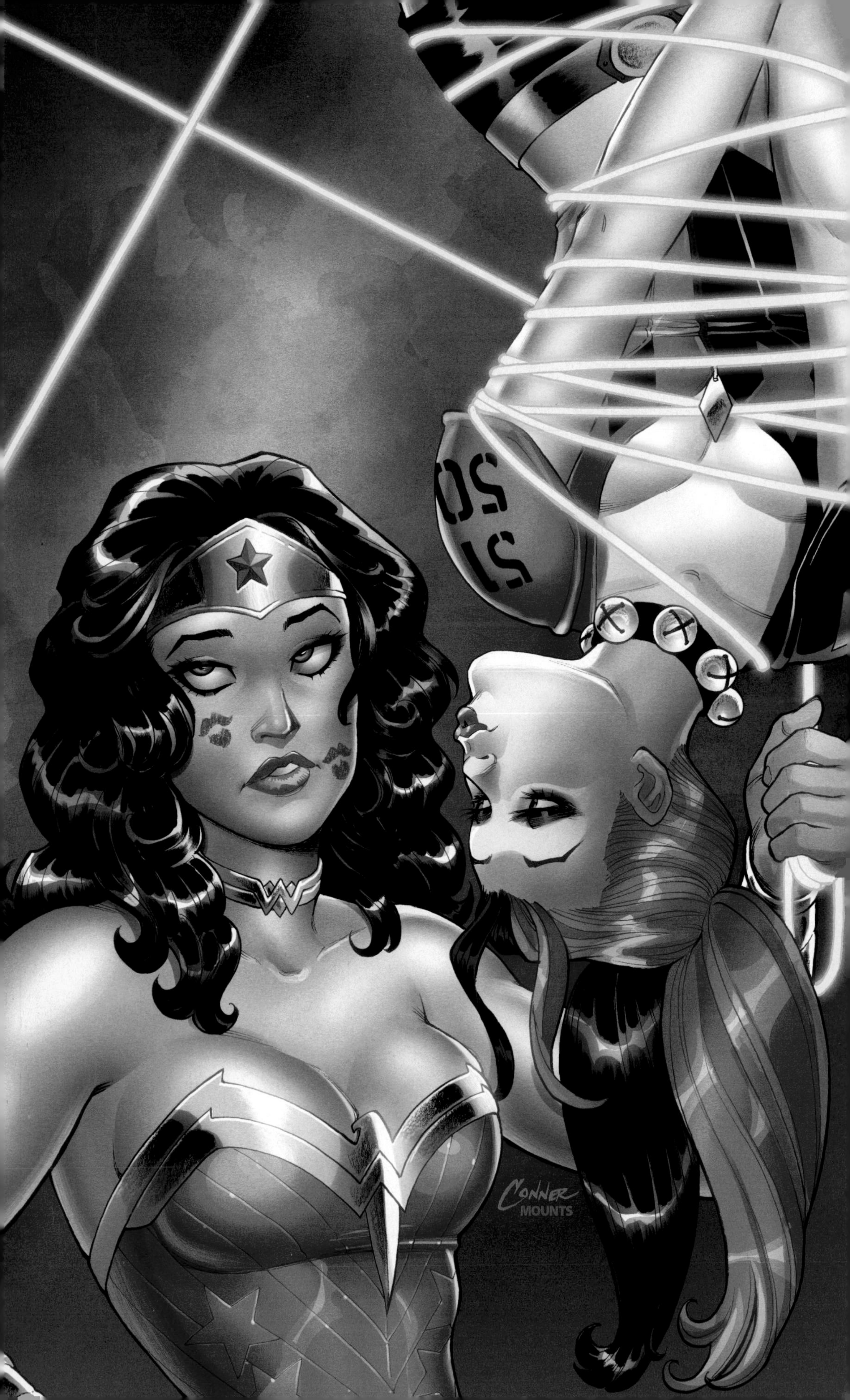
CONNER
MOUNTS

COSTUME REDESIGNS BY
DAVID FINCH

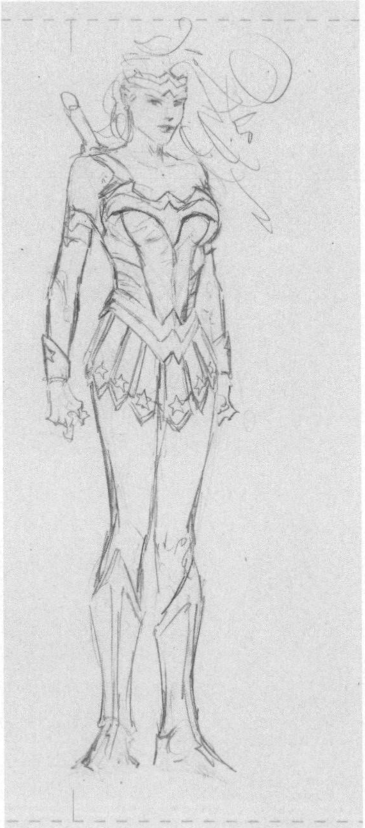

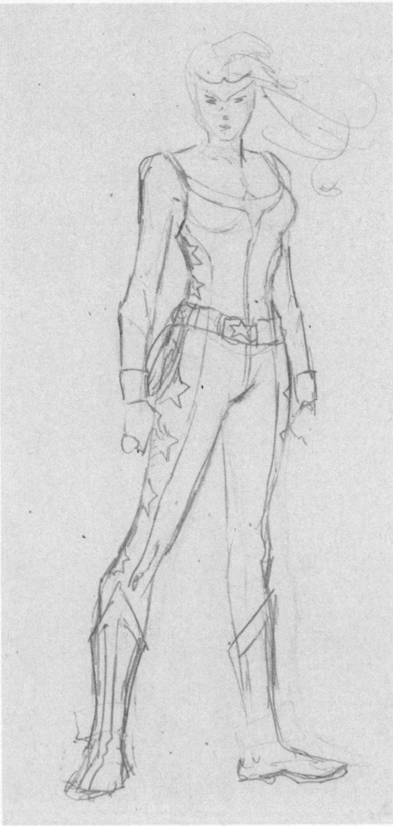

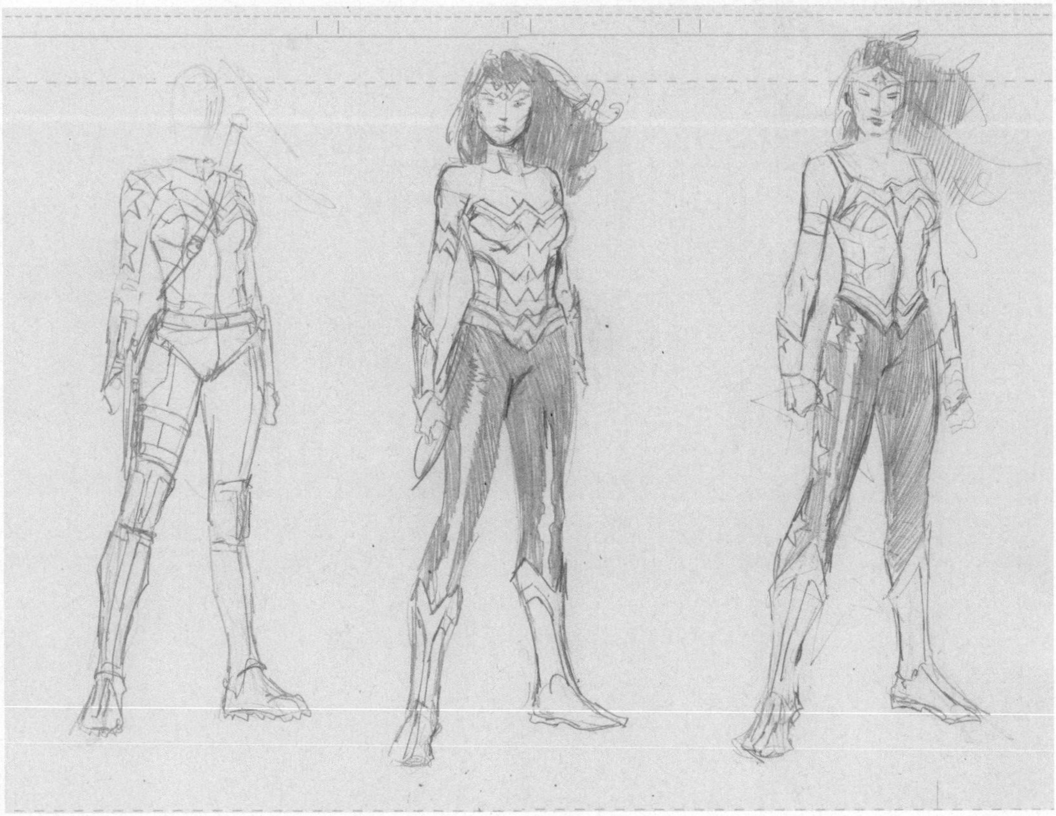

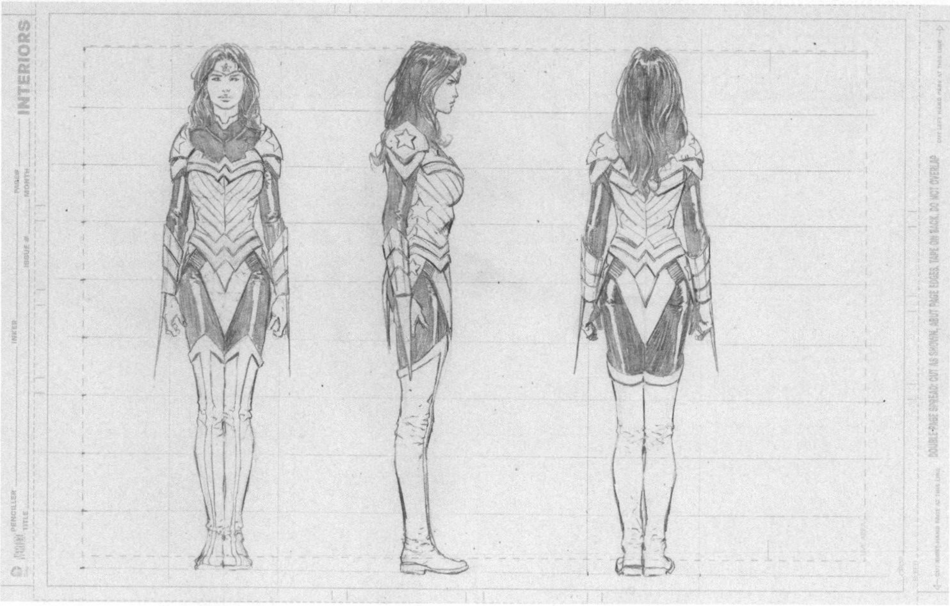
INTERIORS

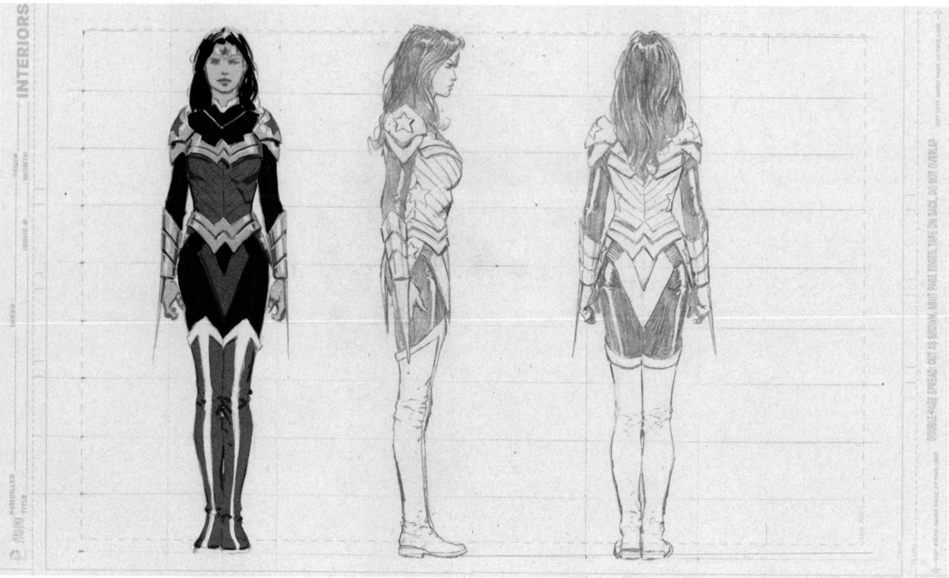
INTERIORS

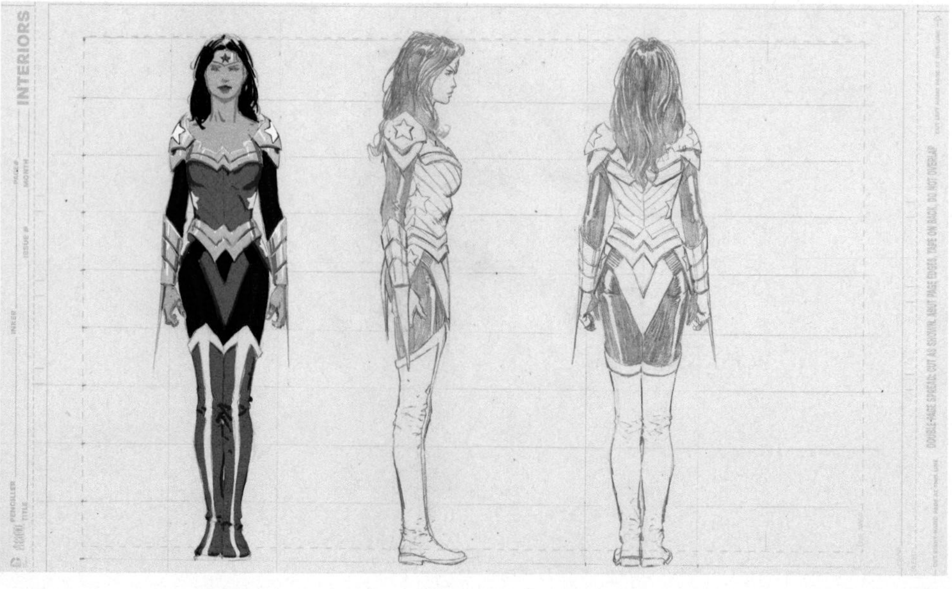
INTERIORS